Church Leader in the Cities

WILLIAM
AUGUSTUS
MUHLENBERG

William Augustus Muhlenberg 1796–1877. A portrait painted in 1836 by Jacob Eicholtz when Muhlenberg was forty years old. At that time he was the head of St. Paul's College. (Courtesy St. Luke's Hospital)

Church Leader in the Cities:

WILLIAM
AUGUSTUS
MUHLENBERG.

Alvin W. Skardon

University of Pennsylvania Press

Philadelphia

LIBRARY OF CONGRESS CATALOG CARD NUMBER: 70-92853

ISBN: 0-8122-7596-9

PRINTED IN THE UNITED STATES OF AMERICA

DESIGNED BY JOHN ANDERSON

To

Genevieve Hooper Skardon

CONTENTS

LIST OF ILLUSTRATIONS

PREFACE

William Augustus Muhlenberg (1796–1877) was an Episcopal clergyman of Philadelphia and New York who was acutely aware of the problems which urbanism was creating in nineteenth-century America. His life work was doubly framed. The first frame was the Episcopal church, in which he exercised his ministry; he is ranked today by Episcopal historians as one of the most influential figures produced by their church in the nineteenth century. The second frame encompassed the two urban centers within which his church lived. Muhlenberg's vision was of a church that penetrated the city with the social ideals of Christianity, ameliorating the evils spawned by the industrial revolution.

As a clergyman in the United Parish in Philadelphia, St. James Church in Lancaster, Pennsylvania, and the Church of the Holy Communion in New York City, his work toward Christian unity foreshadowed the Ecumenical movement which emerged from the cities; his efforts to obtain a more flexible use of the Book of Common Prayer mark him as a pioneer in the Liturgical movement, and his attempts to develop a ritual along "Evangelical Catholic" lines were influential in the Episcopal church and in Protestant churches generally.

His interest in urban problems made him an early advocate of free public schools in Lancaster. In New York he founded St. Luke's Hospital, where he was a pioneer in hospital administration and in developing nursing and social work as professions requiring training and education. He was concerned that the Episcopal church was becoming a church of the affluent, and he established the Church of the Holy Communion as a "free church" without the taint of pauperism. He founded two schools, the Flushing Institute and St. Paul's College, and a newspaper, *The Evangelical Catholic,* and thus had a wide influence on young clergy and on the lay public. At the end of his life he founded St. Johnland, an ecumenical community whose original purpose was to provide adequate housing for industrial workers.

Several historians have explored the subject of the impact of rising urbanism on American society and on American churches; probably the most comprehensive are those of Dr. C. Howard Hopkins, *The Rise of the Social Gospel in American Protestantism*, 1865–1915, which appeared in 1940, and Dr. Aaron I. Abell, *The Urban Impact on American Protestantism*, 1865–1900, published in 1943. Although their emphasis is on the period between 1865 and 1914, they give some space to the clergy and laity who, before the Civil War, saw the problems which urbanism was creating and sought to cope with them. Two contemporary urban historians, Charles N. Glaab and Theodore Brown, have pointed out that Muhlenberg and his colleagues were concerned with the same urban problems in the 1840's and 1850's that we are facing today.

Much of Muhlenberg's work has, therefore, a remarkably contemporary flavor even though he lived in a period when the American public was dominated by rural values and when to the casual observer the nation's greatest challenge arose from the westward movement of population. Muhlenberg, however, sensed the impact that the burgeoning cities were making on American society, and his efforts to cope with their problems may contribute to an understanding of today's urban crisis.

Hopkins and Abell both go into some detail about Muhlenberg and point out that he was a pioneer in recognizing the impact of urbanization on the churches. Episcopal church historians also give considerable attention to Muhlenberg but *primarily* in the role of a denominational leader. Several articles in historical journals have described specific aspects of his life, and there are books dealing with movements in which he participated. There are two full-length biographies by authors who knew him personally and these are valuable as source material.

Yet no definitive life of Muhlenberg has been written and most of the published works suffer from a lack of adequate research. Although Dr. Abell correctly characterizes Muhlenberg as an urban church leader, his treatment is necessarily brief because of the general nature of his book. Other studies are limited to the particular areas of Muhlenberg's life in which their authors were interested, and the two published biographies naturally emphasize those aspects of his life with which their authors were sympathetic. The purpose of this book, therefore, is to present a complete life of Muhlenberg based on adequate research and one which will assess his significance as an urban church leader for his own times and for the present.

To two historians who played a role in the writing of this book an acknowledgement is especially appropriate. The first is Dr. Sidney Mead, my dissertation adviser, formerly professor of the history of American Christianity at the University of Chicago. His patience with my delays, his sharp but sympathetic criticism — which saved me from many foolish errors—and his constant encouragement all helped in the years of research and writing. The second is Dr. Robert Bosher, professor of ecclesiastical history at the General Theological Seminary in New York City, who first pointed out the significance of Muhlenberg and the need for a biography.

Dr. William Manross, professor of American church history at the Philadelphia Divinity School and formerly archivist of the Church Historical Society, was most helpful in locating material. Dr. Theodore Tappert, professor of American church history at the Lutheran Theological Seminary, Mt. Airy, Pennsylvania, helped me on the relation of the Lutheran and Episcopal Churches in the early 19th Century. Dr. Gilbert Doane, of the University of Wisconsin Library, generously allowed me access to the research that he has done on the Kemper Papers. Fr. Frederick C. Joaquin, librarian of Nashotah House, and Mrs. Kemper Jackson of Nashotah, Wisconsin made available hitherto unused material. Dr. Walter P. Stowe, president of the Church Historical Society, offered advice and encouragement throughout the research and writing of this volume. Mr. Andrew Oliver loaned me the letters of Samuel Seabury, his great-grandfather. Miss Olga Wiazemsky, late librarian of St. Luke's Hospital, and Mrs. Agnes E. Ramage, archivist of the Church of the Holy Communion and the Society of St. Johnland, placed at my disposal the records of those institutions. The Rev. Robert Batchelder, rector of St. James, Lancaster, was most helpful in my research in Lancaster, Pennsylvania. Dr. H. Boone Porter, professor of Liturgics at the General Theological Seminary, called my attention to aspects of Muhlenberg's life that I would otherwise have missed.

Numerous other persons rendered valuable advice or assistance. I should like to mention especially Dr. Daniel Boorstin, professor of history at the University of Chicago and a member of my dissertation committee; Dr. Edward Hardy, professor of church history at Berkeley Divinity School; Dr. William Clebsch, formerly professor of church history at the Seminary of the Southwest; Dr. Alexander C. Zabriskie, late dean of the Virginia Theological Seminary; Dr. Richard G. Salomon, late professor of ecclesiastical history at Bexley Hall of Kenyon College; Dr. W. B. McDaniel, librarian of the College of Physicians of Philadelphia; Dr. Robert Handy, professor of church history at Union Theological Seminary in New York; the Rev. D. L. McLean, rector of St. George's Church, Flushing, New York; and the late Dr. Raymond W. Albright, professor of church history at Episcopal Theological Seminary, Cambridge, Massachusetts. Mr. James P. May, director of public relations and development of St. Luke's Hospital, New York City, has been most generous with his time in helping me research the archives of

St. Luke's and in answering my numerous letters. I am also grateful to the many libraries and archives which I visited in preparing this book. Thanks for generous financial assistance is offered to the Church Society for College Work of the Episcopal Church and its former executive director, Dr. Jones B. Shannon.

Despite the contributions of those mentioned above, the opinions expressed in this book are solely the responsibility of the author.

A.W.S.

December 1969

CHAPTER 1

Philadelphia, 1795-1820:
The Urban Background

In the opening years of the nineteenth century the already historic German Lutheran parish of St. Michael and Zion in Philadelphia was convulsed by a bitter controversy. The occasion was the petition of some members that services be held in English as well as in German. The petitioners, after reaffirming their loyalty to the doctrines of the Evangelical Lutheran church, stated that many members of the congregation did not understand German sufficiently well to receive any benefit from the German services. The young people understood German even less and were being lost to the church as a result. They therefore needed sermons and instruction in English. The petitioners assured the congregation that they fully realized that as long as some of the members understood only German that there must also be German language sermons and instruction and that the excellent German hymns should be sung. They went on to point out that the ancestors of the English language people had helped build the church and maintain it. "Our fore-fathers and founders would be deeply disturbed if they saw their children treated as foreigners in the church which they in common with you and us have helped build with much labor and effort."[1]

The petition proposed the continuation of the present German language clergy and the calling of another clergyman who could conduct services in English. The petitioners proposed that this clergyman conduct English services in St. Michael's Church on one Sunday and in Zion Church the following Sunday. (The parish owned two church buildings within a block of each other, a not unusual arrangement during the eigh-

1

teenth and early nineteenth centuries. It was the custom when the original church became too small to construct an additional church building instead of enlarging the old church or building a larger one.)[2]

The members of the German party, however, were adamant in their opposition. They pointed out that all deeds, constitutions, articles of incorporation, records, and so forth, used the term "German Lutheran Church." They denied that even a majority vote of the congregation could authorize English services since the congregation was bound by these documents to use German. Moreover, the reply asserted, Lutheran parents should bring their children up as Germans, they should speak German in their homes, and should send their children to German schools. The German-language party not only constituted a majority of the congregation but also had the backing of their venerable pastor, Justus Henry Christian Helmuth, who had been born and educated in Germany. One of his contemporaries had this to say about him:

> He was a very popular preacher. . . . He preached only in the German language and was a vigorous opposer of the introduction of the English language into our pulpits. In his religious opinions he belonged to the straitest sect of orthodoxy and was less tolerant of differences of sentiment than some of his brethren could have desired.[3]

The struggle had class and ethnic overtones as well. The German party drew many of its supporters from recently arrived immigrants while the English group came from families who had been in America for several generations. Some members of the German party were probably illiterate since they signed the petitions with their mark. The names on the German petitions are almost all of unknown people while the English petitions contain the names of several prominent families. Prejudice about national origins was also involved. The speakers for the German party referred to their opponents as "Irishmen," to the English language as "Irish," and interrupted speeches with shouts of "Throw the Irishman out." Pennsylvania Germans commonly called English-speaking people "Irish" and sometimes referred to the English Language as "Irish" because in the colonial period their principal contacts with English-language culture were with their Scotch-Irish neighbors. Further, the Germans claimed, the English party wanted to bring other races into the church, "even Blacks."[4]

In an effort to force the issue the English party brought Philip Meyer to Philadelphia. He was American-born and a graduate of Columbia College. He had been the pastor of an English Lutheran church in New York and spoke English as his native tongue. His supporters rented a hall at the University of Pennsylvania, and there Pastor Meyer conducted

Lutheran services in English. The crowds that packed the hall and the large classes that he confirmed showed the need for English services, but the dominant party at St. Michael and Zion refused to compromise. The English party finally seceded and founded St. John's English Lutheran Church. This secession did not end the controversy a the older parish. Some English-speaking people did not wish to leave their old parish and their numbers were continually augmented by the young people.[5] The controversy, therefore, continued and erupted into a riot several years later.[6]

The leader of the English party until his death in 1805 was John Peter Gabriel Muhlenberg, who came from a distinguished German-Lutheran

Christ Church, Philadelphia. Painted in 1811 by William Strickland. (Courtesy Historical Society of Pennsylvania)

3

family. His father, Henry Melchior Muhlenberg—great grandfather of the subject of this biography—is regarded as one of the founders of the Lutheran church in the United States. He came to the American colonies from Germany in 1742 to settle in Pennsylvania with his family of three sons and four daughters. As a Lutheran missionary he founded and became the first pastor of St. Michael and Zion. His three sons entered the ministry, but at the outbreak of the revolution, Peter, who was the oldest, enlisted in the Continental Army and became a major-general under Washington. He did not return to the ministry at the end of the war but became a politician and businessman. Frederick Conrad Augustus—usually referred to as Frederick—also left the ministry and became a prominent politician in Pennsylvania. He died in 1801, too early to be involved in the language controversy. The third son, Henry Gottfried Ernst[7]—usually referred to as Henry—remained in the ministry and died in 1815 while pastor of the Lutheran church at Lancaster,

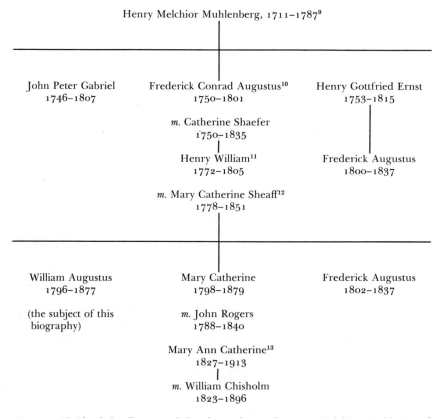

Henry Melchior Muhlenberg, 1711–1787[9]

John Peter Gabriel
1746–1807

Frederick Conrad Augustus[10]
1750–1801

Henry Gottfried Ernst
1753–1815

m. Catherine Shaefer
1750–1835

Henry William[11]
1772–1805

Frederick Augustus
1800–1837

m. Mary Catherine Sheaff[12]
1778–1851

William Augustus
1796–1877

(the subject of this
biography)

Mary Catherine
1798–1879

m. John Rogers
1788–1840

Frederick Augustus
1802–1837

Mary Ann Catherine[13]
1827–1913

m. William Chisholm
1823–1896

Figure 1. Abridged family tree of the descendants of Henry Melchior Muhlenberg.[8]

4

Pennsylvania. In addition to his ministerial career Henry attained an international reputation as a botanist.

One of the arguments of Peter Muhlenberg and the English party at St. Michael and Zion was that the Lutheran church was losing the young people who did not understand German. An excellent example was found among his close relatives. His nephew, Henry William — Frederick's son — had three children: William Augustus — the subject of this book — Frederick Augustus, and Mary Catherine. The marriage of Henry William was performed by Pastor Helmuth[14] and the children were baptized by him. The family were members of St. Michael and Zion parish, but the children were unable to understand the German services. (They appear to be the first generation of Muhlenbergs who knew no German at all.) They, therefore, began to attend the English services of Christ Episcopal Church in the neighborhood. When English Lutheran services were started, Mrs. Muhlenberg tried to persuade her children to attend them but the children were already attached to Christ Church.[15] For this reason, William Augustus Muhlenberg grew up in the Episcopal church instead of the Lutheran church of his fathers.

Henry William Muhlenberg — the father of William Augustus — started out in business with his father, Frederick, as a sugar refiner. Later he went into business on his own as a wine merchant,[16] the family business of his wife's people, the Sheaffs and the Seckels.[17] He apparently prospered for when he died suddenly in 1807, when his son, William Augustus, was eleven years old, he left his wife a substantial fortune. This enabled her to support the children in comfort and to devote her entire time to them.[18] Mrs. Muhlenberg received an additional inheritance from her mother in 1817.[19] The early death of his father apparently cut William Augustus' ties with the Muhlenberg family, for none of its members were then living in Philadelphia. He never mentions his father's people until late in life and then only incidentally. Sometime after 1807 Mrs. Muhlenberg took her family to live with her mother, Mrs. William Sheaff, née Seckel, also a widow, in a house at the corner of Seventh and Market Streets.[20] She also acquired title to the house at this location and to the surrounding land.[21]

William Augustus thus grew up among his mother's people, the Sheaffs and the Seckels (see Figure 2). They constituted a numerous clan in Philadelphia and were for the most part prosperous businessmen or trades people. All of the Seckels listed in Philadelphia's first directory, issued in 1785, are the children of George David Seckel, who died in 1798, leaving his fortune to be divided among them.[22] Most of the Seckels were wine merchants but some had farmland on the outskirts of the city.[23] The most prominent member of this family was Lawrence

Seckel, who is listed as a wine merchant and "grazier." He was the president of the Cattle Society, organized to improve the breed of cattle in Pennsylvania and was a member of the board of managers of both the Philadelphia Hospital and the Philadelphia Dispensary.[24] He was a member of St. Michael and Zion Church and was one of Peter Muhlenberg's supporters in the language controversy.[25] William Augustus spent his vacations as a boy on the farm of Lawrence Seckel.[26]

Lawrence s sister Barbara married William Sheaff, who was also a wine merchant, and their daughter Mary married William Henry Muhlenberg, the father of William Augustus.[27] The wine business was apparently the family occupation of the Sheaffs as well as the Seckels for there are several other Sheaffs listed among the wine merchants of Philadelphia in addition to those mentioned above.[28] A review of the Philadelphia Directories from 1785 to 1805 indicates that these two families had other business interests in addition to their wine shops.[29] They prospered and took an active part in the civic affairs of Philadelphia.[30] The Muhlenbergs are rarely referred to in sources on William Augustus but frequent mention is made of the Sheaffs.[31] Like the Seckels, the Sheaffs were members of the English language party of St. Michael and Zion Church.[32]

The overall family background of William Augustus Muhlenberg is that of a prosperous upper class family which was normally affiliated with the Lutheran church, German in background, and speaking English as its native tongue. There is no trace of German phrases or idioms in the papers of either family. By profession they were wine merchants but some had become prosperous enough to branch out into other fields. Although there is no indication that they were among Philadelphia's aristocracy they were people of consequence among the English-speaking Germans of that city.

An event of some importance in the life of William Augustus took place in 1806. The vestry of the United Parish of Christ Church and St. Peter's, which he and his sister had been attending, decided to build a third church because of the westward movement of population. The committee on a site for the new church reported that the most favorable location was the lot owned by Mrs. Mary Muhlenberg near her home at the corner of Seventh and Market Streets. The vestry then entered into negotiations with George Sheaff, Mrs. Muhlenberg's brother and business agent, and agreed to pay $8,000 for the lot, half was to be paid in cash and half in the form of a mortgage.[33]

This new church was given the name of St. James and from its consecration in 1809 was administered as one of the three churches of the United Parish of Christ, St. Peters and St. James. Each church had its own sexton, clerk, organist, choir, Sunday school, and wardens but all three were under the control of one vestry and were served by one rector and his assistants.[34] The Muhlenberg children now changed from Christ Church to St. James, which was almost next door to their home.[35] Due to the continuing movement of population it soon became the most centrally located church in Philadelphia and was a favorite place for church meetings.[36]

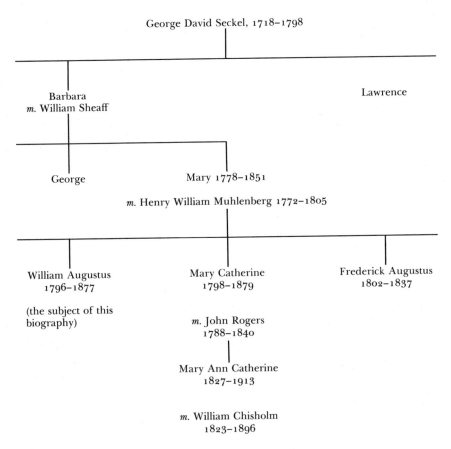

Figure 2. Abridged family tree of the Sheaffs and Seckels, the families of the mother and grandmother of William Augustus Muhlenberg.

From the sparse records of his childhood it seems that young Muhlenberg decided very early to enter the ministry. He was an ardent admirer of Bishop William White, the rector of the United Parish and an enthusiastic attendant at church services. One of his childhood games was to

7

play minister and conduct church services at home. Following the death of his father he lived in a household consisting of his grandmother, mother, younger brother, and sister. It was natural that the clergy should to some extent have taken the place of his father in these early years.[37]

Muhlenberg's education began with a school mistress of whom he had only a slight recollection. He was then sent to a Quaker school—the Society of Friends had a number of excellent elementary schools in Philadelphia—of which he wrote: "My most distinct recollections are that we had to go to Quaker meetings every Thursday morning and sit there quiet for two hours." In 1805, when he was nine years old, his mother entered him in the Philadelphia Academy, a private school for boys operated by Dr. James Abercrombie, Bishop White's assistant in the United Parish.[38] The school had a three-year course, and since the graduating class numbered twelve, the total number attending the school was probably about forty.[39] Dr. Abercrombie stated in his promotional literature that the curriculum of the school provided a complete English education adapted to the peculiar circumstances of the United States. It was designed to prepare a student either to continue his studies in one of the learned professions or to go immediately into business.[40] For Dr. Abercrombie argued that in either case the groundwork of a correct education could be established from a study of English literature. He acknowledged that this "dual purpose" was peculiar to his school but was confident that the prejudice against it inspired by long established custom would eventually be overcome by time and experience.[41]

The subjects taught in the school were grammar, writing, arithmetic, composition, elocution, natural history, geography, and logic. To these some of the students added bookkeeping and mathematics.[42] Young Muhlenberg graduated in 1808 at the age of twelve[43] and at the commencement, which consisted in exercises in elocution on the subject of "Choice of a Profession," he chose the ministry.[44] One of his classmates, Richard H. Mason, also entered the ministry and was ordained with Muhlenberg in 1817.[45]

A distinctive feature of Dr. Abercrombie's school was the formal religious instruction which was in addition to the customary prayers with which the school opened each day. Although a majority of the students were Episcopalians the school was conducted on nondenominational lines. Each student was required to recite on the catechism of his own denomination and every Saturday was required to attend a lecture on "The Leading Principles of Christianity." Observing the ignorance of their church among the Episcopalians, Dr. Abercrombie himself drew up a course of instruction on their catechism.[46]

Information about the Philadelphia Academy is rather meager but there is a great deal about Dr. Abercrombie himself. Although sources on Muhlenberg very rarely mention him, so many of Muhlenberg's ideas were anticipated by Dr. Abercrombie that it is evident that he had a strong, if indirect, influence on his student. He had become a minister of the United Parish in 1796, the year that Muhlenberg was born, and he remained in this position until his retirement in 1833. His ministry thus spans Muhlenberg's entire life in Pennsylvania. In addition to being both a pastor and schoolmaster for Muhlenberg he was also Muhlenberg's colleague on the staff of the United Parish from 1817 to 1820. A short biography of Dr. Abercrombie is in order as the similarity between his ideas and those later developed by Muhlenberg cannot be wholly coincidental.

Dr. James Abercrombie was born in Philadelphia in 1758, his father having been a native of Scotland. He graduated from the College of Philadelphia in 1776 but his plans to study for the ministry were interrupted by illness and the outbreak of the Revolution. He remained in Philadelphia during the British occupation and was on friendly terms with the occupation forces. He was apparently discreet about these matters, however, for there is no record that he was ever persecuted for loyalist sympathies. With the signing of the peace treaty he resumed his studies and was ordained in 1794. Shortly thereafter he became an assistant to Bishop White and remained in this position until his retirement in 1833.[47]

Dr. Abercrombie's brother-in-law wrote that he was noted for his manner of reading the service and was regarded as the best reader of the church services then living. Another contemporary said that his conversation was characterized "by the frank avowal and defense of opinions imbued with the spirit of an early advocacy of Royal Sovereignty in church and state."[48] In 1813 Dr. Abercrombie founded *The Quarterly Theological Magazine,* whose frontispiece carried the quotation "The differences among Christians, about lesser matters, proves the truth of those great fundamental points in which they agree—Bp. Horne." The editors promised that "nothing acrimonious, nothing illiberal, nothing fanatical, and nothing political, will be admitted into its pages."[49] He evidently took this ideal seriously, for of the many controversies in which he became involved none were on religious questions. In addition to his charges to the graduating class of the Philadelphia Academy and his course in religion, he published a textbook on elocution and natural history, and carried on a correspondence with James Boswell in regard to the publication of an American edition of Dr. Johnson's works.[50]

From time to time he composed additional prayers to supplement those in the Book of Common Prayer. He also advocated the singing of a variety of hymns, an unusual practice at that time.[51] He was particularly critical of the dominant part that the clerk took in the services of the church.[52] He abhorred violence, both to man and beast. One of his charges to the graduating class of the Philadelphia Academy is devoted to the duty to be kind to animals.[53] He took the occasion of the death of Alexander Hamilton to deliver a stinging attack on dueling.[54] He also had a very low opinion of military life.[55]

Dr. Abercrombie's magnanimity, so evident in maiters of religion, did not extend to infidels, the French, American supporters of the French Revolution, Thomas Jefferson, and Thomas Paine. His first opportunity to express himself on these subjects came when the president appointed January 9, 1798, as a day of fast. An undeclared war with France was already in progress and formal hostilities seemed inevitable. He prefaced his sermon with the remark that he did not approve of introducing politics into the pulpit, but "uncommon exigencies require unusual exertions." He then pointed out that the American nation itself had become irreligious and immoral. Turning to the French he said, "They have scattered spiritual as well as temporal death throughout the world; spiritual death by their philosophies and temporal death by their armies." The former Loyalist then contrasted France with Great Britain. "From this great country," he said, "we have received the principles of true religion and political wisdom. We have used its constitution which is considered the perfection of civil government as the model for our own." He concluded the sermon with a word of praise for President Adams for "during his administration of the adopted government, he hath done all things well."

Since there were "gross and malevolent misrepresentations of the sentiments contained in the sermon," Dr. Abercrombie found it necessary to publish it.[56] He suffered a similar experience in 1800 when he preached a sermon questioning the advisability of electing Thomas Jefferson, "A Professed Infidel," to the presidency. Again he stated that a clergyman should refrain from politics, except on extraordinary occasions, "but there are periods, particularly under such a government as ours, where there is no established religion ... when the interference and influence of the clergy in behalf of that divine system is unquestionably proper, nay, in my opinion, becomes a duty." Admitting that the personal life and character of Jefferson were above reproach, he exclaimed: "What a monster of a solecism in religion as well as in politics would it be, for a Christian Community, voluntarily, to place at their [sic] head and guide, an acknowledged unbeliever, and of course an enemy to their faith."[57]

Ten years later, Dr. Abercrombie was again called upon to deliver his opinion on infidelity when the valedictorian of the Philadelphia Academy quoted Thomas Paine. Admitting that there was no objection to this particular quotation, Dr. Abercrombie launched into a denunciation of Paine, primarily because of his infidelity and immoral character.[58]

Muhlenberg's first notable reform — overthrowing the clerk at St. James — was anticipated in one of Dr. Abercrombie's sermons. The doctor was an advocate of more hymns, additional prayers to those already in the prayer book, and the saying of the liturgy in an intelligible fashion. In these areas Muhlenberg became a leader. The germ of the Flushing Institute with its flexible curriculum and formal religious instruction can be found in the Philadelphia Academy, and Dr. Abercrombie's liberal attitude toward Christians of other denominations reappears in *The Evangelical Catholic* and in the Memorial movement. Similarly, Muhlenberg reflected Dr. Abercrombie's anglophile and francophobe feelings as well as his antagonism toward "rationalism." In only one respect did Muhlenberg show a marked difference from his old schoolmaster. He showed little interest in politics until the election of 1860 and even then he only cast his vote.

Muhlenberg entered the grammar school of the University of Pennsylvania in 1808 when he was twelve years old.[59] This school was under the immediate care of a master assisted by tutors. There were four grades, the two highest being under the direct supervision of the master. The subjects studied were the rudiments of Latin and Greek. The master received all the tuition money paid by his scholars as salary and lived in one of the houses owned by the university. It was the special duty of the provost and vice-provost of the university to inspect the grammar school regularly.[60] When Muhlenberg entered the school the number of students was sixty-seven but it declined to forty-five in 1812, the year he graduated. The school was operated in the same building as the college department of the university itself.[61] One of the tutors was Benjamin Allen who became prominent in Philadelphia church life during Muhlenberg's early ministry.[62]

There is no evidence that Muhlenberg made any lasting friendships in Dr. Abercrombie's academy, but at the University of Pennsylvania he made several lifelong friends. The first of these he made while he was still in the grammar school. Joseph Engles was a member of a prominent Scotch Presbyterian family of Philadelphia and was a Democrat, something of a francophile, and an admirer of Napoleon.[63] The evidence indicates that Muhlenberg's background was predominantly Federalist, pro-British, and Episcopalian, with some Quaker contacts. Engles was apparently the first person Muhlenberg met who held entirely different views.

He was three years older than Muhlenberg and entered the college

11

the same year that Muhlenberg entered the grammar school.[64] The basis of their friendship appears to have been their common interest in religious matters but their very differences on other subjects enlivened their warm disputes. Engles later became a tutor at the University of Pennsylvania[65] and an agent for the Presbyterian publishing house in Philadelphia.[66] It was his duty in this position to furnish educational and religious material for the westward moving population which also became one of Muhlenberg's interests.[67] His brother, William Morrison Engles, was in the same class as Muhlenberg and became a nationally known Presbyterian clergyman.[68] Joseph Engles died in Philadelphia in 1861. Of him Muhlenberg wrote: "There was no one to whose religious and moral influence I was so much indebted in the days of boyhood and youth as to that of this excellent Presbyterian. We loved each other to the day of his death."

Muhlenberg graduated from the grammar school in 1812 and entered the college of the University of Pennsylvania.[69] The university was at that time a collection of schools of various types. In addition to the grammar school and college there was an English school on the same level as Dr. Abercrombie s Philadelphia Academy, a charity school for poor boys and girls, a medical college, and a law school. Although the Philadelphia Directory stated that the total number of students at the university was over 500 there were only 44 students in the college department. The bulk of the students were apparently in the medical school; it had 270. It was easily the oustanding branch of the university for it had eight professors and held a separate commencement of its own. There was only one professor of law and that school does not appear to have been important.[70]

The college had five professors including the provost and vice-provost, who were expected to supervise the instruction in the grammar, English, and charity schools in addition to their duties in the college. The entire university was housed on the outskirts of the city, its principal building being a large structure originally erected for the use of the president of the United States when it was expected that Philadelphia would be the national capital.

The statutes of the university directed that the course of study include logic, moral philosophy, metaphysics (including natural theology) and the philosophy of the human mind, the classics, belles lettres, mathematics, Latin and Greek classics, Greek and Roman antiquities, geography and history. The professors were also directed to teach such courses in science as were necessary to round out a college education. They were to divide the teaching load among themselves. All students were to assemble every morning in the University Hall for social worship and exercises in public speaking.[71]

12

Although the University of Pennsylvania was nondenominational, the three provosts who were in office during the period of Muhlenberg's attendance were Episcopal clergymen. Likewise, the two clergymen on the board of trustees were Episcopalians: Bishop William White and his assistant minister in the United Parish, Dr. Robert Blackwell. Chief Justice William Tilghman and Horace Binney, two prominent lay Episcopalians, were also on the board.[72] This preponderance of Episcopalians is explained by the fact that of the leading religious groups in Philadelphia, the Quakers had excellent secondary schools but were not interested in higher education; the Lutherans, still predominantly German speaking, were not interested in an English speaking institution; and the Presbyterians, who were both English speaking and interested in higher education, had a rival attraction for their interest in Princeton.[73]

Dr. Edward Potts Cheyney, author of the official history of the University of Pennsylvania, writes that the period from 1800 to 1827, which covers Muhlenberg's student years, was a low-water mark in the history of higher education not only at the University of Pennsylvania but throughout American colleges in general. The evidence abundantly bears him out as far as the University of Pennsylvania is concerned.[74] A major cause of dissension was the relationship between the trustees and the faculty. The trustees supervised the entire operation of the college, leaving the faculty little or no authority. The provost himself was only a figurehead. The trustees drew up elaborate plans of instruction and reserved for themselves the final decision on matters of discipline.[75]

As a result the administration of the university was characterized by disorder approaching anarchy. It is fairly evident from the instances on record that a small group of students managed to create trouble for which the trustees blamed the faculty. On one occasion Joseph Engles, who was now a tutor, was beaten by two students. One of the means of discovering culprits was to require that all students sign a statement that they had not been guilty of a certain act. One such statement bearing Muhlenberg's signature is still in the archives of the university.[76]

The provost was J. N. McDowell, who resigned in 1810 and was succeeded by John Andrews. The latter was an alumnus of the university, already sixty-five years old, and is described as "amiable and learned" but was unable to maintain order.[77] He died suddenly in 1813. Muhlenberg, at least, thought that there was some connection between his sudden death and a prank that the students played on him.[78] He was succeeded by Frederick Beasley, who was only partly successful in stemming the tide of disorder. Conditions remained in an unsatisfactory state until Dr. Beasley was deposed by the board of trustees, and W. H. DeLancey, a minister of the United Parish, was made provost with full powers.[79] Muhlenberg had an affectionate regard for Dr. Beasley, who was still provost in 1815 when he graduated, referring to him in later life as "My old schoolmaster."[80]

In view of the general ineffectiveness of the college during his student days it is probable that Muhlenberg's friends were a more important influence than the faculty or his studies, for in addition to Engles he now met four students whose friendship was also to last throughout his life. These young men reflected the varied cultural life of Philadelphia. Probably the most intimate was Christian Frederic Crusé, who was of German Lutheran background.[81] He later entered the Episcopal ministry and when Muhlenberg founded his school on Long Island, Crusé became a professor there. In later life he was librarian of the General Theological Seminary and in 1862 he went to live at St. Luke's Hospital, of which Muhlenberg was superintendent. Muhlenberg said of him at the time of his death in 1865:

> He was a library in himself . . . and yet not a repository of mere learning, but of learning digested, applied, and illuminated by the light of that which was to him in his inmost mind and heart, the book of books. . . . He had a strong aversion of ecclesiasticism without, however, any leaning towards rationalism . . . He was deeply moved at the wickedness of the late rebellion and for that which lay at the root of it he had utter abhorrence. Nothing so disturbed his equanimity as apologies for that abomination attempted on the ground of Holy Scripture.[82]

A third friend, representing another background, was George Bacon Wood, a Quaker, who after receiving his bachelor of arts degree entered the medical profession and became an outstanding physician in Philadelphia.[83] A speech which he made before the Philomathean Society on "The Early History of the University of Pennsylvania, from its origin to the year 1827" was expanded and later published and is the chief source of information about the University of Pennsylvania during Muhlenberg's student days.[84] His wife was of German Lutheran background and they were married by Philip Meyer, the pastor of the English Lutheran church in Philadelphia. A few days after his wedding Dr. Wood wrote in his diary:

> Received regular notice of my disownment by the Society [of Friends] for accomplishing my marriage by the assistance of a hireling minister with a woman of another religious profession, without the consent of my mother.

Despite this incident he remained a devout Quaker and an uncompromising aristocrat. One of his collateral descendants has written of him:

14

Even in his latter days, as throughout his life, he was always the Aristocrat. It is said that, on one occasion when it was proposed by his nephew that he go home on a streetcar, he replied: 'Horatio, I would have thee know that I never have and never will demean myself by riding in a streetcar. When I ride, I ride in my carriage,' and he walked home.

Dr. Wood was the only member of the group to outlive Muhlenberg. That he shared one of Muhlenberg's pet antipathies, the French, is illustrated by an entry in his diary after a visit to New York in 1827:

But the entertainments after the play were rendered disgusting by the indecent exposure which some recently imported Female Dancers made of their persons. The sense of the better sort of the audience was evinced by many distinct hisses; but these were drowned by the applause of the black-guards in the pit—whom nothing could satisfy but a repetition of the same indelicate scenes. No lady who is at heart really virtuous could encourage the scenes which are tolerated in New York. We know that females in France look upon these things very cooly but we know also the standard of public morals in Paris.[85]

A fourth friend was James Keating whose background, different from that of Muhlenberg and his other friends, further illustrates the varied character of the Philadelphia environment. Keating was a Roman Catholic of part-French descent and came from a family of scientists. He entered politics as a young man but died at the age of twenty-six. Keating, therefore, does not appear in Muhlenberg's later life as do the others.[86]

The most important event in Muhlenberg's college years was the founding of the Philomathean Society, which played an important part in student activities and is still a very active organization.[87] Crusé, Muhlenberg, and Wood were among its founders and were first, second, and third moderators respectively.[88] The college gave the society a large room and two small ones for their meetings. The trustees defrayed the expenses of the society's annual Exhibition which, in 1815, consisted of eight orations interspersed with music.[89]

Upon the fiftieth anniversary of the founding of the society in 1863, Muhlenberg and Crusé were invited to be present but were unable to attend. Dr. Crusé's speech was delivered by the secretary. The proceedings of this occasion do not mention Dr. Wood. Upon his eightieth birthday in 1876, Muhlenberg received a letter of congratulations from the society. After describing the flourishing condition of the society the letter went on:

The walls are hung with photographs of the Senior members, and above the Moderator's desk is a scroll bearing the honored names of the thirteen gentlemen who, in 1813, founded the society. To these gentlemen Philo now expresses her thanks, respect, and admiration.[90]

The leading external event during Muhlenberg's college years was the war with Great Britain which began in 1812, when he entered college, and ended in 1815, when he graduated. As might be expected he greatly deplored the war and this was not due entirely to his pro-British Federalist background. The influence of Quaker thought is clearly shown in his strong feeling for the ideal of nonviolence. He went so far, however, as to work for a day on the fortifications in front of Philadelphia which were being strengthened. He found himself in a quandary, however, over whether to volunteer for military service since he would be eighteen years old in 1815. This dilemma was resolved by the news of peace early in February of that year.[91]

Muhlenberg received his bachelor of arts degree in January, 1815. First honor medal was conferred on George Wood, second on a Mr. Marks, third on Christian Crusé, fourth on Muhlenberg, and fifth on William Engles (Joseph's brother). A sixth medal was not awarded because in Dr. Beasley's estimation no other students were qualified. The Latin salutatory oration was delivered by George Wood, the mathematical by Christian F. Crusé, and the belles-lettres by Muhlenberg. Joseph Engles received the master of arts, and the honorary degree of doctor of laws was conferred on Chief Justice John Marshall, Associate Justice Bushrod Washington, and Rufus King, Senator from New York. Two years later Muhlenberg applied for and received the master of arts degree, which was conferred upon graduates with a bachelor of arts who were recommended by the provost.[92]

While Muhlenberg was at the University of Pennsylvania there were important changes in the United Parish. Robert Blackwell resigned as assistant minister and Jackson Kemper was elected in his place. The new clergyman was of German parentage but had grown up in the Episcopal church. He graduated from Columbia College in 1809 and began studying for holy orders under Bishop John Moore of New York and Dr. John Henry Hobart, then rector of Trinity Church in New York. Due to the illness of Bishop Moore he came to Philadelphia to be ordained to the diaconate by Bishop White and preached his first sermon in St. James Church. His election to the post of assistant minister of the United Parish followed. Three years later he was ordained to the priesthood.[93]

About the same time James Milnor, a lawyer with a Quaker background, entered the ministry from St. James and was for two years an assistant minister in the United Parish. Under the influence of these young clergymen the United Parish began to show more signs of life than it had done since the outbreak of the Revolution. Muhlenberg was one of many who were presented for confirmation by Jackson Kemper.[94] The popularity of Jackson Kemper was shown by a rather amusing incident. He received a call from a Baltimore church, whereupon the vestry immediately raised pew rents 50 per cent to increase his salary. He had already decided to decline the call, however, before the action of the vestry became known. The vestry therefore raised the pew rents 25 per cent and gave all the clergy a small increase in salary.[95]

James Milnor resigned after two years to become rector of St. George's Church in New York. He remained Muhlenberg's close friend and their paths crossed again when Muhlenberg himself moved to New York.[96] Of all the friends that Muhlenberg made during these years, however, Jackson Kemper was undoubtedly the most intimate. Although their paths eventually parted—Kemper found his vocation as a missionary bishop in the west and Muhlenberg as a church leader in New York— they maintained a constant correspondence in regard to the various projects in which they were both interested.[97]

Immediately following his graduation Muhlenberg called on Bishop White to discuss his plans to study for the ministry. Bishop White was, in 1815, not only the bishop of Pennsylvania but also was still the rector of the United Parish, for the diocese of Pennsylvania was unable to support a full-time bishop. He had been rector since 1781 and bishop since 1787 and had therefore been known to Muhlenberg all of his life but this conference seems to have been their first personal meeting. The bishop had been an acquaintance of Muhlenberg's grand uncle, Peter Muhlenberg, who led the English party in the language contro-versy at St. Michael and Zion. He remarked that William Augustus had a hereditary right to the ministry through his greatgrandfather whom he venerated as an elder brother in the ministry.[98]

Bishop White was probably at the height of his prestige in 1815 when this conference took place. His influence on Muhlenberg is profound but less tangible than that of Dr. Abercrombie. Muhlenberg signed his letters to the bishop "Your son in the Gospel" and from time to time quoted him in defense of various stands that he took. A short biography may substantiate this intangible influence.

William White was born in Philadelphia in 1748 of parents from whom he inherited a fortune that made him financially independent and whose prominent social position gave him an established place in Philadelphia society. This position was further strengthened by the fact that he married the daughter of a former mayor of Philadelphia and his sister married Robert Morris "the financier of the Revolution." He received all of his education through the various schools of the newly formed College of Philadelphia of which his father was a trustee. Upon his graduation he studied for holy orders and then went to England to be ordained deacon. He remained there a year studying for the priesthood and took this opportunity to visit his aunts whom he knew to be adherents of the Stuarts. "I did not fail to acknowledge to them that both their brother and his son, although neither of them had ever entered zealously into political parties — were attached to the principles of the British Constitution, as confirmed — not introduced — by the Revolution of 1688," he states in his autobiography.

Upon his return to Philadelphia he supported the revolution and was one of the first to take an oath of allegiance to the new government. He refused, however, to preach "animated" sermons in favor of the war although several of his colleagues did so. He was elected chaplain of the Continental Congress and at the end of the war became rector of Christ Church, the leading Episcopal church in Philadelphia. Before the treaty of peace was signed, however, he published a pamphlet entitled "The Case of the Episcopal Churches Considered." In this pamphlet he advocated the setting up of an American Church independent of the Church of England. Since it was believed that it would be many years before the American church could obtain bishops, he proposed that the church ordain, on its own, a group of priests to carry on the church until bishops could be obtained. This particular proposal created much controversy but the need for it was obviated by the unexpected speed with which the treaty of peace was signed. Most of the other proposals were subsequently carried out. The pamphlet drew considerable attention to its writer and marked him out as a national church leader.

A second problem now presented itself to the church. It was feared that the hostility of American public opinion to bishops would create serious difficulties if bishops should be obtained for the church in the United States. This problem was met by electing three men who had been supporters of the Revolution and one of them was William White. Following his consecration in 1786 he continued as rector of the United Parish as well as discharging the office of bishop of Pennsylvania. He was soon recognized as a leader not only in the church but in civic affairs as well. He was an active member of the board of trustees of the University of Pennsylvania and a lifelong member of the American Philosophical Society. He founded the Episcopal Academy of Philadelphia and led in the formation of the interdenominational Philadelphia Bible Society.

But the projects in which he took the greatest interest were those of a humanitarian nature. A description of Philadelphia published in 1811 lists him on the board of managers of the following institutions: The

18

Philadelphia Dispensary, the Prison Society, the Magdalene Society, and Christ Church Hospital (a home for the aged). Bishop White also founded a free school for poor boys and another for poor girls and was active in projects to help the deaf, dumb and blind. He did not become embroiled in politics as Dr. Abercrombie did but he spoke out on political questions when he believed himself called upon to do so. He drew up and presented several memorials to the state legislature on behalf of prison reform which it appears was his favorite cause, and opposed the legalization of the theater in Philadelphia. When the merchant, Stephen Girard, left a large sum of money to the city for an orphan asylum on condition that no religious instruction or services be permitted, the bishop opposed its acceptance.[99]

In association with Bishop White are frequently found the names of Dr. Benjamin Rush and the Quaker, Roberts Vaux. Although no one man could be called the chief citizen of Philadelphia after the death of Benjamin Franklin, Bishop White was undoubtedly one of its leaders. In this respect he held a position in both church and city somewhat similar to that held in New York by Muhlenberg in the 1850's and 1860's. In his congregation at one time or another were George Washington, Benjamin Franklin, Horace Binney, Joseph Priestley, Chief Justice William Tilghman, Dr. Benjamin Rush, and other national and local figures.[100]

Since there were no theological seminaries of the Episcopal church in 1815 candidates for the ministry studied under the direction of a clergyman. Bishop White appointed Jackson Kemper as the director of Muhlenberg's studies and with two other theological students he read the required books: Paley's *Evidences of Christianity,* Butler's *Analogy,* Stakehouse's *History of the Bible,* and Adam Clark's *Commentary.* They also met every two weeks in the bishop's study to read essays on subjects chosen by the bishop. Muhlenberg received some pastoral training for he constantly accompanied Kemper in his visits to the sick and poor of the city. He wrote in his diary: "Students of Divinity ought to be acquainted with such scenes. Mr. Kemper told me that he had never been in a sickroom before he was called to visit one as a clergyman." He also did lay-reading in two churches outside of Philadelphia, spent six weeks in Huntingdon County, and founded a church in the county seat.[101]

Muhlenberg carried on some studies on his own initiative with his Quaker friend, Dr. George B. Wood, who records in his diary:

> August 8, 1817: It is now more than a year since he [Muhlenberg] and I began to read the classics together.
> August 31, 1817: Muhlenberg and myself recommenced today our usual studies together. Grotius and the Greek Testament will occupy us yet for some time.

September 21, 1817: Muhlenberg and myself have finished the Testament, except the Apcalypse [sic] and have commenced the Dialogues of Lucian.

May 18, 1818: Muhlenberg made me a handsome present of Herodotus in Greek. We are to commence tomorrow a course of history, the first step of which is the author just mentioned.[102]

During his college years he also took up the study of music. No information has been found on who his music teachers were but his training was apparently quite thorough for evidence from several sources indicates that he had a cultivated knowledge of church music and was himself an accomplished musician. He also attended the services of the Roman Catholic church which had a considerable following in Philadelphia. Another source of his knowledge of church music is suggested by the comment of his friend Dr. Robert Abbe:

In August, 1818, we find him on a vacation in Bethlehem, Pennsylvania, among that unique settlemen of German refugees, already a century old, who continue today their annual musical festival. He writes of these 'remarkable religious and musical people,' where all orchestral music was played in schools and churches, by the people, who were like Quakers, in their simplicity! Dr. Muhlenberg s love of fine church music, of Chorals, of Bach, of Gregorian chants, must have been an innate appreciation.[103]

Muhlenberg was ordained to the diaconate by Bishop White in St. Peter's Church on September 21, 1817. Dr. George Wood records in his diary: "September 21, 1817: Muhlenberg was ordained this morning and I went to hear him preach in the afternoon at Christ Church. His text was 'Pray without ceasing.'"[104]

Shortly after his ordination he was elected an assistant to Bishop White by the vestry of the United Parish, a position which he held for three years. This position was on a yearly basis and the vestry re-elected him each year—a motion to make this position permanent was defeated.[105] Muhlenberg thus became a colleague of Bishop White, Dr. Abercrombie, and Jackson Kemper in the ministry of the United Parish. The Philadelphia clergy in these years were thus described by an anonymous writer:

I have very vivid [memories] of Philadelphia; I can remember some incidents as early as 1826. The few clergy in the city were in some respects rather remarkable men. Bishop White's blameless life, his studious habits, his prominent position in the foundation of the American Church, his means and family, all placed him in the forefront of families, as had also Dr. Blackwell. They all had a decided social position. Into this little group of old men, Jackson Kemper, a young deacon entered in 1814. Very handsome, very energetic, and full of zeal, he for some years carried all before him. St. James was then the new, the fashionable, and the energetic parish, and the classes he there prepared for confirmation were remarkable, one numbering one hundred and having among its members some of the most prominent citizens. Mr. Kemper, by his first marriage, became connected with the same elevated social order, but while always retaining the love of his parishioners, and being prominent and influential in all Church work, his pulpit powers have been overestimated.

After some years, however ... he was no longer the only young clergyman. First came James Milnor, a lawyer of distinction. Then Muhlenberg likewise, by all his family highly connected.... But a peculiarity about all of them was that had they not been Clergymen, they would, from their family, manners, etc., have been leaders in society.... I doubt whether there has ever been such a united brotherhood.[106]

Muhlenberg's activity in the United Parish foreshadowed his future. Although he alternated among the three churches he had a particular responsibility for St. James. There he founded a Sunday school which was one of the first in the diocese; he founded a parish Sunday School Society that was the beginning of the diocesan-wide Protestant Episcopal Sunday School Union; and he formed an auxiliary Bible class composed of young men. Bishop White also gave him the charge of the choir and music of St. James Parish, and it was in this connection that Muhlenberg made the first of many drastic reforms. It was customary to hire a layman called the clerk to lead the congregation in making responses and to lead the choir in singing. He usually had a special desk in front of the pulpit. In the course of time, and perhaps influenced by the eighteenth century's fear of "enthusiasm," the clerk came to make the responses alone and he very much dominated the singing as well. Thus the Episcopal church services appeared to consist largely of a dialogue between the clergymen and the clerk, and the singing to be done entirely by the clerk and choir. As early as 1808, Dr. Abercrombie preached a sermon attacking this practice and thus anticipated Muhlenberg's reform.[107]

As might be expected, the attempt to curb the activity of a person like the clerk who was so firmly established by custom and tradition caused considerable commotion. The clerk of St. James was Moses Taylor, who had been in this position for many years, and who had no intention of being dethroned by a young clergyman whom he had known in the parish as a boy. Defeated in a preliminary skirmish, Muhlenberg went to the bishop, who gave him full authority to act. Thereupon Muhlenberg, with his younger brother, went to the church and chopped away the clerk's desk and that dignitary had to sit with the choir. In a short time

21

similar reforms were carried out in the other churches of the United Parish and the movement apparently spread to New York.[108]

Muhlenberg early became conscious of the distinctively class appeal of the Episcopal church, for he records in his diary: "How I wish some plan could be brought about so that the poor might not be excluded from our churches and burial grounds." There was little that the young clergyman could do in this matter since of the income of the United Parish eight thousand dollars came from pew rentals. As an individual he did, however, actively engage in some work among the poor of Philadelphia which brought him into contact with the lower economic groups in the city.[109]

Muhlenberg and Kemper threw themselves into the life of the Episcopal church, which underwent a marked revival after 1815. The first evidence of this revival was the founding of the Society for the Advancement of Christianity in Pennsylvania which continued the work that had been done before the Revolution by the Society for the Propagation of the Gospel in Foreign Parts. The vestry gave Jackson Kemper two leaves of absence to make missionary journeys into the western part of Pennsylvania.[110] Kemper's trips were journeys of discovery according to the report of the society. He found several dormant parishes that could be revived if a clergyman were sent to them as well as a number of lapsed Episcopalians who could be reclaimed. The first objective of the society was, therefore, to revive these dormant parishes. The second was to educate young men for the ministry. The report of the society related that "enthusiasm was not enough for a clergyman—he must have an education. Many qualified young men have been turned down because the means (to educate them) were not available."[111]

The report on Muhlenberg's trip to Huntingdon, Pennsylvania, in 1817 gives an interesting picture of the problems that the Society faced:

> Mr. Muhlenberg, on the fifteenth of August, went to Huntingdon county, where he remained until the fifteenth of September. His principal time was spent in this town, although he visited occasionally one or two other places, viz., Shirlesburgh and the Three Springs settlement. In Huntingdon, Mr. Muhlenberg states: "one fourth of the inhabitants profess to be members of the church. If an Episcopal Clergyman were settled here, without doubt, under present circumstances one third would belong to his flock; many well-disposed persons who have left the church and gone over to other denominations of Christians, particularly to the Methodist Society, speak of their departure merely as temporary. In the town is a neat brick edifice (not yet finished) built cojointly by the Episcopalians and Lutherans, as a place of worship. The prospects of the church about Huntingdon (adds Mr. Muhlenberg) are such that it is a place well worth the attention of the

Society; we may venture to say that an active clergyman would be liberally supported here by a respectable congregation. Many who attended service expressed a heartfelt satisfaction at having an opportunity of worshipping in the way of their fathers, while they look forward with impatience to the time when they will no longer be left as sheep without a shepherd."[112]

In 1819, the report stated that "Easton was visited by the Rev. Mr. Muhlenberg in August who officiated there six times to an attentive congregation."[113]

The society was interested only in Pennsylvania and its activities were restricted to that state by the terms of its charter. The tide of emigration, however, was sweeping far beyond the western areas of the old states. In the fall of 1816, the Episcopal Missionary Society was founded to send missionaries to the Episcopalians in the western states. Like the Advancement Society, it sent a clergyman on a discovery trip, throughout Ohio, Kentucky, and Tennessee. He found few ministers, but many Episcopalians who needed only a clergyman to found a church. The report of this society declared:

> At no period in the annals of our country has the march of emigration been so rapid. For several years past, every road leading to the west has been crowded with emigrants from the southern and eastern states. Many of our Atlantic churches have been deserted amidst the swarm of inhabitants that left their native home, while Episcopal Congregations were carried along. The most remote parts of the western country have thus become peopled with the hardy settlers from the East. Vast numbers went not alone; they took with them their faithful pastors, and religion lent its cheering aid to alleviate the wretchedness of penury and toil. But the Episcopal flock everywhere scattered like sheep without a shepherd, wandered in vain to search that pure fountain whose waters are refreshing to the soul.[114]

It was largely through his association with this society that Jackson Kemper came to his life's work as a missionary in the "western" states. Muhlenberg, although his own interests ran in different channels, was a lifelong supporter of his friend's work.

Both the Advancement Society and the Missionary Society found that the major obstacle to the prosecution of their work was the lack of clergy. A third society was therefore formed in 1818, known as the Education Society. An appeal from the finance committee in 1826 reiterated that many young men wished to enter the ministry but were unable to finance their studies. Other denominations were financing ministerial students through like societies, the appeal pointed out.[115] Another society in the field was the Episcopal Female Tract Society, founded to distribute tracts in the areas in which the two missionary societies were working. This was one of the first groups for women and exemplifies the beginning of women's work in the Episcopal church.[116]

Another effort to meet the demand for more clergy was the establishment of theological seminaries. But here a serious controversy developed. Bishop White and his protégé, Bishop Hobart of New York, believed that the best policy would be for each diocese to have its own seminary, whereas Muhlenberg and Kemper advocated a general seminary supported by the whole church. In this position the latter had the support of several small dioceses which did not have the resources to support seminaries of their own. Under the leadership of the diocese of South Carolina, a general seminary was established in New York but due to the opposition of Bishop Hobart it was transferred to New Haven. The controversy came to a climax when a bequest was received for a general seminary with the stipulation that it must be located in New York. A special general convention was called in 1821 which worked out a compromise satisfactory to both parties. The general seminary was moved back to New York and consolidated with Bishop Hobart's diocesan seminary while Bishop Hobart was given a dominant part in its control.[117]

To publicize these projects, the Episcopalians began the publication of magazines. The first attempt was *The Episcopal Magazine* published in 1820 and 1821. A considerable amount of space was given to the progress of the Episcopal church in Pennsylvania and to articles by Bishop White. This magazine lasted only two years. A more successful attempt was made the following year when *The Church Record* was begun and it became the first weekly publication of the Episcopal church to have any influence. It had several different editors and in 1823 changed its name to *The Philadelphia Recorder*. By 1827 it had 1,200 subscribers. In 1826 a rival paper, *The Church Register,* appeared under the editorship of the Rev. George Weller with Bishop White as its patron. The latter magazine had the endorsement of Jackson Kemper and was interested in promoting the General Theological Seminary and the Missionary Society.[118]

Another organization, founded in 1817, which was an outgrowth of Muhlenberg's Sunday School Society at St. James was the Protestant Episcopal Church Sunday School and Adult School Society. It had the double purpose of educating the poor and giving them religious instruction. By 1819 there were eight such schools in Philadelphia and several outside the city enrolling 1,600 children. In one year the publication committee, composed of Kemper and Muhlenberg, published 2,000 copies of the catechism, the same number of Sunday school hymn books, and 100,000 reward tickets.[119]

Muhlenberg was corresponding secretary and a member of the board of managers of the Sunday School Society as well as one of the two members of its publications committee. He is listed as an officer of the Missionary Society of which his mother was also a member. He, together with his mother and other members of his family, are listed as members of the Advancement Society as early as 1816. His name is listed on the board of managers of this society after 1817 since all clergy living in Philadelphia were members ex officio. The indefatigable Jackson Kemper is listed as an officer of all these organizations.

Prominent in these societies were men whom Muhlenberg had known from boyhood. In addition to Bishop White and Jackson Kemper, there were Dr. Abercrombie, the outspoken assistant minister of the United Parish and head of the Philadelphia Academy; William Tilghman, chief justice of Pennsylvania and senior warden of Christ Church; Dr. Frederick Beasley, provost of the University of Pennsylvania; Benjamin Rush, physician and promoter with Bishop White of philanthropic causes; and Horace Binney, a leading lawyer. He was also now associated with a group of the younger clergy who were coming into the diocese; Benjamin Allen, who had been a master of the grammar school of the University of Pennsylvania, and who became a magazine editor; George Weller, editor of *The Church Register;* George Boyd, also a magazine editor; James Montgomery; W. H. DeLancey, assistant minister of the United Parish and later provost of the University of Pennsylvania; and Samuel H. Turner, later to become a noted biblical scholar.[120]

In evaluating the work of these societies, it must be admitted that their major objective — to cure the clergy shortage — was never achieved. There was always a supply of candidates whenever educational facilities might be available, but the Episcopal church did not have the resources to provide these. Moreover, there was a strong temptation for recently ordained clergy to remain in the East, where economic conditions were more secure but where the shortage of clergy, though real, was less acute.

The progress of the Episcopal church was further impeded by the rise of two parties commonly known as the High Church party and the Low Church party, also known as the Evangelical. The fundamental difference lay in their doctrine as to the ministry. The High Church party held that the episcopal form of government was divinely instituted by Christ himself and that the bishops were successors of the apostles. High Churchmen, therefore, believed that the only valid ministers were those ordained by bishops in the succession of the apostles. The Low Churchmen believed that episcopacy was the best form of church government but denied that it was divinely ordained or that the ordinations not performed by a bishop were invalid. This difference in doctrine led to dif-

25

ferences in policies. The High Churchmen opposed cooperation with interdenominational agencies, such as the American Bible Society, while the Low Churchmen advocated cooperation. The High Churchmen advocated a strict construction of the canons of the church while the Low Churchmen favored a loose construction. The Low Churchmen favored prayer meetings and to a certain degree revivals—but these were opposed by High Churchmen.[121] Kemper, in later life, became a High Churchman.[122] Muhlenberg throughout his life was an Evangelical,[123] but this difference never caused a rupture in their friendship nor prevented them from working together. Bishop White was regarded as an outstanding Low Churchman, and his protégé, Bishop Hobart of New York, was the militant leader of the High Church party.[124]

Jackson Kemper received a leave of absence in 1820 and left Philadelphia for a short time.[125] Muhlenberg also traveled occasionally to New York which was becoming the center of Episcopal church life as well as of the commercial life of the country.[126] The two friends kept in touch with each other by correspondence and their letters give interesting sidelights on the ecclesiastical affairs of their day. Writing to Kemper, while on a visit to New York, Muhlenberg discussed the controversy over the general seminary, which was by now extremely bitter:

> I had a talk with Mr. Turner. He is very much dissatisfied with the last proceedings of the [Theological Seminary] committee. If Bishop H. [Hobart] and Jarvis were to come to an open quarrel before the convention—which might be occasioned by the report of the committee laying the failure of the Seminary to J's, it would be a very unpleasant thing. S . . . says that the Bishop would be surprised to find that Jarvis had a great deal to say, of which he—the Bishop—is ignorant.[127]

Writing from Philadelphia, later in the year, Muhlenberg tells more about the controversy over the seminary:

> They have not done anything about the seminary in New York. Many choose to continue their subscription for New Haven. Hobart is very much disappointed. Richmond, according to his own accounts, is very active in supporting Brownell, and a great obstacle to Bishop Hobart. He wants us to establish a Professorship—a White Scholarship.
> I have asked Bishop White what we are to do. He thinks that we ought to instruct the students among ourselves and in the meanwhile raise a fund. If there is a good prospect of the Seminary at New Haven succeeding, I think the best thing would be to collect money for a professorship or scholarship there. If we are to carry on the Missionary Society—I am afraid we will not be able to do much for the seminary. Everything, you know, is to be obtained from the city. Let me know what you think the best course. The

26

Bishop will probably agree with whatever we think can be executed. He does not speak decisively.[128]

An anonymous pamphlet was published in 1820 attacking the general seminary at New Haven. Muhlenberg believed that the pamphlet had been written by Bishop Hobart or at his instigation.[129] He wrote Kemper concerning this matter:

> I hope for the honor of the Mitre that John Henry [Hobart] can wash his hands in innocence. Turner can tell you what Bp. White thinks of the pamphlet against the general seminary. It will operate in favor of the Institution . . .

> I have talked so much in the presence of Bp. White of the ambition and policy of Bp. Hobart that I wonder the old gentleman is not offended at me. I believe I will say nothing more to him on the subject, as evidentally he is very much attached to Hobart. From Turner you have learnt that Bp. White seems to be rather unfavorable to the seminary.[130]

Writing later in September, Muhlenberg continued on the subject of the pamphlet:

> I sincerely hope that you are mistaken in your suspicions of the Bishop. If you are right, and he is discovered "He has fallen like Lucifer — never to rise again — "the star of his mitre is dimmed — his career is stained with a spot which no after [sic] conduct will ever wash out. Yes, from the bottom of my heart I hope it will prove to be the work of one whose character will not affect the reputation of the church.[131]

Kemper was one of those most active in soliciting funds for the general seminary and in this connection became involved in a personal controversy with Bishop Hobart. The latter finally wrote a long letter explaining remarks that he had made about Kemper.[132]

Although the subject of the seminary was uppermost in their thoughts Muhlenberg wrote about the other projects as well:

> I am very much discouraged at the meeting of the Missionary Society. . . . We want a great deal of zeal to carry on that society. . . . More I am afraid than we can muster in Philadelphia. The managers do not feel the importance of the cause. They regard it as our other . . . [organizations] which have been dragging along at a low pace. Boyd is not sufficiently a man of business or talents to . . . [carry] on such an institution and I feel very inadequate to the work. I don't think it would be advisable to appoint all the members of the convention vice-presidents. I think with you as to the expediency of lessening the number of societies.[133]

27

Concerning one of the church magazines in Philadelphia, he wrote:

> I fear the Episcopal Magazine has nearly reached the term of its existence. Boyd is tired of it and wishes the Missionary Society to take it. But they will not consent, I presume.
>
> The Magazine gets along. It is too *dry* to be popular — says it will be a losing concern — and Boyd I suspect, wants the Missionary Society to take and convert it into a missionary register.[134]

Writing to Jackson Kemper in September 1820 to thank him for a very "newsy" letter Muhlenberg says:

> I don't know when the Post boy has brought me so valuable a letter. As Dr. Franklin has called a little book of his "12 cents worth of wit," so I may truly call this 18 cents worth of news. You, however, are now on the busy spot of our ecclesiastical world — while I am pursuing the even tenor of my way in a city unusually dull. . . . I cannot deny that I am something like the cobbler in the forty thieves — When there is no breeze blowing I like to stir one.[135]

From these letters we get an interesting picture of the situation in the United Parish in 1820. Bishop White was still the rector at the age of seventy-two, and was to continue so until his death in 1837, at the age of eighty-nine.[136] The great qualities of tact, prudence, patience, and deliberation which stood the church in such good stead in the critical years following the Revolution now seemed impediments to the progress of the reviving church. In several of these letters there is a hint of impatience and exasperation on the part of his two youthful assistants; Muhlenberg was now twenty-four years old and Jackson Kemper was thirty-one. They could not understand his fondness for Bishop Hobart, whom Muhlenberg consistently resented on account of his High Church ideas and aggressive tactics. It is not surprising, therefore, that Muhlenberg took the first opportunity to leave the United Parish following his ordination to the priesthood in 1820.

In the formative experiences of the first twenty-four years of Muhlenberg's life, there is an intangible but very real factor that should not be overlooked. This was the city in which he spent those years. The Philadelphia in which Muhlenberg was born in 1796 was still the largest city and the capital of the United States. It was the city in which the continental congresses and the Constitutional Convention had met. In its culture and social order it reflected a civilization both urban and urbane. Benjamin Franklin had died only six years before Muhlenberg was born, and the city which had produced him, and which had in turn been so much influenced by him, still reflected his spirit in its numerous educational, humanitarian, scientific, and intellectual institutions.[137] During the early years of the nineteenth century, Philadelphia began to lose some of its pre-eminence among American cities. In 1800 the national capital was moved to Washington and New York was fast overtaking Philadelphia in population and commerce. As the editor of the *Philadelphia Directory* pointed out:

> Philadelphia . . . is the chief city of the United States in point of size and splendor, though it now fills but the second rank in respect to commercial importance, the trade of America having latterly flowed more freely into the open channels of the bay of New York. It must also yield metropolitan precedence to the doubtful policy of a seat of government far removed from the center of wealth and population, the pendulum of national activity which must long vibrate (perhaps forever) between Baltimore and Philadelphia, and New York, a chain of commercial cities whose vigorous impulse is already accelerated by the bold ramifications of turnpikes and canals.[138]

Philadelphia, however, continued its leadership in other areas during the years of Muhlenberg's boyhood and early manhood. Precedents can be found in Philadelphia for most, if not all, of the projects which Muhlenberg later promoted in New York and many of his ideas reflect this city background. Philadelphia, as an urban center, must be counted an important element in his life.

CHAPTER 2

Lancaster, 1820-1827:
The Experimental Years

Muhlenberg was ordained to the priesthood on October 22, 1820, in Christ Church, and a few weeks later accompanied Bishop White to Lancaster, Pennsylvania, to consecrate the newly constructed St. James Church. He conducted the evening service and made such a favorable impression that the vestry immediately extended him an invitation to become co-rector of the parish. Muhlenberg promptly accepted and entered on his duties in December, 1820.[1]

A Muhlenberg was no stranger to Lancaster. His grandfather, Frederick Augustus Conrad Muhlenberg, spent the last two years of his life there and was buried in the local cemetery.[2] His grand uncle, Henry Ernst Muhlenberg, had been pastor of the local Lutheran church and died in Lancaster in 1815.[3] His cousin, Frederick Augustus Muhlenberg, a prominent physician, was still living there.[4] And indeed, his great-grandfather, Henry Melchior, had visited the Lancaster Lutheran parish on his missionary journeys.[5]

The town, with a population of 8,000 was, in 1820, the second largest community in Pennsylvania and had been the state capital from 1799 to 1812. It had three newspapers, several private and church schools, a theater, and was the home of Franklin College, a German language institution. The religious groups in the area reflected the community's predominantly German population: Mennonites, Amish, Lutherans, Reformed, and Moravians. There were also Roman Catholic, Methodist, Episcopalian, and Jewish groups. Lancaster was connected by a turnpike with Philadelphia and Baltimore and there were several public coaches which traveled daily between these cities.[6] Henry Ernst, William Augustus's grand uncle, had often walked the sixty-two miles from Lancaster to Philadelphia.[7] Travelers were impressed by the German population, the prosperous farms, and the great wagons on the roads.[8] The town provided an advantageous location for young Muhlenberg, enabling him to take an active part in the life of the diocese of Pennsylvania without being under the immediate control of Bishop White.

St. James Church in Lancaster was founded in 1744 and was therefore an old parish, comparatively speaking.[9] It had been dormant for a number of years but about 1820 it revived sufficiently to construct a new building to replace the original structure, which was on the verge of collapse.[10] Muhlenberg was to have charge of the church as co-rector with the current rector, who was too old to care for the church on a full-time basis. It was arranged that Muhlenberg would conduct the services at St. James on three Sundays of the month and on the fourth Sunday would go to a mission at Pequea while the older clergyman took the service at St. James.[11] This arrangement worked fairly well despite the fact that the older clergyman took a dislike to Muhlenberg.[12] The former attended the vestry meetings regularly but otherwise left the work of the parish to his younger associate. He lived through Muhlenberg's stay in Lancaster to make a similar arrangement with his successor.[13]

The two leading professions in the town were iron manufacture and the law. The former was represented in St. James by Robert Coleman and his numerous family, who operated the largest iron works in Pennsylvania.[14] The latter were represented by the family of Jasper Yeates, who had been a prominent lawyer and judge. (He had presided at the trial of the rioters in the language controversy at St. Michael and Zion Church.) Yeates died several years before Muhlenberg came to Lancaster but his widow and daughters became supporters of Muhlenberg while he was there and continued their support of his activities after he moved to New York.[15]

One of the first fruits of Muhlenberg's move to Lancaster was the inauguration of an effort to have the Episcopal church authorize a new and much larger collection of hymns. This project brought him into conflict with Bishop White. This undertaking had a long history. The English Reformation, unlike the German, had produced no great hymns; rather the belief grew up that the only singing proper for churches was the psalms, a number of translations of which were published in the sixteenth century for the use of churches. The most popular of these works in the Church of England was the *New Version of the Psalms of David,* published in 1696, which were fitted to the tunes of Nahum Tate and Nicholas Brady. It is usually known simply as Tate and Brady. This book or similar ones were in use in the colonial Anglican churches up to the time of the Revolution.

Other Protestant churches had been rescued from this rigid adherence to the psalms by the work of Isaac Watts, who frankly gave up the attempt to translate the ancient Hebrew psalms into hymns and introduced instead the writing of modern hymns based on psalms. Soon, however, hymns began to be composed which were free of psalmody altogether. The work of John and Charles Wesley gave a tremendous impetus to the new types of hymns so that by the time of the Revolution they were in use in many Protestant churches.

The leading advocates of hymns in the Episcopal church were Dr. William Smith, a leading Philadelphia clergyman, and Francis Hopkinson, the Philadelphia musician. In 1786 they proposed that fifty-one hymns be added to the American prayer book, but when that book was finally authorized in 1790 the number was reduced to twenty-seven. In the following years, however, the tide of hymnology increased so greatly that the convention of 1808 accepted thirty new hymns over the vigorous objection of Bishop White.[16]

In his memoirs the bishop wrote that he did not doubt the lawfulness of using hymns in church services nor the desirability of having a few well-selected ones on subjects not found in the psalms. But there was little good poetry on sacred subjects outside the Scriptures, he argued, and there was great danger of a selection accommodated to the degree of "animal sensibility" affected by those who were most zealous in the measure. There was another reason for opposing the increase in the number of hymns.

> Some ministers, and other members of this Church, have so strong an inclination to multiply them that, whatever might be in future the number of those allowed there would be at every convention a wish for more. Others are aware of the inconvenience of this continual enlargement, but press for the setting aside of some of those selected, in order to introduce new ones more suited to their taste; not foreseeing that on the same principle there will be in the next convention new proposers of new hymns, and that this will happen without end. There are some religious societies who think it ungodly to introduce into the worship of the sanctuary any other singing than that of the Psalms of David. This is unreasonable; but are not we running into the opposite extreme?[17]

Bishop White followed up these objections with the publication of two articles in the *Christian Journal* entitled: "Thoughts on the Singing of Psalms and Anthems in Churches," signed "Silas." Possibly because of his opposition the fifty-seven hymns which constituted the hymnal, along with *Tate and Brady*, remained unchanged for fifteen years.[18] It

was this collection which was in use when Muhlenberg became an assistant minister to Bishop White in 1817. The bishop himself never permitted hymns to be sung in the United Parish except at Christmas and
Easter, and then only one or two. Muhlenberg wished to go further but
was prevented by Bishop White. Possibly the bishop's opposition was the
result of an early experience with the preaching of George Whitfield
which had given him a strong distaste for "enthusiasm" in religion.[19] As
in the case of the dethroning of the parish clerk, Muhlenberg's reform
was anticipated by Dr. Abercrombie, who was fond of hymns and particularly of a hymn not then in the authorized collection. The latter attempted to get around Bishop White's prohibition of hymn singing by
arranging with the choir that he would end his sermon with the first line
of one of his favorite hymns and the choir would pick up the hymn there
and sing it through. The stunt went over well but it called down on Dr.
Abercrombie the wrath of the bishop. The doctor, who has already
been noted, had a mind of his own, defended his action, the necessity of
hymns, and the beauty of this particular hymn. "As for me," said the
bishop, "whatever thoughts or feelings I want to express . . . I can find
them all in the Psalms of David." Dr. Abercrombie answered that the
"new dispensation" rendered necessary something more than the
Psalms of David could give us. The bishop was not convinced and requested that this incident not be repeated. It never was as long as he was
alive.[20]

Muhlenberg had been in Lancaster less than a year when he wrote
Jackson Kemper:

> I have sent you by mail a little pamphlet on a subject we have frequently
> conversed about. I have forwarded copies to several of my clerical acquaint-
> ances—I trust it will not be thought presumptuous—the subject has long
> lain very near my heart, and this is the only way in which I could do any-
> thing. If you approve of the proposed plan—might not an attempt be made
> in the ensuing convention to carry it into effect. Very little time would be
> consumed—and the appointment of such a committee could not possibly
> do any harm. I need not urge any additional arguments as . . . you feel anx-
> ious on the subject as I do. I can conceive of no improvement to our
> services more beautiful and edifying than a good selection of Evangelical
> Hymns.[21]

The pamphlet to which he referred was entitled *A Plea for Christian
Hymns*,[22] addressed to a friend who was a delegate to the special con-
vention which was meeting in Philadelphia at St. Peter's Church on
October 30, 1821. Muhlenberg was the secretary of the House of
Bishops at this convention as he had been the year before at the regular
convention.

A Plea for Christian Hymns was clearly an attempt to answer Bishop White's arguments, although he was not mentioned by name. Muhlenberg first took up the inadequacy of the psalms for a complete system of Christian worship. While allowing that the psalms were very valuable and that they should have an important part in Christian worship, he pointed out that they were written long before the Christian era and therefore did not mention many of the doctrines of the Christian faith. Muhlenberg admitted that some Christian societies had displayed a great want of taste and a degree of disrespect to the word of God in banishing the psalms altogether from their services but the Episcopal church, in allowing very little else to be sung, had gone to the other extreme. In our singing, "Are we always to be Jews?" he asked.

Muhlenberg asserted that though a few hymns were authorized there was little variety in their subjects, the number was small, and the rubric required one psalm to be sung whenever a hymn was sung, thus precluding a hymn when the congregation sang but once. Furthermore, the psalms were indexed according to classifications which contained many Christian themes but in most cases the psalms merely alluded to the themes and were accompanied by matter foreign to the theme indicated. As Bishop White put it in his pamphlet, the psalms had been accommodated to the theme.[23] In other words, a meaning had been read into a psalm which was not originally intended.

In addition to the fact that the psalms contained no reference to distinctive Christian doctrines, many of them had been composed under peculiar circumstances and were on that account inapplicable to ordinary devotion:

> Thus those professions of innocence, boastings of merit, histories of temporal sufferings, which, in their original use were right and good are evidently unfit for the common purposes of Christian worship. But I will not dwell upon this, or any other of the arguments which occur to my mind, lest you imagine I have not a sufficient regard for this revered portion of the sacred word. I object only to giving it a pre-eminence for which it was never designed. According to the Apostle, the word of God is intended for various purposes. Some parts of it are profitable for *doctrine,* some for *reproof,* and some for *correction in righteousness*—and others (may I not add) for *thanksgiving* and praise. This applies to the Psalter as well as to the other books of Scripture. Portions of it are to be used for doctrine, or reproof, or as history only—and not as exercises of devotion.

The foregoing objections applied particularly to *Tate and Brady,* the version used in the prayer book. Muhlenberg then compared this version with some of Watts' hymns and stated that, although Watts was far from being perfect, nonetheless he had the advantage of being Christian, not Jewish. He called attention to the many portions of Scripture, both in the Old and New Testaments, which could be used as a basis for hymns. As if answering Bishop White's statement that there was little or no good sacred poetry outside of the psalms, he said that Watts, Newton, Cowper, and others had given the world poetry worthy of being sung in any assembly of the saints. He then pointed out:

> The Episcopal Church is more restricted in this respect, than any other society of Christians, excepting the Scotch Presbyterians. It is certain that in the Church of England various compilations are used; and even that in the Roman Catholic communion the hymns and anthems are left to the choice of the clergy. The Lutherans (being a sister church, their example may be of weight) have various hymn books; that most common in the United States contains nearly eight hundred hymns. This is adduced as argument, because the circumstances of the Episcopal Church cannot be so different from those of other communions, that while they find hymns so very necessary, she can profitably dispense with them altogether.

Apparently in answer to Bishop White's argument that the authorization of more hymns would mean interminable arguments in one convention after another, Muhlenberg wrote that the Lutherans and Presbyterians had hymnbooks and yet had no cause for frequently changing their contents. To Bishop White's argument that the greatest care should be taken in admitting new hymns, he countered that if a committee were appointed at this convention it would have ample time, in the two-year interval before the next convention, to consider the new hymns carefully. This document was circulated at the general convention.[24]

No action, however, was taken on the matter. Muhlenberg then began a compilation of hymns on his own initiative which he published under the title of *Church Poetry, being portions of the Psalms in verse and hymns suited to the festivals and fasts and various occasions of the church. Selected and altered from various authors. By William Augustus Muhlenberg, Associate Rector of St. James Church, Lancaster, Philadelphia, Published by S. Potter and Co.* 1823.[25] Evidently he put the volume into use at Lancaster, for the advertisement in the Lancaster papers read "Church Poetry, A Work Containing Psalms and Hymns now used in St. James Church of this city, selected and altered from various authors."[26]

In compiling this collection, Muhlenberg relied heavily on the work of Thomas Cotterill, a Church of England hymnologist. The ninth edition of Cotterill's work was issued by permission of Dr. Edward Harcourt, Archbishop of York, and was dedicated to him.[27] Muhlenberg cited the ninth edition as a precedent for *Church Poetry* and continued Cotterill's practice of revising the work of other hymn writers. Muhlenberg's collection, however, added a number of new hymns and dropped several of Cotterill's hymns. On comparison, the two books are similar but far from identical.

In his preface Muhlenberg remarked that it was generally admitted that the psalmody of the Episcopal church needed reformation. The many new versions of the psalms and the numerous compilations of hymns, some of them under the sanction of the dignitaries of the church, established, he said, the general wish for reformation. This publication was designed to show that such a reformation was practicable.[28] With regard to the editing of the psalms and hymns in *Church Poetry,* he used a great deal of freedom:

> The selection had been made from the works of Tate and Brady, Merish, Watts, Mrs. Steele, Montgomery, Good, Wood, and many others with all of whom great liberty has been taken in the way of alteration. Their compositions have in so many instances been modified and the verses of one blended with those of another in the same Psalm that their names have not been affixed to the portions. Occasionally, to supply a line or verse and rarely a Psalm or Hymn, an attempt has been made at original composition but only when necessity required it.
>
> With respect to the hymns, pains have been taken to adapt them to the various subjects and occasions for which they are needed. They have been selected from a large number of authors with whose works the same freedom has been used as in compiling the Psalms. With the hope of improvement, they have been freely altered — in doing which, great assistance was derived from a "Selection of Psalms and Hymns" published under the patronage of the Archbishop of York, in which many old compositions appear in a new and improved dress. It is hoped that the object constantly in view, in making the compilation, has, in a good degree, been attained — viz., the union of *good poetry* and *evangelical sentiment.*

Muhlenberg also knew of a hymnbook proposed in England under the editorship of Bishop Reginald Heber. This bishop wanted to bring together the poets of England to produce a hymnbook based on the poetry of the time. Muhlenberg says of this project:

> The question may occur, why was not this publication postponed until the appearance of a work said to be in contemplation by the English Poets? But it does not appear that such a work is seriously projected — and if it were, it is questionable whether it would really be an addition to our devotional poetry. Southey, Scott, and Moore might produce elegant verses; but it is doubtful whether they will write many lines of the sort of poetry needed in our congregations. It is to be feared that their harps have not been tuned to the Songs of Zion.[29]

36

The publication of *Church Poetry* may have been an attempt to influence the General Convention of 1823 which met in Philadelphia.[30] Ten days before the opening of the Convention *The Philadelphia Recorder* printed the preface in full.[31] *Church Poetry* had already been put into service in several parishes which caused the comment at the convention that unless the church did something about furnishing an official hymn-book the clergy were likely to take matters into their own hands.[32] Muhlenberg was himself a clerical delegate at the convention and the other two clerical delegates from Pennsylvania were Jackson Kemper and Dr. James Abercrombie. This time the twenty-seven-year-old clergy-man had the convention behind him and a commission was appointed consisting of a number of eminent members among whom were Bishop White, Bishop Hobart, Kemper, Muhlenberg, Dr. Samuel Turner of the General Theological Seminary, and Francis Scott Key.[33] Bishop White, at a subsequent meeting of this committee, read a paper expressing his perennial arguments against introducing more hymns. The committee, however, was undeterred by the arguments of the aged bishop and went forward with its work.[34] When the convention met again in 1826 the hymnal was completed. Its title was *Hymns of the Protestant Episcopal Church in the United States of America set forth in the General Convention of said Church, in the year of our Lord, 1789, 1808,* and *1829*. (It is sometimes referred to as *The Hymnal of 1827* or *The Hymnal of 1828* in source material.)

Even Bishop White admitted that there had been many meetings of the committee and that the members had bestowed great pains upon the work. The most active were Muhlenberg and Henry Ustick Onderdonk, who was placed on the committee after the original appointments were made. These two clergymen paid the cost of publication out of their own pockets and were later reimbursed through the profits from the sale of the hymnbook.[35] In one respect Bishop White's worst fears were realized—the number of hymns was increased from 57 to 213.[36] Another of his fears proved groundless—the work of the committee was accepted as permanent by the Episcopal church and there were no more arguments in the convention about hymns. This hymnal remained the official hymnbook of this church for fifty years and set official endorsement on the use of hymns in the services. Bishop White seems to have caught the significance of the change from the psalm-singing church of his youth to the hymn-singing church of his maturity, for, commenting on this hymnal he says:

> Within my memory . . . there has taken place a most remarkable change in reference to the subject now noticed. When . . . I was a young man, and in England, and when I . . . was there fifteen years after I never in any church,

heard other *metrical* singing than what was either from the version of Stern-hold and Hopkins or from that of Tate and Brady. In this country, it was the same; except on Christmas day and on Easter Sunday, when there were the two hymns now appropriate to those days; which were strictly rubrical; they being no more than passages of scripture, put into the trammels of metre and rhyme. Of late years in England, an unbounded license has taken place in this respect; and even an Archbishop of York has given sanction to a collection of hymns made by one of his clergy. The like liberty has crossed the ocean to this country, in a degree.[37]

The fact that the hymnal was accepted without opposition by all groups in the Episcopal church and remained in effect for such a length of time indicates that Muhlenberg and his associates had correctly gauged the sentiment of the church, and only respect for the aged bishop prevented the adoption of a hymnal sooner.

Concerning this hymnal, an English hymnologist writes:

> To say that English Eighteenth Century dissent furnished a majority of the hymns with Watts, Doddridge, Steele, and Charles Wesley leading is merely to say that it bore the marks of its time. Numerous other writers, older and newer, were also represented. The tone of the book was decidedly Evangelical and quite colorless in ecclesiastical and sacramental directions. It... met in considerable measure the demand of those who had wanted more hymns and to extend the practice of hymn singing in parochial worship. In other communions also the book was favorably regarded, and "Epis. Coll." became a familiar ascription indicating the source of hymns in their hymn book.
>
> The permanent distinction of the hymnal of 1827 is its contribution to English Hymnody. It brought to the fore no less than five American Episcopal Hymn writers, whose hymns have survived. Dr. Onderdonk contributed nine... Dr. Muhlenberg contributed five... George W. Doane contributed two . . . and one each by J. Wallis Eastburn and Francis Scott Key.[38]

Of Muhlenberg's hymns, the first and probably the earliest "I Would Not Live Alway" was the occasion of considerable controversy. There was a popular belief that this hymn was written as a result of his un-happy romance with Sarah Coleman[39] (which is discussed later in this chapter).[40] Muhlenberg always denied that there was any connection between Sarah Coleman and this hymn but the date of her death and the first publication of the hymn suggest the possibility. Sarah Cole-man died in November 1825 and the first known publication of the hymn was in *The Philadelphia Recorder* in June 1826.[41] The hymn had become so popular by 1827 that it was included in the hymnal that the commission was compiling. Muhlenberg's colleagues on the commission did not know that he was the author and it was placed in the hymnbook largely at the insistence of Dr. Henry Ustick Onderdonk. In any case, the hymn soon became a source of embarrassment for he voted against its inclusion in the hymnbook and tried to conceal his authorship.[42] Many years later Jackson Kemper, his most intimate friend, wrote him that he believed Muhlenberg to have written the hymn.[43] Several revisions were published by the author in his later years but they were not successful in displacing the original version.[44]

Of Muhlenberg's five hymns, "I Would Not Live Alway" was by far the most popular, while three others were widely used. During his lifetime he was regarded as a great hymn writer but the verdict of time has been against him. Of his hymns only "Should the Glad Tidings" is in the present hymn book of the Episcopal church. Concerning this hymn, Muhlenberg said that it was composed at the particular request of Bishop Hobart of New York who wanted a hymn that could be sung to a tune "by Avison" which was then very popular. The bishop liked the hymn so well that he had it published and it was sung in Trinity Church, New York, on the following Christmas.[45]

A reading of Muhlenberg's hymns and poetry would indicate that his claim to eminence must rest upon other achievements. But his hymns were very popular during the nineteenth century and contributed greatly to his reputation during his lifetime and for many years after his death. It should be said to his credit, however, that he realized the shortcomings of his most popular hymn "I Would Not Live Always" when his contemporaries did not, and later in life he was to be one of the leaders in reviving classical church music. Likewise his interest in hymnody broadened from its Evangelical base, for he was one of the sponsors of a hymnal in 1861 that included Latin and German hymns. (This topic is further discussed in Chapter 4.) Muhlenberg's enthusiasm for hymnology at Lancaster marked the beginning of a lifelong interest in hymns and church music.

Muhlenberg's work at Lancaster was by no means confined to Hymnody, however. Shortly after his arrival he embarked on a program of education in the church and in the community which for many years he regarded as his life work. Mention has already been made of his activity in religious education at St. James, Philadelphia, and his leadership in the Sunday School Society.[46] This experience he put to good use in Lancaster and, as in the case of his campaign for hymnals, he revealed himself as an accomplished behind the scenes worker.

There was a Union Sunday School already in existence at Lancaster for all English speaking children. One of his first steps was to form a denominational Sunday school for St. James parish. The teachers in the Union School from St. James thereupon withdrew and became teachers in the denominational school. This action created some resentment since the Episcopalians in Lancaster came from the wealthier classes but it was subsequently defended by the teachers themselves for they claimed that the denominational school was more effective than the Union School.[47]

Following the formation of the parochial Sunday school, a Sunday School Society was founded, which affiliated with the Episcopal Sunday School and Adult School Union of Philadelphia. Muhlenberg also persuaded the vestry to erect for its use a separate school building, which was one of the first distinctively Sunday school buildings to be erected in this country by an Episcopal church.[48] The objects of the Sunday School Society were twofold: 1) the religious instruction of the children and 2) the relief of poor members of the church. The first object had to be broadened since it was found necessary to teach some of the children to read and write in order that they might study their Testaments. A lending library was also launched. The first report stated that:

> The school was opened on the 27th of May, 1821, with about 50 scholars; the number has since increased to 150. Forty have committed to memory the Church Catechism—Scripture portions and Hymns are recited every Sunday, by almost all the scholars who can read—and we have the pleasure of stating that some who entered the school ignorant of the alphabet are now able to read in the testament.

To carry out the charitable objects of the Sunday school, the society enacted in its by-laws that

> There shall be appointed from time to time four committees to be called visiting committees, whose duty it shall be to visit the poor of the church residing in the districts for which they shall be severally appointed, and to obtain for them the relief which may be necessary, either from the funds of the society or the charitable collections of the church, and make report to the society.[49]

There was one practice of the Sunday school—that of giving reward tickets—the whole principle of which Muhlenberg was to react against very strongly only a few years later. When he was a member with Kemper of the publication committee of the Sunday School Society, in Philadelphia, they had ordered, among other things, "2,000 reward tickets." It was this practice which was satirized by Mark Twain in *Tom Sawyer*.[50] It was also opposed by Muhlenberg's friends, Roberts Vaux and Joseph Lancaster, in their philosophy of education.[51] But it was evidently in use in St. James for the by-laws of the Sunday school set up a system of rewards and punishments based on tickets. A certain number were awarded for reciting verses from the Bible, hymns, and parts of the catechism, and for good behavior. A corresponding number were forfeited for misbehavior, absences, leaving seats, or forgetting books. Ten blue tickets equaled one red ticket, and a red ticket was worth one cent. A final requirement was that a scholar must recite his tickets, that is, recite the verses for which they had been awarded, before they could be redeemed. It can be seen, therefore, that the system in practice at St. James was similar but not as naive as the system at the church in Hannibal, Missouri, for Tom Sawyer would have been trapped by the final requirement.[52]

In the spring of 1821, Muhlenberg branched out into community activities, of which one was to be his most important work while at Lancaster. He began with two abortive efforts to make books more available. Reflecting the influence of his friend the Quaker philanthropist, Roberts Vaux, he called together a committee to form a Public and Apprentice Library as Vaux had done the previous year in Philadelphia.[53] A little later he tried to form an Athenaeum, a project which

St. James Church, Lancaster, Pennsylvania. Painted by E. H. Hammond, 1844. (Courtesy St. James Church)

was probably suggested by a similar organization in Philadelphia founded by Roberts Vaux, Mathew Carey, and William Tilghman.[54] We hear nothing more of these organizations, and it is probable that they died out, for Muhlenberg became absorbed in an effort to establish a public school system for Lancaster. This project was to have far-reaching results both for Muhlenberg personally and for the community.

While still an assistant minister at the United Parish in Philadelphia Muhlenberg had been appointed a member of the board of controllers of the First School District of Pennsylvania through the influence of Bishop White.[55] The president of the board was Roberts Vaux and the promotion of a public school system appears to have been Vaux's major interest in this period.[56]

The Pennsylvania constitution provided for the erection of a state-wide public school system, but the only step in that direction had been taken in 1809, when a law was passed authorizing the board of assessors of each county to compile a list of children whose parents were unable to pay for their schooling and to circulate it among the teachers in the county. The teachers could then bill the board for the tuition of any child on the list. This procedure put an obvious taint of pauperism on state supported education.[57]

Under the leadership of Roberts Vaux a law was passed in 1818 setting up the city of Philadelphia as the first school district of the state and providing for the instruction of all children in the city, free of charge, thereby removing the stigma attached to the so-called "pauper schools." The law further specified that the schools were to be on the Lancastrian System.[58]

This system was named after an English schoolteacher named Joseph Lancaster. (There is no connection between the name of this man and the name of the city of Lancaster.) Under this system, one or two paid teachers had charge of a school of five or six hundred children. The teachers selected the brightest of the students as "monitors," who did the actual teaching under supervision. Its advantage, at a time when the public had not yet accepted the necessity of large expenditures for public education, was that it enabled numerous children to receive the rudiments of an elementary education on the meager appropriations that the state legislature was willing to make.[59]

Joseph Lancaster had opened a school for poor children in his father's home. Since he was unable to accommodate all applicants he started a system as outlined above. Lancaster was a Quaker and his affiliation with this highly respected group was helpful in promoting his plan. It soon became an international craze spreading not only throughout the British Isles and the United States but also throughout the Continent.[60] Lafayette, for example, is quoted as having said, when he visited the

Lancastrian school in Lancaster, Pennsylvania, that his grandchildren were attending a Lancastrian school in Paris.[61]

Private schools using the Lancastrian plan were already operating in Philadelphia when this became the official system for the public schools established by law in 1818.[62] Lancaster himself came to the United States in that year and in the next few years spent some time in Philadelphia. He organized a model Lancastrian school and delivered lectures on his system.[63] It is quite possible that he met Muhlenberg, who was on the board of controllers.

Roberts Vaux had been warned in advance by a Quaker friend that Lancaster was not in good standing with the Society of Friends and that he was but "too susceptible to vanity."[64] Lancaster was in constant conflict with the board of controllers and his fellow teachers. In a letter to Vaux, Lancaster declared that he wished that he had never seen any of the Philadelphia controllers with the exception of Vaux and one or two others.[65] Whether Muhlenberg was one of the one or two others does not appear in any document but it is noteworthy that Joseph Lancaster is never mentioned in the correspondence between Muhlenberg and Vaux.

When Muhlenberg came to Lancaster in 1820, the Act of 1809 was still the only provision for public education and Philadelphia had the only public school system in the state.[66] Shortly after moving to Lancaster the young clergyman began to work quietly for a more adequate law. His position in this matter was a delicate one for the Lancaster people were still predominantly German and efforts to erect an English school would arouse considerable opposition. On the other hand, Governor Joseph Heister was on record as favoring the Lancastrian system. Furthermore, the money for educational purposes was already appropriated under the earlier act and only needed to be earmarked for the construction and maintenance of a school building by a second act.[67]

Muhlenberg's lobbying was successful. The General Assembly passed an act in 1822, "to provide for the education of children at the public expense within the city and incorporate boroughs of the county of Lancaster."[68] The act directed the Court of Common Pleas of Lancaster County to appoint twelve citizens to be directors of the public schools in Lancaster city, which was denominated the First Section of the Second School District of Pennsylvania. The directors had the power to superintend the schools, erect school houses, appoint teachers, and provide books, stationery, and all things necessary for maintaining and conducting the schools under their control.

Unfortunately, the act for Lancaster, unlike the one setting up the First District (Philadelphia), retained, in part at least, the old pauper provisions instead of admitting all children free:

> The directors may admit into any public school, all such indigent orphan children and the children of indigent parents to be supplied at the public expense as they shall deem expedient and proper; they may also admit children whose parents or guardians are in circumstances to pay for their tuition, either in whole or in part, and shall be at liberty to charge in each individual case any sum which may be agreed upon between the parties . . .

The act further stipulated that the principles of Joseph Lancaster's system of education in its most improved state should be adopted and pursued in all the public schools within the district. A more important provision gave the directors authority to draw on the county treasurer for the erection, establishment, and maintenance of the school.[69]

The Court of Common Pleas in compliance with this act appointed the following as directors: Christian Endress, William Augustus Muhlenberg, William Ashmeade, John Risdel, Adam Reigart, Caspar Schaffner, Jr., Phillip Benedict, George Musser, John Reynolds, Edward Coleman, George B. Porter, and Frederick Augustus Muhlenberg.[70] Of these men, Adam Reigart was to become the chairman of the first board of education under the statewide law which was to supersede the acts of 1822.[71] Edward Coleman, the son of Robert Coleman, was a successful businessman in his own right and a vestryman of St. James Church, and was to figure in Muhlenberg's life in other ways.[72] Frederick Augustus Muhlenberg, a physician, was William Augustus' cousin. He was probably a helpful influence on the board, for he was a leader of the English language party in his church, but was so tactful that he avoided the fight that had taken place at St. Michael and Zion.[73] Christian Endress was elected president of the board and William Augustus Muhlenberg secretary. The board apparently proceeded with dispatch for one year after the passage of the act of 1822 the schoolhouse was completed and two teachers hired. A notice in the *Lancaster Intelligencer* of April 22, 1823, signed by Muhlenberg announced the opening of the school.[74]

The directors submitted their annual report in March, 1824, summarizing the school's first year of operations. There were 460 scholars admitted, 278 boys and 182 girls. The school rooms accommodated 500 scholars. The controversial question of tuition payments was reported as follows:

> A large portion of the . . . [students] are free scholars. A great number pay a small compensation. The directors find that by accepting a very moderate sum for tuition many children are brought within the walls whom their parents would not send as free scholars. . . . Others again pay the full charge for tuition, which, however, is no more than sufficient to raise the income necessary for the support of the school, the appropriation of the legislature from the county funds being inadequate to the object.

44

The report further declared that the current school system was much cheaper than the system established under the law of 1821, in which individual teachers billed the county for their services. The annual expenses of the school were $1,300.00, whereas if all the poor children in the city were taught at public expense the cost would be close to $1,800.00. The two teachers were Alexander Varian and Ann Jamieson.[75] Varian had already had some experience operating a private Lancastrian school before Muhlenberg came to Lancaster. He was a teacher in St. James Sunday School and later was elected to the vestry.[76]

Despite the favorable report given by the directors the school ran into vigorous opposition. The first source of opposition was a perennial one—the fact that the school was still supported partly by tuition fees antagonized the poorer people of the community and gave the school a quasipauper flavor. A second source was the unwillingness of the rural taxpayers to set up additional sections of the Second District. The fact that the school in Lancaster was the only tax-supported school in the county and yet was supported out of the county funds gave some grounds for resistance. The third source, as might be expected, was the German-speaking population, who were answered in the report of 1824:

> In consequence of a late memorial to the legislature complaining that the members of the German Lutheran and Reformed Congregation are not "benefited with the rest of their fellow citizens by the Lancastrian School,' the directors feel called upon to state that the majority of their scholars since the commencement of the institution has always been the children of German Lutheran and German Reformed parents. At present the number of such is upward of one hundred and sixty. If any portion of the community has been benefited more than another by the operation of the public school, it is unquestionably the above named congregations.[77]

The second of these objections, that the rural taxpayers were being unfairly taxed to support a city school, was met by an additional act of the General Assembly, whose preamble indicated a trend to a state-supported system of education. "To provide more effectually for the education of the poor, gratis, and for laying the foundations of a general system of education throughout this commonwealth" the support of the schools in Philadelphia and Lancaster was transferred from the county to the city government. This act was intended to meet the objections of the rural taxpayers and of those who still felt that a pauper stigma was attached to the school.[78]

In the third report, in 1825, the school was described as in excellent condition, the scholars being examined in reading, writing, arithmetic, grammar, geography, and the girls in needlework. Frequent attempts were made to secure the repeal of the act, and at one time John L. Atlee and John Reynolds were authorized by the directors to appear before a legislative committee at Harrisburg to prevent its overthrow. It was generally upheld by the wealthier classes and opposed by the poor.[79] Muhlenberg resigned his position on the board when he left Lancaster in 1826 and his place was taken by his successor, Levi Silliman Ives.

The General Assembly passed a law in 1834 providing for a statewide system of free public schools which is the basis of the present Pennsylvania school system. Lancaster was formally organized under this law four years later. Of the new board, Adam Reigert, its president, and George Musser, its treasurer, had been members of the old board since 1822.[80]

Muhlenberg's connection with the school is an interesting one. Roberts Vaux gave him the credit for founding the school[81] and the correspondence between them during its formation indicates that Muhlenberg was by far the most active member of the board of directors. He seems to have assumed the responsibility of running the school, which he was able to do without difficulty because of his position as secretary of the board. A considerable amount of space has been given to the annual reports because, since he was secretary and since the reports are similar to his other writings, it is quite likely that he wrote them himself.

The correspondence between the Episcopalian rector and the Quaker philanthropist gives an interesting sidelight on the early years of the school at Lancaster. Muhlenberg had evidently been making use of Vaux's interest and experience from the beginning of the project for in the first letter dated January 14, 1822, he writes: "Once more we must trouble you on the business of our public school—your known readiness to serve on such occasions encourages us to ask another favor."[82]

The law setting up the school had been passed only a few days previous to the date of this letter so that it is evident that Muhlenberg had been making plans prior to its passage:

> Mr. Alexander Miller is the architect whom we have employed to erect our school house. He goes to Philadelphia, in order to view the furniture required in a Lancastrian School. Will you, Sir, have the goodness to direct him to the school which you think the best fitted up and give him such information with respect to improvements, if there be any which you think worth commencing.[83]

Muhlenberg wrote again in June 1822 thanking Vaux for his continued interest, and asking for further advice on the arrangement of the school house.[84] In September of that year, Muhlenberg sent Varian to Philadelphia with a letter of introduction to Vaux for the purpose of obtaining training in the Lancastrian System.[85] In February, 1823, another letter gives a list of supplies used in a Lancastrian school.

> I have been requested by the Board of Directors here to trouble you once more, and I trust for the last time with respect to our school. Will you have the goodness to procure for us the slates, pencils, copybooks, lessons, class books, Registers and Monitor's badges (25 staffs for the general monitors, as in the model school); signal bells, etc., in that all the stationery and apparatus (excepting the reward tickets) that would be needed in two schools — 250 scholars each.

> We shall probably send a female teacher to be instructed in the model school. I suppose none receive testimonials of proficiency but those who are fully qualified; the (Lancastrian) system may be much injured and become unpopular when teachers go from the model school if they are not altogether competent. If the controllers feel the least hesitation as [to] the qualifications of a teacher, they ought [to withhold] a testimonial or give a qualified one.[86]

Muhlenberg wrote Vaux one more letter in regard to the supplies and then the correspondence in regard to the details of setting up the school terminated.[87]

Muhlenberg and Vaux kept in touch with each other and three years later they resumed their correspondence although they had evidently seen each other in the meanwhile and discussed the operation of their schools. Muhlenberg had proposed an important change in the Lancastrian system by which a number of permanent monitors would be employed on a salary basis. Muhlenberg sent Vaux a document describing the proposed change and Vaux suggested that he publish it.[88] No copy of this document has been found but the scheme was tried out in the model school in Philadelphia during 1827 and worked so well that it was recommended for the use of schools in other places. Roberts Vaux gave Muhlenberg full credit for this innovation. It was introduced in the Lancaster school on a permanent basis shortly after Muhlenberg left and he himself later used it in a modified form in his school at Flushing, New York.[89]

Another project in which Muhlenberg was interested but which he was never able to undertake was suggested in a letter to Vaux in 1821:

> I was pleased to see in the last report of the Controller an allusion to the all important subject of education in manufactures. I hardly know a matter of higher moment to the real welfare of our country — I hope what you say may have its effect — but I fear none of our legislators will embark in a cause of so questionable popularity — the accomplishment of the object you propose would be worthy of the highest talents — would rank its author

among the benefactors of mankind and would be a project of benevolence not inferior to the abolition of the slave-trade.[90]

The leading event of the school during the time that Muhlenberg was in Lancaster was the visit of Lafayette on his return to the United States in 1825. Lafayette was welcomed to the school by a small boy, James Barrett Kerfoot, whose speech was presumably written by Muhlenberg:

> General: We are happy to welcome you within the walls of our school. We hope that you will always recommend learning and that you will always cherish such valuable institutions as this. Remember that schools are of great importance to a free people and that education is the best security for Virtue, Liberty, and Independence.
> We thank you for your kindness in coming from your native country, France, to help us in getting the liberty we now enjoy. We wish you Health, Honour. and Prosperity as long as you live in this world and in the world to come eternal happiness; and if it is your intention to return to France, we wish you a safe and pleasant voyage.[91]

Muhlenberg summarized his work with the public school system in the valedictory sermon which he delivered when he left Lancaster in 1826:

> This leads me to a topic on which I beg leave to say a few words to my audience as citizens of Lancaster. The only official connection I have had with you in that character has been as a Director of the Public School. Having succeeded in establishing that institution, and always feeling as deeply interested in its concerns as in those of my own parish I would improve this last opportunity of presenting it to your patronage. The school is founded on enlightened principles. Though it has labored under difficulties and has had much opposition to encounter its good effects among us are now generally allowed. It has raised the standard of English education and has offered instruction to numbers who otherwise would have grown up in ignorance. It has also been the means of Moral Reformation.[92]

As early as 1824 Muhlenberg had begun to consider the establishment of a school which would completely embody his ideas. He already had contact with various types of schools: Dr. Abercrombie's Philadelphia Academy, The Grammar School and College of the University of Pennsylvania, the General Theological Seminary, the Lancastrian schools in Philadelphia and Lancaster, and Franklin College[93] in Lancaster. He was also familiar with the Episcopal Academy of Philadelphia although he had no direct contact with it.[94] The forming of the Education Society to finance the studies of candidates for the ministry in

1824 brought from him a letter to Jackson Kemper which shows the trend of his thinking. After expressing hearty approval of the aim of the society he went on to make several specific proposals. First of all the students should study under one teacher and should be subject to the direction of a clergyman who should have some form of official control over them. In his opinion, the period from thirteen to eighteen years of age was the most important in a young man's life, "When habits are acquired, sentiments adopted, and the character of the man is formed."

> Now do not smile when I tell you that I should like to see such a school for young prophets in Lancaster. For I am visionary enough to hope it is practicable. At present we have no classical school in this town but should a competent teacher of the languages and mathematics establish himself here, I have no doubt that in a year or two he would meet with very general good support. This is the opinion of many others beside myself. But no gentleman would be willing to come here and remain long enough to make the experiment. I have wished for sometime to get one but not being able to offer sufficient inducement in the beginning I have never spoken to any individual. But now suppose your society is organized and its auxiliaries are ready to support eight or ten young men—you might select a competent instructor—locate him here and engage to give him as much per ann. for the tuition of each beneficiary. This probably would be enough to enable him to get along until his school received accessions from the neighborhood here—would I think certainly be the case.
>
> As the youth you sent in would generally be no more than boys—there is little vanity in supposing that your humble servant should he be honored would be capable of maintaining over them a superintendenting control and of giving them occasional instruction in branches that would not be the duty of their ordinary teacher.

Muhlenberg made a start by taking two monitors of the Lancastrian school, Libertus Van Bokhelen and James B. Kerfoot, into his home and educating them privately. Of these he wrote:

> The two lads I am educating make most rapid improvement that in a year or two they would be competent for the office of tutor which they would perform gratis—You see the idea I have in my head is simply this—a nursery for the Theological Seminary at Lancaster. . . .
>
> You may communicate the scheme to those of the Brethren you think proper and let me know your sentiments as soon as may be for I should like to know what prospect there is of having a teacher of the languages and mathematics [*settle here*]. . . .

Muhlenberg talked this matter over with friends in Lancaster as well and he came to the conclusion that a school on these lines should be his life work. A rather dramatic episode in his private life, however, may have been the major factor in his decision to leave Lancaster and devote his entire time to establishing such a school.[95]

Miss Ayres, in her biography, makes only a brief mention of Muhlenberg's unhappy romance, which wholly aside from its human interest was a profound influence in shaping his life. Of it, she says only that:

> Most lives have their romance and the one before us was not an exception, of which a separate story might be written, were it to the purpose of these pages. Both the light and the shadow of that romance fell upon the years of earnest work spent in Lancaster, and when Mr. Muhlenberg gave up his charge there, he left behind him the grave of his earthly hopes.
>
> As illustrating a strong element in his character we make a single extract from his private diary in this connection. He had incurred the displeasure of a gentleman whose favor, at the time, was of importance to him, by instituting an evening service; after reviewing for a minute or two, the advantages he would be likely to gain by some concessions in this particular, he adds: "But for no earthly consideration whatever, not even the attainment of the dear object of my heart, will I sacrifice what I believe to be the interest of my church. O Lord, help me.[96]

Lancaster legends as well as secondary sources name Sarah Coleman, daughter of Robert Coleman, as the girl with whom Muhlenberg fell in love. And circumstantial evidence based on primary sources conclusively proves that she was the person involved. The only primary sources that definitely name her are somewhat questionable and are discussed later in this chapter.

The first primary source is the reticent account from the diary (quoted above from Anne Ayres' biography which gives three clues: 1) Muhlenberg had a romance while in Lancaster; 2) the girl involved died before he left; 3) the breaking up of the romance was caused by an argument between Muhlenberg and "a gentleman" over the holding of an evening service. The minutes of St. James Church identify Robert Coleman as the gentleman who objected to the evening services, and Muhlenberg's letters to Jackson Kemper and to the Yeates family speak of an unhappy relationship to the Coleman family. The action of Edward Coleman, Sarah's brother, in offering the vestry five thousand dollars to terminate Muhlenberg's rectorship is further evidence that the person involved came from this family.[97]

Robert Coleman had four daughters, one of whom had married and was living in Philadelphia, a second died before Muhlenberg came to Lancaster, and a third was unmarried and still living when he left. The fourth, Sarah, was the only one who died during his incumbency.

50

The will of Robert Coleman singles out his daughter Sarah in a very striking manner. The only other professional historian who has written on this subject concurs with the conclusion that it was Sarah Coleman who had the romance with Muhlenberg. The evidence is developed in detail below.[98]

In the three years prior to Muhlenberg's coming to Lancaster there occurred a prelude to his romance. Lancaster's wealthiest citizen was Robert Coleman, who was born in North Ireland and came to Pennsylvania as a young man. He built up a fortune in iron manufacturing and took a prominent part in politics. He had a family of four sons and four daughters and at the time of this first incident he was living in Lancaster in semiretirement.

In the summer of 1819 one of Coleman s daughters, Ann, became engaged to James Buchanan, a rising young lawyer. Due to a misunderstanding the engagement was broken and Ann died suddenly on a visit at the home of her married sister in Philadelphia under circumstances strongly suggesting suicide. Present with her at the time of her death was her younger sister, Sarah, who had accompanied her on the trip. Buchanan wrote Robert Coleman a pathetic letter, requesting that he be allowed to view her body before burial and to walk with the mourners at the funeral. Robert Coleman refused to receive the letter, however, and it was returned to Buchanan unopened. Buchanan did have the satisfaction of writing an obituary notice for Ann which was printed in the *Lancaster Journal*. The Coleman family held Buchanan responsible for this tragedy and became his bitter enemy.[99]

Buchanan's tragedy has a place in this biography because of the similar experience of Muhlenberg with Ann Coleman's younger sister, Sarah. Ann died in December, 1819,[100] and Muhlenberg came to Lancaster a year later. The Colemans were at that time the leading family of the parish. It was Robert Coleman who handled the correspondence with Muhlenberg in regard to his coming to St. James, and was one of a committee of three who formally notified him of his election to the rectorship.[101] The Colemans contributed generously to the erection of the new church, Robert being the largest single contributor. He was also the rector warden, the leading lay official of the church, and his son Edward was the registrar of the vestry. Several of Robert Coleman's other sons were members and pewholders.[102] Sarah was a member of the Sunday School Society which Muhlenberg formed.[103] But some time later he introduced the evening service to which her father strongly objected and which resulted in the breaking up of their romance.

The minutes of St. James vestry reflect the course of the controversy. At the April, 1821, vestry election—before the controversy began—

Muhlenberg reappointed Robert Coleman as rector's warden and the vestry elected Charles Smith as their warden. The following year, however, when the controversy had begun, Muhlenberg appointed Charles Smith the rector's warden and the vestry, apparently in an effort to placate the Colemans, elected Robert Coleman their warden. At the following meeting, Edward Coleman, Robert Coleman's son, resigned as registrar of the vestry and George W. Jacobs was elected in his place. Neither of the Colemans ever again attended a vestry meeting while Muhlenberg was rector. At the same meeting, moreover, the question was put by the chairman whether the evening services should continue as heretofore and was decided in the affirmative.[104] This meeting set a pattern which was to continue throughout Muhlenberg's stay in Lancaster. The vestry usually supported Muhlenberg but did everything it could to placate the Colemans.[105] Despite their absence the vestry continued to elect Robert Coleman their warden[106] and both the wardens were elected to represent St. James at the diocesan convention which met in Lancaster in 1823.[107]

So matters continued for two years. In January, 1825, Muhlenberg wrote Jackson Kemper about various church matters and added, among other things: "The Colemans, having withdrawn their support from the church, affects us a little — but I hope ere long to do something in aid of the different institutions of the church." He also appended a postscript:

> As you took such a kind interest in my affairs of late, perhaps I ought to have let you know from me before this — but as nothing of consequence has transpired — and it is a subject which my pen and tongue and mind and heart are sick — I have endeavored to think as little about it as possible — I am perfectly satisfied with what providence has thought best for me.[108]

In that year a series of disasters struck the Coleman family, which affected Muhlenberg as well. Robert Coleman died on August 14, 1825, in the seventy-seventh year of his age. His will was entered at the courthouse on September 3; his four sons were named executors. He divided his estate among his widow and surviving children. There was a special condition, however, attached to Sarah's bequest. He left her property of some value in Lancaster and $50,000 in cash plus a second grant of $50,000, with the following provision:

> And with an anxious view to the future interest, benefit, and support of my said dear daughter Sarah, and to guard against possible difficulties from which none can flatter themselves that they may be certainly exempted and without any other motive, she now being unmarried, I do hereby further give, devise and bequeath to my sons, William Coleman, James

52

Coleman, and my son-in-law, Joseph Hemphill, the sum of fifty thousand dollars...which I order them...to vest...in a productive fund... yielding a quarterly or half yearly interest...to be paid to Sarah or to her husband with her consent. She shall at all times have the right to revoke this consent...and any husband she may hereafter have shall not have power or authority to assign the same or to compel the payment of the...interest or dividend to him...if the said trustees...shall not think it prudent and if the said interest...shall by them be considered as necessary to the support and maintenance of...Sarah and any children she may have.

In case of her death the money was to be divided among her children; if she had no children it was to go to her sisters and their heirs. This provision was the more pointed in that Elizabeth, another unmarried daughter, received her bequest with no strings attached. This will had been drawn up in March, 1822, at the time that the controversy over the evening services began.[109]

On September 27, only a month and a half after Robert Coleman's death, Mary Jane Coleman, the twenty-nine-year-old wife of Edward Coleman, died. And one month later, on November 1, Sarah took a trip to Philadelphia to visit her married sister and there died under circumstances similar to those surrounding the death of her sister Ann in 1819. She, too, was only twenty-four at the time of her death.[110] As in the case of Ann, two obituary notices appeared, one of which was probably written by Muhlenberg.[111]

This incident, together with his growing interest in education, was probably the determining factor in Muhlenberg's decision to leave Lancaster. Six months later he notified the vestry that it was his intention to resign shortly and that he was letting them know so that they would have sufficient time to make a choice of a new pastor. The vestry immediately appointed a committee to call on Muhlenberg and "use all reasonable endeavors to induce his continuance in his present station."[112] The vestry reassembled the following day to hear another letter from Muhlenberg reaffirming the first. A communication was also received from Edward Coleman stating that if all connection between Muhlenberg and St. James was terminated by July the Coleman family would donate five thousand dollars to St. James Church.[113]

The vestry received a formal resignation from Muhlenberg on June 28, 1826. It voted to appoint the wardens a committee to draft an address to him expressing the regret of the vestry at his resignation; their acknowledgement of his services; and that he be furnished a copy of the vestry's proceedings. At the same meeting, however, the vestry voted to inform Edward Coleman that all connection between Muhlenberg and St. James Church had been dissolved by his voluntary resignation and that it was ready to receive the five thousand dollars.

One of the vestrymen objected to this resolution and withdrew from the meeting.[114] Two days later the vestry met again to consider a letter that had been received from the Yeates family, who, during his stay in Lancaster, and in the years following, were Muhlenberg's supporters:

> We, the undersigned members of St. James Church in Lancaster, request the vestry will invite the Rev. William A. Muhlenberg to preach in our church whenever the pulpit is unoccupied — our time being limited precludes our obtaining the signature of the other members of the church — but it is our opinion that these are the sentiments of the majority of the congregation.

A committee was appointed to answer this communication to the effect that Muhlenberg would always have the same courtesy extended to him that is due to every clergyman of the Protestant Episcopal church but that the vestry did not deem it necessary contrary to the usual mode to pass a formal resolution to that effect. James Hopkins requested that his protest be entered on the minutes against this resolution as being disrespectful to the Rev. Mr. Muhlenberg and to Mrs. and the Misses Yeates.[115]

At a July 7 meeting a second letter was received from Edward Coleman, the contents of which are not given in the vestry's minutes. The two wardens, one of whom was Muhlenberg's supporter, James Hopkins, were appointed a committee of two to call on Edward Coleman, in regard to his proposed donation. Their report gives an inside view of what had been going on in the parish.

> The Wardens ... report ... that they have had an interview with Mr. Coleman which embraced all the matters connected with the donation — they regret to state that in their opinion busy bodies and tale bearers have infused an acrimony into this unfortunate business which it would not otherwise have partaken of — This your committee endeavored to assuage by exposing the impositions and contrasting them with plain and simple statement of the truth and although they cannot say they have succeeded in the great object which the vestry have uniformly had in view — the restoration of union and harmony to the church by the reunion of all its members yet they fondly hope that asperities have been softened and a state of moderation and forebearance obtained which will have a tendency to bring back that union and harmony, peace and good will, which is a vital principle of the religion which we profess. As the causes which occasioned the unhappy severance in the church are removed and were in their nature of a transitory character, reason induces us to think that a short time for consideration and reflection will again place us all under the protection of those inestimable blessings which our Holy Church confers upon her true and faithful votaries.[116]

In his valedictory sermon Muhlenberg made only one short reference to this matter: *"A few individuals of one family, indeed, have chosen to absent themselves from our assemblies—BUT THE ALMIGHTY IS WITNESS that they have no just cause for offense."* He made no further reference to the Colemans in his sermon, most of which he devoted to other matters.[117] At its next meeting the vestry voted to publish the sermon.[118] Edward Coleman resumed attending vestry meetings after Muhlenberg left but resigned in April, 1827, probably because his business interests required that he move to Philadelphia.[119] There is no evidence that he ever gave the money to the church. The only further reference that Muhlenberg makes to the Colemans is in a letter to his friends, the Yeateses, in February, 1827:

> I see by one of the Lancaster papers which Mrs. Huffnagle occasionally sends me that the folks have been giving a farewell dinner to my friend Edward C.... Perhaps the time he will have for reflection at sea may lead him to a better mind in some respects.[120]

In both the Buchanan and Muhlenberg cases separate sources complain about the activity of "giddy and indiscreet tongues," and "busybodys and talebearers," which would indicate that Lancaster still had much the atmosphere of a small town.[121]

The primary sources which name Sarah Coleman as the girl with whom Muhlenberg was in love are two letters written over fifty years after the incident. This time lapse opens them to question but all of the contents that can be checked against other source material is found to be accurate. The first of these is a letter written in 1889 by John B. Clemson to Frederick Bird, who visited Muhlenberg in Lancaster in 1826 and to whom Muhlenberg entrusted the copy of the hymn "I Would Not Live Alway" for delivery to the editor of *The Philadelphia Recorder*. Mr. Clemson summarizes the romances of both Buchanan and Muhlenberg as described above but adds the additional bit of information that Ann Coleman, Buchanan's fianceé, "finished her days with a poisonous draught." This is the only documentary evidence that has come to light stating definitely that Ann committed suicide.[122]

The second letter is written by Mrs. J. W. Nevin, also to Frederick Bird, from Lancaster, where she was still living in 1881. She says that she was living in Lancaster during Muhlenberg's pastorate and that she knew all the parties involved. Her account does not mention the controversy over the evening service but otherwise it fits in well with other sources. Writing this letter fifty-five years or more after the events took place, she says:

When Mr. M. was called to St. James Church, Lancaster, the rich man of the congregation was Mr. Robert Coleman who professed himself greatly pleased with the choice of Mr. M., insisted on his making his home in his family for some time and lavished on him all possible attentions, this of course made after great intimacy in his family. At this time Miss Sarah Coleman was under engagement of Marriage to a Mr. Madison of the Virginia Madison family and I account for her fascination with Mr. M. in this way. There was a clique of young ladies her intimate friends who were delighted with the young Minister and constantly talking of him to her naturally interested her mind in him. She felt she had "the inside Track" and when he began to pay her attentions she was flattered by it, and broke off her engagement with Mr. Madison to accept Mr. Muhlenberg's. When there became an understanding between them Mr. Muhlenberg never dreaming that her father would feel any objections, made known his wishes to him, when he was rudely repulsed by Mr. Coleman "that he was after her money and he wasn'ent [*sic*] going to get it" etc.etc. Greatly shocked Mr. Muhlenberg instantly offered to break off all further inter-course, but urged by her Mother's wishes in Mr. M.'s favour Miss C refused to give the matter up — In this embarrassing position things remained a long time — Mr. M. the very soul of honor and truth secretly smarting under such an imputation did not propose marriage — She holding on by throwing herself into all his interests in all of his good works — Mr. M. had taken three boys to educate and she took an especial interest in them — Sending them presents etc. She made no secret of the state of things and I used to think from her buoyancy of manner that she looked upon it in the light of a good joke or flirtation. Things were in this state when she took a bad cold, she was of fragile constitution and the cold settled upon her lungs before her family dreamed of danger. When they awakened to it she was taken to Philadelphia where an eminent Physician was consulted who prescribed a voyage to the south of France. Then arose in the family the difficulty that she had no escort, Mr. M. hearing of this made a proposition to be her escort "either as a friend or husband". It has been said "Avarice is a weakness of age" and it proved true in the case of Mr. Coleman. He was indignant "why did any one want to marry a dying woman but to get her money." The visit to France fell through and Miss C. Died of rapid consumption but I never heard of any one of her intimate friends in Lancaster so much as intimate that she so seriously "took it to heart" as to have affected her health! Miss Coleman had been educated at a French boarding school of high fashion where no religion and very little morality was inculcated and with the Knowledge that she was to be a great heiress. Her accomplishments were external, but with pretty gay and . . . manners she was the very one to attract a shy and sensitive man as was Mr. Muhlen-bergh. It was during this period that Mr. Muhlenbergh wrote "I Would Not Live Alway".

Mrs. Nevins discusses Muhlenberg's authorship of the hymn and mentions later visits to and from Muhlenberg. She also speaks of a dinner party at her home at which both Muhlenberg and Buchanan were present. She says that she knows Baker Clemson whose first wife was a relative of the Colemans. She then returns to her discussion of Muhlenberg's romance:

> I think after Dr. M. went to New York he kept profound silence on the subject—which must have been painful and most mortifying to him and if Drs. Schaff and Washburn "pooh pooh" it, it was because they knew nothing about it, so far as Dr. Schaff was concerned it took place more (perhaps) than twenty years before he came to America and he was not accuainted [sic] with anyone in Lancaster who could have informed him about it.

> Mr. R. Coleman came to America a young adventurer in early [life] and by a fortunate purchase of the Cornwall ore mine at a mere trifle made an immense fortune from it. The business (iron making) being a large one he became with his wealth an important man in the community and asserted his consequence and was what was called a "purse proud" man.[123]

Muhlenberg and Buchanan were both deeply influenced by their unhappy romances. Neither married. Buchanan had planned to settle in Lancaster and continue his lucrative law practice but after Ann's death changed to a political career to find the friends and activity needed to take the place of the family life that he missed. In later life he acquired a household of dependent relatives and became the guardian of his niece, Harriet Lane, who became his hostess at the White House.[124] On Muhlenberg, romance had much the same effect. Not having a family to support he did not find it necessary to settle down into a parish church as did most married clergymen. Instead he was able to devote himself wholeheartedly to the founding of the church institutions with which his name is chiefly associated. These institutions always took on the aspect of a large family with Muhlenberg as the *pater familias*. He, too, accumulated a large household of relatives. His mother lived to a ripe old age and his sister, who was widowed early in life, came to live with him accompanied by her daughter. There always seemed to be an assortment of students and acquaintances whom Muhlenberg housed at various intervals. When he moved to New York his personal household was so large that he could not find a house to accommodate it and had to rent two adjacent houses.[125]

The years which marked a turning point in the life of Muhlenberg saw like changes for his closest friend. Jackson Kemper resigned his post as Bishop White's assistant in 1831 and accepted a call to St. Paul's, Norwalk, Connecticut. His second wife died there and his mother-in-law took over the care of his daughter and two sons. He thus was free to

embark on his life work as a missionary.[126] Bishop White had consecrated twenty-nine bishops before his death in 1836 and the last of
these was Jackson Kemper as "Missionary Bishop of the Northwest."[127]
Muhlenberg, in 1827, moved to the vicinity of New York City, where
he was to spend the rest of his life.

CHAPTER 3

Educator: The Flushing Institute and St. Paul's College

Although the controversy with the Colemans undoubtedly played an important part in Muhlenberg's decision to leave Lancaster, the letters to Jackson Kemper indicate that education had become his absorbing interest. Following his resignation he went to visit his mother and sister, who were living in New York, and then planned a trip abroad, where he hoped to study European schools. His departure was delayed, however, by his desire to see his younger brother, Frederick, who was expected back from Europe. In the interim he accepted an offer to supply at St. George's Parish, Flushing, Long Island, an appointment which he obtained through his old friend, Dr. James Milnor, now rector of St. George's Church, New York City. The vestry immediately elected him rector and he accepted for a period of six months only. Circumstances were to dictate that he should spend the next twenty years of his life in this locality.[1]

Flushing in 1826 was an unincorporated village of 2,000 inhabitants somewhat cut off from the outside world by a marsh over which a causeway had been built. It could be reached from New York by stagecoach or boat. The boat took one hour and made two round trips daily. The town was located on Flushing Bay, an inlet of Long Island Sound, at the farthest point inland accessible to steamboats. It was nine miles from Brooklyn, and one of the instructors at the Flushing Institute made a practice of walking this distance when the weather was favorable. The departure and return of the steamboat were the high points of the day, the occasion for the owners of estates in the neighborhood to gather. Tree nurseries

59

were the areas principal business, and the variety of trees in the town was a result. The steamboat was significantly named the "Linnaeus."[2]

Dr. George Bacon Wood, Muhlenberg's college friend, describes a visit he made to Flushing in 1827. He left Philadelphia by boat for New York, an entire day's trip. On the following day he wrote as follows:

> Desirous of seeing my friend Muhlenberg who has a church at Flushing on Long Island . . . I took Caroline [his wife] on board a steamboat on the East River—which soon bore us to that town. I observed that after we had left the city a few miles behind the shores of Manhattan Island began to assume a more pleasant aspect and many country seats appeared. The shores of Long Island seemed under fine cultivation and very cheerful. Arrived at Flushing we put up at Pecks Hotel where leaving Caroline, I went to call on Mr. M. whom to my great disappointment I found absent. He had gone on a visit to the city and was expected back in the evening. In the evening we returned to New York in the same boat—which in the meantime had made another trip. Just before we embarked I had an opportunity of saying how do you do to Mr. M. who came in the boat from the city.[3]

Flushing like Lancaster was an old town. It had been established by English Quakers who emigrated there while the province was still in the hands of the Dutch. For many years the Episcopalians and the Quakers were the only denominations in the town. St. George's at one time had as its rector Samuel Seabury, the first American Episcopalian bishop.[4] As was true of the other Episcopal churches of this period it derived most of its income from pew rentals; Muhlenberg himself rented a pew there after he resigned to become head of the Flushing Institute.[5]

Muhlenberg was formally elected rector on July 1, 1826, and entered on his duties only a short time later.[6] He continued his normal interest in church work. There was still some editing to do before the new hymnal could be published, and he and Dr. Onderdonk had some difficulty collecting the money they had advanced to finance its publication.[7] He also organized a missionary society for Queens County in which Flushing was located but he had a low opinion of the diocese of New York, for he wrote Jackson Kemper:

> the majority of us are favorable to the project [the Missionary Society] and I think it will be carried. The shame of this Diocese in not doing more for the General Society, . . . I don't want to attraction [attention] to my part of it— You had better, however, say nothing of it there until it is actually done— for you know that in this part of the ecclesiastical world one is taught that charity not only begins at home—but that it almost always stays at home.[8]

His rectorship of St. George's was too short to be noteworthy but he did attempt a reform of the vestry. He was a member of a committee to revise its by-laws and election by secret ballot was introduced. He also established a Sunday school.[9]

Within a year he began to lay plans for the establishment of a school. He had brought with him to Flushing the two boys who had been monitors of his Lancastrian school and who had lived with him in Lancaster.[10] Although he came to Flushing quite by accident he could hardly have chosen a better place to establish a school. Flushing was a secluded spot yet accessible to New York City. It was in a farming country and was located on a bay that had facilities for water sports. It was only a day's journey by boat from Philadelphia, where Muhlenberg hoped to obtain many students because of his connections. He wrote his Lancaster friends, the Yeateses, a description of the proposed school:

> You have often been amused with my talking about my college — and I dare say regarded it as a mere castle in the air — what will you say when I tell you that the castle has lighted on a Hill? — It is even so — or very likely to be so. A number of gentlemen here have determined, by a joint stock, to erect a building according to my ideas, which I am to rent for the interest of the money it costs — probably for less. It is to be placed on a commanding hill near the waterside, whence there is a prospect of the surrounding country almost as fine as that from Bienchuoff's Hill. A more convenient or delightful situation for a college could hardly be desired. The cost of the building will be about fifteen thousand dollars. We are not yet certain that the amount of stocks will be taken — but as ten thousand dollars are subscribed we hope to be able to make up the remainder.[11]

The school was incorporated under the name of the Flushing Institute in January, 1827.[12] Listed as incorporators were a group of important Flushing businessmen.[13] Joseph Bloodgood was a physician and came from a family that was prominent in the tree nursery business.[14] His wife was a member of St. George's and his son Francis entered the ministry and was Muhlenberg's successor at the Church of the Holy Communion.[15] S. B. Nicholl was a physician and a member of the vestry of St. George's.[16] Isaac Peck was an insurance man and a vestryman and treasurer of St. George's; his descendants were still members of the parish in 1956.[17] Thomas Phillips was a vestryman of St. George's.[18] Samuel Willet was a commission merchant and vestryman.[19] Jordan Wright was a New York merchant who after accumulating a fortune of $100,000 decided that this sum was as much money as any man should need and retired to live at Flushing.[20] Thomas H. Thomas was a vestryman of St. George's and a collector of the pew rents.[21]

The school was, therefore, entirely a local enterprise, most of its incorporators having some connection with St. George's Church. They were authorized to issue stock up to 260 shares at fifty dollars per share. Among the shareholders were Muhlenberg himself; J. D. Sheaff, his cousin; Muhlenberg's old antagonist, Bishop Hobart; his friends from Lancaster, Margaret and Catherine Yeates; and George P. Rogers, brother of his sister's husband, who throughout his life was one of Muhlenberg's supporters. Five of the incorporators also bought stock. There seems to have been no one person who was an angel to the school for there were 35 stockholders of the 260 shares; the largest single holding was only 20 shares; and a majority of the stockholders held 5 shares or less.[22]

Muhlenberg gave a detailed description of his plan in a letter to Jackson Kemper who had written him for advice about establishing a similar school near Philadelphia:

> You ought by all means to have a church school in the neighborhood of Philadelphia and on the plan that I have heretofore detailed to you it seems altogether practicable—especially with your funds—your first business would be to look out for some suitable person of approved principles and undoubted competence having a fondness for the education of young persons to take charge of the school—either as a day school or boarding academy—the latter would be infinitely preferable and might be delightfully established in some of the many pleasant situations in the neighborhood of Philadelphia. In thus advising you, however, I am forgetting my own interest, for I calculate on having many of the young people of your flocks at Flushing. Until you find some such individual as I have just mentioned you had better not move in . . . At least I would not like to have my plan tried by a person of any other description. His failure would be disadvantageous to me. You know enough of my system in a general way to induce a teacher (I would rather say a clergyman who had never taught come to think of it) and then I would willingly enter into details. An ordinary day school . . . would be of little service to the church compared with what would arise from a boarding school under proper regulations. Discipline is as important as a branch of education as instruction—there can be little of the latter of a religious nature in a day school.
>
> I dare say you will consider the foregoing as no answer to your request. The truth is I am so full of my own project that in the ways of education I cannot think of anything else—When my institute succeeds I will do everything in my power to form schools on the same plan whenever practicable. I would willingly be a missionary on the subject of Christianity and education. But first I wish to establish a model school—my scheme is an extensive one—but I fear to unravel the whole lest you think me visionary. I wish you could be induced to come spend a few days in Flushing. . . .
>
> As you talk of aiding a classical school, I wish you would aid mine by investing some of your funds in our stock. I have engaged to pay seven percent interest—I would pay ten or fifteen percent if taken in education—$50 a share—I wish you would think of this.[23]

The cornerstone of the Flushing Institute was laid in August, 1827, and the school opened in October, 1828.[24] In the interim Muhlenberg began a vigorous promotion campaign. On the advice of Jackson Kemper he published a prospectus entitled *The Application of Christianity to Education, being the principles and plan of education to be adopted in the Institute at Flushing, L.I.,* in which he propounded his theories of education and gave the plan of the school. The ancient languages, in his opinion, were the best groundwork of liberal learning; therefore Greek was to be the core of the studies of the school. Natural sciences which had currently become so popular were to him a recreation rather than a study. Thus far Muhlenberg was only reproducing the traditional education which he had himself received at the Grammar School and College of the University of Pennsylvania. But he emphasized that mere learning was not enough: the art of study must be taught—the main object of intellectual education is to lead a student to think and acquire knowledge for himself. And this was a fundamental concept in his philosophy—that the means by which a student acquired knowledge were as important as knowledge itself.[25] In developing his philosophy he seems at times to anticipate the ideas of progressive education.[26]

Despite his strong insistence on the importance of Greek, Muhlenberg believed that his "plan," as he was fond of calling it, must be flexible:

Education must accommodate itself more or less to the diversities of natural genius. While the majority of youth give no decisive symptom of what they are designed for in the world, a large minority do. Their readiness in particular branches of knowledge and their total inaptitude for others seem to point to the station which nature has fitted them to fill. For the former class (supposing them to be liberally educated) the usual course of language, mathematics, and philosophy is the best. But in favor of the latter may there not be a deviation from that course, to follow the evident leadings of genius? Why should a boy go double over the declension of nouns and the conjugations of verbs . . . when had he been directed to some department of natural sciences, to the arts or even to practical mechanics, he may have won the distinction of a lad of promise.[27]

This phase of his plan was a development of Dr. Abercrombie's Philadelphia Academy. Muhlenberg recognized that such flexibility had its dangers for under pretense of consulting a boy's genius the teacher might be only humouring his caprice or indulging his indolence. Care would have to be exercised to prevent an abuse of this doctrine which after all only contended that the teacher would consult the various abilities of his students and not, like a mere taskmaster, prescribe alike for them all. Returning to his defense of flexibility in education Muhlenberg said:

Our seminaries look more than they ought to the learned professions as the future sphere of their alumni. (There is too much aim at present to make mere intellectual men.) Almost every parent whose circumstances allow him to indulge the idea looks forward to his son figuring at the bar, lecturing among the faculty, or holding forth in the pulpit, and the prevalent notions of education tend to encourage the absurdity.... We also want practical men ... men of information and principle in all the ranks of society. We want intelligent merchants and manufacturers as well as lawyers and doctors, sensible and pious laymen as well as learned and orthodox clergymen. To furnish these, education must be loosed from the trammels of the monastery and be guided as a handmaid to the practical spirit of the age.[28]

That Muhlenberg practiced this policy is shown by a letter written some years later to the Honorable S. Van Rensselaer, an outstanding New Yorker. Concerning the latter's son, a student at his school, Muhlenberg wrote:

His amiable disposition and good manners make him an agreeable pupil but though not negligent of his studies he has not taste enough for learning to induce him to any very close application. His studies are Latin, Greek, arithmetic, algebra with some attention to English reading and composition. If you would prefer that his attention should be directed to some of the more *immediately* practical branches of an English education, in place of any of the above, have the goodness to intimate your wishes and it shall be attended to.[29]

To carry out this plan the school offered "a thorough English education" including mathematics, natural history, and philosophy as far as these studies could be advantageously pursued; vocal music, instrumental music, and drawing when the student had a marked talent for them; Latin and Greek or Spanish and French according to whether the pupil was destined for the counting room or the college. The classical course could be continued until it was the equivalent of a collegiate one. "No pains will be spared to make well grounded scholars in the dead languages. But when a boy is no more than a smatterer, with his parents consent, his attention will be directed to something else."[30]

As for moral education Muhlenberg considered his school distinctive. Most schools were concerned with literature and science but devoted no time to moral education. These schools admitted that Christian principles should not be neglected but these were not regarded as a concern of the school. Under his plan moral education would be on an equality with intellectual education. Moreover, moral education must be based on Christianity, and the Bible must be the subject of systematic instruction.[31]

The Flushing Institute Building. (Courtesy Queensboro Public Library)

At this point Muhlenberg grappled with the problem that has so often confronted American educators — how to provide moral education in schools which derive their support from a pluralistic society. He frankly admitted that one of the reasons for the neglect of scriptural instruction in our schools was the obvious difficulty of adapting it to the conflicting creeds of the patrons. He had already had some experience with this problem. Dr. Abercrombie had met it by operating his school along nondenominational lines but requiring each student to recite in the catechism of his particular denomination and to listen every Saturday to a talk on general principles of Christianity. Dr. Abercrombie, it should also be remembered, had drawn up a formal course of religious instruction for the Episcopalians in his school. At the Grammar School and College of the University of Pennsylvania there had been social worship conducted by the provost along with exercises in public speaking. Muhlenberg had again encountered this difficulty in his public school at Lancaster and had discerned the trend which would eventually lead to a nondenominational public school system in which religious teaching would be eliminated. If on the other hand the scriptures were to be taught in a nondenominational school there was danger of latitudinarianism in trying to please all points of view.[32]

Muhlenberg met the problem by making his school frankly denominational:

> The danger of latitudinarianism will not exist in an establishment professedly Episcopal; in which the religious instruction will, of course, conform to what the principal esteems to be the sentiments of the church in which he ministers.
>
> In applying Christianity thoroughly to education it must be viewed in some one of its existing forms. We cannot take it in the abstract. We cannot deal only in the few general principles which are acknowledged by all denominations. To make the proposed experiment fairly Christianity must be taught as it is professed by some particular church. Such a course will be perfectly understood by the public; and is certainly less liable to objection than the contrary one of latitudinarianism in profession but sectarianism in practice. On this subject the Roman Catholics are consistent. Their faith is sedulously interwoven with their education—hence the secret of their constancy in its profession.[33]

Physical education was an important part of Muhlenberg's plan. The schedule of his school called for studies and recitations in the mornings, exercise of various sorts to occupy the entire afternoon, and studies again at night:

> Proper physical education is a powerful auxiliary to moral discipline. "Let a boy have his due share of exercise, let his diet be simple and wholesome, let certain hours be appropriated to manly sports and he will return contented to his books. And when he retires to his chambers it will be to sleep, not to concert mischief or corrupt his companions. College rebellions are nothing wonderful...Except by the exemplary few the hours allotted to study will never be wholly given to it. Hence a large proportion of idle time naturally generates occasional riot. The redundancy of animal spirits common to early years will vent itself. Let it be worked off in the gymnasium and it will not explode in rebellion.[34]

The major sports at the Flushing Institute were water sports in summer and ice skating and sledding in winter. The boys also had individual plots for growing vegetables or flowers. No evidence has come to light that the school was equipped with a gymnasium although there is one mention of a gymnastic pole. Sources on the school abound in descriptions of boating, swimming, ice skating, sledding, and gardening.[35]

In this respect Muhlenberg was definitely in advance of his time. Commenting on student riots at this time a historian of American social and cultural life says:

> A contributing factor was the absence of any organized program of athletics. Instead of the emphasis on sports often criticized in the twentieth

century, foreign visitors of this period commented on the absence of any attempt by the Colleges to provide exercise for the students.[36]

In regard to moral discipline Muhlenberg emphasized again that the means used were as important as the ends sought. It would be easy, he admits, to maintain order by the use of severe corporal punishment and to induce students to study hard by promoting competition and offering prizes. But a better way to maintain order was to have the environment of the school so organized as to give little inducement to disorder or rebellion. Perhaps here Muhlenberg remembered the state of near anarchy at the University of Pennsylvania during his own student years. His school was organized to avoid such a condition. He hired the professors, tutors, and governess, controlled the admission of the students, and had the final authority in disciplining them. The entire school lived in one large building and the students when not in class were under the supervision of the tutors in their hours of recreation and of study. There was one tutor for every nine students. Flushing was a secluded spot which offered little or no opportunity for mischief and, as has already been noted, the boys had ample opportunity for recreation. "The government of the school should be mild and affectionate yet steady and uniform."[37]

Reproof and admonition should always be administered in private and corrective discipline should be chosen and regulated with a view to implanting principles. Forfeiture of privileges and confinements were the most common penalties; corporal punishment was not entirely abolished but was used sparingly. The principal, however, reserved the right to remove a boy from the school if he turned out to be incorrigible or if he was a bad influence on his fellow students. Students should be taught to value the approbation of the wise and the good around them as the reward for excellence in studies and any reward given should be such as might seem to be only the fruits of excellence. The offering of rewards and prizes which could be attained only by a few and which disappointed many others should be avoided.[38]

The physical plant was planned to implement these principles. The school building was neo-classic in design and consisted of three stories and a basement. There were columns in front of the building and it was surrounded by six acres of wooded grounds. It contained a recitation hall, dormitories, lecture rooms, and dining hall. The tutors and unmarried professors lived in the dormitories with the students.[39]

Muhlenberg was the principal of the school, and lived with his mother in an apartment in the school building. (Mrs. Muhlenberg seems to have taken little part in the life of the school and was opposed to the whole project.) A number of the professors were clergymen, some of whom

subsequently attained prominence in the church. The tutors were usually young men at least seventeen years of age who were candidates for
the ministry and who in return for their services received advanced instruction and their living expenses. They were an outgrowth of Muhlenberg's experiments in education at Lancaster, where he had started the
practice of having paid monitors. There was also a governess who had
charge of domestic arrangements. "This station will be filled by a lady
every way qualified for it, from whom the pupils will meet with as much
maternal kindness and attention as they would be likely to find anywhere abroad." The school year began October 1 and extended through
July. There was only a two-month vacation.[40]

With a twenty-four-page prospectus along these lines Muhlenberg began his promotion campaign. In February of 1828 he wrote to Jackson
Kemper:

> I have forwarded to most of the clergy in Philadelphia a copy of my pam-
> phlet prepared as you suggested—I have omitted, however, much of the
> minutiae of the Plan which was detailed at St. Peters vestry room and sub-
> stituted other matter more likely to be generally read. The objections to
> publishing the plan minutely (in addition to the probability of its not being
> understood fully) is that some might attempt to carry it into practice and
> failing denounce it as inefficient.
>
> May I put you to the trouble of expressing your views of the undertaking
> as far as they be favorable on paper and of getting the names of such affixed
> to it as you can see conveniently—a few subscribed to something pretty
> strong and decided will be better than many to an equivocal Sertimonae.
>
> I have written to Bp. White desiring him to favor me with an answer
> which I expect to use as a certificate of his approbation. If you have an op-
> portunity will you give him a hint to make it as serviceable to me as his con-
> science will allow.
>
> The only apology I can offer for saddling you with this communication is
> the cause we both live to support. I have a good deal at stake, a rent of
> $1,400, that I am naturally anxious to obtain all the countenance I can get—
> and which I am more ready to ask as the profits of the concern will be
> sacredly devoted to the cause of Christian Education and the support of
> missions—the school will be the same grade as the famous one at North-
> hampton—and that to be established by the Dwights—but as you see $50
> less a year. My charge is lower than that of any seminary in this neighbor-
> hood of the same respectability.[41]

Another letter went to his Quaker friend, Roberts Vaux:

> I send you by mail a copy of my school project—Christian Education I
> believe to be the "one thing needful" of the present day!! [I am] tired of
> talking to others about schemes for reformation [so] I have resolved to do

what I can in the good cause myself—with regard to the proposed institution as an Episcopal School, you will have your own opinion (perceiving too, I trust, that if Christianity is to be thoroughly applied to the business of education it must be taken in some of its existing modes)—but with respect to the modified monitorial system which is to be practiced, if you feel free to give it, I should like to have your written opinion in a letter which I might publicly use—I am determined to do my best to make the system proceed—to that end I will employ none as tutors or monitors but the most exemplary lads. The advantages I offer will command much.

Then, probably to appease Vaux's Quaker prejudice against hireling ministers, he wrote:

In order to remove the suspicions of being actuated in this undertaking by motives unworthy of a Gospel minister the profits of the school will be devoted ... entirely to the cause of missions and Christian Education.[42]

The next letter went to Bishop White couched in the most respectful language beginning "Rt. Rev. and Venerated Sir" and concluding "your Son in the Gospel" but containing the same information given in a more familiar vein to Jackson Kemper.[43] Somewhat later he invited Bishop White to visit the school.[44] Similar letters went out to all bishops and prominent clergy. In his promotion Muhlenberg tried to avoid being drawn into the High-Church—Low-Church controversy which was particularly warm in Pennsylvania. There, Muhlenberg's hymn-committee colleague, Henry Ustick Onderdonk, had been elected bishop in a bitter fight. Writing to Jackson Kemper Muhlenberg said: "If I should be so fortunate as to get the patronage of both parties I suppose you will not blame me, provided I do so by fair means—the same story is told to both."[45] At first it appeared that he would be successful—Bishop Hobart the militant leader of the High Church party in whose diocese Muhlenberg was now a clergyman expressed himself as truly pleased with the venture and bought fifty shares of stock.[46] Perhaps Muhlenberg feared that the denominational character of the school might prejudice the Low Churchmen for, after discussing this matter in the body of his Prospectus, he appended an additional note:

The author anticipates but one objection to his system—that which will be styled its sectarianism. If by this is meant that it will promote among its subjects an attachment to the principles of the Protestant Episcopal Church, the charge is admitted. As an Episcopal Clergyman, having a course of religious instruction under his control, he naturally expects that such more or less will be the effect. It cannot be otherwise. His duty in this respect will be the same in the school as it is in the pulpit. In interweaving Christianity with education, of course, the former will be exhibited as it appears in those institutions which he believes to be entirely scriptual and which he is solemnly bound to support.

But if by sectarianism be meant any approach to that spirit which identifies the pale of salvation with the boundary of a certain church; or to that which does not distinguish between essentials and non-essentials, as the objects of zeal, in a particular form of Christianity; or to that which does not recognize in the principles of truth and virtue a bond of union superior to that of any visible forms; in a word, if it be bigotry he disclaims it. It is not the spirit of his church. It is not the spirit of the brightest ornaments of that church. It is not the spirit of the Gospel. He adopts the trite maxim of a Father: "In rebus necessariis, unitas; in non-necessariis, libertas; in omnibus, charitas." [In essentials unity, in non-essentials, liberty; in all things, charity.][47]

Following the publication of the prospectus, Bishop Hobart's opinion of the school seemed to change. He did not answer Muhlenberg's letter and the list of endorsements had to be published without one from him. Muhlenberg wrote to Kemper that:

From almost all the Bishops and clergy to whom I have written on the subject of my school I have received favorable replies. Our little archbishop here, since reading my pamphlet, has expressed no opinion—though in conversation before he expressed himself [as] highly pleased with the undertaking—took some of the stock, etc. I would have published my recommendations before, had I received something from him.[48]

Unknown to Muhlenberg a correspondence was going on between Bishop Hobart and Bishop Croes of New Jersey. The latter had received Muhlenberg's letter but before replying he wrote Bishop Hobart:

The plan I like though I do not think it practicable in every respect. The difficulty with me is, Can Mr. M. be depended on as a sound churchman? And is he not in some way connected with or under the influence of Dr. M-l-r? [This reference is to Dr. James Milnor, Muhlenberg's friend and the leader of the Low-Church party in New York.] If it be an institution of that nature it may do a great deal of mischief in your Diocese. The reason of my writing to you on the subject is to hear from you, whether you approve of it and have confidence in Mr. M. that it will not be made an instrument of disseminating Puritan principles in your diocese. As he has requested me to give my opinion of the plan, etc. and suffer him to make it public, the answer you give me I shall consider perfectly confidential. . . . If you have no fears I shall encourage it with pleasure.[49]

Since no copy of Muhlenberg's pamphlet has been found it is not known whether he received endorsements from Roberts Vaux, Bishop

Hobart, and Bishop Croes. In the course of time, however, both Hobart and Croes gave their approval; Hobart visited the school for a confirmation class and strongly endorsed the project in his convention address of 1829[50] and Bishop Croes sent his son there to be educated.[51] Possibly the appointment of Samuel Seabury as chaplain helped to dissipate Hobart's opposition for Dr. Seabury was the grandson of a famous High Church bishop.[52] With the opening of the institute in October, 1828, Muhlenberg handed in his resignation as rector of St. George's but he and Samuel Seabury continued to conduct services there until a new rector was elected.[53]

There is very little information on the early years of the school but it is evident that it was successful from the start. Three years after its founding Muhlenberg took the occasion of its first commencement to advertise its success with a public examination of the students. He also delivered an address entitled "Christian Education" which was published in pamphlet form and served as a description of the school. In this pamphlet he reaffirmed the stand taken in the original prospectus concerning rewards and punishments. No artificial stimulants to study such as prizes were used. No spirit of rivalry was excited. The degrees of the scale by which standing in scholarship was graduated was fixed and had no reference to the merits of the pupils as compared with one another. The first place that each was exhorted to strive for was not a point which continually receded from the approaches of all except the most talented competitor but a permanent station so broad as to admit all the successful aspirants and yet so elevated as to render the reaching of it a sufficiently vigorous reward.

> The means of getting the students to study are as important as the end because of the benefit that the means have on moral character. The effect, however, of exclusively Christian Discipline in a seminary of learning . . . is not so much to make one or two prodigies as to increase the average quantum of industry; to raise the standard of proficiency among the many of moderate abilities rather than to multiply the opportunities of distinction for the gifted few.[54]

The discipline and moral atmosphere of the school were satisfactory, the report stated, due to the circumstances surrounding the school and to the sound principles on which it was conducted. The general government of the school was wholly paternal in its character, administered in the spirit of kindness and condescension, supported chiefly by private admonition and avoiding more anxiously the extreme of rigor than that of indulgence. If the mildness of the regimen maintained had not kept some minor evils in check this disadvantage had been more than counterbalanced by the contentment, mutual good will, and cheerful obedience which characterized in general the members of the school family. Whenever a pupil proved refractory, injurious to his companions, or too troublesome to his instructors he was separated from the institution. Of the 103 names upon the roll of the institution since its commencement twelve had been stricken off in this way.[55]

Pains were taken to give interest to the services in the chapel. The observance of the Lord's day was enforced on the one hand with a moderation which perceives the danger of rendering its duties tedious and irksome; yet on the other with a strictness which would guard against the opposite and more common error, of allowing it to relax into a mere holiday for indulgence.[56]

Muhlenberg then took up several problems which had arisen since the beginning of the school. He deplored unnecessary absences and advised against withdrawing students for short periods. He found that the students had difficulty readjusting when they returned. Sometime later in the history of the school he required a written promise from parents that they would not even ask for their sons to be given a leave of absence except in cases of extreme emergency.[57] The school gave a two-month vacation which Muhlenberg regarded as too long for the students but too short for the instructors. Plans were therefore being made to shorten the vacation period. A further difficulty in regard to vacation periods, Muhlenberg said, was that parents tended to over indulge their sons during the vacation and they thus came to regard their life at the school as a term of imprisonment and their vacation as a period of liberty.[58] Some years later he published a *Tabella Sacra for the Vacation;* it contained a brief address on religious duties during vacation, a table of daily Bible lessons, prayers, hymns, and a help to self-examination.[59] There had been no changes in the plan of study outlined in the prospectus:

> The course of study proceeds upon the established opinion that the classics and pure mathematics afford the surest ground work for solid education. There is no want of schools which substitute modern languages and natural science for the severer disciplines. Schools are multiplying to meet the demand for "practical education." In the zeal for the diffusion of knowledge and for leveling it to the intellectual abilities of all classes some care must be had for the interest of liberal education.[60]

There were several important rules and regulations. The privacy of correspondence between students and parents was guaranteed but the principal had the right to read all other mail both outgoing and incoming. Students must keep an account of the money they received from their parents through the principal's office and must exhibit it upon request of the principal. There was no need, however, to send boys money because everything that they needed was furnished through the school and there was little that they could buy in Flushing. The principal also had the right to prohibit books and magazines in the school which he thought were detrimental to its good order. The uniform dress of the school was a plain suit of dark blue or gray cloth, black vest, and stock, for winter; and white vest and pantaloons for summer. The tuition charge was $250 which covered all expenses except books, stationery, and instruction in French and instrumental music.[61]

Further information about the routine of the school is found in *The Journal of the Flushing Institute,* a monthly publication. The ordinary day began with the waking bell, at ten minutes before six. Then came the roll call and prayers in the chapel, after which the boys had their breakfast. The morning was spent in study and recitations. The five afternoon hours were spent in recreation, study, recitation, recreation and study, respectively. Evenings were times for reading and relaxation. Chapel ended the day at nine o'clock. On Saturday afternoon the boys amused themselves. Sunday was a day of many religious activities. After roll call, at six o'clock, came chapel and then breakfast. Following this were scripture lessons and questions in the chapel. After an hour's work memorizing Bible passages the boys went to chapel once more for a service and sermon at half past ten o'clock. After dinner they spent half an hour preparing answers to questions on the sermon. At two o'clock they recited scripture lessons. At half past three they had chapel again. From seven to eight o'clock religious meetings were held in either the chapel or in the rooms of the instructors. The day ended with prayers at nine o'clock. Instead of report cards Muhlenberg printed a page in the *Journal* giving each student's grades. Each student was assigned an initial which was known only to the principal, teachers, and his parents.[62]

It has already been noted that Muhlenberg drew upon several sources for his "Plan". Dr. Abercrombie, Roberts Vaux, and Joseph Lancaster seem to be the men who directly influenced him and, in the promotion literature, a further influence appears. Muhlenberg refers to "the famous school at Northhampton"[63] which followed the lines of a Swiss school.

The institution of the Fellenberg at Berne was founded by a Swiss nobleman, Philip Emmanuel von Fellenberg, to educate children made orphans by the French Revolution.[64] The school rapidly attained an international reputation and attracted numerous visitors including two American scholars then studying in Europe: George Bancroft and Joseph Green Cogswell. These two men after their return to the United States decided to found a school at Northampton, Massachusetts, to be known as the Round Hill School and the principles of which were copied from the Fellenberg school.[65]

They published a prospectus in 1823 and a description in 1826,[66] but the chief source of information concerning the Round Hill School is an elaborate description in a pamphlet written by Cogswell in 1831. This school was remarkably successful in its short life. The list of students indicates that they came from prominent families not only in New York and New England but from all sections of the United States.[67]

A search of the papers of Cogswell and Bancroft in the manuscript room of the New York Public Library does not reveal any evidence that Muhlenberg contacted these men in forming plans for his school nor does the catalogue of Muhlenberg's library indicate that he had any of the publications of or about Fellenberg or the Round Hill School. The evidence is nonetheless fairly convincing that Muhlenberg was influenced by these two schools to some degree. The similarity between them and his school as outlined in his *Application of Christianity to Education* and *Christian Education* is striking.

Among the similarities may be mentioned the concept of the school as a large family with the headmaster as the *pater familias*, the system of rewards and punishments, the emphasis on classical education with flexibility for those who seemed incapable of profiting by such education, the recognition of the importance of athletics (adequate physical activity) and the rather frank appeal to families in the upper economic levels. Further Muhlenberg not only referred to "The Celebrated School at Northhampton" in his promotional literature but was personally acquainted with Cogswell. It is not known when this acquaintance began but when Bishop Ives of North Carolina decided to found a boys school in his diocese he visited both the Round Hill School and the Flushing Institute. Finding that Cogswell was discouraged with the prospects of the Round Hill School the bishop persuaded him to give it up and come to Raleigh to be principal of his school which was modeled on the Flushing Institute.[68] When this venture also failed Muhlenberg recommended Cogswell to Bishop Kemper for a school out west.[69] A comparison of the student list of Flushing Institute and St. Paul's College with that of Round Hill School also indicates that many families who formerly sent their sons to the Round Hill School transferred to Muhlenberg's school when the former was disbanded.[70] Cogswell later found his major interest in life to be library science and is regarded as one of the founders of the New York Public Library System.[71] While in this position he was a member of the Board of Visitors of St. Paul's College which grew out of the Flushing Institute.[72] So that while there is no direct evidence that Muhlenberg was consciously influenced by these schools the similarities were such that a young Englishman, Thomas K. Wharton, who taught at the Flushing Institute, wrote in his diary:

74

The general features of the system [at the Flushing Institute] both moral and educational were taken from the famous institution of the Fellenberg at Berne in Switzerland—whose views our excellent principal has fully espoused and elaborated in his establishment with great success.[73]

Wharton came to this country with his parents, brother, and sister from England in 1830 and settled in Ohio. He showed such marked talent in drawing that his parents sent him to New York to continue his studies. He appears to have been an instantaneous success for he was received in the literary and artistic circles of New York and made a number of influential friends. He kept an extensive diary which is of great interest as a picture of New York life of the 1830's. He became a protégé of Colonel Sylvanus Thayer, superintendent of West Point, and through him met Muhlenberg who employed him as a teacher of drawing at the Flushing Institute. Wharton chiefly valued this position because it gave him a secluded spot to which he could withdraw but at the same time was close enough to New York to have easy access to his friends, one of whom was Washington Irving. He often walked from Flushing to the ferry boat landing at Brooklyn.[74]

Since he was neither a clergyman nor a ministerial candidate he was not one of the inner circle of Muhlenberg's staff at Flushing. The following extracts from the portions of his diary dealing with the Flushing Institute would indicate, through the testimony of a sympathetic outsider, that Muhlenberg had succeeded in establishing the type of school he so often discussed in his letters to Jackson Kemper. Wharton thus describes his life at Flushing:

December, 1832. I took the little steamboat "Linnaeus" and landed at Whitestone dock where I found a light country carriage to take me and my luggage to Flushing (some three miles off). Mr. Muhlenberg gave me a cordial welcome to the institution, introduced me to the professors, and in a few days time I found myself fully established in my new home, surrounded by intelligent, well-educated, and gentlemanly companions and ready to enter upon my new duties and studies with alacrity—there were about 60 or 70 students and a finer set of boys it would be hard to find or under more complete or paternal discipline—in fact—the institute compared to one large family with Mr. Muhlenberg, the principal, at its head, and the several professors and instructors many of them very young men educated in the institution, were more like elder brothers and companions of the pupils than the austere taskmasters who usually fill these responsible posts—all seemed to look up to Mr. Muhlenberg with affection and reverence—and I never saw a scholastic establishment where a firm and methodical system of control was more happily blended with the strictest regard to the happiness and improvement of the inmates—[Here follows the reference to Fellenberg and a description of the buildings of the school.]

75

December 26, 1832. At eight o'clock two stages and a carriage started full of boys for the city and at 9½ St. Clair and I followed on foot. The day was frosty and we preferred walking...I met Mr. I. Diller our Professor of Mathematics and walked about the city with him.

December 28, 1832. In the evening the "Eunomian Society" held its 4th anniversary—Mr. Muhlenberg delivered a very neat address on their motto "Ecce Quercus." Mr. Seabury followed and Libertus van Bokkelen closed the meeting with a short and appropriate speech. The "study" was tastefully decorated for the occasion.

January 1, 1833. After service all repaired to the drawing room to pay Mrs. Muhlenberg the accustomed New Year's visit and partake of her New Year's refreshments—and at half past we sat down to a bountiful New Year's Dinner. . . . In the afternoon chess, draughts, backgammon, etc. were put into requisition . . . Towards evening Messers Diller, Brenneman, and I took a glass of wine and cake with Mr. and Mrs. Seabury in the village and returned in time for evening prayers.

January 5, 1833. The communicants of the Institute, Messers Fetter, Diller, Franklin, Kerfoot and myself met at Mr. Seabury's in the evening for devotional exercises, the sacrament will be administered tomorrow.

January 14, 1833. At 8 PM Messers Seabury, Diller, Barton, Babcock, Franklin, Kerfoot, and myself met in Mr. Diller's room for religious exercises and improving conversation.

January 17, 1833. In the afternoon I called at Mr. Seabury's and after fortifying ourselves against the keen air with a glass of wine we walked out together until after sunset—he hoped I would join a literary association about to be formed among the instructors and invited me to attend a meeting to be held tomorrow evening for organization—which I shall do with pleasure.

January 21, 1833. Sunday—Mr. Muhlenberg preached an excellent discourse on "Death" and in the afternoon read a tract contrasting the last moments of the infidel Hume with those of the eminent Dr. Finley of Princeton, N.J.

February 21, 1833. I commenced today with my class in Descriptive Geometry consisting of Messers L. van Bokkelen and John B. Kerfoot, James West, and Henry Sergeant—all young men of great promise.

February 22, 1833 . . . Earlier in the day we had a very solemn and different duty to perform—the funeral of Mr. Seabury's brother who has been wasting away for some time past, it is supposed from unceasing application to study.

February 23, 1833... Last evening Mr. Seabury delivered his inaugural on taking the chair as President of the Eumathean Society which we have just formed for our mutual improvement in polite literature.

April 21, 1833. Dr. M. [probably Frederick] played the organ today as he does so every now and then and his execution is delightful, indeed his musical talents are of a very superior order. He seems much younger than his brother [William Augustus].

July 21, 1833. As next Sunday will be the last of the session the communion will be administered and the term closed in a manner constitently [sic] with the character of the institution.

The calm retirement of this place is well calculated to keep alive a spirit of devotion, it is also a great aid to the formation of studious habits—next session I propose by a proper course of mathematics to qualify myself to combine instruction in the "exact sciences" with my profession as a painter and no where could I enjoy greater advantages for such an object than at Flushing.

July 26, 1833. This is an admirable Institution and doubtless much genuine piety exists here ... It is apparent that more good order and diligence need not be desired—none of those improper expressions so common among schoolboys seem current here—and there is but little of those petty quarrels, bickering and ill-will which disgrace all large assemblies of youth—the general sentiment here seems against them.

During the vacation period Wharton received the news of his mother's death. (His parents at this time lived in Ohio.) He was allowed some time off and then wrote:

In a few days I resumed my duties and studies at the Flushing Institute—everyone seemed to sympathize deeply with me in my bereavement and I soon felt more than ever that I was really among kindred spirits whose society was congenial to me and from whom I felt also that I should be unwilling even with ever so strong inducements to part.

The session of 1833–34 glided away happily and usefully at the Flushing Institute. Alternate duties, studies and recreation and pleasant visits at intervals to my friends in the city—I became very much attached to that kind of life and to the friends I made at Flushing. And I had sufficient leisure and inducement to follow up my favorite employment of painting in connection with classical and other pursuits.

This statement concludes Wharton's comments about the Flushing Institute. He later became a successful architect in New Orleans where he died in 1862.[75]

The institute was a financial success in that Muhlenberg managed to pay off all his debts but in regard to profits he reported that:

> As in the original Prospectus of the Institute it was stated that all the profits arising from the patronage of the same should be devoted to the support of Missions, this seems the proper place for observing that as yet no profits have been realized. The amount expended by the Institution has been greater than that received by it, and this without the allowance of any salary to the principal.[76]

The success of the institute encouraged Muhlenberg to proceed with his plan to establish a college. He, therefore, in 1836 bought a farm of 100 acres on a point of land at the entrance to the Flushing Bay on the East River about four miles north of Flushing.[77] In the same year he published a prospectus for the college to be named St. Paul's.[78] He had originally planned to withdraw from the Flushing Institute altogether and devote his entire time to the college but so strong were the protests of the parents who had sons at the institute that he decided to combine the two institutions. He therefore turned the institute building over to the stockholders and relinquished all connection with it.[79]

His plans for St. Paul's required an effort to obtain wide support for the college. The Flushing Institute had been conducted as a private venture by Muhlenberg with the backing of businessmen in Flushing and his personal friends and family.[80] In the prospectus of St. Paul's issued in 1836 he frankly appealed for contributions from alumni, parents, and the church at large. The organization of the college government reflected this change. A board of visitors was set up appointed by the bishop of New York. Among the other clerical members were Muhlenberg's old friend Dr. James Milnor of St. George's, New York City; Samuel Seabury, the former chaplain at the Flushing Institute and now editor of *The Churchman*, a leading Episcopal magazine; and Jonathan Wainwright, who was later to become a member of the faculty. Among the lay members were Abel T. Anderson of New York, who was later to become the father-in-law of Muhlenberg's protégé, James Barrett Kerfoot, and Joseph G. Cogswell, the founder of the Round Hill School at Northampton, now a member of the staff of the Astor Library in New York.[81]

To give effect to this new purpose a constitution of the college was drawn up which required that the religious instruction be in accordance with the doctrines of the Episcopal church and that the government of the college be vested in the rector and the professors. A further article stated that:

The college shall be subjected to the visitation and inspection of the Bishop of the Diocese of New York as the official visitor of the same and of a Board of Associate Visitors to be appointed by the Bishop.

The Board of Associate Visitors shall consist of eight clergymen of the Protestant Episcopal Church and six communicant laymen of the same to be appointed by the Bishop of the Diocese of New York.

The Bishop and Board of Visitors shall approve of the studies of the Institution. They shall cause an examination of the students to be made in their presence at least once a year—they shall make an annual report to the church of the state of the institution and they shall grant testimonials of Scholarship, good morals, and soundness in the Christian Faith to such students as may be recommended to them by the faculty for such a testimonial and in their judgment are deserving of the same.[82]

The rector was to be appointed by the trustees of the college by and with the consent of the bishop and the board of associate visitors. The professors were appointed by the rector with the advice and consent of the trustees but the rector had the right to appoint outright all subordinate officers. Salaries were fixed by the trustees.[83] This closer connection with the church was part of a move to obtain financial assistance from the diocese of New York. It failed, however, for Muhlenberg was never able to obtain support beyond his own circle of relatives and friends.[84]

Despite the imposing array of visitors the real authority over the college was vested in the board of trustees. These were named in the Act of Incorporation as follows: Muhlenberg; his two protégés, Kerfoot and Van Bokkelen; John G. Barton, who succeeded Muhlenberg as principal of the college; George Rogers, Muhlenberg's sister's brother-in-law; Isaac Peck, businessman and vestryman of St. George's Church, Flushing; and Benjamin Ogden, physician and friend of Muhlenberg. The trustees were thus all close associates of Muhlenberg and through them he could control the college.[85]

The studies of the college department were much the same as those at the University of Pennsylvania. Muhlenberg himself held the title of "Senior of the Collegiate Family and Professor of the Evidences and Ethics of Christianity." The combined college and grammar school at its height had 116 students and fifteen professors, instructors, and other officers. There were three classes at the collegiate level and four at the grammar school level. In 1838 the junior class in the college (the highest) had five students, the sophomore eleven, and the freshman fourteen. In the grammar school the first class had twelve, the second class had fifteen, the third class had sixteen, and the introductory class had twenty-seven.[86]

New York contributed by far the largest number of students — forty-four; Pennsylvania contributed thirteen, all of them from either Philadelphia or Lancaster; South Carolina came next with eight; then Maryland with four. There were scattered students from Louisiana, Virginia, Michigan, Massachusetts, the District of Columbia, Missouri, Georgia, North Carolina, Arkansas, Florida, Connecticut, New Jersey, Kentucky, and the West Indies.[87]

The establishment of the college gave Muhlenberg an opportunity to push two of his cherished plans: first to provide scholarships for young men who planned to enter the ministry or teaching and second, to provide a supply of missionaries for his old friend Jackson Kemper. In these two projects he reflects his earlier interests in the Missionary Society and in the Education Society in Philadelphia.

> As the college may now be regarded as completely established as an Institution of the Church it is hoped that churchmen will give it their patronage by making donations towards the founding of scholarships particularly for the benefit of young men desiring an education as instructors and clergymen. In no way perhaps can a more valuable service be rendered to the church with the same amount of money. All donations to be paid to J. G. Barton, Esq. College Point, N.Y. Treasurer of the Corporation.

The catalogue of 1838 announced the establishment of a fund for the education of teachers:

> Few objects are of more immediate interest to the church or to the country at large than the education of enlightened Christian teachers. It is second only to the education of the clergy and is equally the proper business of the church. Provision for it should be permanent and large. Christianity, in order to retain her ascendancy in the land, must train up capable and conscientious instructors, as well as learned and faithful ministers. The pastor and the teacher should go hand in hand. It is the policy of infidelity to sever them: let it be the wisdom and patriotism of Christianity to unite them, until everywhere the Church, the College, and the School be regarded as a common cause.[88]

Under the provisions of the fund the principal was to be loaned to St. Paul's College and for every $1,500 so loaned the college was to educate one student qualified to become an instructor. A statement of the fund in 1838 showed $4,500 contributed by eleven persons. Most of the contributions came from Long Island. The exceptions were one from the Sheaff family in Philadelphia; one from Muhlenberg's old Quaker friend, Dr. George Bacon Wood; and two from his friends in Lancaster, the Yeates sisters. The following year the catalogue announced the setting up of six scholarship funds: the Barton Scholarship; the Flushing

80

Scholarship by sundry individuals of Flushing; the College Point Scholarship by an individual of College Point; the Chapel Scholarship, by sundry alumni of the Institution; the Philadelphia Scholarship, chiefly by two individual Philadelphians; and the Lancaster Scholarship—by sundry individuals of Lancaster. Here again it appears that five out of the six scholarships were due to Muhlenberg's personal influence. One of the stipulations for the holders of these scholarships was that they must spend some time as missionaries in the "new" regions of the west following ordination.[89]

Muhlenberg also envisioned an addition to St. Paul's College to be known as Cadet's Hall which would be to the church what West Point and Annapolis were to the Army and Navy. Possibly his friendship with Colonel Thayer and his associations with West Point suggested this idea. Writing to Jackson Kemper he said:

> Before long, I hope, also . . . [to] realize the plan of Cadet's Hall, I feel sure that I could send you eight or ten [men] every year. The Church must . . . [agree] on a Mission school for the west—in which young men should receive their education gratis, on condition of their serving as missionaries and teachers at least four or five years under Western bishops. Having served that long the majority would settle in the west—on some accounts a mission school for the West would do better in the neighborhood of New York than anywhere else.

These plans never got beyond the talking stage as far as Muhlenberg was concerned but they may have influenced James Lloyd Breck in his project at Nashotah as noted later in this chapter.[90]

Muhlenberg continued the close relationship between himself as the head of the school and the individual students at St. Paul's College that he had begun at the Flushing Institute. Extracts from several letters and the catalogue illustrate this policy. Writing to Bishop Kemper about an entering student, he said: "Young Ashurst may come about the tenth of May. . . . I should like him to be accompanied by some friend with whom I could have a personal interview and from whom I might learn the peculiar disposition, talents, etc. of the boy." Writing again to the bishop some years later he discussed a student who was having difficulties at the school:

> I thank you for your letter about William Ashurst as it lets me know what the family thinks. I am very well acquainted with his own feelings as in conversation I give him opportunities of speaking without disguise; which he does very freely. For a long time he has had nothing to do with Manual Fetter so that I am at a loss to account for his complaints of him. — He has quarreled with all his schoolmasters—with Mr. Seabury as much as

with the younger teachers. Within a couple of weeks he seems to be better satisfied. The whole difficulty is his hatred of being controlled. He has been treated with extreme indulgence — I mean comparatively — but to satisfy him he must be allowed to study or not as the humor takes him. I do not despair of bringing him to a proper state of mind for which you may be well assured I will not fail to labor and pray. It would indeed, as you say, be a great triumph of the Christian System to subdue such a boy. I shall see the family during the vacation and have a full conversation with them.

The catalogue of St. Paul's College also laid down a policy in regard to promotion and expulsion:

> A pupil is not obliged to remain a certain period in one class but is promoted according to his progess.
> If the school after a reasonable time fails of its proper effect upon him his parents are requested to withdraw him. Very rarely a boy is formally expelled. It is a serious thing to inflict such a disgrace upon him so early in life. Another system may be suited to his disposition and he should have a fair chance of starting anew. We endeavour therefore to part with a boy when we cannot retain him with as much delicacy as the circumstances will allow both for the sake of the parents and that whatever good he may have derived from us may not be destroyed by the harshness of violent rupture.

Writing to Stephen Van Rensselaer concerning his son he said:

> Remember me to Wextrous who I hope will be pleased with his new school — His departure from the Institute was rather sudden — Indeed it is the first instance I believe in which a pupil has left with so little notification.[91]

St. Paul's College soon ran into serious problems. When Muhlenberg started the project in 1836 he had received pledges from friends and supporters through which he believed that he could finance his buildings. The cornerstone of the college was laid in 1836 with appropriate ceremonies by Bishop Onderdonk, Bishop Hobart's successor. A disastrous financial panic struck the country in 1837, however, and several of Muhlenberg's supporters were unable to make good their pledges. The foundations of the college building were already laid but the construction came to a halt when Muhlenberg ran out of money. He therefore erected temporary wooden buildings and the college and grammar school were opened in 1837. He was never able to raise the money to complete the college building, and the temporary buildings remained to the end.[92]

The second obstacle was related to the first. In the prospectus of St. Paul's College issued in 1836 it was promised that:

> Provision will be made for obtaining from competent authority the usual collegiate degrees of Bachelor and Master of Arts, for those students who shall successfully prosecute the entire course of study.

In a note to this statement Muhlenberg added:

> The writer has not changed the estimate, which he has heretofore expressed, of college honors, especially as they are diminishing in value, (little as it already is) by the increase of institutions everywhere that confer them. But as they may be desired by many parents for their children, arrangements, it is believed, can be made for securing them to such as shall really deserve them.[93]

In attempting to obtain degree granting powers for his college, however, he met difficulties from the Board of Regents of the University of New York. An exchange of correspondence between Muhlenberg and the Hon. G. C. Verplank, chairman of the Board of Regents in December, 1838 indicates that the lack of an adequate endowment was the reason for the reluctance of the Board to give degree granting powers. Muhlenberg suggested several alternatives but Verplank was apparently unable to do anything about this matter.[94] Muhlenberg again wrote him in 1839 for St. Paul's would have a graduating class in 1840. The best that Verplank could do was to suggest that as a "Body of Scientific and Learned Men" the college faculty should grant diplomas but Muhlenberg feared that this would be "a usurpation in the Empire of letters."[95] He finally gave up the attempt to obtain degree-granting powers and applied for incorporation in 1840 without them.

The language of the act of incorporation passed by the state legislature clearly limits the scope of St. Paul's. It was called a "literary institution" instead of a college, the trustees were referred to as "proprietors," its object was declared to be "the promotion of education," and the legislature reserved the right to alter or repeal the act at any time. A partial solution of the problem of degrees was found, however, by having the graduating class of St. Paul's go to Maryland and receive degrees from St. James College then under the presidency of Muhlenberg's protégé, John Barrett Kerfoot.[96]

A third problem which Muhlenberg faced at St. Paul's was the maintenance of discipline. The good order which was such a notable feature of the Flushing Institute disappeared at College Point. Several sources speak of vandalism, rowdy conduct, and insubordination at the new college. So often did Sam and Lewis Kemper who were students there mention this matter in letters to their father that Bishop Kemper finally wrote Muhlenberg for information.[97] This inquiry brought the following candid response:

My dear Bishop:

I thank you for your letter—I wish that all parents were equally candid— Sam's fears were excited probably by the mischief of some of the boys whose fun it is to "stuff" as they call it—a new comer—particularly if he be "green" —another epithet in their vocabulary to denote the innocence of a home-boy yet a stranger to school life. Alas! that it is so—but I have long since found that the beau ideal of a Christian School—and the thing in practice— have some striking variations. Home—a pious home—I have ever said is the only true Christian School—To contrive the best substitute is the labor of my life—If we have not come as near to it as is practicable—it has not been for want of endeavor—or multiplication of means and appliances to supply the defect which is more or less inseparable from a public school. The "Big-boys" will always lord it over the "little ones"—but at present I am confident there is very little of such tyranny. Those who know what schools generally are in that respect would say there is none—and with us the persecuted boy has always the opportunity of protection in his prefect or Instructor of which—from the familiarity existing between the parties he can avail him-self without odium—there is no Anti-Christian party—in the school—but human nature is not so far transformed among us that "he that is after the flesh will not persecute him that is after the spirit." The case mentioned by Anson Blake was an outrage on decency that I believe the boys themselves would resent. As to the number on their knees in the Dormitory Sam was mistaken—and little Craig's nickname of "Bishop" was given rather in good nature than malice.

Still I deny not [that] I have some [numbers] of the [wicked] ones and at the end of every year I get rid of as many as I can.[98]

His failure to raise money for an endowment and permanent build-ings, the refusal of the Regents to give St. Paul's degree-granting powers, and his disciplinary problems may have been factors in his decision to relinquish the project altogether and to enter into a wider sphere of activity. But there were undoubtedly other reasons. The proximity of his schools to New York City, now the center of the church as well as the economic life of the nation had drawn him into broader fields of inter-est. When, in 1844, circumstances made it possible for him to enter more fully into the life of the metropolis he decided to resign the college into the hands of his associates and to accept the position of Pastor of the projected Church of the Holy Communion. Muhlenberg remained at the college while superintending the construction of the church, and when the church was completed he formally resigned the rectorship. A personal letter appeared in the catalogue of 1846 explaining the change:

As I am about to enter upon a pastoral charge in the city of New York I beg leave to inform all whom it may concern that there will be no interruption in consequence of St. Paul's College. The duties of the Rectorship will devolve upon Mr. J. G. Barton, now the vice-Rector, and the other departments of the Institution will continue to be filled as they are at present. There will be no change except my own removal—and that will not be an entire separation, as I propose to retain such a pastoral care of the boys as can be administered by weekly visits during the greater part of the session. While, of course, I can never be indifferent, or refuse any assistance in my power, to the object of so many years' solicitude and care, it will be understood that the responsibility of the future management of the Institution will rest with those who have the immediate charge of it. They have been long and faithfully devoted to its interests as a service for the Church; and the increase of zeal and activity to be naturally called forth by their increased obligations, will, I trust, give promise of the perpetuity of the School such as could not be afforded by my own continuance at its head.[99]

St. Paul's did not long survive Muhlenberg's departure. A local historian[100] suggests that the principle reason was the loss of Muhlenberg himself. The school had been built so much around him that without his distinguished name and engaging personality it could not attract students. In this respect it shared a fate similar to the Round Hill School at Northampton after the departure of Cogswell. The property passed into the hands of his niece, whose family built a private residence on the foundations of the never-completed college building. The site is today a park maintained by the town of College Point.[101]

The apparent success of the Flushing Institute and St. Paul's College led to a number of imitations, and several failed as Muhlenberg had foreseen. Despite these failures, however, Muhlenberg's reputation grew because so many schools and colleges were started in conscious imitation of his schools.

The first instance was that of Dr. G. W. Doane, Bishop of New Jersey, who proposed that Muhlenberg head a diocesan school project. Bishop Doane was a High Churchman who believed in a considerable measure of ecclesiastical control. Muhlenberg replied as follows:

.... Whenever I have contemplated a removal, it has always been to the northward. Political considerations induce me to prefer New England, and somewhere on the sound, in Connecticut, has been long, in my imagination, the ultimate location of my college. Candor, however, dictates another answer. The seminary proposed for your diocese, doubtless, is designed to be subject to specific ecclesiastical control. I am never restless under government but such arrangement might interfere materially with the prosecution of my plans, and would impair too much my freedom of action in the enterprise. Attachment to the Episcopal Church and submission to her proper authority will I hope, always characterize any institution of which I may have the charge, but the security for these must be found only in the consistency of my character as an Episcopalian—whatever it may be—and in my duty as a Presbyter of the church. In a word, I prefer the independence of a *private* Institution.[102]

Bishop Doane then embarked upon a school project on his own which ended in financial failure and the bishop's trial before an ecclesiastical court for maladministration of funds. Bishop John Henry Hopkins of Vermont also founded a boys' school which was swept away in the panic of 1837.[103] Bishop Gadsden of South Carolina who had visited College Point[104] and was a friend of Muhlenberg's attempted to found a boys' school which collapsed in the same depression.[105]

Bishop Levi Silliman Ives, who succeeded Muhlenberg as the rector at Lancaster and who later became bishop of North Carolina had no more success. He visited both the Flushing Institute and the Round Hill School and persuaded Joseph Cogswell to give up the latter and return with him to Raleigh to found the Episcopal School for Boys. This school which Bishop Doane referred to as "the first real Episcopal School" was deliberately modeled after the Flushing Institute. Like many of its contemporaries it did not survive the depression of 1837; its buildings, however, were later used for a girls' school, St. Mary's, which is still in existence.[106]

Jackson Kemper, Muhlenberg's old friend, was somewhat more successful but he also had his difficulties. His predecessors in the field had found that it was difficult to persuade Episcopal clergymen to volunteer for work in the west. He therefore attempted to found a college to train local men for the ministry. With this end in view he wrote a letter to Muhlenberg asking his assistance in obtaining clergymen to establish such a college who would be willing to go around begging for it. Muhlenberg's answer highlights the difficulties of recruitment:

I have read your letter with deep interest—and would to God I could reply to it as you wish. But where are the men you describe to be found? I scarcely know of one, whom I would care to associate with myself much less one qualified for the important work you have in hand: Qualifications of mind and talent and tact . . . are not [rare] but the qualification of single-minded devotion to the 'despicable [sic] business of education' is singularly [lacking] except indeed in those who have no other qualifications. We talk of living for the welfare of men—but who does it? The young parson burning with zeal for the glory of God takes his first step into matrimony and makes it his first care, as of course he then ought, to provide for his wife and the forthcoming little ones—How can you expect him to go to Missouri to be a beggar...The vow of poverty requires the vow of celibacy. No sir, depend on it, our young ministers are but half in earnest—they make very good parish ministers—they have a valuable conservative influence in society—but as to living for the one thing professed to be the single object of their aim (for at least a while) they know little of it—and until we have an order of monks to that effect—I fear that begging will be no particular inducement to remove to the West. I wish I had one to spare you.[107]

In the same year Kemper decided to establish a college in St. Louis and applied to the Missouri legislature for a charter for Missouri College. The legislature gave the trustees the charter but with the stipulation that the college use some other name since the legislature had hopes of founding a University of Missouri. Much to the embarrassment of the bishop the trustees named the new institution "Kemper College."[108] At the beginning their begging was quite successful for they raised $20,000 with which they purchased a plot of land and erected a building.[109] In their promotional literature they compared Kemper College to St. Paul's. Typical of this literature is the following circular:

> You are requested to attend a meeting of the friends of the Episcopal Church to be held in St. James Church on Sunday evening 18 May, at 8 o'clock to take into consideration the propriety of establishing at "Kemper College" near St. Louis in Missouri a "Bishop White Professorship."
>
> The institution, now in its infancy, is conducted upon the admirable plan of St. Paul's College at Flushing, Long Island, New York of which the Rev. Dr. Muhlenberg is president and like it is intended to secure to the youth of our country a thorough education under the constant guidance of Christian principles; with the additional object confessedly of the first importance, of preparing pious natives of the West for the arduous duties of the ministry.[110]

The college for some time prospered but faculty dissension, maladministration, and bank failures in the East finally wrecked it. In at least one respect, however, church educators had learned by experience: there is no more mention of profits. Kemper offered the presidency of his college to Muhlenberg and later tried to have him made bishop of Missouri. Muhlenberg declined both of these proposals.[111]

Of Muhlenberg's other colleagues Bishop Otey of Tennessee was one who visited College Point in 1854[112] and some years later became a founder of the University of the South at Sewanee, Tennessee. His model, however, was Oxford University, England, rather than St. Paul's, College Point.[113]

A number of the faculty members attained distinction after they left St. Paul's. Mention has already been made of Muhlenberg's lifelong friend, Dr. Christian F. Crusé. He was assistant professor of Greek and Latin languages[114] and occupied a position at Flushing not unlike that of George Bancroft at Round Hill School.[115] Dr. Francis L. Hawks, a lawyer before entering the ministry, appropriately enough taught rhetoric and oratory.[116] He later founded St. Thomas' Hall at Flushing with the apparent intent of competing with St. Paul's. He failed disastrously,[117] however, and had to leave the state to escape prosecution for his debts. Despite these unpleasant incidents he was a man of considerable significance. He later became the first president of the University of Louisiana, now Tulane University, and was a pioneer in the field of American church history. He was rated one of the ablest preachers in the Episcopal church.[118] Muhlenberg does not appear to have borne him any ill-will.[119]

Dr. Jebediah Vincent Huntington, who taught philosophy at St. Paul's, attained considerable repute as a poet and novelist.[120] Dr. Samuel Roosevelt Johnson was for twenty years on the faculty of the General Theological Seminary.[121] Dr. Samuel Seabury, Muhlenberg's first assistant and chaplain, left the school to become editor of *The Churchman*, probably the most influential Episcopal church magazine of the period. He later became rector of the Church of the Annunciation where he put into effect some of the practices that Muhlenberg initiated at Flushing.[122] Jonathan Mayhew Wainwright collaborated with Muhlenberg as early as 1826 on a collection of hymn tunes. It is not known when he became a member of the faculty of St. Paul's but when Muhlenberg took his trip to Europe, Dr. Wainwright was left in charge of the college. He became an eminent clergyman and bishop of New York from 1852 to 1854.[123]

The students of Muhlenberg were, however, the chief instruments in his expanding influence. Probably the most important of these was James Barrett Kerfoot. He was born in Ireland but his parents moved to this country when he was a small child and settled in Lancaster, Pennsylvania. His father died when he was nine years old and young Kerfoot came under the care of Muhlenberg. He attended the Lancastrian school and was the small boy chosen to deliver the address of welcome to Lafayette. He was one of the two students that Muhlenberg brought with him to Flushing from Lancaster and his expenses were defrayed by one of the Yeates sisters. He later became an instructor in Greek and Latin and chaplain at St. Paul's College.[124] He also served as Muhlenberg's administrative assistant and was his choice to be in charge of Cadet's Hall.[125]

88

As has already been noted, Muhlenberg turned down an offer from Bishop G. W. Doane to establish a school in his diocese. But the popularity of St. Paul's College by 1841 apparently led him to believe that the time was now ripe to begin the third phase of his plan—that of establishing other schools on the model of St. Paul's. The opportunity came in 1841 when he was approached by Bishop W. R. Whittingham, now bishop of Maryland, but formerly a professor at the General Theological Seminary and a member of the board of visitors of St. Paul's, to establish a branch in Maryland. Muhlenberg accordingly wrote Bishop Whittingham giving his ideas on the proper way to establish a church college:

> The more I think of the proposed branch of our institution in your diocese, the more disposed I feel to attempt to realize it.
>
> I believe it would operate favorably on the cause of education in various ways, and not the least by showing the true way of beginning a Church School. I have often wished for an opportunity of starting *de novo,* with a few select men and with perfect independence as to patronage. This, it appears to me, we could do at "Fountain Rock." We would send out a colony of pious, intelligent, respectable young fellows, with Kerfoot at their head, who would care nothing about their support and enter upon their work con amore. They would be the soul of the thing and gradually they would generate the body around them. I have the whole arranged in my mind and I believe we would realize the very beau ideal of a Catholic School—something of a kind which has not been realized in this part of the world. You smile, I dare say, but I know what can be done. I mean a genuine Church School, not a great literary institution...I esteem it of essential importance that our engagement should be wholly with yourself and not at all with the gentlemen who have purchased the property at Hagerstown. Our entire independence will be indispensable to our success, at least to that kind of success which will be permanently and really desirable. We must appear rather indifferent to patronage and popularity while we leave nothing undone to deserve it....[126]

Muhlenberg made a visit to Maryland and met with the building committee. He was disturbed to find that little had been done and that the school was not going to be opened under the ideal conditions which he had outlined in his letter. The building committee had not met and there was some doubt of their obtaining the requisite funds. Moreover, there was one serious drawback in regard to the site:

> I cannot help adding that for a school I should have preferred a location that would have afforded the variety of wood and water for the amusement of the boys. I feel a little doubt about the management of them, confined as they will be on a plain lot of twenty acres, no swimming or rambling in the woods in summer, or skating in winter.[127]

Kerfoot, however, began St. James under better circumstances than most colleges in this period. He already had experience as a teacher and college administrator. And he had a corps of teachers drawn from St. Paul's and his brother, Samuel, who had some business experience to act as curator. Throughout the entire life of the school he had Muhlenberg to depend on for advice and encouragement. The financial support was not as complete as he and Muhlenberg had hoped but there they had the backing of Bishop Whittingham. The young teachers had to work without salary for the first year and many of their supplies were purchased on credit. Matters, however, were so arranged that the opening of the school was definitely decided upon.[128]

Several changes in the original plan were made. Instead of operating St. James as a branch of St. Paul's it became an independent institution with Kerfoot as its head and Muhlenberg withdrew from any personal connection with it. But he maintained a keen interest in the school and came to Maryland to lay the cornerstone of a new building and to again expound his philosophy of education as he had done at the laying of the cornerstone of St. Paul's.[129] A second change was the marriage of Kerfoot; Bishop Whittingham wrote him:

> I heard with great surprise, the other day, that your calculations were not to lead the life of a celibate at the Hall. It was perfectly new to me, as my dreams had been all of a brotherhood, such as that at St. Paul's.[130]

Kerfoot replied:

> I will live . . . a celibate for the year. If after that I marry, my marriage will at the least bring no expense on that or in any other enterprise. . . . My expectation indeed was expressed to lay aside the monk's cowl when all seemed right for it.[131]

Kerfoot was married in September, 1842, by Muhlenberg to Eliza Anderson. She was the sister of Kip Anderson, a fellow student at St. Paul's College and an instructor at St. James.[132]

St. James College went through many vicissitudes but appeared to be firmly established at the outbreak of the Civil War. After the demise of St. Paul's it became the prototype of a church college. As already noted Kerfoot accompanied Muhlenberg on his visit to Europe in 1843. The Civil War forced the closing of the school but later it was reopened as a secondary school and continues in existence to this day. Upon the closing, Kerfoot became president of Trinity College, Hartford, Connecticut, and a short time later was elected first bishop of Pittsburgh. To the end of his life he remained a High Churchman while Muhlenberg became more Broad Church in his sympathies. This difference of opinion, however, never disrupted their personal friendship.[133]

The man who was to be the most noted exemplar of Muhlenberg's ideas, however, was not Kerfoot but Henry Augustus Coit. He was a student at St. Paul's College during Muhlenberg's last years there and later went to St. James as a teacher under Kerfoot. From there he became headmaster of a school in Lancaster, Pennsylvania. Shortly thereafter he was invited by a group of laymen headed by a Boston philanthropist, Dr. George Cheyne Shattuck, to found a boys school at Concord, New Hampshire. Dr. Shattuck had been a student at the Round Hill School and was particularly interested in founding a similar school in the New England area which his son could attend. Dr. Coit, therefore, started out with all the prerequisites of the successful founder of a school—teaching experience, school administrative experience, and financial backing. He likewise had both Muhlenberg and Kerfoot to call upon for advice, and Muhlenberg himself visited the school. As his assistant he had his younger brother, Joseph H. Coit, who had been educated at St. James. In the years following the Civil War, St. Paul's School at Concord, New Hampshire, became the best known example of a Muhlenberg school.[134]

Writing of the Muhlenberg influence at St. Paul's in the 1880's one of its alumni says in his autobiography:

> In its beginning St. Paul's School simply meant Dr. Henry Augustus Coit, who might well have said, L'Ecole, C'est Moi. He had derived his ideals from Dr. William Augustus Muhlenberg of St. Paul's College, Flushing, which he attended; and of a number who in various places followed the Muhlenberg tradition, Dr. Coit gave it its fullest and most permanent embodiment. Dr. Muhlenberg's school was a family of boys, of which he was "school-father," the spiritual guide, friend, and father-confessor of his school-sons, not merely schoolmaster: and everything was dominated by his own personality. He had a genius for appraising the moral and mental value of external surroundings, the use of color and music in young lives, was an artist in his use of religious services, and although there was no talk about "psychology" in his day, he knew all about boy's souls and how to get at them. What Dr. Muhlenberg was at St. Paul's on Long Island, Dr. Coit was at St. Paul's in New Hampshire. There were differences but the type was the same. Dr. Coit was the more scholarly and a brilliant teacher. But in each school the headmaster's personality dominated and left its impress chiefly by giving a standard of spiritual values.[135]

A student who tried to carry out Muhlenberg's idea of Cadet's Hall and of a teaching monastic order was James Lloyd Breck. He was born in Philadelphia in 1818, the nephew of Samuel Breck, a leader in the public school movement in Pennsylvania. His father died at an early age and his mother sent him to the Flushing Institute. When the institute was merged into St. Paul's College he transferred to the University

91

of Pennsylvania. He took his theological training at the General Theological Seminary from which he graduated in 1841.[136]

Breck was confirmed at the Flushing Institute and there made his decision to enter the ministry. He also seriously considered taking a vow of celibacy. Writing from Flushing in 1834 to his uncle Muhlenberg said:

> James is an excellent boy. His persevering industry, amiable disposition, and I may now add consistent piety, afford promise that the wishes of his parent and instructors will not be disappointed.[137]

At the General Theological Seminary he came under the influence of Dr. W. R. Whittingham, bishop-elect of Maryland, who had some idea of instituting a monastic teaching order as has already been described in connection with Kerfoot. In the spring of 1841 Jackson Kemper came to the seminary and made an appeal for missionaries. One of the students, J. W. Miles from South Carolina, drew up a proposal to establish a semimonastic missionary order and several students appeared interested. When the young men started out for Wisconsin only three of the original group were prepared to go: William Adams, John Henry Hobart (son of the bishop), and James Lloyd Breck.[138] They invited John Barrett Kerfoot to be their superior but he had just concluded his agreement with Bishop Whittingham and was unable to accept. F. F. Peake who had been sent East on a recruitment trip by Bishop Kemper in 1841 wrote that he had talked with Muhlenberg and Kerfoot without result but that the bishop could depend upon the three celibates and referred to them as "semi-Jesuits."[139]

The three sent out to Wisconsin in 1842 settled on a tract of land provided for them by Bishop Kemper at Nashotah Lakes. When it was found impossible to obtain an experienced clergyman Breck was elected the superior of the mission. He thus began his work with none of the prerequisites for a successful educational project. He had neither teaching nor administrative experience nor yet adequate financial backing. In the first year of the mission Hobart had to withdraw and return east due to rheumatism brought on by exposure and some years later William Adams also withdrew after a quarrel with Breck. He later returned through the mediation of Bishop Kemper as a teacher but not as a member of the brotherhood. He married the bishop's daughter, Elizabeth, and gave fifty years of his life to teaching at the Nashotah Seminary. When the enormous Northwest Territory was split up into dioceses, Bishop Kemper himself accepted the bishopric of Wisconsin and moved to a farmhouse near Nashotah. He was thus able to give a greater degree of attention to Nashotah and of advice and counsel to Breck.[140]

Writing in 1848 to the Rev. William G. French, the superior of a similar community at Valle Crucis in North Carolina under the sponsorship of Bishop Ives, Breck thus describes the Nashotah Mission after it had been in existence for six years:

> Your ill buildings, etc. can scarcely be inferior to our own—these are not the things sought after by ourselves—we refused an effort (on the part of the Rev. Dr. Muhlenberg) to raise up to $5,000 to erect a permanent building—indeed our frailness is so great that I fear to advance too rapidly.[141]

Despite his inexperience, his inability to get along with his associates, his devotion to the idea of forming a monastic community against all odds, and his singular lack of tact, Breck nonetheless laid the foundations of the present Nashotah House. First of all he was free from the illusion entertained by so many of his contemporaries that the way to begin a college was to erect a large building on the top of a hill. He further refused to allow Muhlenberg and others to make public appeals on his behalf. He attempted to make Nashotah self-supporting through the work of the teachers and the part-time labor of the students. Despite the defection of his two colleagues he worked toward this ideal as long as he remained at Nashotah.[142]

Muhlenberg maintained a keen interest in his former student. When he founded the Church of the Holy Communion he made it a center for raising money and recruiting missionaries for the western missions. He once wrote Jackson Kemper that he regarded Nashotah as the only real mission of the church and referred to Breck as "the missionary." Muhlenberg himself made two visits to Nashotah in July, 1847, and in June, 1852.[143] He was apparently fired with enthusiasm on his first visit for two months later we have the following anguished letter from Breck to Bishop Kemper:

> I was grieved to learn of the intentions of Dr. Muhlenberg—I have written to him an earnest letter which he will perhaps show you, sir, imploring him not to publish anything about Nashotah as an appeal for one dollar. I know it will injure us greatly—neither would I have him preach from city to city in our behalf—his instructions when helping us were to meet a few christian men in private and petition them to which I did not object, but to this, I do solemnly and I hope you will, Rt. Rev. and Dear Father, call at once upon Dr. M. and silence all petitioning in Nashotah's behalf unless in the last mentioned resort.[144]

In a postscript to another letter a few days later he wrote:

> I wrote a day or two since to object to the publication of any pamphlet or any appeal in the public papers on the subject of buildings for Nashotah— these little cells answer every purpose, except discipline and health.[145]

Lewis Kemper, Jackson Kemper's son, was living at Muhlenberg's home in New York while attending Columbia College. He was preparing to come out to Nashotah to teach and he shared Muhlenberg's concern for the well being of the Nashotah Mission. In particular they did not want it to be confused with the Anglo-Catholic group under the sponsorship of Bishop Ives at Valle Crucis in North Carolina. (For a discussion of the controversy over the Anglo-Catholics see Chapter VIII.) When Bishop Ives preached a sermon at the Church of the Holy Communion on behalf of the Valle Crucis community, Lewis, on the advice of Muhlenberg, wrote a letter to *The Churchman* and sent an explanatory note to his father:

> The Sunday after you left Bp. Ives preached here for the aid of Valle Crucis and as in his sermon he said some things which might be misunderstood and thus be prejudicial to the Nashotah Mission. I spoke to the Dr. [Muhlenberg] on the subject and he suggested that the best way to prevent any bad effect would be to put a few lines in the "Churchman." He thought it would be well to take some notice of it for as many of his congregation take a warm interest in Nashotah and he hopes to increase it, he wished them to understand it thoroughly.[146]

Another difficulty arose over William Passmore, an alumnus of St. Paul's College. He was a long time acquaintance of Muhlenberg's, having been the son of the first mayor of Lancaster. Muhlenberg suspected him of having leanings towards Roman Catholicism and was reluctant to send him out to Nashotah. Breck wrote to Bishop Kemper about this matter:

> [I expect] the Rev. Mr. Davis to leave in April or June next not on account of any difficulty here but on account of his intended marriage. Please inform Dr. M. of this. He will thereby be more persuaded of the Rev. Wm. Passmore's duty to join us certainly by that time.[147]

After graduating from St. Paul's, Passmore had gone to Valle Crucis to complete his theological studies. Bishop Ives wrote Kemper concerning him:

> As I learn that Dr. Muhlenberg has written you about our young friend Passmore who has been designed for Nashotah—setting forth some difficulties he has had on the subject of Romanism, I hasten to discharge a pleasant duty in his behalf by assuring you that these difficulties are at an end. That circumstances brought him under my influence and instructions which by God's grace have been instrumental to his entire rescue from tendencies towards Rome. He has been with me for some days; and as I find that he needs more knowledge and discrimination on points which

94

separate us from that communion, I feel it my duty to keep him in my diocese some two or three months when I trust he will be prepared for Priest's Orders. After he receives them should you feel satisfied of his fitness for Nashotah he will stand ready to join that institution as he is under promise to do. But should you be doubtful about him for that place, I shall be most happy to retain him for Valle Crucis as I feel every confidence in his stability. It is true that he stands where I confess myself to stand, on the true Catholic ground which Dr. Pusey has for sometime occupied. But I think that he stands there more firmly than ever.

Do write me on this subject just as you feel and make any request in regard to Passmore that your mind may suggest. I shall attend to it with every pleasure—as I feel the same interest for Nashotah as I feel for Valle Crucis.[148]

Passmore never went to Wisconsin; he was later the rector of a church in Vicksburg and died there during an epidemic. His brother, Joseph, graduated from St. Paul's and for a time practiced law but later went to teach at St. James under Kerfoot. There he entered the ministry and went out to Racine College, another institution founded by Bishop Kemper and modeled on St. James.[149]

Although Nashotah seemed firmly established, Breck's troubles increased largely due to his attempt to maintain the strict discipline that he had inherited from the Flushing Institute.[150] Finally in December, 1849, Bishop Kemper sent him to New York to have a consultation with Muhlenberg and wrote the latter as follows:

Try to make Breck deeply evangelical. He must now pursue the straight path the church points out. I have done and borne much for him and thereby proved my love. He is capable of winning all hearts and doing much good. But he must give up private interpretations—have a few general rules and govern as a father. Say to him all that affection dictates. He and Nashotah are inseparably connected. His path is a glorious one and he can pursue it to the satisfaction of us all. I will not interfere with the government of Nashotah and will move to Nashotah if I can.[151]

The consultation did not come out as Bishop Kemper anticipated. Muhlenberg, finding that Breck's position at Nashotah had become too difficult, tried at first to persuade him to return to New York and take up some work on the East Side.[152] Breck, however, wanted to remain in the West and apparently on Muhlenberg's advice decided to give up his work at Nashotah and move on to Minnesota and there attempt to put into practice the monastic ideal to which he was so devoted.[153] This decision did not please Bishop Kemper but he was able to get a new president for Nashotah under whose conservative administration Nashotah frankly abandoned the semimonastic regime of Breck and settled down to a quiet existence as the seminary for the Wisconsin area.[154]

Breck, still unwilling to give up the idea of a monastic community, wrote his brother some years later that:

> Our associate mission consisting of the Rev. Timothy Wilcoxson, J. A. Merrick (Deacon) and the Rev. J. L. Breck was organized in the Church of the Holy Communion, New York, by the Rev. Dr. Muhlenberg on Trinity Sunday, 1850 and we entered Minnesota on St. John's Baptist Day of the same year.[155]

With the experience of Nashotah behind him Breck managed to found a number of institutions including the Seabury Divinity School at Faribault, Minnesota. He also pioneered in establishing missions among the Indians. But in 1867 J. P. T. Kip, the missionary Bishop of California (who had met Muhlenberg at Nashotah with Breck in 1847), called on Breck and proposed that he establish a mission in California. With the reluctant consent of Bishop Whipple he resigned his work in Minnesota and returned to New York to organize his third venture.[156]

Again Breck's mission was organized at a formal service in the Church of the Holy Communion on October 9, 1867, and the missionaries arrived in California in November of that year. He immediately proceeded to found a grammar school, college, and divinity school but in a few years this ambitious project collapsed due to lack of financial support. One of the lay members of the board of trustees, however, George W. Gibbs, had his interest stimulated by Breck and some years later he was one of the leaders in the founding of the present Church Divinity School of the Pacific.[157] Breck eventually gave up the idea of establishing a monastic community and himself married a woman mission worker. Like Kerfoot he named one of his sons William Augustus Muhlenberg Breck.[158] Breck died in 1876.

Throughout his life he bore testimony to the influence that Muhlenberg, St. Paul's College, and the Church of the Holy Communion had upon him. He regarded Muhlenberg as the real founder of Nashotah House. In a letter to the members of the faculty of St. Paul's College he said: "I do... state that our Reverend Father, the founder of your school and through me by the help of God, of this house also..."[159] and in a second letter to them:

> I cannot go back to the first formation of this House and mission and trace them to their present growth. I would, however, state that so far as either depends upon myself, the germ was first nurtured in St. Paul's, at that time the "Flushing Institute." For this reason, as well as from the known object of our Brotherhood, the members of your own Fraternity must feel

a deep interest in us. They have at various times given conclusive proof of such interest.[160]

Writing to the congregation of the Church of the Holy Communion to thank them for their donation to his Indian Mission in Minnesota Breck said:

It was in the Church of the Holy Communion, New York . . . that the associate Mission for Minnesota was formed. In May next six years will have passed since your venerable pastor and my spiritual father blessed us in the name of the Lord, as we stood before him in the Sanctuary, ready to depart for another unoccupied field of labor for the West.[161]

And speaking of the California Mission he wrote his brother: "I wish to spend the Feast Day at the Church of the Holy Communion, New York. It was there that this mission was organized . . ."[162] Likewise he continued various ritualistic practices he learned from Muhlenberg. In regard to church decorations he wrote:

The adult is quite as greatly influenced by the story of Christmas but in a somewhat different way but nevertheless quite as much as children are, who all admit to be readily and permanently impressed by these means. How distinctly shall I always remember the Christmas early Matin Service of St. Paul's College which at the age of thirteen I attended.[163]

He started a similar ritual at Nashotah and some years later he wrote from the Indian Mission in Minnesota:

Christmas was full of religious privileges. Our little mission house was illuminated and the appropriate Matin Service of Dr. Muhlenberg at St. Paul's College next used at Nashotah, then at St. Paul, Minn., and now in the Indian Mission . . . beautifully introduced the great subject of the day.[164]

Of Muhlenberg's students three became bishops. Mention has already been made of Kerfoot, who became first bishop of Pittsburgh and was a High Churchman. A second was Gregory Thurston Bedell, who entered the Flushing Institute as a small boy and remained until he was seventeen. He became assistant bishop of Ohio in 1859 and bishop in 1873. He was a leader of the most extreme wing of the Low Church party.[165] The third bishop was William H. Odenheimer, who after leaving St. Paul's College became rector of St. Peter's Church, Philadelphia. (St. Peter's was formerly one of the United Churches under Bishop White but they had now become separate parishes.) He succeeded Muhlenberg's old friend Bishop Doane as Bishop of New Jersey in 1859 and was a leader of the High Church party. He was also a hymnographer of considerable reputation.[166]

97

Milo Mahan who had been chaplain and professor of ancient languages at St. Paul's became a leader of the Anglo-Catholic movement. He was ordained by Bishop Ives in the Church of the Holy Communion in 1846 and served as assistant to Dr. Seabury at the Church of the Annunciation in 1848. As was the case with other High Churchmen of his time he was pro-Southern and opposed endorsement of the Union Cause in the Civil War.[167]

A remarkable case of dramatic irony is to be found in the life of another student, George Hendrick Houghton. Mention has been made of Muhlenberg's lifelong aversion for the theater but this student was to be connected with the theatrical profession in a unique manner. Houghton taught at St. Paul's College while he studied theology privately under Muhlenberg and became a curate at the Church of the Holy Communion when it first opened. In April, 1849, he established a mission which he called the Church of the Transfiguration for the poorer members of the community in the neighborhood of the fashionable Church of the Atonement.[168]

The incident which was to link Houghton's name with the theatrical profession occurred in 1870. George Holland, a famous actor and comedian, died in that year, and his son together with the actor Joseph Jefferson called on the Rev. William T. Sabine, rector of the Church of the Atonement, to arrange for the funeral. When Mr. Sabine learned that Holland had been an actor he refused to have the funeral in the church. Jefferson then asked if there was any church in the neighborhood which would have it. Mr. Sabine replied that there was "a little church around the corner." Jefferson and Holland went around the corner to Houghton's church and arranged for the funeral. As a result of this incident the Church of the Transfiguration became nationally known as "The Little Church around the Corner" and became intimately linked with the profession which Muhlenberg so detested.[169]

Another clergyman whose influence was more in line with Muhlenberg's outlook was John Ireland Tucker. He came to Flushing Institute at the age of thirteen and as one of his classmates put it: "Dr. Muhlenberg always tested the musical capabilities of a new pupil and of course soon discovered those of "Jack Tucker" as we always called him."[170] Commenting on this practice Muhlenberg said in the school catalogue:

Music is not cultivated merely as an accomplishment but as an auxiliary in moral education. All the pupils are instructed in singing either to take their part in the choir or to unite in the service of the congregation in general. The chanting of the musical parts of the service by boys, as practiced from the beginning of the institution, it is hoped will be generally adopted in our churches, and so obviate the necessity for hiring female singers. To train boys to this and give them a taste for sacred music is one branch of Church Education.[171]

Tucker was soon the leader of the boys' choir and after leaving Flushing continued his musical education. He became the rector of the Church of the Holy Cross, Troy, New York, a post which he held throughout his life. He early became a leader in the movement for the improvement of church music—a movement which was his major interest and with which his name is closely associated. He continued his friendship with Muhlenberg after leaving Flushing.[172]

Muhlenberg emphasized that his school was intended to educate men for all walks of life, not just the ministry, but it is for the clergymen it produced that it is best known. He estimated that of the 900 students who attended the Flushing Institute and St. Paul's College 50 had entered the ministry.[173] Of the laymen who became prominent probably the most important was John Jay, grandson of the statesman of the same name and the son of Judge William Jay, an abolitionist leader and moral crusader. Jay—like his father an antislavery leader—took part in the seven-year fight to admit St. Philip's Church, an all Negro parish, into the diocese of New York;[174] he also acted as counsel for Negro fugitives after the enactment of the Fugitive Slave Laws; and he framed resolutions for a New York meeting called to oppose the repeal of the Missouri Compromise. He was one of the founders of the Republican party, favored the enlistment of Negroes in the Union Army, supported the Proclamation of Emancipation and the adoption of the Thirteenth Amendment. He opposed state aid for Roman Catholic parochial schools but served as secretary of the Irish Relief Committee. He was a historian of some ability.[175] Throughout his life he was a devoted friend and supporter of Muhlenberg.[176] Other eminent lay alumni were Samuel D. Babcock, President of the Chamber of Commerce of New York City and the critic, Richard Grant White. Miss Ayres states that "others lead at the bar or in medical life."[177] Many of the students came from prominent families. The college catalogue lists such names as Biddle from Philadelphia; Mikel, Manigault, Bailey, and Rutledge from South Carolina; Van Rensselaer from New York; and Habersham from Georgia. From Maryland came Charles Key, son of Muhlenberg's hymn-committee colleague, Francis Scott Key.[178]

Despite the closing of St. Paul's College so soon after Muhlenberg left, the alumni and former faculty members continued to be a strong group of Muhlenberg supporters. This was particularly true of those from New York City, but there were others scattered throughout the nation. His personal reputation thus made the Church of the Holy Communion a national project from its very beginning.[179]

CHAPTER 4

The Church of the Holy Communion:
A Pioneer Institutional Parish

The New York to which Muhlenberg came in 1845 was an interesting contrast to the Philadelphia which he left in 1820. It had long since outstripped Philadelphia in population as well as in commercial activity. As early as 1820[1] it equaled Philadelphia in population and in the succeeding years grew more rapidly. In the thirty years from 1845 to 1875 — the period of Muhlenberg's greatest influence and activity — the population jumped from 750,000 to 1,500,000[2]. In 1845, the built-up section of the city extended to present Fourteenth Street with scattered houses extended as far north as present Twenty-second Street.[3]

Three aspects of New York which impressed observers in 1850 were the unparalleled commercial prosperity of the city; its enormous increase in population; and the large percentage of the population that was foreign born, particularly German and Irish. The preface to a New York guide published in 1853 reads:

> The first half of the nineteenth century closed upon the city of New York leaving it in the full tide of commercial prosperity. Its population by an unparalleled increase had attained to more than half a million and its suburbs contained nearly half as many more. Of the new part of the inhabitants a large portion were of foreign birth chiefly natives of Ireland and Germany. The influence of these strangers has doubtless been unfavorable to the morals and manners of society though there is reason to believe that the assimilating tendencies of our institutions will rapidly remedy these imported evils. For these social evils some compensation is

100

offered in the form of labor as these foreigners now perform most of the heavy service required by the public and private improvement of the city.[4]

Again in 1855 we read:

Of the whole area of Manhattan Island about one fifth part at the southern extremity is occupied by the compactly-built portion of the city. Another fifth part is covered by the partially regulated outskirts. Of the remaining portion some parts are still covered with the primeval forests or are under tillage; others are cities of suburban villages or of gentlemen's county-seats and of a variety of benevolent institutions. As far up as Fourteenth Street or nearly three miles from the Battery the whole area is densely occupied by buildings. From that line to 42nd St. the ground is only partially built upon, the population being less and less dense according to the distance up-town. In nearly all the portions, however, the streets are opened but many of these are but partially regulated.[5]

The Church of the Holy Communion, at the corner of Sixth Avenue and Twentieth Street, New York. (Courtesy Church of the Holy Communion)

A fourth aspect less frequently mentioned was the growth of great slum areas in the heart of the city. In this respect New York had a peculiar difficulty: It was located on Manhattan, a long narrow island. By 1845 the entire island had been organized as the county and city of New York but, as the quotation above indicates, as late as 1850 only the southern one-fifth of the island was occupied. On the outskirts of the city lived squatters who made their living by rag collecting, working in manure factories, and in other marginal occupations. Immediately adjacent to the undeveloped areas were the homes of the wealthy, more of which were continually added to the north. South of the wealthy section the housing steadily deteriorated into great slums. The problem of housing, difficult enough in the average American city, was chronic in New York because the city had only one way to expand — northward along the narrow neck of Manhattan Island.[6]

Muhlenberg came to New York uniquely qualified to be a leader in the largest city of the United States. During his early life and ministry he lived in the environment of Philadelphia, America's then leading city, and therefore had firsthand experience in the problems of a large and rapidly growing urban center. He had had parochial experience in Lancaster and the administrative experience of operating the Flushing Institute and St. Paul's College. Although he expended his inheritance in the operation of these schools he still had the financial backing of his wealthy and devoted sister. He came from one of the nation's best known families. In previous generations it had produced a political leader, a military hero, a leading scientist, and several important clergymen and in the present generation continued to produce outstanding citizens. He also had a measure of fame in his own right. He first came to nationwide attention in the church through his activity in compiling the hymnal of 1826. His own hymns were well known, in particular the unfortunate "I Would Not Live Alway." His educational ventures on Long Island had brought him before church leaders from all parts of the country and his students had come from almost every diocese of the Episcopal church. It is not surprising, therefore, that his arrival in New York created something of a stir in church circles not only locally but throughout the nation.

In the twenty years following Muhlenberg performed the most significant work of his life. It was in this relatively brief period that he established an institutional church, founded an order of deaconesses, opened a church hospital, began a movement towards church unity, started church social work, promoted the reform of church ritual and music, and gave a notable impulse to church life in general. These great twenty years came to an end around 1865, when, as a relatively old man (he was sixty-nine years old in that year) he withdrew from active church life and became absorbed in St. Johnland, the last of his projects. This withdrawal was probably occasioned by a lack of sympathy for trends in church affairs following the close of the Civil War. The twenty years which are now to be described are those which gave his ministry its distinctively urban character.

Muhlenberg was fifty years old when he began his New York ministry but he was already a city man and even to some extent a New Yorker. His early life in Philadelphia, then the leading urban center of the country, and the proximity of his schools to New York had drawn him into the urban environment from the beginning. As early as 1835 he had published a proposal for church unity entitled *Hints on Catholic Union* which attracted little attention at the time but which was the germ of the Memorial which he presented to the House of Bishops in 1853 (see Chapter 9). He was involved in the business life of New York through his efforts to raise money for his schools. The two magazines which he published during his years as an educator — *The Journal of the Institute at Flushing* and *The Journal of St. Paul's College* — were far broader in subject matter than the interest of the schools alone would have required. They foreshadowed many of his activities in the years after he left Flushing. Muhlenberg also attended the conventions of the diocese of New York and was involved in the sensational trial of its bishop (see Chapter 8).

He acquired an insight into the economic life of the city. On the occasion of one of New York's periodic great fires (in 1835), he preached a sermon which attracted wide attention. It should be remembered that a great fire in New York could be plainly seen from Flushing. After remarking on the "entertainment value" of the fire and the evidence that it afforded of the inability of man to control the forces of nature, he went on:

> I am disposed to look upon this terrible destruction as a solemn rebuke from Heaven of that *inordinate spirit of money making,* which marks our country in general and its commercial cities in particular...When there is a prevalent sin in a community and there comes a sore calamity directly affecting the means of that sin, then we make no mistake, certainly no dangerous one if we consider the calamity as a judgement upon that sin. Now the inordinate spirit of money making is a prevalent sin in our community, and the late calamity has fallen directly upon its means — upon its chief theater of action — and therefore we may consider it as a visitation of Providence on this particular sin: the voice of God reproving this inordinate spirit of money making; THE REBUKE OF THE LORD WITH FLAMES OF FIRE.

Muhlenberg admitted that money could be made by fair means. The importer of goods, the owner of real estate, the lender of money, and the retail dealer could carry on honest trade and grow richer every day. Since the present generation spent money faster it must make money faster and its superior art must do in days what its father's plodding labor did in years:

> But it is the false capital—the unreal sale—the maneuvers in stocks—the lottery of speculation and the various combinations of chance and cunning which turn business into a mere game that are preferred by the multitude who are in haste to be rich. If it be said that no one step in any such operations as those I have alluded to can be proved to be immoral (which on the principles of the New Testament I am not prepared to admit), yet it will not be denied that their spirit is not that of open honesty, that their tendency is unfavorable to a nice feeling of moral virtue in the community, and that, in the effect which they have of accustoming the conscience to dealings of a more and more doubtful character, they are wholly at variance with the genius of Christianity.
>
> And how will some other practices stand the test of Christianity, that are common in the money-making world? For instance, when the seller disposes of his wares, not at their real value, but for whatever he can make his customer believe to be their value—when the seller withholds information from the buyer, that would be greatly to his advantage, but would probably prevent a bargain—on the other hand, when the buyer hastens to purchase an article which he has learned has suddenly risen in value, before the seller has time to receive the information—when the seller by any of the common artifices of traffic endeavors to mislead the judgment of the customer, and throw him off his guard...Will these things...bear for a moment the light of Christianity? In plain terms are they not sins; and the sins of every day and every hour in the world of trade?
>
> When intelligence affecting stocks or property is circulated on slight foundation, and advantage taken of the lower prices which it has produced; or, to refer to but one more of the many examples at hand, when a private monopoly is formed for the purpose of creating a scarcity of a particular article and then demanding exorbitant prices for it; and this although the unreal scarcity may occasion distress and suffering in a part of the community. How, again, will such things bear the light of Christianity? Not at all. Let the answer be candid—they are not to be tried by the maxims of trade, and trade has maxims of its own. These are perfectly understood. The buyer and seller expect no candor from one another, and the object of each is to get the better of the other wherever he can. Merchant's honesty is one thing and Christian honesty is another.
>
> And here we see the magnitude of the sin. We see what an utter exclusion there is of the morality of Jesus Christ; we see how the world has substituted a morality of its own; how these eternal laws of justice: "Thou

104

shalt love thy neighbor as thyself," "Whatever ye would that men should do unto you do ye even so unto them," are interpreted to have no bearing on the intercourse of men in trade. How candor and sincerity are repudiated in the markets, and the superior laws take precedence; "Get rich, by fair means, if possible, but by all means get rich"—"Keep all you get, and get all you can." Such principles indeed are part of the selfish heart of man; but they are developed more or less by circumstances, and it is in our great commercial marts that we see them carried out to their full extent. Where there is such violence of competition; where every post of business is thronged, and nothing that opens the least chance of securing the great prize in view is left untried; where cunning contends with cunning and skill with skill; there we see into what licentious extremes this selfishness will run;—how little rotten morality will avail to save men from making shipwreck of a good conscience, and how to the eye that brings all things to the measurement of the Gospel, there may appear iniquity enough for the Lord to "rebuke with flames of fire."

The current love of money, he continued, did not grow out of a love of money for its own sake but for what it procured—adventure, indulgence, distinction, amusement—and whatever it put within our reach; such a passion was the inglorious distinction of our own age and country.

It grows naturally out of the extraordinary facilities afforded by the resources and government of our country in connection with the practical applications of science peculiar to the age.

You may see it [money-mania] everywhere; you may hear it everywhere. Listen to a conversation wherever you will, and nine times out of ten money is the topic. It is the leading and all absorbing theme. The state of the stocks; the advance of property; the last speculation; how much can be realized? What did it cost? [These] are changes incessantly rung, not only in the markets but in our parlors, at our firesides, at our meals, aye, and in our churches, too.

In his peroration he saw conclusive evidence that the fire was a judgment of God on New York for its "money-mania." He expressed the hope that the destroyed section of the city would soon be rebuilt. He acknowledged that there was much good in the city but he hoped that the fire would be understood as a rebuke of the Lord for past sins.[7] Muhlenberg returned to this theme again in a sermon published in 1840 entitled *The Voice of the Church and the Times Chiefly addressed to Churchmen in the Middle and Upper Walks of Life*[8] which reiterated the line of thought of his earlier sermon on the great fire of 1835.

Of the New York Episcopal clergy one of the leaders was Dr. James Milnor, rector of St. George's Church, an old friend of Muhlenberg who had come from St. James, Philadelphia. Dr. Milnor died shortly after Muhlenberg came to New York and his successor was Stephen Tyng, whose father had been a Philadelphia clergyman. Gregory T. Bedell, also the son of a Philadelphia clergyman and one of Muhlenberg's first students at Flushing Institute, was rector of the Church of the Ascension. Christian Crusé, Muhlenberg's college friend and a former professor at St. Paul's College, was rector of St. Simon's, a German congregation. Jacob W. Diller, former professor of mathematics at St. Paul's College, was rector of St. Luke's Church, Brooklyn. Samuel Seabury, the first chaplain of the Flushing Institute, was rector of the Church of the Annunciation and editor of *The Churchman*. John I. Tucker, who had been outstanding in the boys' choir of Flushing Institute, was now in charge of the Church of the Holy Cross, Troy, New York. A few years later Dr. Francis Hawks, by now regarded as one of the great preachers of the Episcopal church, became rector of Calvary Church. Dr. John F. Schroeder, who had been rector of St. Ann's Hall at Flushing and one of Muhlenberg's commencement speakers, came to New York as the rector of the Church of the Crucifixion.[9]

The most conspicuous feature of the Episcopal church in New York was its costly churches. Outstanding among these was Trinity, which had managed to retain its endowments after the revolution, and these, having increased enormously in value, made the parish the wealthiest in the city. As was the case with the United Parish in Philadelphia, it owned several church buildings and had several clergy on its staff. One of these was Dr. Jonathan Wainwright, Muhlenberg's colleague on the faculty of St. Paul's College. In 1840 Trinity Church building was found to have deteriorated so greatly that it was necessary to demolish it and erect a new structure. The parish accordingly took advantage of this opportunity to build a church surpassing in magnificence anything known in New York. It also broke with the prevailing fashion in church architecture by employing Richard Upjohn as architect. Upjohn was one of the leaders of the Gothic revival and he designed the new Trinity Church in Gothic style. Church buildings in the years preceding this revival were usually Georgian or Neo-classic, so that the revival brought in a more "churchly" type of building. The example of Trinity Church was quickly followed by other parishes so that a directory of churches in New York could report that the Episcopalians had not only the largest number of churches in New York but also the costliest.[10]

The immediate occasion for Muhlenberg's coming to New York was a proposal by his sister, Mrs. John Rogers, that she finance the building

106

of a new church in which all pews would be free and of which Muhlenberg would be the first pastor. Mrs. Rogers' husband had been a wealthy citizen of New York and had himself planned this project. He died before he could carry it out but left a large fortune to his widow with the understanding that she would do so. In consultation with her brother she decided on a site at the corner of Sixth Avenue and Twentieth Street in what was then almost the geographic center of lower Manhattan Island.[11] In this project Muhlenberg saw an opportunity to enter a broad field which would give his ideas on church development greater scope. He therefore accepted his sister's proposal and much of the planning for the new church was done under his supervision.[12]

Following the example of Trinity Church, Muhlenberg employed Upjohn to design the new church, which was named the Church of the Holy Communion. In this Muhlenberg was patronizing the leading architect of his day and following the latest trend in church architecture. Upjohn's biographer says:

The Church of the Holy Communion, New York on the corner of Sixth Avenue and Twentieth Street . . . is a wholly charming example of Upjohn's style. Begun in 1844 and completed in the next year it adopts the decorated style in fairly simple form. The slender tower on the corner, with its bottleneck battlements top sets off what was once a little country church. In fact early lithographs show it surrounded by trees with no great office buildings to challenge and dwarf it in size and of course with no elevated railroad to distract attention from the rural charm of the little building.[13]

Of Upjohn's place in the history of American architecture another historian writes:

But Upjohn, it must never be forgotten, was not an architect who happened to be an Episcopalian, but an Episcopalian who happened to be an architect. There could be no mistaking his reverence, a fervent High Churchman, he was so sensitive to the beauty of ritual that he often bewildered those who leaned toward the Low Church by his dogmatic insistence on deep chancels and every other architectural device that might enhance the mystery of the service . . . Perhaps Upjohn was happier designing the Church of the Holy Communion on Sixth Avenue and Twentieth Street. Though he had to be satisfied with a single aisle, instead of the three at Ascension, he introduced the cruciform plan, subtly accented by a corner tower and secured the deep chancel on which he set his heart.[14]

In the interior design, however, Muhlenberg was definitely in advance of his time. Most of the Episcopal churches at the beginning of the nineteenth century were exceedingly plain. The communion table at one end

of the church was usually an ordinary four-legged table with no ornaments on it, and it was enclosed by a railing. In front of the table was
a pulpit and reading desk which effectively cut off the congregation's
view of the communion table. Thus the congregation was unable for
the most part to see any of the communion service and could see the
clergyman only when he delivered the sermon. A small professional
choir in a gallery in the rear of the church furnished the music. The
clergyman wore a black preaching gown except when celebrating the
Holy Communion; then he went into the vestry room and put on a
white surplice and black scarf. In order to relieve the drabness of the
building some of the wealthy churches began to use various devices
of a theatrical nature, such as rich hangings, decorations of various
kinds, and scenic illusions, making the interior of the church resemble
a pagan temple. Any attempt to modify the traditional interior arrangements and decorations were regarded as Romish. An English observer
comments:

> On the whole, I think it may be said with truth, that in America the
> Episcopal Churches greatly exceed those of all other denominations in
> elegance and finish. In many instances the expense of the internal decora-
> tion is even carried to the verge of extravagance and beyond the limits
> of correct taste. There are churches which rather resemble splendid
> drawing rooms. Handsome carpets cover every part of the floor; the
> pews are luxuriously cushioned in a manner calculated to invite repose;
> while splendid embroided pulpit hangings, superb services of Communion
> plate and a profusion of silk and velvet, of gilding and of painting, excite
> the curiosity of the stranger more than devotion.[15]

In regard to the interior of the church that his friend Seabury built
some years previously, Muhlenberg wrote:

> I think you could hardly have misunderstood me about the painting
> on the rear wall of the Chancel—I have said from the beginning that a
> window is by all means to be preferred—but if that cannot be—and you
> have no objection to a scenic illusion—then I propose a continuation of the
> architecture in perspective—at the same time I observed that I would not
> on any account tolerate mere stage effect in a church of my own—I have
> no doubt it would be admired—it might be made very striking and beauti-
> ful—but it would be worthy of the theater—not of the church. With
> respect to the plan of the church in general I objected to the propor-
> tions—as long as they are retained it is impossible to make a good church—
> If I were obliged to build on your ground, I would either abandon the
> idea of a Gothic structure altogether or adopt such proportions as are
> required to give effect to that style of architecture.[16]

Yet a trend had already started in the Episcopal church away from the type of interior arrangements described above which were still dominant in the 1840's and 1850's. At the east end of the Church of the Holy Communion was an altar raised above the rest of the church with a cross and an open Bible on it. To one side was a small pulpit and on the other side a reading desk. Every member of the congregation could both see and hear all that went on in the church. Muhlenberg discarded entirely the preaching gown and conducted all the services in surplice and scarf.[17]

In addition to rearranging the interior of the church, Muhlenberg began improvements in the church services. The customary service lasting two hours or more consisted of three offices: Morning Prayer, the Litany, the Ante-communion, and a sermon. Although these were three separate and distinct services, there had grown up through the years the custom of holding them all together, thus producing a long and tiring service. He decided to hold several different services on the same day and instituted the practice of having a celebration of the Holy Communion every Sunday as well as on weekdays when the occasion required. This innovation was so startling that it created wide comment. When Holy Communion was celebrated only once a month, only those who could arrange to be present on that day at that time could attend, but with more frequent celebrations, it was possible for servants and other people who worked on Sundays to attend.[18]

Muhlenberg brought to New York his lifelong interest in church music. At St. James, Philadelphia, he had charge of a boys' choir and as noted in Chapter 3 he made instruction in singing a part of a boy's education in his schools. The students were trained to sing in the choir or to take part in congregational singing. He hoped that this custom would be generally followed in parish churches and that it would eliminate the necessity of hiring female singers. In New York he put this idea into operation. Instead of the usual professional choir he organized a boys' choir which occupied the gallery in the transepts on one side of the church with the organ on the other. Muhlenberg was also an ardent advocate of congregational singing, and the Church of the Holy Communion became famous for the way that the congregation joined in the worship.[19] He started training the choir even before the church opened[20] and once the church was successfully launched he printed a series of Pastoral Tracts to assist the congregation. The third of these was a tract entitled *Anthems and Devotions for Passion Week and Easter...intended for the use of the members of the Church of the Holy Communion.* This tract contained in addition *A Litany of the*

Passion which consisted of a series of collects with a response at the end of each collect. In the same year he began the publication of chant books, usually in collaboration with his friend, Dr. Jonathan Wainwright. The prefaces to these books gave the encouragement of congregational singing as their purpose.[21]

These efforts drew the attention of the church at large, for in 1856, the House of Bishops appointed a committee of three persons skilled in sacred music to prepare a book of psalm and hymn tunes and chants and anthems for the use of congregations. The committee consisted of Muhlenberg, G. T. Bedell—an alumnus of the Flushing Institute—and G. J. Geer. The members commented in the preface that they would have hesitated to accept this project if they had known how much work was involved.[22]

Despite this remark Muhlenberg was one of a group who drew up another hymnbook published in 1861 designed to supplement the official one. Among this group, in addition to Muhlenberg, were found Bishop George Burgess of Maine, M. A. deWolfe Howe of Pennsylvania, Cleveland Coxe of Maryland, and a Professor Wharton of Kenyon College. This hymnbook in a certain way was as significant a contribution to hymnology as was Muhlenberg's *Church Poetry* in 1823, for it introduced German and Latin hymns as well as English hymn writers of the sixteenth, seventeenth, and eighteenth centuries. It also included contemporary hymns, among them the hymns of Reginald Heber, the English bishop whose proposed hymnbook had been rejected by Muhlenberg in 1826 as not being sufficiently evangelical. This book thus responded to a demand for a broader hymnody and paved the way for a further revision and enlargement of the hymnbook.[23] Muhlenberg's reputation had become so widely recognized in the field of church music that he was called upon to give lectures on congregational singing in various churches in the city. In *The Evangelical Catholic*, November 10, 1853, for example, there appears this advertisement:

VOCAL MUSIC—It is proposed to give a course of instruction in vocal music by Mr. J. A. Johnson, Chorister of the Church of the Holy Communion and Mr. Bourganier from Paris in the Chapel of New York University. The course will be opened by an introductory lecture by the Rev. Dr. Muhlenberg...Persons interested in the promotion of congregational psalmody are especially invited to attend.

In the same issue, Muhlenberg printed an editorial commending the lecture.[24] There are numerous other instances of remarks about Muhlenberg's knowledge of music, his voice, and his ability as a musician.[25]

In another issue of *The Evangelical Catholic* Muhlenberg commented on the current style in preaching:

Public taste is at this moment wielding a mighty influence upon the pulpit.... The primary, all-prevailing conditions of acceptable preaching are that a clergyman should have good rhetoric at his command, and a good voice wherewith to impart the proper effect to said rhetoric. The clergyman who pleases is one who is best able to construct sentences well rounded or else well supplied with pointed antitheses.... The first particular noticed is the preacher's style, the second thing his manner, the last thing the substance of discourse. This last is usually disposed of in a sentence.... The subject matter of a sermon is overlooked.... The notion or expectation of deriving real instruction from the pulpit has in a measure become obsolete. Especially is this true of City Churches and of those in the neighborhood of cities.

People do not want what is called "Deep Preaching" [a young clergyman] is told to pay more attention to his style than to anything else. A good style will secure him at once a good income. [Young Clergymen] spend most of their time polishing their sermons, spending hours and days in this way, which should be sacred to thought and study. They are in imminent danger of becoming mere platitudes, word mongers, dealers in unmeaning generalities.

According to this view, then, the reigning public taste at the present makes decidedly against the real power of the pulpit. It does its utmost to convert it into a rhetorical rostrum. It lures young men from the noble pathway of thought; represses that independent investigation which imparts real force to sermons, and occupies them with sounds and shows.

Let us have more substance; let the people clamor for thought and for instruction, as is now done for style and manner; let their standard here be as high as possible, and then complaints of starveling essays and dry disquisitions will not be heard so constantly from the more thoughtful portions of the church. The ministry will be spurred to nobler preparation of their discourses; will feel more deeply the sacred character of the message they are commissioned to announce; and the duty of preaching will be restored to its true normal rank.[26]

Other sources amply support Muhlenberg's analysis of the fashions then current in preaching. The leading Episcopal preacher in New York was Muhlenberg's old colleague at St. Paul's College, Dr. Francis Hawks. Of him a contemporary wrote:

As a preacher [Dr. Hawks] was greatly indebted to the musical instrument that he carried in his throat. To hear him preach was like listening to the harmonies of a grand organ, with its varied stops and solemn sub-bass and tremulous pathetic reeds.... I would not say that Dr. Hawks was not a great preacher.... I would simply intimate that almost anything would sound impressive if it were spoken by Dr. Hawks.[27]

Of another of the Episcopal clergy a contemporary says: "The Rev. Dr. Higbie... unites the graces of an accomplished rhetorician to the

111

charms of a singularly tuneful voice and an engaging manner."[28] Of Muhlenberg himself an associate said:

> He never did justice to himself, however, and always underestimated his own abilities as a preacher. Yet who that has heard him ever thought him dull? He was always interesting and sometimes eloquent. He preached to achieve results and not to win applause. To him the pulpit was not the throne of the orator, but the chair of the preacher of the Gospel of Jesus Christ. In fact he possessed the prophetic spirit, for he was a fearless preacher of the word and will of God.[29]

A number of Muhlenberg's sermons have been preserved in *Evangelical Catholic Papers* and summaries of others are given in the diaries of Thomas Wharton and Henry Dana Ward.[30] A reading of these indicates that Muhlenberg practiced what he preached. His sermons were obviously not written for effect but emphasized content. He did not draw the great crowds that Dr. Hawks drew but those who heard him were impressed with his sincerity. He gave weekly lectures in the evening to supplement his sermons and published both in the form of tracts.[31] The evidence also indicates that he had a voice with remarkable carrying power. When he became pastor-superintendent of St. Luke's Hospital he conducted daily services in the chapel. The hospital was so built that each ward had one door opening on the chapel and Muhlenberg's voice could be distinctly heard throughout the entire hospital.[32]

The characteristic for which the Church of the Holy Communion was best known and which created the widest comment was the free pew system. It had become almost the universal practice in the Episcopal church to finance the construction of new churches by selling the pews in advance and then levying an assessment against the pew holders to defray the operating expenses of the church.[33] Even Jackson Kemper used this system in the mission field.[34] Muhlenberg was thoroughly acquainted with the system because it had been in operation in every church with which he had been connected. A contemporary English visitor wrote thus of its effects:

> It is a radical fault in the American [Episcopal] church, and if countenanced, must work a rottenness in her bones, that she often times is so exhibited, that the poor are repelled from her communion. It is lamentable to see how this wretched policy sometimes drives whole communities of emigrant English families into the ranks of dissent. A church is erected, the whole floor occupied with pews which are luxuriously furnished and sold or let at prices which exclude every poor member of the Church from the Sacred precincts, and in some cases, gives to non-Episcopalians of

means and wealth the controlling influence in the parish affairs! It is true that by the Canon of the Church every Episcopalian resident within certain fixed boundaries is a parishioner, and claims by ecclesiastical right the services of and the spiritual care of the Rector, yet what accommodation is made for the poorer churchmen and their families to worship God in ninety-nine out of every hundred churches which are built? Have the poor of the American Episcopal Church the gospel preached to them? No! Not in fifty parishes out of the twelve hundred which are provided with temples—not in fifty of them on a fair computation.

The constitution, canons, and prayerbook and the pretensions of the Episcopal Church do not in any place recognize such a thing as a rich man's church—a genteel denomination—a fashionable sect. Episcopacy is declared to be a divine institution; nay, in some of her formularies and many of her standards, as essential to the very being of a true church; the exclusive validity of her sacraments, is constantly maintained by her clergy and laity; and liturgical worship is pronounced the only edifying one. Yet with these large claims Church privileges are in effect extended only to the rich; whilst the poor are suffered to wander into the mazes of ruinous schism and even of scepticism. This fact in relation to the American church which I record in the deepest sorrow, it must be admitted, is a strong argument in favour of an ENDOWED NATIONAL RELIGION.[35]

Not only were the poor excluded from the church, but the vestry, the lay governing body, was elected by the pew holders. The vestry in turn elected the parish's representatives to the diocesan convention which in turn elected the diocese's representative to the national convention. Thus the pew system not only excluded the poor from seats in the local parish church, but also meant that the entire lay representation in the church would be dominated by the pew holders.[36]

Thoughtful church members early saw the consequences of this system. As early as 1822 an article appeared in *The Gospel Advocate* offering a plan for free churches,[37] and the first attempt to found a free church of which there is any record occurred the following year in Charleston, South Carolina. Describing the consecration of St. Stephen's Chapel, *The Christian Journal and Literary Register* said:

> This neat and well furnished building reared by the pious liberality of Episcopalians in this city, is intended exclusively for persons who are unable to obtain seats in the other churches; for seamen and others; all the seats are free and the worshipers will be subject to no expense. Services will be performed by a missionary.[38]

This paragraph sums up an aspect of the Free Church movement which was to characterize it for many years to come: Free churches were charities and a pauper taint attached to them.

The same magazine published in 1826 an article entitled "Thoughts on the Establishment of a Free Church in New York."[39] In 1831, the Protestant Episcopal City Mission Society was founded for the purpose of providing free sittings in mission churches "for a large class of Episcopalians and others disposed to become members of the Church who were at that time virtually excluded from the Parish Churches—the class referred to comprising the families of poorer mechanics, widows, merchants, clerks, journeymen, apprentices, domestics, and others, unable to pay for sittings, besides strangers, emigrants, etc."[40] The first example of a free church in the diocese of New York occurred in 1833 when St. Mary's, Manhattanville, announced in its annual report, "There are no pew rents in this church."[41] (The term free church has several different meanings in American church history. It is here used rather narrowly to mean only a church all of whose pews were free.) St. Mary's however, was a small rural church north of New York.[42] In the same year the Free Church of the Epiphany was founded by the Mission Society and therefore can lay claim to being the first free Episcopal church in New York City. It was still, however, a mission and charity church with the inevitable pauper taint.[43]

A new type of free church appeared in 1835. Bishop Onderdonk of New York in his address to the convention of that year told of the establishment of St. Paul's free church in Brooklyn. This was a different matter altogether for it was the first free church on record which was neither a mission nor a charity but was a self-supporting church. In his address the bishop endorsed three types of churches: the free mission church supported by the gifts of outsiders, the free self-supporting church, and the church supported by pew rents or sales. He seemed to think that all three were legitimate for he stated that people who could afford to do so should pay for their pews.[44] Prior to 1845 there are records of other free churches being organized in New York. The Mission Society, which had financed free churches, was dissolved in 1847 on the ground that its work was now being taken over by individual parishes which were providing free sittings for providing the poor in their congregations. The supporters of the society questioned the wisdom of the dissolution, however, because

> the most destitute portions of the city are ever most distant from that parochial supervision to which alone they are now entrusted. It is obvious, that in such a widespread city of strangers as New York has now become, without some general missionary care, irrespective of bounds, much of its spiritual destitution must be unknown and many, very many whom the church is bound to care for, wholly neglected.[45]

It is therefore inaccurate to say that the Church of the Holy Communion was the first free Episcopal church in the United States. There

114

were already free churches both subsidized and self-supporting. It is true, however, that the latter had to struggle for existence and to a certain extent depended on outside help. Although recognized as full-fledged parishes they were unable to accept their share in general church work.[46] What Muhlenberg did do in establishing and becoming rector of the Church of the Holy Communion was to give the free church movement a dignity and prestige that it had formerly lacked. Backed by his own distinguished name, the wealth of his sister, and a few parishioners, he managed to give a new impetus to the movement. That this was a major purpose in establishing this parish there can be little doubt. The sentence of consecration in addition to the usual statements added:

And I hereby pronounce the seats of the same church open and free to all persons . . . the pious builder and proprietor thereof, Mary Ann C. Rogers, having by solemn covenant . . . devoted the same forever to this sacred use and secured it by a lawful trust from desecration to any other use whatever . . . (note: the provision for free and open seats in the above sentence, is not to be so construed as to prevent the formation of a regular and settled congregation. Such is the understanding of the Bishop.)[47]

Muhlenberg then considered the problem of a vestry or board of trustees. There were two acts of New York State for incorporating Episcopal churches. One provided for the pew system and a second provided for the incorporation of free mission churches[48] but there was no act for the incorporation of self-supporting "free" churches. Muhlenberg therefore applied to the legislature for a special act incorporating the church. Writing to a friend in 1847 he said:

I hoped in reply to your letter to be able to inform you of the complete organization of the Church of the Holy Communion—but we were disappointed by the legislature in consequence of the new constitution. We have good prospects, however, of getting something better than we thought it expedient to apply for . . . The plan is to convey the property of the church to a close corporation—on conditions to be expressed in the instrument or deed—or conveyance [which will] forever secure it to the original purpose. The minister is to be chosen by the trustees and the male communicants of a certain standing in the congregation—I wish to give the people some voice in the call of their pastor, but in the safest way—when an election is to be made the communicants of the prescribed qualifications could appoint deputies (the same in number as the trustees), who jointly with the trustees should make the choice—finally to be confirmed by the Bishop. For the support of the Minister we may have some endowments, after awhile, but we mean to rely mainly on the offertory—I am endeavoring to get the people to realize the idea of offerings—which in the minds of the majority has no [meaning]. I regard that part of the communion service as invaluable—and a special provision in favor of what we call free churches.[49]

115

Muhlenberg was thus attempting to establish a parish which not only had free pews but was also free of other evils of pew holder domination. The combination of trustees and elected deputies outlined above would eliminate the vestry controlled by the pew holders. In a still more drastic move he announced that the parish would not send delegates to the diocesan convention — that the parish would be united to the rest of the church through the relationship of the parish and the bishop. This move grew out of Muhlenberg's dislike of the domination of the lay house by representatives who were elected by the pew holders of the parish.[50]

Muhlenberg had a lifelong familiarity with the evils of the system. The United Parish in Philadelphia derived the major part of its income from pew rents. The church at Lancaster had been similarly supported and this factor played a major part in the conflict with the Coleman family.[51] As one communicant of the parish pointed out, the fact that the Coleman family owned several pews gave them an influence in the parish far out of proportion to their number.[52] When he served his short term as rector of St. George's, Flushing, Muhlenberg attempted to reorganize the vestry. Yet he himself rented a pew in the Flushing church[53] after he resigned to start the Flushing Institute. When he came to New York, therefore, he had ample experience in the operation of this system.

Throughout Muhlenberg's pastorate at the Church of the Holy Communion it was listed as one of the churches in the diocese of New York but was not listed as a member of the convention. Muhlenberg himself did attend but was listed as "pastor" of the Church of the Holy Communion rather than the more authoritarian "rector" — the title commonly used.[54] He also ran into a number of problems which beset the free churches of his day. In his first pastoral he said:

> The burden of support of the Church is still left to fall too much upon a few individuals; but the people are beginning to see that they must share in it generally and accordingly they have, of late, contributed more liberally at the weekly offering.[55]

That he did not entirely escape the desire of members of his congregation to have special seats is shown by the following entry from the Ward *Diary*:

> Attended all day at the Church of the Holy Communion. Have hitherto sat near the pulpit; but yesterday Dr. Muhlenberg called to say that we were occupying seats which some of his earliest and best supports had been accustomed to use from the beginning of the church. I confessed my ignor-

ance of the name of one of them — my willingness to take another position — and excuse for having sat there was his own advice to take a front seat which I had done as nearly as possible. He assigned me a place about two-thirds of the way down the church and there my family with me today sat.[56]

That Muhlenberg succeeded in his endeavors can be shown from several sources. An English visitor writing of his church says:

A great impetus had already been given to ritual improvement and to the promotion of a more real congregational interest and participation in Divine Service by the devoted pastor of the Church of the Holy Communion, in New York, the Rev. Dr. Muhlenberg.

One of its peculiarities from the first and one of its great recommendations was its being a free church rejecting the odious and mischievous pew system — having all its seats open, unappropriated, and free; another was its adopting a division of the services; and another its having a Choral Service along with other correct and devotional ritual observances, new to Americans and eminently calculated, as the result proved, to secure a large and earnest minded congregation.

There is always a celebration of the Holy Communion on Sunday and the number of communicants weekly is very considerable. At Morning and Evening Prayer both the canticles and Psalms are chanted in a superior style, there being a good choir placed in one of the transepts, the organ being in the other. As well as these attractive services, there is excellent preaching. No wonder, therefore, the church, being also free, is generally filled to overflowing — often, indeed, crowds go away, unable to obtain even standing room.[57]

A further interesting account comes from the diary of Henry Dana Ward. In at least one respect he was strongly sympathetic with Muhlenberg for he himself had founded St. Jude's free church and had for several years endeavored to take care of a congregation of poor people, principally immigrants. This church had been unable to pay him a living salary — despite a grant from Trinity parish — and he made his living by running a girls' school in his home. This latter venture was so successful that when differences erupted which forced him to resign, he devoted his full time to the girls' school. He, together with his family and boarding students, attended the Church of the Holy Communion which was in the vicinity of the school.[58] Although at first critical of Muhlenberg, he was eventually won over:

Sept. 18, 1853:
We attended Dr. Muhlenberg's church liking him but not his fancies or his peculiarities with one exception which is the chanting of the Psalter and the Creed.

117

Oct. 12, 1853:

Attended at the Church of the Holy Communion all day. Sometimes come to think I may yet prefer a part of the service at Dr. M. more than the whole elsewhere, there is so much heart in the devotion and praise.

Oct. 26, 1853:

Attended all day at the Church of the Holy Communion and my feeling was "it is good to be here.... The power of the chanting and life of the singing is what fires my love for the worship of God in this church more than others.[59]

The Church of the Holy Communion itself was located in the six-teenth ward of New York at the corner of Sixth Avenue and Twentieth Street. The built-up areas of the city were subdivided into wards one through fifteen; the sixteenth ward covered the area which was in proc-ess of being built up. Its boundaries were Fourteenth Street on the south to present-day Forty-second Street on the north and east, and west it extended across the whole of Manhattan Island from the Hudson River to the East River.[60]

This tremendous ward was not, of course, intended to be permanent but rather to give some municipal organization to the people living there. In the following year it was divided into two wards and subse-quently subdivided again.[61] The state of New York, as was its policy, took its decennial census in 1845 and this census together with maps gives an interesting picture of the area. A built-up section extended to Six-teenth Street within four blocks of the church building. The simple Gothic structure fitted in well with its surroundings. Contemporary drawings show it in vacant land with a house or two in the distance.[62]

The census shows that the sixteenth ward had the largest population of any one ward but this was undoubtedly due to its large extent. More significant was the fact that one-fourth of this population were un-naturalized aliens and that the largest single group of foreign born came from "Great Britain and Dependencies." There is no breakdown of the figures for this entry but the large immigration from South Ireland had already begun and many of these people were probably Irish Roman Catholics. The frequent references to English and Irish Protestants in source materials indicate that these groups were also numerous. The Germans were the second largest foreign-born group but were far inferior numerically to English-speaking group.[63]

The census shows further that there was practically no farming in this section of the city although a large number of the people kept cows and hogs, possibly for domestic consumption. There were twenty-six manufacturing establishments of which twenty were manure factories. There were already five Episcopal churches in the ward and seventeen of other denominations.[64] The General Theological Seminary that Muhlenberg had championed so ardently as a young clergyman in Philadelphia was on Ninth Avenue only three blocks away. The building of the church excited the interest of the seminarians and its proximity gave Muhlenberg some influence over the future leaders of the church.[65]

It is probable that many if not most of the inhabitants of this ward were poverty stricken squatters who made their living by collecting and selling rags, bones, manure, or working in other marginal occupations. most significant of all the facts garnered by the census was that a majority of the registered paupers in the entire city lived in this one ward.[66]

The area, however, did not long remain in this condition and during the years of Muhlenberg's ministry it changed rather markedly. Parts of it were soon inhabited by prosperous people while others contained large pockets of immigrants and poor native born Americans. A sharp distinction was made among the other Episcopal churches between those that catered to the poor and those that catered to the prosperous. The Church of the Holy Communion embraced wealthy, and poor, and in-between in one congregation—a condition which was unique among the Episcopal churches of New York City.[67]

To meet the needs of the many poverty stricken people in his neighborhood Muhlenberg began a program which was later to develop into the many-sided institutional church of the post-Civil War era. He founded a church dispensary where the poverty-stricken could obtain free medicine and medical advice. For those needing medical care he founded a parish infirmary which was to develop into St. Luke's Hospital (this topic is more fully developed in Chapter 6); he founded a fresh air fund to send slum-dwellers on vacations during the summer; he visited the prisons and public hospitals in the neighborhood; he founded an employment society for the assistance of the poor women of the congregation; and in a yearly Christmas party for the neighborhood children he introduced and popularized the custom of having a Christmas tree. He also continued his interest in education by organizing a parish school for boys and girls. To implement this work he founded a society of deaconesses which he called the Sisterhood of the Holy Communion. (This topic is more fully developed in Chapter 5.)[68]

Muhlenberg's efforts were not, moreover, confined to the Church of the Holy Communion. He threw his influence and energy behind a rising tide of interest in social work which was becoming evident throughout the Diocese of New York. St. Luke's Home for Old People was founded in 1852 and listed him as one of its chief supporters.[69] A Home for Incurables was started in 1865 with Muhlenberg on the board of managers.[70] He endeavored to use the old buildings of St. Paul's College as an orphanage.[71] The account of another social service that he promoted is given in the following excerpt from the bishop's address in 1865: "In the Church of the Holy Communion, after a lecture on the subject by the Rev. Dr. Muhlenberg, I presided at a meeting of gentlemen whom I had summoned to consider what further could be done for the recovery of fallen women and to diminish the dangers to which the friendless are exposed."[72] This meeting resulted in the establishment of an institution known as the Midnight Mission for the purpose of rehabilitating prostitutes. Muhlenberg delivered a sermon entitled "The Woman and Her Accusers; A Plea for the Midnight Mission," which he repeated in several of the churches of New York and Brooklyn. It was then printed and went through several editions. This mission was founded in 1866 and grew out of the City Mission Society.[73] In one description the statement appears that "The Mission owes much to several clergymen but the name of the Rev. Dr. Muhlenberg should be especially mentioned whose sermon in behalf of the Mission has been repeated in several churches, and has already yielded the treasury nearly the sum of $3,000."[74]

In this sermon Muhlenberg did not condemn the prostitutes themselves but rather the social order that forced them into this way of earning a living. He drew on his own experience in work in the slums to illustrate this point. In particular he emphasized the plight of the immigrant woman who was thrown on the street as the result of her inability to earn a living and of poverty-stricken native-born women who were victimized. The general plan of the mission was to have a house of refuge in the red-light district to help such women.[75] Some years later a House of Mercy was founded which was preventive in character giving aid to women before they should resort to prostitution.[76]

The Bishop in his annual address of 1864 could say that "within the last ten years, various institutions of the Church—St. Luke's Hospital, the New York Orphan Asylum, St. Luke's Home for Aged and Infirm Women, the Church Charity Foundation of Brooklyn, the House of Mercy, the Sheltering Arms—have come into existence."[77] Another interesting development was that St. Michael's parish, whose rector was closely associated with Muhlenberg, developed policies which were later identified with the institutional church. This development coincided so closely with that of the Church of the Holy Communion that it is difficult to say whether St. Michael's was influenced by Muhlenberg or whether it happened to start on its course about the same time. In any event the relationship between Muhlenberg and Thomas McClure Peters, rector of St. Michael's, was particularly close. Speaking of this friendship, Peters' son, who succeeded his father as rector of St. Michael's says:

Mr. Peters was in close sympathy with Dr. Muhlenberg, and their views in many respects were so similar that it is not surprising that the record of St. Michael's should in much resemble that of the Holy Communion. The early Communion, weekly celebrations, and daily prayer was established at St. Michael's about or not long after 1862, when they were still counted as marks of an "advanced church." Christmas trees Mr. Peters had started while still at St. Mary's, Manhattanville.[78]

In Collaboration with Mr. Peters, Muhlenberg was able to see another dream come true. Not only had he wanted a free church but also free cemetery where the poor could be buried. Quoting Mr. Peters' son:

> In 1852 Dr. Muhlenberg joined with the Rev. Mr. Peters . . . to establish a free burial ground on Long Island, where patients from St. Luke's were also buried. A cemetery was bought and St. Luke's Hospital, the Churches of the Holy Communion, the Holy Apostles, Trinity, and the Sheltering Arms gave free graves.

> Our church, I believe stands alone among all Christian bodies in this city in having a ground in which the pastors of her thirty free congregations or the missionaries to hospital and asylum can receive without purchase, resting place for their dead.[79]

On another occasion Dr. Peters planned a home for children from broken families which he wanted to call St. Johns. Muhlenberg objected to this title because he himself was planning the community of St. Johnland. Dr. Peters offered to forego this title if Muhlenberg would find a better one for his project. Muhlenberg suggested The Shelter and Dr. Peters changed this to The Sheltering Arms.[80]

During his pastorate at the Church of the Holy Communion a talent of Muhlenberg's which had emerged in Flushing becomes conspicuous. This was his ability to interest wealthy businessmen in his projects. The most outstanding example was Robert Minturn (1805–1866), who was Muhlenberg's closest friend from his coming to New York to Minturn's death in 1866. Minturn was the son and grandson of prosperous New Englanders who had moved their business from Norwalk, Connecticut, to New York. Minturn greatly expanded his inherited fortune. Under the name of Grinnell, Minturn and Co., his firm attained a secure position as one of the largest of the New York commerical houses. It specialized in trade with Europe, Latin America, and China but had business connections all over the world. It shared with the Welds of Boston the honor of being the largest American shipowners of the day. Minturn's company ran regular packet lines to Liverpool and London and owned some of the finest of the American Clipper Ships.

Minturn had already begun a career of good works before Muhlenberg came to New York. He was a member of the Board of Commissioners of Immigration which did much to protect the newly arrived immigrant, and he was one of the founders of the Association for Improving the Condition of the Poor. He was a leader in the founding of the Republican Party and was a friend of Abraham Lincoln. His wife has been credited with the idea of establishing Central Park and he supported her in this project. In church affairs he was a member of the Church of the Holy Communion, a supporter of Bishop Kemper's missionary efforts, the first president of the board of directors of St. Luke's Hospital, and treasurer of the Episcopal Freedmen's Aid Society. He was a supporter of the free church movement and of the efforts of Muhlenberg and Dr. Peters to provide free burial grounds.[81]

Second only to Minturn was John D. Wolfe (1792–1872), a New York businessman of German parentage who made his fortune in the hardware business and later expanded it by investments in real estate. He was already regarded as one of New York's wealthiest businessmen when, at the age of fifty, he decided to retire and devote the balance of his life to philanthropy. Wolfe shared with Muhlenberg an interest in church and educational activities in the west. He founded schools in Colorado and Kansas, gave a building to the theological school of Kenyon College in Ohio, and made numerous contributions to church and educational activities in other western states. Among Muhlenberg's projects he was an active supporter of St. Luke's Hospital and was particularly interested in St. Johnland. Wolfe built a cottage for the Sheltering Arms and was one of the founders of the Home for Incurables. He was president of the American Museum of Natural History and a member of the board of directors of the Working Woman's Protective Union. His wife was a member of the Lorillard family and his daughter, who never married, inherited both the Wolfe and part of the Lorillard fortunes. She continued her father's philanthropic interests.[82]

There were also Adam Norrie, treasurer of St. Luke's Hospital;[83] Mr. and Mrs. John H. Swift—members of the Church of the Holy Communion—who gave the first large gift to the parish in the form of a house for the sisterhood, and who were supporters of St. Luke's and St. Johnland;[84] William B. Astor (1792–1875), who gave St. Luke's its largest contribution in its first fund drive, and who was on the boards of St. Luke's and St. Johnland (upon his death in 1875 he left a fortune of fifty million dollars and was reputed to be the wealthiest man in the United States);[85] and the banker, J. P. Morgan, who was on the board of directors of St. Johnland.[86] Relatives by marriage were William Chisholm who married Muhlenberg's niece; George P. Rogers, brother-in-law of his sister;[87] and members of the Rhinelander and Stewart families who were related to his sister by marriage.[88]

Although deeply immersed in the activities of church work in the nation's largest city, Muhlenberg did not forget his old friend Jackson Kemper. He made the Church of the Holy Communion the center for missionaries going to and from the West and raised money for Kemper and Breck. Bishop Kemper made the Church of the Holy Communion his headquarters when he was in New York and seems to have regarded Muhlenberg as his agent in the East. Lewis Kemper, the bishop's son, lived at Muhlenberg's house while attending Columbia College.[89] All sources indicate, however, that deep as was Muhlenberg's interest in these missionary efforts, his absorbing interest was in the teeming metropolis.

Muhlenberg withdrew from the active direction of the Church of the Holy Communion in 1859 in order to devote his whole time to St. Luke's Hospital, which had its beginnings in the parish infirmary.[90] But this did not mean a complete withdrawal from the parish for he continued a sort of pastoral oversight. (The property of the church was still in the name of his sister.)[91] His successor was Francis Effingham Lawrence, who came from a family at St. George's, Flushing, was a graduate of the Flushing Institute and had been Muhlenberg's assistant at the church.[92]

The tide of population continued to engulf the church's neighborhood so that by 1869 it had become almost exclusively an upper-class section and on the communicant list of the parish appeared such names as Astor, Delano, Fabri, Roosevelt, Schemerhorn, and Van Rensselaer.[93] The church continued to developed as an institutional parish. The New York legislature passed an act for the incorporation of societies to establish free churches in 1854 but the parish did not become incorporated until 1867. Incorporation papers were then taken out declaring that the purpose of the parish was "to maintain a house for the worship of Almighty God according to the Catholic faith, whole and undefiled, and to be forever used as a free church.[94] The papers of incorporation were later amended to add the following paragraph: "Such church to be and forever to remain a Protestant Episcopal Church in Communion with and subject to the Jurisdiction, constitution, laws and canons of the Protestant Episcopal church in the state of New York."[95] The original incorporators were Muhlenberg, Dr. Francis Effingham Lawrence, George P. Rogers, John H. Smith, George T. Schermerhorn, Edgar H. Richards, and William E. Chisholm.[96] At the first meeting of the trustees in 1868 Muhlenberg was elected president. He then presented a deed to the trustees on behalf of Mrs. Rogers for the entire church property with the proviso that Mrs. Rogers should continue to use the rectory for the balance of her life.[97] The Church of the Holy Communion applied for admission to the Diocesan Convention in 1873.[98]

Despite the fact that it was now in an upper-class district the parish continued its institutional work. The church budget for 1874 included items for funerals, a parish school, home for the aged, dispensary, sisters' work, fresh air fund, Sunday school, employment society, Thanksgiving dinner, parish physician, and diocesan missions.[99] Henry Mottet was elected rector to succeed Dr. Lawrence in 1879. Mr. Mottet's parents were members of the Church of the Holy Communion and he grew up in the parish. He also served as a curate under Dr. Lawrence.[100] During Dr. Mottet's rectorship, the parish neighborhood began to change into tenements. Under his leadership the church continued to be a fully developed "institutional church" with numerous activities for the benefit of the people living in its neighborhood.[101]

Summarizing Muhlenberg's work at the Church of the Holy Communion his friend, Dr. Harwood, said:

> The Church of the Holy Communion became thus an institution. It represented a free gospel, systematic work for the poor. Its name meant not the sacrament but communion, Christian brotherhood. One found there beauty in the forms of worship, congregational singing, and devout church music. Dr. Muhlenberg was known as the influential champion of the free church system; as the successful organizer of work for the poor; as the apostle to the sick and needy, working perhaps in the out-door field more through others than personally.[102]

CHAPTER 5

Practical Christianity:

Deaconesses and Sisterhoods

Bishop Jackson Kemper while on his missionary travels in 1841 wrote to his daughter, Elizabeth, then living with her maternal grandparents in Philadelphia:

> The subject of female association upon true Christian principles something like the deaconesses of the primitive church, is deserving of examination and would, I think, if properly presented to the members of the church, meet with much approbation—active employment should be constantly arrived at—either in attending to the poor and sick—or in educating youths—suppose you get from the library the life of Archbishop Sharpe of York and examine...the plan which you will find, I think, in the 2nd Volume, for the establishment of Protestant Nunneries—in fact if you have time I wish you would copy it off for me and send it in a letter to St. Louis.[1]

Elizabeth Kemper dutifully copied the entire article and sent it on to her father. It was a proposal drawn up in 1737 for instituting Protestant convents in the Church of England and was addressed to the Rev. Thomas Sharpe sometime before he became archbishop of York. This convent was to be set up in the bishopric of Durham on a trial basis. The difference between Protestant nuns and Roman Catholic nuns was carefully defined. Protestant nuns were not to take vows and had the right to leave the order by giving "timely notice." They were not to have superiors or an independent organization of their own but were to work under the supervision of the bishop of the diocese in which they were located. The convent would not be for marriageable young women but

125

for "gentlewomen and ladies of quality who have passed the first bloom of life and are still single." Such women the writer said often lack useful employment of their time and are the subject of ridicule because of their unmarried state. Widowed ladies would likewise be eligible for membership. These Protestant nuns were to be actively employed in doing good works.[2]

Muhlenberg himself had occasionally suggested some kind of teaching order of men who would take temporary vows of celibacy and go to the western part of the United States as missionaries. His project of Cadet's Hall also was to be run by a teaching order whose members would take temporary vows. The faculty of St. Paul's College had been vaguely organized as a semimonastic brotherhood. Muhlenberg knew of the efforts of his friend Bishop Ives of North Carolina to form a monastic community. He knew too of the influence of Bishop Whittington of Maryland, who promoted the idea of a monastic order among students at the General Theological Seminary and of the plans of Breck at Nashotah.[3] But up to the time of his coming to the Church of the Holy Communion these plans had involved only orders for men. Muhlenberg may have talked with Jackson Kemper about Archbishop Sharpe's proposal. The sisterhood that he founded was remarkably similar to it.

There is no definite evidence, however, as to how Muhlenberg first evolved the idea of a Protestant sisterhood. He knew of the Episcopal Female Tract Society in Philadelphia, and while rector of St. James, Lancaster, he had been active in obtaining the assistance of the women in parish work. He thereby became one of the first clergymen to mobilize the woman power of the church. He was familiar with the work of the Sisters of Charity, a religious order of women in the Roman Catholic church. That order was founded by a Mrs. Elizabeth Seton who had originally been an Episcopalian and a member of Trinity Church, New York. Upon her conversion to Roman Catholicism she organized this sisterhood and it grew rapidly. It specialized in education, hospitals, and charitable works and was a major factor in cementing the loyalty of immigrant groups to the Roman Catholic church.[4] Although Muhlenberg condemned its discipline, vows, and doctrine he had only praise for its work. He sometimes referred to his sisterhood as Protestant Sisters of Charity.[5]

His ideas on this subject were probably crystalized by Anne Ayres, a young woman whom he met about 1845, the year before the Church of the Holy Communion opened. She was born in London in 1816 but came to this country with her mother when she was twenty. She had a good education and brought letters of introduction to New York businessmen who helped her obtain students for a private school. Among the students were Muhlenberg's niece, Mary Ann Rogers, and daughters of some of his friends. Muhlenberg was at that time still rector of St. Paul's College and Miss Ayres came to College Point as the guest of his sister and niece. One Sunday Muhlenberg preached a sermon on Jephtha's vow and it was this sermon that led Miss Ayres to consecrate her life to charity. On All Saints' Day in the same year (1845) Muhlenberg received Miss Ayres in a quiet service as a Sister of the Holy Communion. For eight years she was the only member of the sisterhood; in 1853 a Miss Brevoot joined, and the order was regularly organized as The Sisterhood of the Holy Communion; in 1854 a Sister Catherine joined and in 1857, Miss Harriet Starr Cannon.[6]

The sisters first established a parish school for girls and when the cholera epidemic of 1849 broke out they worked in the emergency hospitals. A parish infirmary was established in a tenement in 1853 and three years later the Infirmary and Dispensary Building presented by John H. Swift was finished and to this building the Sisters moved. They continued doing parish work until the opening of St. Luke's Hospital in 1859.[7]

Sister Anne [Ayres], First Sister and House Mother, biographer of Muhlenberg. (Courtesy St. Luke's Hospital)

127

Sister Anne described the work of the sisterhood in its early years in a pamphlet written in 1867. Its members were called sisters not in imitation of Roman Catholic nuns but because this term indicated their relationship to each other. Muhlenberg said that they might also be called deaconesses but that that term had an ecclesiastical meaning which he did not think accurate. He insisted on the terms sister and sisterhood because these two terms accurately described the true character of the organization. Miss Ayres (Sister Anne) stated that the sisters lived together in an organization because in this way they could work more efficiently. At one time provision was made for associate or nonresident sisters but that experiment failed.[8]

From the beginning the sisterhood was engaged in teaching, nursing, and social work. The infirmary took care of a total of eighty patients, principally incurables, there were no hired nurses. Fourteen hundred patients received prescriptions at the parish dispensary together with clothing, sick diet, and nursing at their homes as needed. Seventy children were taught every day and partly clothed in the parish school. One hundred and fifty poor families received aid, of whom only one hundred belonged to the parish. In a further appeal for more candidates for the sisterhood, Sister Anne wrote:

> Look at the quantity of work waiting for some of us to do, among the miserable young vagrants in our streets, in the thousand wretched houses within view of our own comfortable dwellings, in our prisons, our penitentiaries, our hospitals and other asylums.

In the same pamphlet she outlined how similar sisterhoods should be organized. Membership in sisterhoods should be for a specific period and should be renewable at the end of that period. Sisterhoods in general should be organized according to the type of work their particular order planned to undertake. Sisters should have their home in the institutions in which they were working and board, laundry, and room should be furnished by the institution. Personal expenses should be provided for by the sister herself or her friends but the institution should set up a fund to help those who had no means of their own. An elder or superintending sister should take care of the general affairs of the sisterhood. A few rules of the society should have to do with hours of work and rest, food, and clothing. Each associate on her admission to full membership should subscribe to the rules and should be bound by them as long as she continued in the society. The prescribed term should be three years preceded by a probationary term of six months. A candidate should be accepted by the sister superintendent and by vote of the other sisters.[9]

The idea of sisterhoods on this plan received wide publicity during the controversy over the Muhlenberg Memorial in 1853–1856 (see Chapter 8). One of the questions raised was whether there was a place for Protestant sisterhoods and in its final report the committee offered the following opinion:

And here we are constrained to call attention to the wasted energy and unemployed power of the women of the Church. The Sisters of Charity in the Romish Communion are worth, perhaps, more to their cause than the combined wealth of their Hierarchy—the learning of their priesthood, and the self-sacrificing zeal of their missionaries. The Providential government of the world leaves everywhere a large number of unmarried and unemployed females, and this appears to point the Church to a wise appropriation of their peculiar talents or gifts, in the cause of Christ and humanity. The associated charity and benevolence of Christian sisterhoods which we have in mind, is the very opposite of the hermitage and the nunnery. Instead of a criminal and cowardly withdrawal from the world and the duties which the wants and distresses of humanity may claim, it is the voluntary consecration to Christ of all the powers of the body and the soul in the active performance of the most tender, the most endearing, and yet the most neglected offices of charity. Many have seen and many lament our loss in this respect: but individual zeal and effort can effect but little in the way of providing a remedy. The constituted authorities of the Church must take hold of the subject—deal with it without reserve—combine efforts in the cause, and give direction to it without fear of man.[10]

The sisterhood, however, ran into a major obstacle in the 1850's. The impact of the Tractarian Movement (see Chapter 8) was now being felt in the United States as well as in England. In the latter country sisterhoods were being formed openly on the model of the Roman Catholic orders. The word sisterhood therefore denoted a species of Romanism to the public. But Muhlenberg refused to change the name to deaconess or some other one less offensive. He published in 1852 two letters on Protestant sisterhoods defending them because they had neither vows nor superiors, because they did good works, and were Protestant in doctrine and life.[11] Muhlenberg made a trip to England in 1855 to inspect sisterhoods and hospitals and had this comment to make on his visit to an Anglo-Catholic sisterhood:

Went out to Clewer and had a long talk with the 'Sister Superior' as she is styled. . . . They are doing great good, I am sure, but their religious system lacks in the Evangelical element. . . . They depend too much upon training. Every penitent unless dismissed, becomes a communicant of the Church. The Sisters go to confession, not however, compulsively. They keep the Canonical hours, thus meeting for prayer six times a day. On the whole it is too much a copying of the Roman Sisterhood.[12]

Typical of the reaction of the average Protestant of the 1850's was that of Henry Dana Ward, the diarist:

Jan. 15, 1854. In the sermon of the morning Dr. Muhlenberg spoke of the seven years experience and growth of the Church in very modest and appropriate manner. When he named the sisterhood I could have groaned: for that is an experiment that has failed in every age and climate since the early church and I have no heart for attempting to introduce vows of celibacy and poverty in our Church...Jan. 29, 1854. Before church I went into Dr. M's study where he spoke of "The Sisterhood of his Church as the best thing belonging to it." "I did not know until a month or two since, Doctor, that you had such a thing in your church; and when informed," I said, "such had been too long and too often tried to leave any hope of success."

"Not so," he replied, "they are neither long tried nor often. They are German Lutheran and French Calvinistic, but not Roman, neither Anglican."

"They take Vows?"

"Not at all; they are free, always, free to leave when they please. While in the sisterhood, they conform to its laws, which do not require vows but habits of virtue, piety, and charity."

This put a new face on the matter and he followed it by handing me a copy of his pamphlet explaining the case—which I have read this evening with satisfaction.[13.]

Muhlenberg could point to a parallel development in the Lutheran church. In 1836 a German pastor, Theodore Fliedner, founded an order of deaconesses at Kaiserwerth in Germany, where Florence Nightingale went for training. These deaconesses specialized in hospitals, orphanages, and other works of charity. In 1846 a young Lutheran clergyman, W. A. Passavant, who had become interested in church institutional work, visited Pastor Fliedner and upon his return to the United States founded a hospital in Pittsburgh with four deaconesses. Muhlenberg cited the example of this order to defend his own sisterhood from the charges of Romanism. Pastor Fliedner himself visited the United States and met Muhlenberg in New York.[14]

The work of Pastor Passavant in developing Lutheran deaconesses parallels that of Muhlenberg in the Episcopal church. Yet while the Sisterhood of the Holy Communion resembled the institution of the Lutheran Deaconesses at Kaiserwerth it does not appear that the former was copied from the latter but rather that each was founded independently. In spirit and principle, however, the two are remarkably alike.[15] Passavant's biographer recorded that "Passavant and William Augustus Muhlenberg were friends and it is likely that in establishing the American branch of the Lutheran order of deaconesses and the Episcopal

Sisterhood of the Holy Communion they influenced each other."[16] Miss Ayres later published a pamphlet entitled *Evangelical Sisterhoods* which contained a section entitled "Questions for Self-Examination, selected and slightly altered from a series prepared by Pastor Fliedner, with special reference to Deaconesses employed in hospitals."[17] Muhlenberg also published a letter from Passavant which he had apparently solicited describing the hospital and deaconesses in Pittsburgh.[18]

Despite his efforts, however, the sisterhood continued to suffer from the stigma of Romanism. The excitement of the Tractarian Movement was intense and the managers of St. Luke's Hospital who were in process of raising a building fund were adverse to having the hospital associated in the public mind with the sisterhood. So far did this feeling go that the board of managers adopted a resolution that when the hospital was opened the sisterhood was to have nothing to do with it. This was done despite the fact that the sisterhood had largely founded and operated the parish infirmary out of which St. Luke's Hospital grew. Muhlenberg managed to have this resolution repealed, and when the hospital was finally opened in 1859 the sisterhood moved in and took over its interior management.[19] In the second annual report dated 1860, Dr. Edward B. Dalton, the resident physician, stated:

> In reply to frequent inquiries as to the success of nursing by volunteer ladies, it may be mentioned that members of the medical staff, connected for many years with other hospitals, express their conviction of its great superiority both in ameliorating the condition of the patient and facilitating the efforts of the physician. As among the especial indications of this—the rapid recovery of patients who have been subjects of surgical operation has been observed; the fact, too, that consumptive cases survive for a much longer period than in other institutions and the record (of no deaths) in the children's department.[20]

A second objection may have arisen from the fact that nurses in the New York City hospitals were customarily prisoners from the jails and served out their terms by working in the hospitals. Many of these were "ten-day women" who had been arrested on the streets of New York for prostitution. Public opinion may have regarded it as astonishing that respectable young women were taking over an occupation associated with criminals and prostitutes.[21] Not surprising, perhaps, is the fact that reports on the condition of public hospitals described the nurses as "intemperate persons."[22]

The sisters did not drop their social work when they moved to St. Luke's. Muhlenberg instructed them to secure in connection with each patient's history, details as to source of income, number of children in the family, and other information about the patient's environment. If the patient was a wage earner, the head nurse, on her first moment off duty, was instructed to go to the patient's home, size up the situation, and if necessary see that the family was provided with food and other necessities as it had been observed that a patient responded to treatment much better if he was not worrying about his family at home.[23]

In addition the sisterhood made a beginning in nursing education by training the probationary sisters in their duties. A document in the archives of St. Luke's Hospital describes the system developed by the sisters:

> One peculiarity which distinguishes the management of St. Luke's from that of other hospitals around us, is its system of nursing.
>
> The fundamental idea is not the substitution of voluntary for paid labor, for we have also our hired nurses, but it is the interposition between the Physician and his patients of educated Christian women, who voluntarily perform certain duties more responsibly than can be entrusted to paid nurses. It is the substitution of intelligent, appreciative, critical assistance on the part of the Sisterhood, for the unquestioning routine obedience of nurses; and it has all the advantages which increased intelligence always has in any work.
>
> The system is too well known to be described here; but a few words may be offered upon it.
>
> Every Ward is in charge of a Sister, who has under her two day nurses, and one for the night. She has had some instruction in medicines. Attached to her ward is a drug-closet containing such *materia medica* as is most likely to be used, and all prescriptions are put up and administered by herself. For example: if a man is ordered twenty drops of Tinct. Opii, three times a day, three single doses are prepared, and taken to him by the Sister.
>
> There are two advantages in this over the ordinary method. First, as no medicines are ordered in quantity, but each dose is prepared and given separately, there is no waste — nothing is left over to be thrown away. Secondly, greater safety and accuracy are secured. Patients cannot be trusted with their own medicine. They cannot be made to understand the fallacy of the argument, that if a tea-spoonful of anything will cure a man slowly, the whole bottle will do it immediately. It is not an unheard of thing for an elegantly disguised and flavored medicine to be rubbed on an injured limb and for the cooling lotion, ordered at the same time, to be faithfully taken in teaspoonful doses after meals. To avoid such gross mistakes as these, it is customary in hospitals for the nurse to administer the medicines according to distinctly marked directions on the bottle. This works well and mistakes are rare. But to have the medicine given by one who is herself responsible for its proper administration and preparation, who is required by the Rules of the Sisterhood to understand its nature, the ordinary dose, and its expected effect, and who is honest and faithful enough to report immediately any mistake which may occur, shuts up many sources of error and danger.

132

Besides the administration of medicine the feeding of patients is a duty in which the advantages of the Sister's services are clearly seen. Whether the patient is to have House or extra diet is, of course, ordered by the Physician. But a sick man's appetite is a very changeable thing and patients will be dissatisfied. When they complain to the nurse, he or she is powerless and the matter is referred to the Physician. It is to obviate these annoyances, and to meet the capricious desires of the patient with a corresponding flexibility of resources, that the Sister is ready to act in the matter. It is her duty and pleasure to find what each patient can eat and she has ability to obtain it for him. The matter of extras is quite a business with the Sisters after every meal in their private dining-room where the provisions are sent up and distributed by them with careful discrimination for their patients.

The diet orders once given hold good from day to day, through weeks or months, till changed. The general direction is the duty of the Physicians; the practical labor, and the complaints are the portion of the Sister. And here as in the administration of medicine, one of two persons is always responsible for errors, either the Doctor who gave the order, or the Sister who did not carry it out.[24]

Strongly as Muhlenberg opposed the Catholic conception of the sisterhood with its vows, religious devotions, and strict rules, he involuntarily had an important part in founding the first and at the present time the largest order of nuns in the American Episcopal church. As already noted he received Harriet Starr Cannon into the Sisterhood of the Holy Communion—a woman of strong and forceful character. She won Muhlenberg's respect and for six years was engaged in the work of the sisterhood. But about 1862 dissension arose because some of the sisters under the leadership of Sister Harriet Starr Cannon wanted to organize the Sisterhood of the Holy Communion along the lines of a Catholic order. Sister Anne resigned her position upon finding that her ideas in regard to the methods and government were disapproved by some, if not most, of its members. Muhlenberg thereupon declared the sisterhood dissolved by the withdrawal of its head and proposed a new organization, a company of Christian Ladies, who should work under Miss Ayres as matron of the hospital.

Miss Cannon and her associates felt that they had been badly treated by Muhlenberg and withdrew from association with his work. It was precisely the time when these women found themselves without an occupation that Dr. Thomas McClure Peters, rector of St. Michael's and Muhlenberg's close friend, was looking for someone to operate the House of Mercy, an institution to rehabilitate prostitutes. Through his intimate friendship with Muhlenberg, Dr. Peters knew and admired the sisters who worked at St. Luke's, but others associated with him looked somewhat askance at the women who were felt to have deserted

St. Luke's. Dr. Peters in this emergency turned to them not withstanding to take charge of the House of Mercy and in the following year enlisted their services to operate the Sheltering Arms as well. While they resented Muhlenberg for the treatment they had received, he, on his part, was thoroughly convinced of their capacity and their value as workers and was happy that Dr. Peters should accept their assistance in his projects.[25]

The above version of this dispute is based on the account given by John Punnett Peters, son of Muhlenberg's friend, and also a friend of the sisters. A somewhat different version is given in the recently published history of the Sisterhood of St. Mary by Sister Mary Hillary, who apparently drew on sources not available to this author.

But the sands of human personality proved to be an unsound foundation upon which to build a growing Sisterhood. The Sisters complained of erratic and autocratic direction; Sister Anne responded with increasing demands and tightened controls. She opposed their suggestion that the Sisterhood adopt the corporate organization and the traditional ways of the conventual life. Early in the winter of 1862-63, United Sister Louisa Cooper and Probationary Sister Amelia Asten left the hospital to avoid further discord. Sister Anne concluded that two courses of action lay open before her: she must conform to the Sisters' requests or she must resign her office. She decided to resign and announced her decision to the Sisterhood. At once Dr. Muhlenberg, to the consternation of the sisters, informed them that the Sisterhood was ipso facto dissolved. The work at St. Luke's Hospital was to be continued under Miss Ayres as matron with such Sisters as chose to remain. Before the change could be made, however, Sister Anne angrily ordered Sisters Harriet and Mary off the premises and their appeal to Dr. Muhlenberg met with his refusal to interfere.

Accordingly, four Sisters left St. Luke's Hospital early in the morning of April 9, 1863 — Harriet Cannon, Mary Heartt, Jane Haight, and Sarah Bridge.

The Sisters never became reconciled to their abrupt departure from St. Luke's. Sister Harriet grieved to part without a word of farewell from people with whom she had worked for seven years. She returned the following day to attempt a reconciliation but Sister Anne declined to see her. As time went on, Sister Harriet recalled with pleasure the hard work and jokes and fun they had had together at St. Luke's. She always ended with a lament over the estrangement from Sister Anne. 'If only she could have trusted me...' The two women were estranged for many years but were eventually reconciled.

Toward the end of Sister Anne's life Mother Harriet went to visit her, somewhat apprehensively, not certain how she would be received. Her fears were groundless, however. Both had been certain of being wronged, but both had learned to forgive. Sister Anne received her guest with great kindness and the two talked together calmly and quietly. At Sister Anne's funeral Mother Harriet was among those who stood beside the grave.[26]

Both Dr. Peters and the sisters came to the conclusion that in order to make their work effective, there should be a permanent organization of the sisterhood. He therefore laid the matter before Bishop Potter of New York and suggested the appointment of a committee to consider this matter. Upon the recommendation of this committee the bishop received these women as the first members of the Sisterhood of St. Mary, a society for the "performance of all spiritual and corporal works of mercy which a woman may perform, especially the care of the sick and the education of the young."

The establishment of a sisterhood on the Catholic model in the Episcopal church created great excitement in New York due possibly to the existence of another period of controversy between the Catholic and Protestant parties. The Protestant party was so inflamed over this incident that the Sisters of St. Mary were forced to give up their work at the House of Mercy and the Sheltering Arms — which were supported by public donations — and to found institutions under their own control. Possibly in reaction to this controversy, Sister Anne published a pamphlet in 1864 in defense of the Evangelical type of sisterhood and issued a revised edition of her pamphlets on Evangelical sisterhoods in 1867.[27]

Muhlenberg's sisterhood was again reorganized in 1873 to be called the Sisterhood of St. Luke and St. John because it now was working with him in a further project, The Society of St. Johnland. There were also a sufficient number of sisters to reconstitute the Sisterhood of the Holy Communion which returned to parochial work at the Church of the Holy Communion. It was a matter of gratification to Muhlenberg and Sister Anne that similar sisterhoods in other parts of the country were being organized.[28]

Sister Anne retired in 1878, one year after the death of Muhlenberg, but remained a guest of the hospital until her death. Muhlenberg was succeeded as pastor-superintendent of St. Luke's by George Stuart Baker, whose wife had at one time been a member of the sisterhood and who was made house mother. She served in this position until 1888 carrying on the traditions and policies of Muhlenberg and Sister Anne.[29]

In the years following the death of Muhlenberg and the retirement of Sister Anne the character of nursing at St. Luke's changed with the expansion of the hospital. The sisterhood failed to grow rapidly enough and recourse was finally had to hired nurses who were professionally

Sister Harriet [Starr Cannon] in the "plain ordinary dress of a gentlewoman" prescribed for the Sisters of the Holy Communion. (Courtesy The Community of St. Mary)

trained. Sometime after 1877, Miss Jessica Reid, a graduate of the Boston City Hospital, was placed in charge of nursing but the sisters continued to work along with the paid nurses. In 1892 Miss Walstein Thompson became head of the nursing department. She was in her own person the link between the past and present as she had been prepared for the work under the old regime of Episcopal sisters. St. Luke's thus made the transition from the period when nursing was part of a voluntary religious vocation to the day when it became a full-fledged profession requiring at least three years of specialized preparation beyond the cultural prerequisites for entrance.[30]

Both Hopkins and Abell, authorities on the urban impact on the Protestant churches, discuss the important role that deaconesses played in Protestant social work after the Civil War and cite Muhlenberg as a pioneer.[31] The deaconesses specialized in nursing, social work, and teaching until these fields were developed into salaried professions. Muhlenberg's part in this development is summarized by Bishop Horatio Potter in his pastoral address of 1865:

> It is due to the venerable and beloved founder of St. Luke's Hospital, the Rev. Dr. Muhlenberg, so well known among us for works of piety and charity to record the fact that he first in our church in this diocese, if not in this country, called to his aid and organized into a permanent agency, devoted Christian women who desired to be set apart and associated together in the manner and for the sacred purposes to which reference has been made, though in their case more especially for the care of the sick.[32]

CHAPTER 6

Practical Christianity:
St. Luke's Hospital

Private church hospitals in New York originated in attempts to meet the problems of the immigrant. It is true that the city operated municipal hospitals but these were pauper hospitals which were combination hospitals and poor houses.[1] As noted in Chapter 5, the nurses were prisoners who served out their terms by nursing in these hospitals and reports described them as intemperate persons.[2] The poverty-stricken immigrant who did not want to endure the humiliation of going to the pauper hospital but who could not be treated in his overcrowded tenement was the principal sufferer. The first attempt to set up a private hospital was a Jewish hospital which, according to the census of 1845, involved a total of seventeen people, patients and staff combined.[3] Another attempt was made in 1846 by Moses Marcus, an English priest who was working among the British immigrants in New York. He proposed the building of a church and hospital to be known as the church and Hospital of St. George the Martyr. For this purpose he received a gift of land from the city of New York under the terms of which Trinity Church, in return for this donation, renounced its claims on certain property held by the city. This project, however, was never realized.[4]

In the meanwhile the Roman Catholic Sisters of Charity of St. Vincent de Paul founded St. Vincent's Hospital in 1849 in a three-story house that could accommodate thirty patients. A few years later the adjoining house was rented and fitted up as a hospital. This could accommodate seventy patients. In 1856 the sisters rented a building which had formerly been an orphan asylum and could accommodate about

138

150 patients. This hospital received approximately two-thirds of its income from paying patients and the balance from contributions, city grants, and funds raised by fairs and floral festivals.[5] Another Jewish hospital was opened in 1855 which could accommodate sixty patients comfortably.[6]

It could not escape the notice of Muhlenberg that a hospital was badly needed for the numerous British immigrants in New York, many of whom were Anglicans and were therefore the peculiar responsibility of the Episcopal church. In the second year of his pastorate at the Church of the Holy Communion he announced that one-half of the offering on St. Luke's Day would be set aside to start a hospital building fund. One-half of this collection netted $32.00.[7] Sometime during the next few years a tenement was rented and fitted up as a parish infirmary and in 1856 a building for this purpose was presented to the parish by Mr. and Mrs. John Swift.[8] The patients were for the most part immigrants, principally from Ireland and Englnnd, with a sprinkling of native born Americans.[9] An outbreak of cholera in 1849 required the establishment of a chain of emergency hospitals throughout the city and the conditions which Muhlenberg observed in these made a deep impression on him. Possibly this epidemic impelled him to make a more vigorous attempt to build an adequate hospital.

A general collection was taken up in the diocese of New York on St. Luke's Day, 1849, and the sermon which Muhlenberg delivered in several different churches was published. In this sermon he outlined his project in some detail:

> The first object will be to secure a site of ground, somewhere in the upper and open part of the city, sufficiently large for an extensive establishment. The building is to be built in such a manner as to allow for extensions as needed and as necessary funds shall be obtained. The institution thus may begin its operation on a small scale, if that be necessary and enlarge them as it shall come in possession of the means. But in the first instance sufficient ground must be had to admit of the extension of the hospital.
>
> The means of the maintenance of the hospital will be derived from annual donations, subscriptions, collections in churches, and such like sources. If the income arising be small, the number of beneficiaries likewise will be small. The latter will be increased only with the increase of the former. Thus the undertaking may proceed prudently and without incurring debt, both in the erection of buildings and in the support of the institution.
>
> Individuals or congregations making sufficient donations will be entitled to send patients to the Hospital. They may endow a bed and alcove or a ward in the same manner that scholarships are founded in literary institutions — For this purpose as time goes on, there will no doubt be endowments by means of legacies, etc.[10]

139

Muhlenberg also proposed that a part of the building in time might be used for the relief of destitute persons in temporary distress giving the example of Christ Church Hospital, Philadelphia.[11] The plan of the hospital building should be such that the wards could open into the chapel by means of doors or windows at their termination.[12]

Incorporation papers were filed in May of the same year under the provisions of an act entitled "An Act for the Incorporation of Benevolent, Charitable, Scientific, and Missionary Societies," passed in April, 1848. The incorporators were for the most part Muhlenberg's friends and supporters: L. M. Hoffman, John H. Swift, Robert B. Minturn, Joseph D. B. Curtis, Benjamin Ogden, George P. Rogers. Others were James Warren, William H. Hobart, M.D., Samuel Davis, Edward McVicker, John Punnett, and Henry C. Hobart.[13]

The managers obtained the site formerly owned by the Church of St. George the Martyr by a joint act of the Corporation of New York and Trinity Church, the original donors. A complicated legal problem arose which was not solved until 1852.[14] With this problem out of the way an appeal was launched for $100,000.

Muhlenberg then editorialized on a familiar theme:

> "So Large a Sum" for a house of mercy in a City like this, which despises small sums in which the largest enterprises of a secular character are daily entered into, when the common talk is about extravagant projects, extravagant houses, extravagant ornaments; the wonder being where all the money comes from to indulge to such a degree our luxurious habits and pampered tastes—a city in which the emulation [sic] to spend money is as great as it is to acquire it—into whose lap Europe is emptying her choicest specimens of luxury and virtue, because she is becoming too poor to retain them—a city in fact in which Dives appears to have run mad.[15]

A subscription was begun the following year and 158 persons contributed. The largest single gift was $13,000 from William B. Astor. Other amounts were from two who gave $10,000 each, down to 63 who gave amounts of less than $100.[16]

The managers ran into other difficulties and the cornerstone was not laid by the provisional bishop of New York until May, 1854.[17] The architect of the building was John W. Ritch.[18] The first part of the building to be completed was the chapel which was used for services while the other parts were being built.[19]

With this hospital project definitely launched, Muhlenberg took a second trip to England in 1855 to study hospitals abroad. He left in April and returned in October. He first went to London to visit the hospitals there. He wrote to a friend describing his visit to one of them:

I spent several hours in St. Bartholomew's Hospital. One of the chaplains, a most excellent and earnest man, accompanied me through every part of it. He complained of Dickens in his otherwise admirable description of the institution ignoring the religious provisions of the same; and well he might complain. There are four chaplains, two of them in residence attending on the sick. Service is read every day in each of the wards. Suitable prayers in large print on a card are hung over the bed of each patient. Biblical texts are painted on the walls. All the sisters but one are communicants of the Church and those I spoke to seemed to be good women. The Christian Character of the place is evident at a glance, and if all the Chaplains are like the one who went about with us, nothing on that score is wanting. The most ample space is allowed for the beds, there not being more than twenty-two or twenty-four in each ward which is divided into two compartments leaving to each ten or twelve patients in a room some forty feet long by twenty-five in width. Each ward has the services of four nurses including the Sister. The atmosphere was as fresh as in our little Infirmary and the cleanliness everywhere is beautiful. If the other hospitals of London are in like condition, and I am told they are, London has more to boast of than I imagined.

St. Luke's Hospital—the original building. (Courtesy St. Luke's Hospital)

141

He visited the other hospitals in London as well as in Paris apparently attempting to pick up as much information as he could in preparation for the organization of St. Luke's.[20.]

Patients were first received in the new building in May, 1858, and on this occasion the sermon in the chapel was preached by Samuel Cooke, rector of St. Bartholomew's Church. He took his text from the fifth chapter of St. John's Gospel, comparing St. Luke's to the pool of Bethesda where people came to be healed. He ended on the practical note that, now that the building was completed, it was necessary to raise an endowment for the support of the hospital.[21] For its first year the hospital had Dr. David Eigenbrodt as its resident physician. He was the son of a professor at the General Theological Seminary and who donated his services free of charge.[22] The number of the board of managers was increased in 1891 from thirteen to thirty-one.[23] Among its officers were the familiar names of Muhlenberg's supporters: Robert Minturn, president; Murray Hoffman, vice-president; Cyrus Curtis, vice-president; Adam Norrie, treasurer; T. W. Ogden, secretary. Among the members were names which appear on other Muhlenberg projects: John Caswell, J. H. Swift, S. D. Babock, H. C. Smythe, H. C. Hobart, George P. Rogers, and Benjamin Ogden. Ex-officio members were the mayor of New York, the British consul, the president of the Board of Aldermen, and the president of the Board of Councilmen. The clerical board of the hospital was made up of the newly elected bishop, Horatio Potter; William Berian, rector of Trinity Church; Samuel Seabury, editor of *The Churchman;* Stephen Tyng, rector of St. George's Church; W. E. Eigenbrodt, father of the resident physician; G. T. Bedell, rector of the Church of the Ascension; and Samuel Cooke, rector of St. Bartholomew's.[24]

The money raised by the first building drive proved inadequate and a second drive was therefore authorized in 1858. This time there were 432 contributors of whom all were individuals except fourteen. The latter group included churches, business firms, and organizations, one of which was the Anglo-American Emigrant Society of London.[25] An interesting gift was a painting of the Three Marys at the Tomb by the fashionable artist Daniel Huntington. It was to be sold and the proceeds were to be given to the building fund. Contributions in kind came from individuals, churches, hospital associations, and Bible societies.[26]

Previous reports had been made from 1850 to 1858 of an informal character, but the report of 1859 was the first of a comprehensive nature. It represented the first full year of operation and it gave an interesting picture of the beginning of the hospital. The building was on Fifth Avenue between Fifty-fourth and Fifty-fifth Streets on a plot 200 feet wide and 400 feet long. The principal front was on Fifty-fourth Street facing south and extending from east to west, 280 feet in length. The general plan of the building was a narrow parallelogram with a wing at each end and a central chapel flanked with towers. It was built of square red brick. The central chapel was the distinctive feature of the hospital. It was three stories high and could seat 350 persons.[27] A large photograph of the original building shows that the architecture was Gothic and suggested, as Muhlenberg put it, that St. Luke's was not only a church hospital but a hospital church.

Although no evidence has been found to suggest deliberate imitation the interior plan bears a striking similarity to the Philadelphia General Hospital.[28] A form of central heating and central ventilation was put into effect. The general outline of the building was designed to produce fresh air in every part of the house, and sunlight in all the apartments occupied by the sick. The wards and private rooms had a southern exposure with windows opening on a lawn 100 feet by 400 feet. Space for moderate exercise without exposure to the weather was afforded by the long corridors between the wards and the outer walls. With steam heat in winter and unimpeded circulation of air during the summer, a moderate temperature was maintained throughout the hospital at all times. The apparatus for airing the house, the report stated, had been of an experimental nature and proved entirely adequate justifying the original cost. The entire cost of the building was nearly $200,000.[29] Concerning the religious organization of the hospital Muhlenberg wrote:

A good idea of the interior economy of the Hospital might be found by considering it as a family under a paternal and sisterly care and in its religious bearing, it will be understood, it is regarded as that of a congregation under the care of the pastor. The patients, when they come here, enter a hospital church as well as a church hospital. This they find, not only in the religious order of the house, but in the very construction of the building. The principal wards are the "long drawn aisles" of the central church—in each of the aisles every morning there are prayers with reading of the Holy Scriptures and family lectures, for which the patients who are well enough gather near the Desk, forming a congregation often quite as large as at the "daily Service" in some of our great churches nor less earnest in their devotions. . . . In the evening the service is held in the chapel.

All who are able come in and occupy their seats while those in beds can still be participants in the Service, the open doors allowing a free passage for the Speaker's voice, as he stands midway between them, to be distinctly heard at the extreme end of the wards. For this purpose, the acoustic properties of the house have surpassed expectations. It is at "Evensong," when the whole household is assembled, that the idea of a congregation of the sick and well uniting in the same act of worship is fully realized.

143

On Sunday morning there is a regular Church Service and sermon for the House generally. The Communion is administered once a month in the chapel and when occasion requires in the wards.[30]

St. Luke's was definitely a free or charity hospital. Although it never turned a patient away for lack of money some method had to be devised to pay for each patient. The adequate endowment for which Muhlenberg hoped never became a reality perhaps because of the outbreak of the Civil War only two years after the hospital opened its doors. The hospital derived its income from a variety of sources — gifts of individuals, collections in churches, gifts in kind from those who did not have money to contribute. Some income was derived from the endowment of charity beds by individuals or support of hospital beds by churches. St. Luke's Hospital Associations were founded in several parishes; their duties were not only to raise money for hospital beds but to seek out those in the parish who needed hospitalization.

At the end of the first year the managers could report that its income fully met expenditures:

> Let associations continue to be formed; let the more able and liberal friends of the hospital engage to support one patient each; let the congregations give us annual collections, or what is more desired, let their members become annual subscribers — and the hospital will fulfill its mission of charity, and suitable applicants will never be turned away from its doors — as thus far none have been.[31]

At first it appeared that the admission of patients would be on a denominational basis for Muhlenberg wrote: "In receiving patients, members of the Protestant Episcopal Church will be preferred, but not to the exclusion of others (so far as there may be room for them) who are willing to accept the ministrations of the Church."

This policy was never carried out and from its opening the hospital admitted patients of any or no religion.[32] Muhlenberg took the same stand in regard to denominationalism that he took in regard to his schools. A Christian hospital had to have one denomination to look after its religious activities, and since the supporters of St. Luke's were all of the Episcopal church that should be the denomination which took the responsibility for the religious activities.[33]

In regard to the medical aspects of the hospital's activities the manager's report endeavored to account for the large number of deaths:

> [In a] large proportion of the cases, the disease was pulmonary consumption — to provide for the incurably ill particularly of this class, was one of the objects of the hospital and therein to supply an urgent want in the Community. With the exception of the Bellevue Hospital and the small Roman

144

Catholic Hospital of St. Vincent's, there was no resort for consumptives, so numerous in our climate, whence St. Luke's as a church institution felt bound to open its door to them. Several have been received who had first applied to the New York hospital for admission having been directed here by the excellent superintendent of that venerable institution, which by its rules confines itself in Medical cases to those not beyound the reach of the physician's skill. The reason for excluding incurables there, it might be thought, should equally operate here but it must be recollected that here spiritual as well as physical care is an object, for which there is more opportunity in slow than in acute diseases. A Hospital which offers medicine for the soul cannot dispense them only on condition that the medicines for the body shall avail. At any rate, as long as there is room, incurables, within certain limits, will be eligible for admission.[34]

In the early years of the hospital a majority of the patients in the hospital were Episcopalians but the pattern soon settled into that which continued for the rest of Muhlenberg's life: Episcopalians remained the largest single group among the patients but they were never again a majority. Patients from other Protestant denominations seem to have been satisfied with the religious services of the hospital although they had the right to be visited by their own clergy if they wished.[35] Speaking of the German patients in whom he had a sentimental interest Muhlenberg said:

> Judging from them it would seem that there cannot be all the infidelity we hear of among German immigrants; but the inference rather is that, in their sickness, they recur to the Faith of their earlier days. They express no doubts but gladly recognize the religion of their Fatherland. This is a fact that might be used with their vaunting rationalist and free-thinking leaders. Let them know that their disciples disappear in the hospital.[36]

A more difficult problem rose with the Roman Catholic patients who were one of the largest single groups at the hospital. They, as did the Protestants, had the right to have their own clergy call on them. Muhlenberg resented the practice of the Roman Catholic priests of warning their patients to have nothing to do with the religious services of the hospital. Of this problem Muhlenberg wrote:

> Among my parishioners, so to call them, there are always a number of our Roman Catholic brethren—They attend services—of course the preaching and teaching in a place like this consist less in exposing peculiar error than in enforcing common truth. Hence a sensible Roman Catholic woman who was a most attentive listener and a devout worshipper in chapel made the remark "I believe all that I hear, but I don't hear all I believe."...
> Other clergymen who ignore our ministry and would feel bound to warn their sick against it, of course, are out of place in our wards. But

even they are not excluded from emergencies. For example in a case of sudden accident when the sufferer or his friends desire the office of a priest of their own, no objection is ever made.

Muhlenberg, probably in company with most Protestants of his day, regarded the Roman Catholic church as a hopelessly corrupt sector of Christendom and remarked in his reports on how many of the patients had been "liberated" from "the Bondage of Romanism."[37]

The hospital's original purpose was reflected in the fact that foreign-born patients outnumbered native-born Americans from the very beginning. Of this group by far the greater number were Irish but there is no breakdown in the hospital's records as to how many were Protestant North Irish and how many were Roman Catholic South Irish. If, however, the number of Roman Catholic patients is deducted in any given year from the number of Irish reported it is evident that a majority of the Irish were Protestant North Irishmen. Germans as might be expected constituted the second largest national group in the hospital.[38]

Financing of the hospital was a recurrent problem. Muhlenberg and his associates realized that for the hospital to continue as a free hospital an adequate endowment was essential.[39] The coming of the Civil War probably kept the hospital from attaining this goal but it was in a fairly prosperous condition in its early years since in both 1859 and 1860 the managers could report a slight operating surplus.[40] Following the war the hospital began to show a deficit at the end of each year with monotonous regularity and this condition continued throughout Muhlenberg's lifetime.[41] There were several factors involved. As the building grew older maintenance costs increased;[42] as the city grew there was a greater demand for its charitable services, which required some expansion;[43] once the novelty of the hospital began to wear off, interest in it dropped bringing corresponding decrease in the contributions which had maintained it in its early years.[44] An important factor in this decrease may have been a source of some gratification to Muhlenberg, however, for the building of St. Luke's had stimulated church charities in the Episcopal church throughout the Diocese of New York. As the diocese and the various parishes developed their own projects they had less time and money to contribute to St. Luke's.[45]

Still another factor was the widespread belief that St. Luke's was a wealthy institution that needed no contributions. Speaking of this notion Muhlenberg said:

> These adverse things are due chiefly to the prevalent impression that
> St. Luke's is a wealthy institution, possessing or commanding ample

means—it is high time that this most injurious misapprehension was corrected—and especially in consideration of the further fact, that all the while the demands upon the charity of the Hospital are increasing, never so incessant and urgent as now. Applications for gratuitous admission come in from all quarters—not only in writing which, thus made, would leave us the chance of declining if we thought proper, but the sick themselves are sent to our doors exhibiting their extremity, and imploring not to be turned away. So far as they are at all eligible subjects, what can be done but to put their names on the Registers. The agents of other charities, City Missionaries of all denominations, Bible women, good Brethren in the city, and the country far and wide around, submitting pitiable beings in their parishes but offering nothing for their bed and board, all seem to think that our "Noble Institution" as they call it—for we have no lack of praise—stands with wide open portals inviting admission without money and without price. Of the present occupants of our wards there are forty for whom we receive equivalent in pay, which is partly explained by the fact that the interest of the endowment for a Charity Bed is far from being enough for its support.[46]

The bishop of the diocese instituted Hospital Sunday in 1877, a day on which the Episcopal churches took up a collection for the benefit of St. Luke's and this brought in a steady income.[47] This practice was eventually broadened to include all hospitals in New York of any denomination.[48] In the last years of Muhlenberg's life a number of the wealthier members of the board made contributions toward the establishment of an endowment fund in the hope that before his death the hospital might be established on a sound financial basis.[49] Another factor not generally credited by Muhlenberg's admirers must also be considered. In the closing years of his life immediately following the Civil War, Muhlenberg became involved in another project, the founding of St. Johnland (see Chapter 11). No doubt there was a need for some such institution as St. Johnland but after 1864 it did absorb a large part of Muhlenberg's energy and divided his supporters. This division may have been a major factor in the continued financial weakness of St. Luke's.

Of the types of medical cases that came into the hospital many were attributable to the continued rapid growth of the city northward along Manhattan Island:

> The great activity in raising new buildings, blasting rocks for foundations, sewers, etc., and the frequent and rapid passage of railway trains through the crowded thoroughfares in this vicinity, are, and will continue to be fruitful causes of accidents of a serious nature which require immediate hospital treatment.[50]

Cases of sudden injury, requiring immediate care, are received at once and if need be without charge. No cases of contagious diseases are admitted. Incurable cases, needing the particular benefits of the Hospital, are received their continuance being extended from month to month, at the discretion of the executive committee. These patients have their places in the general wards. None are received who cannot be conveniently treated there or who from the nature of their disease, would occasion discomfort to their neighbors. Chronic cases will not be retained longer than medical treatment and nursing are essential to the relief or amelioration of suffering—that is to say, after the acute attack has subsided, and the patient is restored to the ordinary health of persons in his condition. The hospital is not a home for chronic invalids, except in peculiar circumstances.[51]

About three hundred applications for admission have been refused as ineligible—such as confirmed paralysis, remedyless cancer, delerium tremens—and various contagious diseases. In declining these we have often occasioned surprise as well as disappointment and sometimes displeasure. Again and again intelligent persons have gone away, indignantly asking what the Hospital was meant for, because we would not receive persons, in whom they were interested, wholly incapable of relief. Of confirmed paralytics alone, if we had admitted all who have been urged upon us, our beds would have been nearly filled with place for no others. Hence not only a house but a most capacious one, is needed for the many who, while we sincerely commiserate their condition, are, in justice to the design of our Institution, beyond the reach of its hospitality.[52]

The nineteenth annual report in 1877 listed patients of 176 different occupations—the largest groups were carpenters, clerks, cooks, domestics, dressmakers, drivers, housekeepers, house workers, laborers, laundresses, nurses, painters, salesmen, seamstresses, and shoemakers.[53] Another class that made frequent use of the hospital were young people living in boarding houses. Most of these had come to the city to work and when sick had no one to care for them.[54] The boarding house was apparently a new phenomenon and also distinctively American, for the English visitor, Waylen, in his *Ecclesiastical Reminiscences,* gave a detailed description of the one in which he lived in New York.[55]

Muhlenberg faced another problem of interest to the fields of hospital administration and medical research. In a memorandum to the board of managers in 1870 or 1871 describing the qualifications that the board should look for in his successor he expressed his opinion of the use of patients for medical research:

> Then, we must call to mind the distinctive feature of the Hospital in its having a resident family, which gives it its domestic character and keeps up kindly and wholesome influences as well as good order. In ordinary hospitals the professional staff is the supreme authority. Between

the doctors and the patients there are only the hired nurses; in St. Luke's Hospital there is the family—the House Father, and the House Mother, and the Sisters. These have an interest in the patients, sympathize with them in a way that cannot be expected from those who deal with them only professionally. Let these latter be as kind and sympathizing as possible, still hospital patients should not be left wholly in professional hands. They cannot help regarding the patients as more or less subjects for their—I will not say experiments—but for testing new treatment to an extent for which they would not feel free in private practice.

One of the objects of a hospital, they contend, is for the advancement of science, and if, in so using it, occasionally the patients suffer, still it is for good, on the whole. Let this be so, but let there be also a safeguard in the other direction, in favor of the patients, by an interposing authority. In a word, I maintain that the physicians and surgeons in such a hospital as ours should stand towards the patients in the same relation that they do toward those in the respectable families that they visit, in order to which, the hospital households should be considered a family, in which the patients are the sick guests, and visited as such by the physicians.

This is the theory. Of course it will be greatly modified in practice, both on the family and the doctor's side, but it must not be lost sight of. If not the visiting staff, at least the young residents, must be held in check. You will remember how often I have dwelt upon the importance of having an experienced medical officer of the House, and how we have failed to obtain one. The next best thing is to secure younger men. The best we can get, for a liberal compensation, is a Head of the House whose right to keep the young physicians to their duty they will acknowledge. But that right they will not acknowledge in a mere superintendent. He must be a man carrying more weight and influence than such an official is likely to possess. Take, for example, surgical operations in which there is great risk of life. The surgeon is conscientious and states the probabilities to the patient, but advises its being done. The patient, from the nature of the malady, must die, at any rate, or have a protracted existence of suffering. He may recover from the operation and enjoy a good term of life afterwards. What shall he do? The chances in regard to the operation of life and death are equal or those of the latter much greater, or the operation is confessedly an extremely dangerous, though not hopeless, one. The patient wants advice—disinterested advice—from a competent friend, and that he ought to have in the House Father or House Mother of the Hospital, with whom supposing the acquiescence of the patient, the decision ought to rest. But in the old New York Hospital, for instance, when would the surgeon have allowed the superintendent to put in his word in such cases as I have supposed? They have never questioned my right and more than once I have exercised it to their disappointment.[56]

The Civil War touched St. Luke's closely on two occasions. For a time it took care of two hundred sick or wounded soldiers under an agreement with the War Department. Muhlenberg refused to allow the whole hospital to be used for this purpose because he believed that the hospital should continue to care for civilians as well.[57] The second occasion was more dramatic. The city was plunged into anarchy by draft riots in 1863. These originated among the foreign born in the city when they were threatened with conscription. There were charges of inequities in the enforcement of conscription and there were rumors that the jobs of the conscripts would be taken by Negroes. The announcement that the conscription laws would be put into force set off the riot which lasted for several days. The chief targets of the rioters were public buildings.[58] St. Luke's was one of the buildings marked for destruction because it had taken in a wounded policeman, but it was apparently saved by Muhlenberg's presence of mind. When sometime later a wounded rioter was brought in for treatment by members of the mob, Muhlenberg announced to them that the hospital was open to any injured person regardless of whether he was a policeman or a rioter. This statement appeared to change the attitude of the crowd and they formed a guard to prevent the hospital from being destroyed. Muhlenberg then took the opportunity to preach a sermon on the theme that they could better express their grievances by nonviolent rather than violent means.[59]

A number of important though intangible results flowed from the building of St. Luke's Hospital. Its example led to an increased interest in church charities in New York; church hospitals with evangelical sisterhoods were organized in other cities; its appeal for mass contributions inaugurated a new era in church financing which slowly supplanted the old system of selling pews or depending on contributions from a few wealthy individuals. But there was one far-reaching effect to which Muhlenberg himself called attention. Although Christians were bitterly divided on theological matters they could unite on works of charity. This argument was emphatically advanced in the promotional literature for St. Luke's at a time when American Protestanism in general and the Episcopal church in particular were split into contending theological camps. In an editorial in *The Evangelical Catholic,* Muhlenberg asserted that although Christians might be divided on theological matters they could unite on good works which might be the basis of eventual unity. He held up St. Luke's Hospital as an example.[60] On his clerical board there were representatives of all parties in the church, two of whom, Samuel Seabury and Stephen Tyng, were probably the most belligerent leaders of their respective factions.[61]

The significance of St. Luke's in Muhlenberg's life and work is best summarized in a statement by his friend, the poet-journalist, William Cullen Bryant:

150

Other men have accumulated wealth that they might found hospitals, he accumulated the hospital fund as such — never owning it and therefore never giving it. The charitable institutions which he founded were to him what family and friends and personal prosperity are to men generally — and — dying as he did, poor — in St. Luke's Hospital — He died a grandly successful man.[62]

CHAPTER 7

Journalist:

The Evangelical Catholic

The New York of the 1840's and 1850's was characterized by a remarkable flowering of the press. There were twelve daily papers in 1841 and over one hundred weekly publications. Muhlenberg knew personally two of the leading newspapermen of New York, Henry Jarvis Raymond of *The New York Times* and William Cullen Bryant of *The New York Evening Post*.[1] The invention of the two-penny newspaper which was distributed by boys made the newspapers not only the molders of public opinion and the average citizen's source of news but also, in view of the shortcomings of the public school system, the leading means of popular education.[2] Muhlenberg had long wished to publish a church paper but was deterred by the opposition of his mother, who had been pleased with his decision to enter the ministry but had opposed his plans to become a schoolmaster or newspaperman. She died in June, 1851, and three months later the first issue of *The Evangelical Catholic* appeared. It was printed by Stanford and Swords, an old and well-established church publishing house.[3]

Muhlenberg's principal purpose was to publish a paper for the general public. In the first issue he wrote that the journal would be published every other Saturday at one dollar per year. As soon as the subscription list met expenses, however, it would be issued every Saturday—"the object being to afford a weekly paper at a rate within the reach of all."[4] A second purpose of *The Evangelical Catholic* was to diminish partisan strife by furnishing the church with a paper which was above party. The bitterly partisan tone of the Episcopal Church

Price ONE DOLLAR per Annum, or TWELVE AND A HALF CENTS per Number.

THE

Evangelical Catholic.

A MONTHLY PAPER

Devoted Chiefly to Matters of Practical Christianity.

" For His Body's Sake, which is the Church."

VOL. I.   SATURDAY, JUNE 19, 1852.   No. 20.

Contents.

NEW-YORK:

PUBLISHED BY STANFORD AND SWORDS, 137 BROADWAY.

1852.

Front page and table of contents of *The Evangelical Catholic*. (Courtesy General Theological Seminary)

Press had become so marked that it had been rebuked in a pastoral letter by the House of Bishops.[5] Commenting on this purpose Muhlenberg wrote that the editors planned to be pacificators rather than polemicists. They would avoid controversy as far as possible but would endeavor to call for action on grounds on which all were in agreement.

But controversial material would not be ruled out entirely:

Although . . . we shall rather decline controversy, we would not put a veto on discussion in our columns, on topics either doctrinal or practical provided that it be conducted with Christian temper and decorum. We expect to have correspondents differing on many points from ourselves and from one another; but if they cannot express their differences with the courtesy common to debates of the world; if they must deal in offensive personalities . . . we shall decline their favors. The "odium Theologicum" shall never discharge its venom on our pages. Zeal for truth will not be accepted in apology for lack of decency. Our readers shall never have occasion to lay down the paper, quoting ironically the saying of old, "See how these Christians love one another." We have no fear that this understanding will lessen the number of desirable correspondents.[6]

The third purpose was the most important of the three in the context of Muhlenberg's life and work and was the one which Muhlenberg most stressed. *The Evangelical Catholic* was "A . . . paper devoted chiefly to matters of Practical Christianity." By this term Muhlenberg meant the efforts of the church to meet the needs of the poverty stricken people of the cities. The paper carried many articles on free churches, free hospitals, sisterhoods, slums, the rehabilitation of prostitutes, Church charities, and the like. As in the promotion of St. Luke's Hospital he believed that Christians could unite in good works regardless of their doctrinal differences. "Whatever be the importance of points of difference among us we are all sufficiently sound in the faith to be far more abundant in the fruits of good works." Expanding this idea he wrote:

Especially we hope to be of some service in fixing the concern of the Church more intently on a sphere of action in which though it demands her chief care, she has been confessedly too idle. We mean the field of domestic missions which lies immediately about our doors; we mean the ministering of the Gospel to the souls, and to the bodies too, of the thousands who have no name in the world and are so unknown to the Church — the poor and the ignorant, the destitute and afflicted to whom the Gospel was first preached, and who surely have more than a residuary claim on the appointed dispenser of the Gospel. Would that it be our privilege to wake up the Church to a deeper consciousness of her mission in that regard; and to a conviction, also, that only by an earnest discharge of it will men be satisfied that she has a mission. Hence the increase of charitable foundations among us; Church asylums for the destitute, the stranger, or the sick; houses of God open on equal terms to the rich and the poor; free schools for training the young to something more than the service of the world; missions to the highways and hedges; whatever brings the Gospel, with its blessings for this life as well as that which is to come, more in contact with the masses of the population on whose affections the Church at present has so faint a hold, we shall hail as the best of signs of the times. We are not socialists as the word is now understood; but we confess to the socialism of brotherhood in Christ....[7]

The issuance of the paper had other consequences which Muhlenberg probably did not foresee. The general public had supposed that he was a member of the Tractarian party but his editorials showed that he had little sympathy with the exclusive claims of that party. *The Evangelical Catholic* thus cleared the way for a recognition of Muhlenberg as a church leader above party. A second important consequence resulted from the work of Dr. Edwin Harwood, the first of Muhlenberg's assistant editors. Here was a man familiar with scholarly developments in England and in Germany—and was a pioneer in the introduction of biblical criticism in the Episcopal church. He collaborated with Dr. Phillip Schaff in translating from German a series of biblical studies and his learned articles supplemented his articles on "practical christianity."[8]

The Evangelical Catholic was published for slightly over two years— first as a biweekly and later as a weekly. There were many unsigned articles which were probably written by Muhlenberg, and the other articles were signed only by the initials of their authors. Those signed E. H. are presumably by Dr. Harwood and those signed T. T. by T. Tracy, Dr. Harwood's successor. Many articles are reprints from other papers. No attempt has been made in this chapter to identify the various contributors but rather to present the subject matter of the paper as the product of Muhlenberg and his associates. Here it is possible to study and appraise Muhlenberg's opinions at the height of his career.

As might be expected, a number of articles reflected Muhlenberg's lifelong interest in western missionary work. Occasional letters were received from James Lloyd Breck which the paper published in full. Breck was then working among the Indians of Minnesota. This was the first distinctly missionary work in which the Episcopal church engaged since it involved the actual conversion of non-Christians to Christianity rather than merely the organizing of congregations of already confirmed church members who had moved westward. In one editorial Muhlenberg said: "A highly interesting letter from the missionary Breck. Do read it, if only to keep alive your sympathies with one who has done more than any man amongst us as a propagandist of the faith." Muhlenberg consistently referred to Breck as "The Missionary." He likewise kept up his interest in Nashotah House which was under the presidency of A. D. Cole, Breck's successor. In addition he publicized Kenyon College in Ohio, which, like Nashotah, had been established to educate clergy for the West.[9]

A new interest had developed for he now gave space to foreign missions. He noted the consecration of a bishop for Africa:

> It shows we are in earnest in doing something towards paying the mighty debt we owe especially to that quarter of the heathen world. . . . There is no disparagement of other foreign missions in saying that Africa has a pre-eminent claim on American Christians. The reasons occur to everyone. Bishop Payne has lately delivered an address before the Alumni of the Virginia Theological Seminary where he was educated, and whence, to the credit of the Institution be it acknowledged, nearly all our foreign missionaries have come. Will our general seminary allow this to be always so? Why should this school of the prophets do more for Heathendom, than the school of the whole church? All our associations being with the latter, it is only a godly jealousy which prompts the question.

He took note of the translation of the Bible into Chinese and of the tour of the United States by a Chinese Christian.[10]

Muhlenberg's interest in public education displayed in his years at Lancaster was by no means dead. He wrote of the decision of the vestry of Trinity Church, New York, to make a perpetual grant of $3,000 a year to Geneva—now Hobart—College in order that it could become a free college, that is, one in which no tuition was charged.[11] He was also alert to the public school system of New York City but here his interest was in religious teaching in the schools. He had already touched at least once before on the problem of religious instruction in the public schools of our multi-denominational society. In *The Evangelical Catholic* he wrote an article entitled "The Grand Defect of our Public Schools Supplied" in which he anticipated the present day policy of released time:

> Why could not the following means be adopted for providing the children in our Public Schools with religious instruction? Let the secular teaching of the schools be ended some two or three hours before the usual time of dismission, say at eleven o'clock. At that time let the scholars all be divided into sections, according to the several religious denominations to which their parents belong, and then given in charge to suitable persons, to be conducted to their respective churches or Sunday School rooms, there to be catechized or taught in whatever manner thought best, the principles of their faith. Those who would not be included in these sections should be detained at the schoolhouse for whatever instruction the authorities might appoint. They would have not been allowed to run free. No holiday or easier duty should be gained by their escaping from the sections. All finding themselves obliged either to stay in school or go to catechism, the minority belonging to no denomination would soon become very small.[12]

It was natural that Muhlenberg should use *The Evangelical Catholic* to promote one of his favorite causes—that of free churches. This was still a controversial topic because such institutions were still regarded primarily as charitable. Even Bishop Onderdonk, one of their staunchest supporters, believed that if a church member became prosperous he should rent or buy a pew.[13] Muhlenberg thought that the entire system was morally wrong for rich and poor alike, and should be done away with completely. In this contention he was sharply attacked by a letters-to-the-editor writer who claimed that the poor were being pauperized by the free churches and that the acquisition of a church pew was a sign of dignity toward which the poor should strive. Muhlenberg replied to these letters editorially and an extended controversy ensued with neither writer convincing the other.[14]

In a further defense of free churches Muhlenberg wrote:

[Of] The Church of the Epiphany, New York, the Rector told us, only the other day, that he had at least one hundred families, who have not only been drawn to the Church because of its free pews, but who would be driven from it if they were assessed at any rates, however low. They give voluntarily on Sundays what they can afford. They are of the laboring classes of our own citizens but have no idea that they are compromising their independence by attending a free church. . . . After an experience of twenty years, the Rector is convinced of the efficacy of the system, and thinks its extension over the whole city would be the best possible expedient for bringing the poor into our churches.

More than forty families attend the Church of the Holy Communion, who would statedly go nowhere if they had to pay pew rent. The difficulty in this church is, not that the poor will not come to it but they are kept out of it too much by persons who avail themselves of its privileges, but unfortunately feel no obligation to contribute to its support. This evil, however, arises out of circumstances independent of the freeness of the church and so makes nothing against the system. We refer also to St. Stephen's Chapel, Boston, to the Church of the Advent whose late lamented pastor could have answered our correspondence with facts. . . . (Our correspondent, however, labors under the notion of a free church as an eleemosynary provision for the poor alone which we endeavored to correct in our last article) and no wonder that he maintains that it will be rejected by the laboring classes. But what if our churches were free—as we trust they will be one day, will the laboring classes still eschew them?[15]

The paper published examples of the spread of the free church system. St. Michael's, Bloomingdale, became a free church whose rector was Muhlenberg's good friend, Dr. Peters. Trinity Church announced that the magnificent new chapel that it was building uptown would be a free church. And the Diocese of Western New York took action to make all of its new churches free churches.[16]

A matter of great concern to the paper was the steady movement of Protestant churches out of the densely populated, poverty-stricken lower Manhattan area which occurred as their members moved uptown. It commented that this movement left the 200,000 inhabitants of the older section of the city without as much care as would have been available in India. A case in point was that of Zion Church:

> Saving a Church from Desecration: A meeting of a number of the clergy of the city was held on Tuesday last in the Sunday School room of St. John's Church, to take measures for the purchasing and sustaining of Zion Church about to be vacated by its congregation, and in danger of being sold to the highest bidder. It was proposed to make it a free church and establish in connection with it, a home for destitute females, especially the poor sewing women. The subject elicited the same hearty and united feeling that showed itself at the meeting for the Bishop-elect is chairman, and he also presided at the meeting.
>
> What is everybody's business is nobody's business — so it was with the threatened sale of Zion Church. Everybody said it would be a sin and a shame and contented themselves with saying so, until the Rev. Mr. Peters took the matter in hand and had the meeting called which, we trust, will issue in the desired result.

An editorial a few issues later warned that the failure of this project would mean the withdrawal of the church from the Five Points area, the poorest section of New York City. And the following issue contained the brief announcement: "We learn with sorrow and shame, that Zion Church of this city has just been sold to the Romanists. Price, $35,000."[17]

Another church concern was the long struggle by St. Philips — an all Negro parish — for admission to the New York Diocesan Convention. The fight was led by Muhlenberg's old student, John Jay, who was editorially supported by *The Evangelical Catholic*. The controversy continued over a period of years; a committee was appointed to consider the matter and brought in a majority report against and a minority report for admission, the latter written by Jay. Backing the stand of the minority report was a letter from a correspondent of *The Evangelical Catholic* telling of the admission of Negro parishes and clergy in New Jersey, Pennsylvania, and Michigan. Muhlenberg's editorial comment: "Councils of the Catholic Church excluding congregations because of their color. O Marvelous Catholicity!"[18]

It is not surprising to find that *The Evangelical Catholic* promoted the cause of St. Luke's Hospital and defended the appropriateness of sisterhoods in a Protestant church. It also promoted other church institutions. In commenting on a report of the New York Academy of Medicine, Muhlenberg suggested:

> Let every congregation of any size have its own physician for visiting its poor, or the poor which it may consider within its bounds and agree with some convenient apothecary to supply medicines on the order of the physician. This would be a simple arrangement, and quite practicable with most of our congregations; nor would it be attended with much expense. Physicians would not be backward to undertake the duty either gratuitously or for a moderate salary, and druggists would be ready to make up prescriptions for little more than the cost of the articles. One great advantage of the plan would be that doctors and clergymen might thus act in concert, and with mutual satisfaction, in their ministration to the sick poor. Each, too, would serve to keep the other in mind of his duty and enable him to discharge it with better success. In many cases important benefits would result from an understanding between the bodily and the spiritual physician, which is now impracticable but often felt by both parties to be extremely desirable.
>
> We know of one congregation in which this course had been adopted greatly to the comfort of the poor, and at a comparatively trifling cost. We commend it to the thoughts of our brethren who minister in cities particularly to those who have large numbers of poor among their parishoners. We think they must see the need of Church dispensaries as well as of Church Hospitals. The Church, among us, has only begun her mission in such works.[19]

He was able to report the establishment of an orphanage in New York and of a church hospital in Philadelphia. His interest in institutions for the rehabilitation of prostitutes, expressed later in his sermons for the Midnight Mission, is reflected in a number of articles on the institutions which he had visited in England. The paper also reported on the work of the Episcopal clergy in New York City's public institutions.[20]

Muhlenberg reported the formation of the Protestant Episcopal Mutual Benefit Society. An article in *The Evangelical Catholic* read:

> We ask the attention of our readers to the following statement of the objects of the P.E. Mutual Benefit Society. As an effort to make brotherhood in the churches a tangible and practical thing, we heartily wish the institution a large increase of the prosperity which it has already attained. . . .
> Its present members, clerical and lay, are of no one party in the Church and this is another reason why we bid the Society "Good Luck" in the name of the Lord.

The objects of the society were first of all to look after the mutual care and relief of its members when sick or physically disabled; to secure Christian burial for deceased members; to help their widows and orphans; to minister according to its ability to the relief of sick strangers and to the destitute of its own communion. In practical terms it supplied sickness benefits, funeral expenses, and pensions.[21]

The Evangelical Catholic did not deal only with charitable institutions and missions; it was concerned with the position of the Episcopal church in American society in general. The announcement that all Protestant denominations except the Episcopal church would engage in street preaching brought forth a series of editorials which examined the whole attitude of the church toward the lower economic groups:

> We are ministers it may be said, of the Protestant Episcopal Church; and the work of the Protestant Episcopal Church may not lie among the multitudes at large. To look out for their salvation devolves rather upon other bodies of Christians, upon the different "persuasions" who are more fitted for it, and know how to go about it. There is a division of labor among the working bodies of Christendom. Our share is that of guarding and defending the truths of Christianity and bringing them to bear upon the more staid and enlightened sort of people. Our province, as a branch of the Church, is that of Conservators. We are not pioneers. Others may do the rougher work of evangelizing the rude and ignorant; it is ours to refine them after they have gone through the process which prepares them for our more gentle hands. Let others cry aloud and spare not among the base and ignoble of the garrets and cellars, while we administer the soothing influences of religion to souls of a more genial stamp, within the precincts of the sanctuary.
>
> Now this is an intelligible view of the business of our church, and one which we have no doubt is tacitly accepted by not a few of her members; seeing that "the church" is the place for themselves, they think it quite in order that their domestics should go to some of the "meeting houses." We understand such Protestant Episcopalians. It is a very good thing in its way. Nay, our church, considered as appointed to a special trust, that of conserving the great truths of the Gospel, holds a most important post in these days of private judgement and self-well, and it might be shown that in this regard, Protestant Christendom is not a little in her debt.

Muhlenberg questioned whether this was a satisfactory view of the church and asserted that it would not be so regarded by a majority of the clergy and of the serious minded laity. Yet there were undoubtedly many church members who would not openly avow it though they tacitly agreed with it. "Actions," wrote Muhlenberg, "speak louder than words." He charged that the church's actions spoke no equivocal language, that it followed policies which attracted only the upper economic groups and repelled the masses of people. Even its missionaries in the West reported that it was the better sort of people who were drawn to the church in the new communities. While cargoes of human beings were transported by the thousands along the rivers of the West no large portion of them were being gathered in. The posts occupied were where there was or promised to be a thriving population.

It was in the cities that Muhlenberg found the most striking evidence that the church's appeal was primarily to the middle and upper classes. New church buildings were always placed where prosperous people were moving in and where the developer had donated the site for the building because it would increase the value of his property. In contrast to the advance of the church in the prosperous developing sections of the city Muhlenberg examined the church in the poverty-stricken sections of New York. He pointed out that the area bounded by the East River, Broadway, and Ninth Street was the most densely settled part of New York and that in the last fifteen years only one Episcopal church had been erected there and that only with the greatest difficulty. In this area was the notorious Five Points section, which all the denominations had avoided until the Methodists went in and began a revolution there. When we said that the Episcopal church was keeping pace with the advancing population, Muhlenberg pointed out, we meant in the "Court End" of town.

Not only did the location of the new churches exclusively in the prosperous section exclude the poor, the method of financing had a like tendency. Many times a church was built as a purely business operation by securing to those engaged in the enterprise a fair quid pro quo in the form of pews. Pews were auctioned off to build the church and assessments made on them to support it. Thus a poor person entering one of the churches was encroaching on purchased rights. Since the church would not go out into the streets to reach the masses, would not build free churches, or throw churches open to the poor, it was not surprising that the world concluded that the church was not interested in preaching the Gospel to the poor. Muhlenberg did not doubt the sympathy of Episcopalians for the poor nor their generosity when approached for contributions for charitable objects. "An open generous heart is one of the marks of the genuine churchman; and yet he might think it awkward to have a shabby fellow sitting in his pew and is but little disturbed at his dependents receiving their religious instruction from some sectarian preacher as on the whole best suited to persons in their rank of life.

Muhlenberg concluded the editorial by suggesting that since the Episcopal church showed so little interest in the masses there might well be a widespread belief in the church that her mission was not to them.[22]

Muhlenberg did not try to develop a full-scale social philosophy but in an editorial endorsing the Shirt-Sewers Union he came nearer to summarizing his social thought than in any of his other writings:

> When men come to see that Christianity is not simply a fact or a doctrine or a set of doctrines, to be preached and believed but also an institution for the spiritual and temporal benefit of mankind, having not the truth but the incarnate Lord of Truth for its living center, when they learn that it is the universal Brotherhood of which "the Word was made flesh," Christ Jesus was the elder brother, they will see that it, and it alone, is the remedy for the social evils of the world.
>
> Brotherhood — Brotherhood in Christ, this is the grand lesson we all have to master — we church-folk no less than others. This is the vivifying truth which must regenerate our Church zeal. It will dissolve our stiff and mechanical ecclesiasticism . . . and will make us truly churches of the primitive stamp.[23]

He took the occasion of a sermon before the Mutual Benefit Society to expound his ideas further. Taking as his text the account in the Book of Acts which described the early church in which all goods were held in common, he suggested that this was the first recorded instance of a mutual aid society. Here was charity based on a common creed. "Here was the basis of their charity; there was a community of good; individual interests were merged in the common good; none wanted, all were rich because no one was allowed to be poor."

Muhlenberg hastened to assure his hearers, however, that the holding of goods in common was not an essential part of the Christian faith. This practice, he said, was adopted under peculiar circumstances and was not intended for all types of society. A common fund today, he said, would beget indolence and dependence and could not be supported without a violation of God's law. Moreover, the gradations in social life were of divine appointment and none but a visionary theorist would think of changing them. But while the modes of its manifestation might vary according to the wants of each age, yet the spirit of true charity must ever remain the same.[24]

The Evangelical Catholic hailed another Episcopalian periodical, *The Church Review,* for articles which were "fresh and spirited." It particularly recommended two entitled "The Church and the Times" and "Modern Theories of Social Progress."[25] In the following issue it reproduced in its entirety an article from *The Church Review* entitled "Christianity and the Social Questions of the Age." This article paralleled the editorial of *The Evangelical Catholic* on street-preaching. The spirit of caste, the editorial stated, is as rife in Christian Europe and America as it ever was in pagan Greece and Rome. Christians are classified in the arrangements of public worship with painful exactness according to their position in society. It is not to be expected that all distinction of rank can be annihilated. The writer agreed with Muhlenberg that there were some laws of social intercourse which separate the lower from the upper classes and which serve the comfort of the former as much as they do the taste of the latter. It would distress both parties alike if these rules and customs should be done away. But the gulf which now separates them is certainly wider and more impassable than it need be. The writer then continued in much the same vein as the editorials in *The Evangelical Catholic:*

> Neither is it right that the church should stand passively by and look with either disdain or fear upon the movements now in agitation for the elevation of the lower class of laborers, and for the rescue of those who lie lower still from the miseries of pauperism; to shrink with horror at the enormities of socialism is not "The whole duty of man." To tremble at the growing power of "Trade Unions" is not the most dignified attitude for a Christian. The Church has a work to do down in those lower regions where these movements originate, which thus far has been rarely noticed in her convention debates and never in her legislation. The most imperative work now incumbent on the Church lies in that direction. We say this deliberately and unqualifiedly. These dangerous movements among the poor are not to be rudely repressed, and they cannot be summarily arrested. They originate in a stern state of want, sometimes in a hopeless despair, which Christians must relieve or take the consequences. It will not do for the well-fed and prosperous disciple to say "Those poor wretches have the same opportunity to rise in the world that any of us have; I was poor once and I am rich now"; There are tens of thousands even in our own community, who can no more rise from their degradation without some new action in the social state, than they could understand our "popular preachers" without an interpreter. They must be helped to their feet or they can never stand upright. The causes of pauperism, of crime, and of atheistic convulsions must be explored. The probable effects of the increasing inequality in the distribution of wealth must be carefully investigated.

The writer found it alarming that most of the reform movements among the laboring class were associated with "infidelity." Were revolutions, great discoveries, augmented science, and new forms of policy to be regarded as mechanics of depravity? If Christians relinquished the amelioration demanded by humanity and the regulation of the present world into the hands of infidels, it required no very acute vision to see where the Church would be found a half century from now. She must identify herself with the masses of the people if she would save either them or herself.[26]

In an early issue of *The Evangelical Catholic* the editors wrote a long review of a book entitled *New Themes for the Protestant Clergy* which had been published anonymously:

> Thoroughly Protestant in his modes of thought, accepting in the gross, Protestant Orthodoxy as accurate, he complains that it is but a skeleton of sound propositions to which Protestantism is devoted. It lacks charity; it lacks humanity; and is thus dead to the true spirit of Christianity ... Instead of seeking the poor, the sorrowing or the outcast, the depraved and abandoned, he declares that Protestantism contents itself with teaching the dry husks of theology — with drilling the understanding into acquiescence with certain accredited formulas — with pronouncing orations on Sundays to respectable well-behaved persons, who listen seated in their cushioned pews. He may exaggerate the evils around us in this particular. But this is a subject which requires strong statement. We are so secure, so well satisfied, that nothing but the image of a gigantic sin can startle us from our propriety. It is a protest against the Phariseeism of the day, against its heartless formalism, against its frigid theology, which this man is here uttering. We are very unwillingly prevented from further observations upon his production at present. The length of the extracts compels us to abstain. The book is sold by Stanford and Swords, of this city; buy it and read it.[27]

The book in question was written by a Presbyterian layman, Stephen Colwell of Philadelphia, and is one of the earliest attempts to call the attention of the Protestant churches to the problems created by urbanization and industrialization.[28] A reading of the long extracts given in *The Evangelical Catholic* indicates that here was another example of a contemporary whose ideas ran parallel to those of Muhlenberg yet who developed them independently. The editors of *The Evangelical Catholic* asserted that they did not know the name of the author.

Other articles cited specific cases. The paper was concerned with the plight of the dressmakers and needlewomen of the city. It carried an appeal for assistance from the Shirt-Sewers Union:

> Forced by direct necessity through want of employment and starvation wages when we had work to do, some few of our present number combined together in the month of April last and organized into an Association styled the Shirt-Sewer's Co-operative Union. Our aims and objects were, to work together for mutual benefit, to share the profits accruing from our industry according to our ability and willingness to do, instead of being, as formerly, compelled to give the *Lions Share* of our labor to an employer. Briefly it was an experiment and it has succeeded. We have demonstrated the fact to our cast down and suffering sisters that full double the wages can be earned by less hours of toil, under our new plan of combination, than under the old arrangement. When our numbers were limited and the work light we were unable to pay our way; but as our members increased with the demand for

labor our profits increased leaving us at present a net profit of ten percent over the prices paid to the members. A statement of the prices of work given by employers and that paid by the association will serve to show the advantages we have already gained by combination.[29]

The Evangelical Catholic not only printed this statement but published a commendatory editorial in which it endorsed this particular union. It added that this endorsement did not commit the paper to the support of the general principle of cooperative unions among the laboring classes. The editors wanted more time to examine this subject. But in the present instance it seemed wholly unobjectionable and was the only means of abating a misery which no good man could hear of and not feel compelled to do something. "It has that great recommendation of a plan of benevolences, that it enables the poor to help themselves." The editorial commented on the fact that two churchmen, R. B. Minturn and J. H. Swift, were on the committee of collection. These two men were also long-time supporters of Muhlenberg's projects.[30]

A series of articles on the condition of the poor ran in *The Evangelical Catholic*. They emphasized the frightful conditions under which the poor lived and compared them with the extravagance of the upper classes.[31] This extract appeared from the *New York Daily Times*: "In our late visit to these rag-pickers in the Eleventh Ward, we again came upon important facts in relation to rents. This I desire especially to call to the attention of our businessmen."[32] After commenting on the condition of the houses, the high rents, and the enormous profits that the landlords were making, the writer added:

We call upon Christian merchants in New York to look at these things. If such enormous profits can be made of these great colony houses for the poor, why cannot some benevolent man step forward and build healthful, convenient, and cheerful houses and still derive a profit which shall make his investment no poor one. Would it not be a humane and Christian mode of employing capital?[33]

Muhlenberg wrote articles describing various attempts to solve the housing problem. He quoted a *Tribune* article on "Homes for the Poor" which described a project to build decent homes at rentals the poor could afford. Another article told of the building of Prince Albert's Model Homes for Poor Families at Hyde Park, London, a housing project designed for families of manufacturing or mercantile operatives. Still another described the Price Patent Candle Factory, an extensive establishment in London, in the hands of an incorporated company—which besides its chemical science and mechanical ingenuity, showed a high degree of moral interest in its admirable provisions for the education of the children in its work. "There is an account of the training schools of the factory, by a writer in Fraser's magazine, part of which we transfer to our pages . . . confident that it will prove interesting to our readers."[34]

The editors of *The Evangelical Catholic* were familiar with unions and strikes, but as noted above they preferred to reserve judgment even on cooperative unions. However, a long article did appear, written by T. Tracy, the associate editor—the only attempt to go into the problem in detail. He wrote feelingly of the plight of the laboring class in the large cities. He pointed out that after long and arduous toil the laboring man at the end of the week found his pay insufficient to buy the bare necessities of life. On the other hand, the capital of the rich could be used to the almost immediate aggrandizement of its possessors. At the same time the poor became poorer:

> Such may be the practical working of the steam-engine—to produce the millionaire and the pauper. To get a patent and buy machinery and have the means of competing, may bring wealth to the capitalist, almost with the facility of romance, while the poor, crowding to the place of work, and having everything even the garden vegetable to purchase, cause an advance in all items of living in the market, in proportion to the increase of population and demand and thus they injure themselves. They find everyday their old wages to be less and less capable of sustaining them. . . .
>
> In such cases may we not ask whether the words of Solomon are not to be heeded, when he declares that he cannot be innocent who makes haste to get rich; whether our present steam-engine system does not cause an exception to the general rule of the relations in society and whether the capitalist, under such circumstances, is a friend of the poor, if mercy is not considered as well as profit.

What then could the poor do? They found that as prosperity increased the cost of living also increased. Since the capitalist continued to obtain higher prices for the commodity that he produced why should not the laborer in turn receive higher wages? "Such is the hinge or heart of the whole question between the employer and laborer—capital and work—a question of the greatest magnitude in our country."

Mr. Tracy did not believe that strikes were the solution to the problem. "Do not the operatives know that they—and a good many higher in life than they—are at the mercy of the capitalist? That in every commercial region money is the most powerful agent to influence the community? That there is a law of the kingdom of traffic? Will it do any good to exasperate the employers?"

Mr. Tracy saw no hope in strikes. He had observed rather closely

a recent strike of the painters which he said had consisted of "all dec-
lamation and crimination." How then could the operatives deal with
the operators? Their only hope was to reason with them by publishing
facts and statistics, showing that the prices that the operators were
charging were not only advancing to keep up with the cost of produc-
tion, but increasing profits as well, while the increased prices were
driving the operatives down in the economic scale. Then the capitalist
could see for himself whether the one was ascending while the other
was descending:

> Whether the riches of the one are owing to the poverty of the other;
> whether one class in the community rises on the ruins of the other; whether
> capital will indeed need adjustment from extraneous sources. If it be true
> that this system of labor requires the poor everyday to be less prosperous,
> while the capitalist everyday becomes more so, something manifestly
> is wrong.

Having stated the question what was the answer? Here Mr. Tracy
gave an answer that was characteristic of Muhlenberg and his associates:
the workers must appeal to the Christian philanthropy of the capitalist:

> Should these statistics show that there is an imminent danger of such
> being the relations of the rich and poor of our times — that it is the tendency
> of our system, may we not ask them, as Christians and citizens and philan-
> thropists, and especially as capitalists, whose business and success tend to
> make the poor poorer; to give — not pay the wages and fulfill the contract
> punctually at every close of the month — but to give absolutely and largely
> to help those poor; to build the church and the schoolhouse, and replenish
> the treasury of the church; to relieve those on whose decaying strength,
> and by whom, according to the present law of the business world, they are
> fast becoming rich.[35]

Although the greater part of *The Evangelical Catholic* was devoted to
matters of practical Christianity there were also articles on the intellectual interest of the church of the day which reflected the scholarly
influence of Dr. Edwin Harwood. The paper took note of two lecturers:
Ralph Waldo Emerson and Theodore Parker. A New York paper was
quoted by *The Evangelical Catholic* as to Emerson's lecture:

> This gentleman known to fame as a Lecturer, Essayist, etc., read a
> lecture to a large audience in the Tabernacle last Tuesday evening. The
> subject was Power. It was a rambling, desultory performance, filled with
> common place thoughts, but characterized by a terse and occasionally
> brilliant style. It was a sort of deification of the rude physical forces of man.

167

Soul, as such, seemed to be excluded from the lecturer's categories. It was Hegelianism—in so far as it could be said to belong to any known philosophical school—run mad. Emerson's moral man is a superlatively selfish man—a thoroughly ungodly man—a man who is to obey his impulses just as they come. As a literary performance, it was unworthy the real genius of the writer, as a moral exhibition it was abominable. Yet the audience was delighted. Hundreds of men hung upon his words, as if they were very oracles of wisdom. The fewer we have of such lectures the better, both for the literary taste and the morals of the people.[36]

The paper quoted the *Boston Daily Advertiser,* which gave some extracts of Parker's sermons which "exhibit rank infidelity":

The Boston Daily Advertiser gives some extracts from recently published sermons of Mr. Parker, which exhibit rank infidelity. He says: "I do not believe there ever was a miracle, or ever will be. I do not believe in the miraculous inspiration of the Old Testament. I do not believe that the Old Testament was God's first word nor that the New Testament was His last. The Scriptures are no finality to me. Inspiration is a perpetual fact. . . . I do not believe the miraculous origin of the Hebrew Church, or the Buddhist Church or the Christian Church; nor the miraculous character of Jesus. I do not take the Bible for master, nor yet the Church; nor yet Jesus ,or my master. I feel not at all bound to believe what the Church says is true, nor what any writer in the Old or New Testament declares true; and I am ready to believe that Jesus taught as I think, eternal torment, the existence of a devil, and that he himself should ere long come back in the clouds of heaven. I do not accept these things on his authority. I try all things by the human faculties." And this is the man who is sent for, far and near, to lecture before Lyceums to our youth.[37]

Of Robert Owen, the paper was even more critical:

A more signal exhibition of that great law which so often punishes unbelief by consigning the proud intellect to the most abject credulity has seldom been afforded than by Robert Owen's late letter to the Queen. That patriarch of Socialism after spending nearly his whole life in trying to persuade himself and others that he had "a mission" to found a new state of society in which religion, law, marriage, and private property should be unknown; after preaching disbelief in the very existence of God, and declaring fanciful notions and prejudices, has now come out as the herald of a new faith, lately spawned on that western soil, prolific of heresies and delusions. . . . Robert Owens proclaims his faith in "spirit rappings" and not only so, but is a "medium" himself and has obtained revelations from the spirit of her Majesty's late royal father, the Duke of Kent.[38]

An original contribution was a long article on the influence of Sir Walter Scott by Dr. Harwood:

> Until the novels of Sir Walter Scott had begun to exercise a plastic influence upon the public taste it was the fashion to regard the Middle Ages as a dismal swamp. . . . The novels of Sr. W. Scott effected, however, a complete revolution in the public taste. It became the fashion to go into ecstacies at the thought of mailed knights and fair ladies, of feudal castles and feudal institutions, of the crusades, and of all the marked peculiarities of those ages. Men began to build new country seats which should look old as soon as finished, and wear from the start a medieval aspect. . . . Maudlin young gentlemen and ladies sighed over the flat prosaic days which began to usher in the reign of steam; they bemoaned their stars because they were not born seven or eight hundred years ago. Poets found subjects for their songs in the ages of chivalry and the crusades. In our own boyhood, not a college exhibition "went off" without some glorification of medieval institutions. In this respect it was simply a fancy; it did not enter within the domain of faith or practice. In fact, a ruined Melrose was more romantic than an actual church with its crowds, worshippers, with its relics and high altar, and mystic candlesticks and censers.[39]

Charles Dickens, however, posed a dilemma for *The Evangelical Catholic*. As a spokesman for the poor in England he had the paper's sympathies but he was not a believer in traditional Christianity:

> There are few features of the literature of the day which give us more concern than the wrong bias, too visible in much that has come from the pen or appeared under the sanction of that popular writer, Charles Dickens. Where the cause of suffering humanity is to be pleaded; where the sorrows of God's languishing and ill-treated poor are to be sketched, who could plead more touchingly, who could sketch more powerfully than Dickens? How sad is it, then, that the gifted apostle of humanity would not be in his sphere, an apostle of Christ's religion too. That religion is the only sure basis of philanthropy. . . . We generally find, moreover, that the mere philanthropist soon tires of his work . . . Acting as he does from other than genuine religious principle, and without a view to the recompense of the heavenly reward, he has not the Christian's unfailing motive to preserve unweariedly in labors of love, under everything calculated to vex and to disgust him.[40]

A contemporary movement which both interested and puzzled the editors of *The Evangelical Catholic* was the Mercersberg movement in the German Reformed Church—a movement that compares with the Tractarian Movement in the Episcopal church (see Chapter VIII). It was led by Dr. John W. Nevin, a professor at the German Reformed

Seminary at Mercersberg, Pennsylvania. The first item appeared when the Synod of the German Reformed Church rejected the resignation of Dr. Nevin, assured him of its unabated confidence and pledged him its support. *The Evangelical Catholic* regarded this act as an endorsement of Dr. Nevin's theology by the German Reformed church and found it alarming.[41]

Nonetheless, a few weeks later the paper published an article by Dr. Nevin entitled "From the Mystical Presence."[42] And later still it commented:

> In Dr. Nevin's article on early Christianity, instead of hurling condemnation at the Fathers, he does his utmost to show that they in the main rightly conceived the true meaning and substance of Christianity, and that their Christianity, instead of resembling our Evangelical Protestantism was entirely unlike it and bore strong marks of affinity with even the modern Roman Catholic system. There is a vast deal of assertion upon Dr. Nevin's part in these articles—an air of authority, amounting almost to arrogance, as if he wished to convey the impression, "Question what I say and I will brand you publicly as a fool."[43]

In a subsequent issue *The Evangelical Catholic* pointed out that Dr. Nevin denied that the early church was a perfect model as did the Anglo-Catholics. "Protestantism is an advance upon what went before but is in itself only transitional. We must look to the Church of the future, which shall absorb into one glorious whole the truth of the old Catholic form such as we have in Rome and the truth of Protestantism."[44]

The Evangelical Catholic asserted that Dr. Nevin offered nothing in the place of what he demolished. Another issue carried an article on the *Mercersberg Quarterly Review,* the organ of the Mercersberg Movement. In it the opinion was expressed that Dr. Nevin would not join the Roman Catholic church as some Protestants feared.[45] The final article related to this subject announced the election of Dr. Phillip Schaff as president of Franklin and Marshall College, with which the German Reformed Seminary had merged. Dr. Schaff was a distinguished church historian and is today regarded as the founder of American church history as a field of study. He was at this time identified with the Mercersberg Movement but later he moved to New York, where he became a close friend of Muhlenberg. Dr. Schaff held Muhlenberg up as an example of a Broad Churchman and Muhlenberg dedicated a collection of his hymns to Dr. Schaff.[46]

There was, however, a contemporary movement in England to which the editors of *The Evangelical Catholic* gave their wholehearted approval—this was the Christian Socialist movement under the leadership of

Charles Kingsley and Frederick Dennison Maurice—a movement within the Church of England designed to apply the principles of Christianity to the social order. Merged with, and in some ways indistinguishable from the Christian Socialist movement, was the Broad Church movement which advocated greater freedom of theological opinion particularly in regard to the acceptance of biblical criticism. Maurice and Dr. Thomas Arnold of Rugby were regarded as the leaders of the second movement. It was probably inevitable that charges of socialism and unorthodox theological opinion should be brought against these men.[47] Speaking of Kingsley, *The Evangelical Catholic* said:

> At the request of several of our subscribers, we give them another sermon from Mr. Kingsley, author of "Alton Locke." In this implied commendation of this original and spirited writer, we would not be understood as receiving all the views he presents in his several works—and in his sermon from Mr. Kingsley, author of "Alton Locke." In this implied comexplanation; but on the whole they are among the best plain discourses, adapted to the times that we know of.[48]

The Christian Socialists had advocated preaching in plain ordinary English and this was discussed in *The Evangelical Catholic*'s next comment on Kingsley's sermons:

> They are by no means model sermons, but they have the charm of freshness and naturalness—they come in contact with the minds of ordinary men by addressing them in the language of ordinary life—they are free from technicalities of religionism and ecclesiasticism—and so far they are worthy of imitation. They are manly, earnest talks to plain people, in words which such people use, about common and everyday matters. Mr. Kingsley sometimes, indeed, carries this too far—he is sometimes too familiar for the sacredness of his theme—too natural for one treating of the supernatural; but the prevalent fault of preachers is all the other way. Hence sermons are proverbially dry reading. Hence so many who are lively and engaging in conversation are dull in the pulpit. With their dread of any unorthodox expression and their staid notions of the dignity of the pulpit, they deal so much in stale and trite phraseology, that whatever be their subject, it seems the thrice-told tale.
>
> Bishop Whittingham, when lately in England, spent several hours with Mr. K. at his house, and as the Bishop informed us, was much pleased with him, and considers him in the main, sound in the faith.[49]

A further comment on Kingsley's sermons from the paper states: "Others of his discourses are more explicit on the great articles of the faith, in which he might be suspected of heterodoxy. The Socialists claim Mr. Kingsley. The foregoing is not the teaching of Socialists in these parts."[50]

These reprints of Kingsley's sermons evidently received some attention, for an editorial entitled "Sermons by the Author of *Alton Locke*," ran thus:

> In our past numbers we have published several of the Village Sermons, by the Rev. Mr. Kingsley, which attracted considerable attention, and have now led to the publication of the whole volume by Mr. Hooker of Philadelphia. They are twenty-five in number, and mostly of the same interesting character as those we printed. We cannot doubt they will meet with a steady sale. While we are not ready to assent to everything expressed in them, they abound in wholesome, practical thoughts adapted to the times and delivered in a style of uncommon ease and vivacity. These sermons deserve to be read by the clergy as well as the laity, as specimens of fresh and lively composition, free from the technical language of theology and the hackneyed phrases of popular religionism. Mr. Kingsley comes down to the level of his audience — yet without lowering himself. He speaks like a man in earnest — discourses of everyday matters in the terms of everyday — caring mainly to be understood by his hearers, and to let them feel that he really means what he says. An elaborator of pulpit essays, according to Dr. Blair's receipt, would indeed be shocked by some homely talk — we are beginning, however, to review our notions of the dignity of the pulpit, and Mr. Kingsley's sermons are opportune for that purpose.[51]

As to Maurice, Muhlenberg called on him during his first visit to England and referred to him as a "lovely person."[52] Since on that visit Muhlenberg was preoccupied with problems rising out of the Tractarian Movement, he did not leave any account of this conversation. In an early number of *The Evangelical Catholic* he quoted "Maurice On the Prayerbook."[53] Maurice, however, was a scholar who anticipated both the impact of biblical criticism and of Darwinism. Upon the reprinting of certain articles on the Old Testament the paper commented, "The following is from Mr. Maurice's new work on the Old Testament. Everything from Mr. M's pen bears marks of thoughtful, profound earnestness."[54] In 1853 Muhlenberg made a second visit to England and spent more time with Maurice. (This visit is discussed in Chapter 8.)

Darwin did not publish his *Origin of Species* until 1859, some six years after *The Evangelical Catholic* ceased publication, but some of his ideas were anticipated by the geologist Sir Charles Lyell — particularly in the questioning of literal acceptance of the account of the creation found in the Book of Genesis. In a series of published sermons Maurice accepted the view that the first chapter of Genesis could not be taken literally. These sermons were reviewed in an editorial probably written by Dr. Harwood:

> This volume has not met with the attention it deserves. The first sermon is quite unpromising. It is peculiar and at first sight furnishes some ground for the sharp assertion of the Westminster Review, that Mr. Maurice believes in Moses and in Sir Charles Lyell. If, however, Mr. Maurice be right, we reply—and why not? But is he right? That is the question. The general verdict of the Christianity of the day would, perhaps, answer this question in the negative. The subject is the creation, a difficult one surely. For either geology is wrong, or else Moses is wrong, or else we misunderstand Moses. Mr. Maurice says, in the main, that geology is not wrong; that Moses is not wrong; but we are.
>
> Scriptural readers and commentators have insisted that the Mosaic history of Creation shall be the history of the formation of the material earth, though there is not a single sentence in the Sacred writing in which the slightest allusion is made to the formation. They have insisted that the week must refer to the time as measured by the sun, though distinct words and the whole context of the discourse negative such a supposition.
>
> Such then is Mr. Maurice's view of the narrative of the creation in the book of Genesis. He denies it to refer primarily to the phenomenal world; affirms it to be a record of *the act of God* considered apart from and anterior to the actual palpable existence of "the things which do appear." This certainly is very intelligible. It requires no special faculty of discernment to perceive the force of the distinction between God's act in himself and the outward phenomenal results of that act. The only question is whether such distinction actually occurred to the historian, and whether it is actually stated. It is not stated, of course, in the language of schools, but is it really stated? If Mr. Maurice fails to convince his readers that it is stated, it is very certain that his reasoning cannot be thrown aside summarily. It deserves consideration, is calm and reverential. His interpretation is immeasurably more satisfactory than that which has become quite fashionable since Geology has been thundering its dicta at the portals of Scripture. It is more reasonable and natural and easy than the view, which proceeding from the notion that the material phenomenal world is the theme of discourse in the first chapters of Genesis, chooses to interpret the days by a period of a thousand years. If the narrative be literal and after the fashion of our modern materialistic notions, how can we in the name of all honesty make an exception in favor of the duration of the *days of creation?* This is of special force when we consider that these very days are among the heaviest difficulties in the accepted view of the signification of the Chapter. In stretching them to such a length, we are using questionable means to save the credit of the book. We must say that we prefer Mr. Maurice's view. It is unusual; but it is so because so many are encased in cast iron materialistic traditions which they are compelled to swallow from childhood—a mixture of Scotch metaphysics and bad philology.[55]

173

Muhlenberg himself editorially endorsed Maurice's point of view:

> The Two Beginnings. Those of our readers who are troubled at the assertions which are now so confidently made by certain naturalists that the Mosaic date of the creation is irreconcilable with the now known facts in geology, will do well to read the article in our present number with the above title. The solution which it proposes of the difficulty is a very simple one and is sustained by the language of the sacred text.[56]

Commenting on the influence of German theology in England, Dr. Harwood predicted that eventually it would be absorbed into the English church system:

> Already does the *Remembrancer* speak of the Germanizers, already do the papers show that a cloud, no larger indeed than a man's hand, just now, has appeared above the horizon of the English Church. There is no reason to fear that English Churchmen will run German-mad. A great body of them probably will, before long, adopt the results of German Theological science on the orthodox side . . . but that England or the English Church will pass through the crisis from which German Christianity has begun to recover strikes us almost as a moral impossibility.
>
> Not fearing any widespread disastrous defections from the laity we sincerely join in the hope expressed by the *Remembrancer* . . . that the English Church may have English Commentators, home bred expounders of the Word, sacred philologists imbued with her spirit but in order to be truly effective, the English must take up the pursuit at the present point to which German science has brought it and go forward in an independent way; and surrounded by and recognizing the value of the labors of those critics who at this moment professedly occupy the forefront in the department of biblical interpretation — E.H.[57]

As already noted Dr. Harwood had collaborated with Dr. Phillip Schaff on the translation of a series of books on biblical criticism from Germany and was apparently well informed on theological developments in that country. Muhlenberg may also have been influenced by Dr. Samuel Turner, who had entered the ministry under the influence of Bishop White and whom Muhlenberg had known as a colleague in Philadelphia.[58] Dr. Turner was a professor of biblical learning and interpretation at the General Theological Seminary during the years that Muhlenberg was at the Church of the Holy Communion. It should be remembered that this seminary — in which Muhlenberg had taken an intense interest — was only three blocks from the Church of the Holy Communion. Dr. Turner was one of the earliest scholars to recognize the importance of German developments in the field of biblical criticism.[59]

The Evangelical Catholic printed several chapters from the biography of Dr. Thomas Arnold, another Broad Church leader whom Muhlenberg held in high esteem. There was, however, no editorial comment on Dr. Arnold's biography.[60] (For further discussion of the Broad Church Movement see Chapter 8.)

Other articles reflected Muhlenberg's varied interests. A long article denounced spiritualism;[61] another advocated a greater variety in church services; others gave religious news both domestic and foreign.[62] A large part of the contents were reprints from other periodicals, particularly English ones.[63]

Dr. Edwin Harwood resigned his position as associate editor in 1853,[64] and his place was taken by T. Tracy.[65] He in turn resigned after a short time because he could not agree with the memorial which Muhlenberg presented to the House of Bishops in that year.[66] From that time on, Muhlenberg edited the paper alone. There is no way of knowing exactly what was the extent of its influence. The persons writing of it were largely Muhlenberg's friends such as Breck,[67] Bishop Kemper,[68] and Dr. Croswell of the Church of the Advent,[69] Boston. The last issue was that of December 30, 1853. No announcement was made of its discontinuance; many years later Muhlenberg thought of reviving it but that was the last time it was mentioned in any of his papers.[70] Possibly the memorial which he presented in 1853 absorbed all of his time and energy.

Summarizing the influence of *The Evangelical Catholic*, Dr. Harwood wrote:

The Evangelical Catholic was a genuine surprise, and the surprise culminated when it was discovered that Dr. Muhlenberg had no doctrinal affiliation with the party to which it had been assumed that he belonged. It was found that he was thoroughly Protestant both in his beliefs and in his sympathies. Catholic he claimed to be, because he held to the historic Church, with its creed and sacraments, and ministry and type of worship: Evangelical, because the Scriptures were the sole ultimate rule of faith and practice. He advocated great freedom of thought within the faith of Christ. This was the position he laid down, and upon which he stood before the church and country. Standing upon it resolutely he found, and others began to find also, that he thenceforth surely, and without any qualification, began to acquire the confidence of the community and he became a recognized power in New York and throughout the church.[71]

175

CHAPTER 8

Theology, the Liturgical Movement,
and Tractarianism

An examination of Muhlenberg's theological views leads to the conclusion that although he made no claims to being a professional theologian he held to a fairly consistent theology throughout his life. He began his ministry and continued as an Evangelical without ever being a party man and he often varied from the Low Churchmen of his time. Thus he could accept so-called Catholic elements of which his fellow Evangelicals would be suspicious. He regarded the Roman Catholic church as a hopelessly corrupt branch of Christendom and outside the pale as far as reunion was concerned—a view concurred in by popular Protestant opinion. He had a horror of infidelity particularly as he perceived it among the Germans and of rationalism without ever defining exactly what he meant by these terms. Only one mention of Unitarianism has been found in this research and that only incidental,[1] but he regarded all orthodox Protestant denominations as part of Catholic Christianity. He believed the Episcopal church to be doctrinally the most nearly complete of the churches, without denying the Catholicity of other Protestant denominations or passing judgment on the validity of their ministries.[2] However, he rejected the claim of the High Church party that the Episcopal church was the only legitimate church in the United States because he felt that despite its doctrinal correctness it was distinctively a class church which reached only a small segment of the population. On the other hand, the other Protestant churches, although not as doctrinally complete as the Episcopal church, nonetheless could justly claim Catholicity because of their ability to reach the masses.

176

Muhlenberg began his ministry strongly influenced by two Low Church leaders, Bishop White and Dr. James Milnor, and two High Churchmen, Dr. James Abercrombie and Bishop Kemper. He deplored the violence of the attacks by Low Churchmen on Bishop Hobart, the High Church leader, although he himself was critical of the bishop. When Benjamin Allen, the editor of a Low Church paper in Philadelphia, made an attack on Bishop Hobart, Muhlenberg wrote Jackson Kemper:

> I don't wonder that Hobart's sermon excited the wrath of the Radicals [Low Churchmen] but to reprove him as Allen has done reminds me (as I have just told Allen in my letter to him) of a woman whom I once saw beating her child for using profane language while she swore outrageously at every blow herself.[3]

But Muhlenberg himself on more than one occasion expressed sharp criticism of Bishop Hobart and the High Church Party. The Diocese of New York which prided itself on its sound (i.e., High) Churchmanship came in for some caustic remarks from him in a letter to Kemper for its lack of real religion:

> Ash Wednesday was solemnized by a most dashing ball by one of the members of Grace Church. The "weeping, fasting, and praying of Lent" is to be kept up with a succession of such holy festivities by the Children of Grace and worshipers of Trinity—however I believe Philadelphia is not much better. I mention these facts because they are in the center of Episcopacy, the metropolitical [sic] see where all the rites, and ceremonies, and . . . [?] and articles and Canons and ancient practices and edifying forms are insisted upon to the last Iota.
>
> On mentioning the inconsistency of such gaiety with the requisitions of the Church—a New Yorker answered, "Yes but we needed the ornaments of our Church for a Ballroom." I was in hopes it would not have been told in Gath.
>
> I hope I can look with an equal eye "upon my own things and those of others." I hope I have charity enough to judge impartially of my own Church—But indeed I cannot alter my opinion as to the real state of religion in the principal parishes of the city. There is not vital godliness (begging the Bishop's pardon) where is not zeal enough in the cause of religion to give the Church in New York that high standing . . . which she demands and assumes [sic]. We hear indeed a great deal about the earmarks of religion, about caution and prudence in maintaining the dignity of our profession, and danger of ostentation in preaching told [sic] by the truths of the Gospel. But "Jesus Christ and Him crucified." (I feel that I am saying a great deal—I feel that I am making a heavy charge)—held forth in simplicity and truth—Perhaps I am censorious—I may be guilty of the same er-

177

rors (in either way) which I discover in others—I hope my judgment is wrong—From what I can learn the Sunday schools in Grace and Trinity Parishes are in poor condition—Except St. John's Church I believe there is not a weekly adult school in any of the Churches.[4]

But more often Muhlenberg had a tendency to poke fun at party differences:

Has Montgomery been able yet to reconcile his High Church and Evangelical principles? A strange mixture! That would keep a man constantly— we would think—in a sort of Theological Gripes.[5]

Many years later he wrote in a similar vein to Ellie Bowman, daughter of an old friend, Bishop Samuel Bowman. This bishop was a High Churchman and a former rector of St. James, Lancaster.[6] Ellie had received a proposal of marriage from Bishop Thomas H. Vail, who was a proponent of the comprehensive church idea[7]—as was Muhlenberg. She wrote Muhlenberg for advice and his reply showed his attitude in the prime of life (1857) toward church parties:

My dear Ellie: So good a Bishop's daughter deserves to be a good Bishop's wife—and a good Bishop he is. I highly esteem him. As to *his* low Churchmanship—the only thing he believes you don't like in him—it is not lower than the prayerbook—which of course is wide enough. And if you do have some good . . . [?] Argumentation, it will only give that variety which is the "Spice of Life"—even matrimonial life—for you to think perfectly alike in all things wouldn't be half so pleasant—of this I am sure, that if our Communion ever attains to the place in the land which we hope for her it will be by the prevalence among her clergy of such views of her politics and policy as are held by Bishop Vail. Excuse my brief, brief letter—were it twice as long, I could not more heartily give you my blessing, "May you so live together in this life that in the world to come you may attain life everlasting."[8]

In his valedictory sermon at Lancaster Muhlenberg discussed his own theological beliefs in some detail:

While the doctrine of justification by faith alone has thus been maintained as the peculiar glory of the Gospel, you have been shown that such justifying faith is an active principle of holiness; that good works spring from it of necessity, and belong to it in the same manner as fruit belongs to the tree on which it hangs. Comparing Christian virtue to the human system, faith is the soul, the vital principle; while good works are the body. Thus they are the feet running in the ways of righteousness, the hands busy in deeds of love, the eyes lifted heavenward in devotion, the tongue speaking the words of truth, charity, and peace and glorifying the name of the creator.[9]

But this emphasis on Justification by Faith did not definitely align him with the Low Church party, for as he later pointed out even a High Churchman such as Bishop Whittingham held to this doctrine.[10]

Muhlenberg's difficulties with Bishop Hobart over his school at Flushing have already been recounted and he was a member of an association of clergymen in New York which drew the bishop's censure.[11] Up to the time of the opening of St. Paul's College, Muhlenberg was thus generally regarded as a member of the Low Church or Evangelical party.

But he also had close friendships with members of the High Church party. In addition to Dr. James Abercrombie, his old schoolmaster,[12] there was Dr. Frederick Beasley, the provost of the University of Pennsylvania.[13] As the years went on Jackson Kemper became a High Churchman and may have influenced Muhlenberg to a certain extent.[14] Similarly when Muhlenberg opened the Flushing Institute he had Samuel Seabury, grandson of a famous High Church bishop as his assistant, a man whose very name was a symbol of High Churchmanship.[15] Samuel Roosevelt Johnson, also a High Churchman, was on the faculty of St. Paul's College.[16] With Samuel Seabury, Muhlenberg was on terms of close friendship.[17] Under the influence of these men many of Muhlenberg's students became High Churchmen including his protégé, John Barrett Kerfoot.[18] So Muhlenberg, although identified with the Evangelical party, had close friends in the other camp. Even Muhlenberg's hostility toward Bishop Hobart diminished toward the close of the bishop's life.[19]

Muhlenberg regarded theological disputations as of little use. Rather, the course for Christians in general and Episcopalians in particular was to unite on projects which were common to all Christians regardless of their theological differences. In the event that theological controversies could not be avoided they should be conducted without name calling and without impugning the integrity of one's opponents.[20] It would have been difficult, however, for any person of prominence to avoid the bitter theological controversy which raged in the Episcopal church in the period 1840–1860 and even Muhlenberg was drawn in, although involuntarily. But it is an excellent index to his character that he managed to remain a figure above party while maintaining the respect of members of all parties.

The occasion for the controversy was a movement which began at Oxford University in England in 1833 under the leadership of three clergymen: E. B. Pusey, John Keble, and John Henry Newman. This movement has been variously named the Oxford movement from the university of its origin and the Tractarian movement because of the use its leader made of tracts. Its followers were also known as Puseyites from the name of its principal leader. Later it was broadly referred to as the Anglo-Catholic movement. It will be referred to in this book as the Tractarian movement in its early stages and the Anglo-Catholic movement in its later stages.

The movement was a revival of the old High Church Party of Hobart in the United States and of Archbishop Laud in England but with new emphases and interpretations. It accepted the exclusive claims of the High Churchmen as far as the protestant ministries were concerned but took a new view of the Roman Catholic and Greek Orthodox churches. It regarded both of these churches as branches of the one true Catholic church of which the Anglican church was the English-speaking branch. Like the old High Church party it emphasized the authority of the priesthood and the importance of the sacraments but it went further and began to reintroduce ceremonial and ritualistic practices which had died out of the Anglican church and which were regarded as evidence of an affinity to Roman Catholicism. Discarding the earlier attitude toward Roman Catholicism, the Tractarians did not regard that church as hopelessly corrupt but believed that it had much that was admirable both in doctrine and ceremonial. Newman precipitated a bitter controversy when he published a tract claiming that Roman Catholic doctrines could be reconciled with the Anglican church's Thirty-Nine Articles, for these articles had formerly been regarded as the Anglican church's chief bulwark against Roman Catholicism. The conversion of Newman to the Roman Catholic church in 1845 seemed final proof to the opponents of the Tractarians that they represented a Romeward movement.[21]

Although Muhlenberg had always been an opponent of the old High Church party, he was deeply influenced by Tractarianism—probably because several of the interests which he had developed independently coincided with Tractarian ideas. The first publication of the Tracts made a profound impression on the members of the faculty of St. Paul's College. They discussed them in private and Muhlenberg, although not influenced as much as his colleagues, nonetheless used them as sermon material at the evening services. Without being able to accept them wholeheartedly he sympathized with their deep religious orientation, something that he missed in the old-fashioned High Churchmen.[22] Likewise, even before the ritualistic phase of the movement began, Muhlenberg had introduced various ritualistic practices at Flushing Institute and St. Paul's College. On church festivals he censed the chapel before the service, on Easter and Christmas the chapel was decorated with flowers, and on Good Friday it was draped in black. On Christmas

180

there was a picture of the Nativity on the altar and on Easter a picture of the Resurrection. For the early services which were held before daylight the chapel was lit with candles.[23] These customs were apparently the basis of charges that Muhlenberg was introducing Romish practices at his school.[24]

Muhlenberg himself was familiar with Roman Catholic ritual for he had attended services of that church in Philadelphia as a boy and young man and it was probably there that he acquired his knowledge of ritual. Miss Ayres summarizes his diary regarding this boyhood experience:

> He records that at seven o'clock on Christmas morning he went into St. Mary's [Roman Catholic] and "all the chapels" and then to morning service at St. James [Episcopal] which he found decorated "as well as might be" but evidently not to his satisfaction. . . . He enjoys it all and regrets at night that the day is over. "O dies felicissima" "Dies dilecta" he exclaims. . . . At the same time he laments that the services were not richer and fuller. "If I were an Archbishop the churches on this most holy day should shine with brilliancy, not poor laurel only. I would have the altar in white, a large painting representing the Nativity, wreaths of cedar and laurel to hide the walls, a choir with loud bursting organ and a thousand voices should sing their Alleluias, Churches I would have builded in the most magnificent manner," etc. etc.

Later on in life as a college boy he wrote:

> I took occasional opportunities of going to the Roman Church and for several years made a point of attending early Christmas Mass in the old Roman Catholic Church on the corner of Sixth and Spruce Streets, Philadelphia. "Venite adoremus, venite adoremus" how it rang in my ears and I cannot tell how much its echoes have had to do with the early Christmas services in which so many have rejoiced with me in the course of my ministry.[25]

He introduced the custom of singing parts of the service and using a boys' choir at his schools.[26] These were the practices about which Elizabeth Kemper wrote her father. She was then living in Philadelphia and her two brothers were attending St. Paul's College:

> He [Sam Kemper] says that they have prayers at noon besides the morning and evening prayers which he thinks very good. And they sing on their knees! He says that they are very much like Roman Catholics there! but says we must not tell anyone lest they should hear it. The other day he heard one of the teachers ask the other whether he thought the sermon they heard would hurt the boys which question Sam says he can't understand. They ought, I think, to be rather careful in making their remarks before the boys. I suppose it is Oxford and all Oxford there.[27]

Since many of Muhlenberg's associates at his schools such as Samuel Seabury, Milo Mahan, George Houghton, W. H. Odenheimer, James Lloyd Breck, John Barrett Kerfoot, J. V. Huntingdon, and Samuel Roosevelt Johnson sympathized with the new movement, Muhlenberg himself may very well have been considered one of their number.[28]

The Tractarian movement had a double impact on the American Episcopal church. This church along with the rest of American Protestantism was greatly alarmed by the expanding influence of the Roman Catholic church reinforced as it was by Irish and German immigration. In addition that church had a forceful and aggressive leader in Archbishop John Hughes of New York.[29] It thus appeared that all Protestantism had an enemy in the Roman Catholic church but that the Episcopal church, had in addition—to use twentieth-century terminology—a fifth column in its own ranks.[30]

Muhlenberg took a trip to England in 1843 principally to interview the leaders of the Tractarian movement. In letters which he wrote his friend Samuel Seabury, now editor of *The Churchman,* he reported the gossip which he heard on all sides. One of the high points of his trip was his call on Dr. Pusey:

> I called on Dr. Pusey soon after getting to Oxford—and though he was quite sick, he very politely admitted me on the introduction of the Bishop's general letter—His books and papers were much in the same order as your own. He was lying on a sofa wrapped in cloaks—the poor man looked melancholy so that I did not venture to stay long. He at first thought I had come to beg—when relieved of the impression he talked freely—inquired about persons and things in America—particularly of Bishop Doane—dwelt upon the want of men in the Church of inferior education to labor among the poor—did not allude to his own situation—in reference to his sermon—but expressed in a general way and in the same gentle patient manner that appears in his writings—his confidence in God as the protector of the Church. Copeland came in to whom he introduced me for attentions which it was not in his power to render—I left him with the impression that he is a sincere and devout man.[31]

A more interesting visit was his call on Newman himself. Of this period in his life Newman states in his *Apologia* that "From the end of 1841, I was on my death bed as regards my membership with the Anglican Church though at the time I became aware of it only by degrees." He was, in July, 1843, when Muhlenberg visited him, the rector of the church at Littlemore, a short distance from Oxford. Commenting on intruders at Littlemore he said "Doctors of Divinity dived into the hidden recesses of that private tenement uninvited, and drew domestic conclusions from what they saw there." In February he made a formal retraction of all remarks he had made against the Church of Rome. In March of that year he planned to give up his position as a clergyman of the Church of England and become a lay communicant.[32] This may, to a certain extent, explain his attitude as reported by Muhlenberg:

> I went out to Littlemore—three miles from Oxford—to see Newman—after service in his little church—I introduced myself to him—and nothing could exceed his gracious reception of me—He took me to his humble abode where everything is remarkably neat and equally plain—I gave him Wainwright's letter and showed him the letter from the Bishop—he was extremely affable—asked a great many questions—talked only on indifferent topics—He gave that answer to every question I put [sic] and seemed not inclined to express opinions. He was perfectly simple and unaffected in his manners—He received some things I said with so much modesty that he seemed really like an humble man—If I had to judge I should say he had much of the gentleness and meekness of Christ—and yet he was very *cautious*—he lacks not the wisdom of the serpent any more than the harmlessness of the dove. He gave me a very pressing invitation to come to breakfast with my friends, at Oriel College which of course we accepted. Several gentlemen were there to meet us so that I had no opportunity for anything but the more general conversation. He never committed himself—I am sure I could repeat nothing he has said that could be turned against him to his disadvantage. He was more kind and polite at table—all attention—and when I bade him good morning—he shook my hand very cordially—but said not a word about seeing me again—although I had more than once intimated I wanted information from him on several points—He is not transparent—Richmond must have sharper eyes than mine—If he could see through him.[33]

Muhlenberg called on Newman again however on his return to Oxford in September and recorded in his diary:

> Sept. 16. took a fly with K. to Littlemore, Newman again very gracious. Had heard of me, he said, from Mozely and by letter from Dr. Seabury. Appeared very glad to see me, invited K. and myself *right off* to dine with him at Oriel.
> Sunday, Sept. 17. Heard Mr. Newman at St. Mary's from Isaiah 'all things new' (completely himself)...Dined with him in the common room at Oriel ... He asked questions about the American Church. Said 'that as so many of our clergymen came over from the Dissenters he thought they might be likely to go further, i.e. Rome? He bade us good-by, very kindly. Welcomes the coming, speeds the parting guests. K— thinks I am too suspicious of Newman.[34]

Two months after Muhlenberg's visit Newman resigned his rectorship at Littlemore and gave up all clerical duty in the Church of England.

Later in that year he wrote that he began to despair of the Church of England and that what he wrote and did was influenced by a mere wish not to injure it and not by the wish to benefit it. In October, 1843, he wrote a friend stating that he had begun to believe that the Church of Rome was the Catholic church. He then began the writing of his book on *Doctrinal Development* which led him into the Roman Catholic church. He was received into that church on October 8, 1845, approximately two years after Muhlenberg's visit.[35]

In the New York Diocesan Convention of 1841, Bishop Benjamin T. Onderdonk, the successor of Bishop Hobart, called for a fair-minded and judicious view of the "Oxford Men."[36] In the following year he was called upon to handle a highly controversial case within his own diocese. A young student at the General Theological Seminary by the name of Arthur Carey, who had been influenced by the Tractarian Movement, was denounced by some of the clergy for holding Roman Catholic doctrines. The bishop appointed a commission to examine Carey, which subjected him to an exhaustive examination. The majority returned a verdict in favor of Carey while a minority brought in a report upholding the original charges. The bishop therefore proceeded to ordain Carey but at the ordination service two clergymen arose and repeated their charges. The bishop, however, replied that these charges had already been adequately considered and continued with the service. Carey, who had been in ill health, took a voyage to the Caribbean where he died aboard ship—the result, his friends said, of this "persecution."[37]

Seabury and Muhlenberg were evidently close friends of Carey, for shortly after Carey's death Muhlenberg wrote Seabury:

> I meant to visit you as a mourning friend, hardly however, to condole with you—for surely we may rather thank God that a life so ripe for heaven was no longer detained on earth—I expect to be in again this week when nothing shall prevent my calling—and I beg you not to misunderstand my not coming yesterday—I was particularly anxious to see you after hearing of your sermon—it made different impressions of course, in different minds—some thought it only a natural expression of your feeling—and a very solemn and eloquent one—others while they sympathized with what you said wished that you had not referred so strongly to his persecution as the cause of his death. The use of the collect for St. Stephen's Day, has been principally spoken of—and I hope you will excuse me for saying, that knowing how it would be understood it would better [have] been omitted. You might, however, go much further in your own church—considering all the circumstances, than probably you might think of doing more publicly—perhaps it was well—the sermon was the first burst of your feelings—perhaps it was well that you had not the opportunity of giving vent to it in the *Churchman*—By the next paper your emotions will

184

have somewhat subsided—you will have time to reflect not only if what you say is true but also how it will *be taken* —and what will be the effects upon the Church—You have declared for peace—So do nothing which will renew the war—write as that sweet spirit now at rest, would bid you— could he indite your words.—Remember too that everybody can say and enough so say "—poor C—was murdered—how must S and A feel?" This is in the mouth of everybody—Therefore *you* need not say it—to abstain from saying it will have far more effect—and accomplish your object more certainly—will be a dignified and Christian forbearance— ... It is due to the memory of your friend not to seem to use it for any un- hallowed purpose—I make this last remark from hearing a person say, who was told of your sermon—"Seabury now intends to make political capital out of C—'s death." It is for the conspiracies of the world, not for the congregation of the saints, to rouse their fellows to vengeance, over the corpse of their fallen friend—God forbid I should think you capable of that but you might appear to the world to do it—Excuse me, my dear friend, you know my motives—I may be weak and . . [?] but I am sincere—I would express more precisely what I mean if I had time—Burn this—Sincerely W.A.M.[38]

A more bitter controversy soon developed in which Muhlenberg was directly involved. Bishop Onderdonk had apparently acted in a too familiar manner with some of the women of his diocese. The common sense verdict in this affair was summed up by Jackson Kemper who stated that the bishop had been indiscreet and deserved a reprimand and admonition from his fellow bishops but that there was no evidence that the bishop had any immoral or criminal intent.[39] Muhlenberg was more critical of the bishop than Kemper although on the whole he agreed with him. Muhlenberg had been an unwitting factor in bringing on the controversy.

A Long Island clergyman and friend of Muhlenberg, Henry Beare, had been angered by the bishop's conduct toward his wife, and Muhlen- berg and his friends Jonathan Wainwright and James Milnor called on the bishop in a group to discuss this matter with him.[40] The bishop on this first visit vigorously protested his innocence but when the clergy- men called again, this time in company with Beare, he admitted the truth of Beare's complaint but claimed that his actions had been mis- interpreted. Despite the careful manner in which Muhlenberg and his friends conducted themselves this matter seems to have become known in the church.[41]

Bishop Onderdonk was tried for immoral conduct by the House of Bishops in New York in 1844 under a charge signed by three of his fellow bishops.[42] The High Church party was convinced that the Low Churchmen were attacking the bishop because of his sympathetic attitude toward the Tractarian movement and his decision in the Carey case.[43] Muhlenberg was called to testify and told of his two calls on the bishop. Jackson Kemper, a defender of the accused bishop, stated that all parties agreed that Muhlenberg had done exactly what a clergyman should do in such circumstances.[44] The verdict by the House of Bishops was reached, however, largely on a party basis. Most of the High Churchmen upheld the bishop's innocence and most of the Low Churchmen found him guilty. A third group held the bishop guilty but did not believe that he should be deposed. A lesser sentence of indefinite suspension from the ministry was therefore agreed upon.[45]

Seabury, through the columns of *The Churchman,* was one of the most ardent defenders of the bishop. Muhlenberg at first was inclined to view the trial in a somewhat facetious light as evidenced by the following letter to Seabury:

> I hear you think I am miserably lacking in sympathy for our persecuted Bishop—but I assure you that I have felt quite happy since you told me they have made so little of Beare's case—I intend to see B—before coming to the City, if I can—not, you may be sure, to revive his original feelings—I want to do only what is right—and no work of supererogation—so you take care that there is no super-interrogation—at the trial—Keith made me laugh today by a pun which I told him would run well in verse:
> "Everyone to his liking" we always allow
> Nor blame the old woman for kissing the cow
> So sure 'twas a harmless though funny affair
> That a Bishop should fancy to kiss a She-Bear
> *Burn this* I charge you.[46]
>
> Yours
W. A. M.

Shortly after writing this letter Muhlenberg heard of the bishop's sentence. About the same time Seabury's father died so that from Muhlenberg's next letter all facetiousness had gone. He first extended his condolences to Seabury on the death of his father and then went into a discussion of Bishop Onderdonk's trial. Although Muhlenberg had been more critical of the bishop than Seabury and Kemper he deplored the harshness of the sentence. "They have dealt hardly with the Bishop—Whatever I may think of the Justice of the verdict, in itself, I am sure there is no mercy in the sentence." Muhlenberg recommended that the clergy of New York accept the verdict and after an interval petition the House of Bishops to terminate the sentence of indefinite suspension.

> This would be stooping indeed—but I tell you the stooping will do us no harm—we have been carrying our heads too high—we have been self-

confident and boasting—we have been proud of the advancement of the Diocese in "Sound Churchmanship" while there has been no manifestation of the first signs of genuine churchmanship.—we wanted humbling and God has humbled us—in mercy—let us take care that we take it not in harshness.[47]

The next letter written three days later reveals a strain in the friendship between the two men: "I do not flatter myself that anything I can say in the present juncture of our church will have much weight with you—I know precisely the length and breadth that I measure on your scale," Muhlenberg wrote his friend. Nonetheless he proceeded to give Seabury advice. He pointed out that in the present excited state of opinion the welfare of the church depended on Seabury as editor of *The Churchman* more than on any other one man. "What will the next *Churchman* say?" is now the question that everyone asks of his neighbor with fearful anxiety. He therefore exhorted Seabury to rise above minor considerations and speak as the counselor of the church. Then in several pages he again recommended the course of action suggested in his earlier letter, that after a "cooling off" period the diocese should petition for a restoration of the bishop. He again pointed out that the troubles of the diocese might be considered a judgment on its pride:

We have been grouping on the high ground we have taken—we have been vaunting our catholicism—because forsooth we have built magnificent churches—(But not hospitals—or schools—or orphan houses)—and have the altar in the right position—and put gilt crosses on our prayer-books—and sing the Gregorian chants, etc.—

On the other hand if the diocese followed the course he suggested, then:

The Bishop and clergy will be more united than ever—and then our "Catholicism" would be something more than it now is—a pretty dilettantism with some—a sectarian pride with others—and with the rest a cold conservatism—I could write a great deal—but you have my mind "valear quantrum valear." I write in haste from the fullness of my heart, and not without prayer to the Father of light—affectionately.[48]

The suspension of the Bishop left the Diocese of New York in a quandary for the canons were vague as to how a diocese was to be administered during the suspension of its bishop. Bishop Onderdonk accepted the suspension but refused to resign on the grounds that such an action would be an admission of guilt. The diocese therefore considered the plan of electing a provisional bishop who would administer its affairs until this dilemma was resolved.[49] So strong was partisan feeling, however, that not until seven years later was it possible to elect a provisional bishop.

When Muhlenberg moved to New York the Carey case was only two years old, the bishop had just been suspended, and in October of that year the news was received of Newman's conversion to the Roman Catholic church. Speaking of the state of the Episcopal church at that time, Dr. Edwin Harwood, Muhlenberg's close friend and collaborator, says:

> When Dr. Muhlenberg began his pastorate at the Holy Communion, the Protestant Episcopal Church was, and had been for several years, in a state of great commotion. The storms of today are feeble in comparison. Doctrinal controversy and personal scandals had produced only bitterness, anger, malice, and an evil temper. The thoroughly Protestant portion of the church and numbers of Christians not of our communion, were alike exasperated and alarmed at the drift towards Rome. When, at last, John Henry Newman, author of Tract No. 90, a publication which had alarmed churchmen everywhere—when Mr. Newman, the darling leader of the new movement, the eloquent preacher, the devout theologian, deserted the Church of England and joined the Church of Rome, there was actual consternation in the High-Church Party, and they were compelled beside to listen to the taunts of many of their Low-Church brethren, who were not loath nor slow in saying, "We told you so." The atmosphere of the whole church was heated; the temper of the laity had become suspicious; New York was divided into two hostile camps; Theology and scandal, "Puseyism," and the process against Bishop Onderdonk produced the most painful confusion; and everyone felt that the Church had received a check which could not be neutralized nor forgotten for years. It was at this apparently most inauspicious season that Dr. Muhlenberg began his ministry in New York. He had come to New York, moreover, with an enthusiastic feeling for certain phases of church life and peculiarities of worship which were extremely distasteful to the Low-Churchmen but to which High-Churchmen gave sympathy and support.[50]

The opening of the Church of the Holy Communion was therefore regarded by public opinion as a major triumph for Puseyism because many of the so-called novelties which Muhlenberg introduced at the church were associated with that party. He therefore attracted to the church those people who were interested in the latest sensations while he was regarded with suspicion by the great mass of old-fashioned laity. He was naturally the object of much gossip and it was assumed that he was very Romish. Dr. Harwood thus summarizes his position in the years following his coming to New York.

Between the years of 1847 and 1851 his personal associations were largely with clergymen and others who sympathized with that movement [the Tractarian] and I venture the assertion, with all caution, however, that during those years, while the work and the services in the Church of the Holy Communion were attracting such general notice, Dr. Muhlenberg had not clearly defined either to himself or to others his doctrinal position.[51]

Other comments indicate that Muhlenberg was generally regarded as a member of the Tractarian party. Thus Fr. Clarence Walworth writing of his student days at the General Theological Seminary, only a few blocks from the Church of the Holy Communion, says:

[The] Rev. Dr. Muhlenberg whose beautiful church on the corner of Twentieth Street and Fifth Avenue, New York City, was building in 1843 was eagerly watched by us seminarians. We looked upon the worthy doctor as neither low nor high, nor dry, but as true Catholic in the romantic sense of the word. He was particularly a favorite among students of the ritualistic type. He was admired then as a poet, with a keen taste for church architecture, author of the beautiful hymn "I Would Not Live Alway," now known also as the founder of St. Luke's Hospital, under the care of Episcopalian nuns.[52]

Dr. Clinton Locke, speaking of his seminary days in the 1850's, says:

Our highest exponent of ceremonial and ritual was the Church of the Holy Communion, then considered the extremest height possible, and its extremes consisted of a proper altar with a cross and flowers, and a choir of unvested boys who chanted the Psalter.[53]

Possibly it was to combat these preconceptions concerning himself and his parish that Muhlenberg issued a series of tracts explaining and defending those aspects of the parish which were considered novelties by his contemporaries. The first of these tracts was entitled *The Catholic Faith. Whole and Undefiled*—one of his favorite expressions—and was an excerpt from a sermon preached shortly after the church was consecrated. In it he attempted to define his position in regard to the relationship of the Episcopal church and other Protestant churches. He first endeavored to show that the Catholic faith was contained in the Apostles' and Nicene Creeds which were in the Book of Common Prayer. He then went on:

Some of the older religious bodies around us perhaps have not departed materially from the Catholic Faith, inasmuch as in their confessions they explicitly teach the doctrines of the Apostles' and Nicene Creeds. But they do not hold it in connection with what we believe to be a duly constituted ministry and have given up the old "forms of sound words," which have ever been the safeguards of the Faith. While we cannot make one with them without a compromise of our principles, and exposing ourselves to the dangers from which they have suffered, we are not called upon to say how far they are, or are not, parts of the one Catholic Church. There is no necessity for our defining the ecclesiastical position of our neighbors— it is sufficient for us to be satisfied of our own. Let us thank God that, in his good time, this is so clear. We cannot doubt that we have the essential elementary points of a true Church. We have the Holy Scriptures and (for their right interpretations in the fundamentals of the faith) we have the universal creeds; we have the Christian Ministry, as it has come down to us in an unbroken series of ordinations, from those on whom the great High Priest at first laid hands; we have the Holy Sacraments; we have incorporated in our services parts of the most ancient liturgies; we have various "forms of sound words." To these we will hold fast, as we would keep the Catholic Faith whole, we will suffer no deductions from them, as we would shun the least chance of apostasy from the truth. We will adhere to them as we value the well being of our souls. No considerations of expediency, or liberality, or charity (falsely so-called) shall persuade us to give up one jot or title of them. Doing so our duty in the matter is done— although we may not perceive the demonstration that every Christian community in the land, beside our own, is out of the pale of the Catholic Church.[54]

With this statement the Tractarians would on the whole have agreed, but they would have dissented sharply from Muhlenberg over the statement that other Protestant churches were not outside the pale of the Catholic church. For it was fundamental to Tractarian theology that groups of Christians which did not possess the Apostolic succession had in fact "unchurched" themselves and could not be regarded as being within the Catholic faith at all.[55]

Muhlenberg goes on to define his attitude toward the Thirty-Nine Articles, around which raged one of the chief controversies in regard to the Tractarian movement:

> These are the articles of our Church, in which she declares her dissent from the Church of Rome, and I have recited them, partly for the purpose of saying that I hope they will ever be received in this congregation in their plain and obvious meaning.—in the "natural" sense of the words—and with such an interpretation (whenever one is needed) as is afforded by the Liturgy and offices of the Book of Common Prayer.[56]

Commenting then on the official title of the Episcopal church which contained the word "Protestant"—always a sore point with the Tractarians and their successors the Anglo-Catholics—he said:

This, my brethren, is a Protestant Church. On that point I wish to utter no ambiguous language. It was consecrated as a Protestant Church; and when it ceases to be such, the conditions of its donations will be violated. Not that I regard the term Protestant as a very desirable appellation for a branch of the Catholic Church. I wish that our Protestant Episcopal Communion in this country had a name more indicative of its positive character, and significant of its connection with the Church at large. At present, however, we are hardly in a situation to designate ourselves by any more primitive style. Were our zeal and practice more worthy of our principles; had our professions of churchmanship less of a sectarian character, heart and hand, in giving actual existence to the church contemplated in the Prayer Book, we should find ourselves gradually becoming, and being recognized by others as an *American Catholic Church*. But in any event, as long as there is a spiritual power in Christendom, exercising an usurped control far and wide over the earth, active and energetic among ourselves, aiming at universal dominion, which it demands in the name of Christ, and insisting on false doctrines as the Gospel—while this lasts, there is meaning, in those who contend for the Catholic Faith undefiled, in calling themselves Protestants. The honor of the name indeed has been sadly tarnished. It has been employed to cover the boldest heresies and the wildest extravagancies of religious licentiousness—but as long as we read of Martyrs, Confessors, and Saints glorying in it and adorning it; as long as our Mother Church of England is not ashamed of it, and her truest sons have used it as a watchword of the "liberty wherewith Christ hath made us free," as long as the works of the great theologians and scholars, who have illustrated the principles of the Reformation are part and parcel of the literature of the English tongue, the name of Protestant can never be wholly an inglorious name.[57]

Muhlenberg then took a stand in regard to Roman Catholicism which is very near the Tractarian belief that there were elements in that church which were good and should be imitated and that practices should not be prohibited merely because they were used by that church:

I am far from thinking that the errors and corruptions of the Roman Church are the only danger to which we are exposed. Much less do I think that we are to secure ourselves by taking our position in as opposite a direction as possible. In the cycle of opinions, by constantly receding from one set of errors, we may only be returning to them in another form. Hence while I have a deep conviction that the system against which our church lifts her voice, is far wide of the simplicity of the "Truth as it is in Jesus," and is, in its practical tendency, dangerous to the soul (though that tendency be more or less counteracted by the virtue of the truth also held in the system) you shall never hear from me that indiscriminate denunciation of Roman Catholics which some may demand as a proof of soundness in the faith. This test of orthodoxy will not be exhibited here.

I shall never think it my duty to disparage the works of mercy and charity, of self-denial and devotion which we might rather emulate, because they are the fruits of the faith, with corrupt admixtures. Nor shall I hesitate to uphold any Catholic Truths and practices, which are really such, merely because of the evils to which they have given occasion.[58]

He then in summary defined his attitude toward the Book of Common Prayer:

Lastly we pledge ourselves to the Catholic faith as set forth in the Book of Common Prayer. Under this head much might be said pertinent to the object of this discourse; but it may be the more readily omitted, as opportunities for it will be frequently occurring. At present I would only observe that in the conduct of the services of this Church, we hope to make a good use of all the provisions of the Prayer Book, as the appointed means of building us up in our most holy faith. While there will be conformity to the strictness of the letter, its evident intention will also be a guide in the use of it; and whatever liberty it allows will be employed in accordance with and in fuller development of its spirit. If in any customs and practices we chance to differ from our fellow churchmen elsewhere, let it not be set down to a mere desire for change — much less to a spirit of innovation. The sincere endeavor will be to do justice to the service according to its original design, and to conform it, by such means as are allowable, to the varying seasons of the ecclesiastical year. If our whole nature is to be consecrated to God, then it is right to interest the imagination as well as the understanding and the affections in the worship of His holy temple.[59]

Having defined his position on the leading theological controversies of his time, Muhlenberg then proceeded to explain various practices in which the Church of the Holy Communion differed from other Episcopalian parishes. The most conspicuous of these was the central position of the altar which dominated the whole interior of the church with the pulpit at the side instead of in the center. In the second tract entitled *Reasons Why the Holy Table or Altar Should be a Distinct and Principal Object in a Christian Church*, he wrote:

A Christian Church is a house for the worship of God, through our Lord Jesus Christ. Now, let us consider what such a church is, reducing it to its utmost simplicity. It might consist of only four walls and a roof. It might be one plain and open room, containing no article whatever, except a table. No seats, no pulpit, no reading desk — for the people and minister might either stand or kneel. But the Holy Communion must be administered, as that is the highest act of worship of God, through our Lord Jesus Christ — and for that a table is necessary. A Christian Church, then, reduced to its naked form, is an open room containing a table. Or to go still further, if the congregation worship under the open canopy of heaven, still the

Table must be there. It might be a board laid upon the ground, still it would be the Table or Board of the Lord. In erecting a Church, then, whatever we do in the way of convenience or ornament, we must not lose sight of that which is the distinctive feature—the essential part—of a Christian Church. The Holy Table will be a conspicuous and prominent object, to mark, decidedly and at once, the Christianity of the place.

But again what is this table? It is a Holy Table, by reason of the Holy service in which it is used. The rite there celebrated is the Holy Supper; the sacred feast which is the bond of the holy communion of the Faithful— hence the Holy Table. But according to the liturgical order of the Church, there is a solemn offering of the elements of God, as a memorial of the sacrifice of the death of Christ. There is a commemorative and symbolical oblation, and then the table becomes an Altar. As we ever associate it with the Eucharist, which is a commemoration of the death of Christ, it stands forth in the church, a visible memorial of the atonement as a great and central truth of our religion.[60]

The next tract took up the posture of the minister in prayer. In most Episcopal churches the reading desk was turned toward the people but in the Church of the Holy Communion the minister turned toward the altar when he led the prayers. Defending this practice, Muhlenberg said:

Taking the foregoing view of the Altar, we see why the congregation should be turned in that direction, particularly when engaged in prayer. [Why then] should the minister turn towards the people when he prays? Because of custom? I answer—it is the custom of those who use extempo-rary prayer which often savors as much of address to the people as to the Deity; but is not the custom in Liturgical worship, over Christendom at large.[61]

The same reasons therefore were valid for the people that were valid for the minister's facing the altar when he led the prayers. It was more natural, more favorable to the devotion of the minister and more favor-able to uttering the prayers as prayers. When facing the people the minister is more apt to use the voice of a preacher. The very language of the objection makes it a suspicious one, "turning the back to the people as if some intentional disrespect was done to them. . . . The secret of offence at the practice in question, in some minds may be an unde-fined feeling that it seems to slight the supremacy of the people. The popular custom is essentially and consistently congregational." Another view of the matter which had never occurred to him was suggested by a person who observed that "the ministers should be careful how they turn their backs upon those from whom they get their bread and butter."[62]

Muhlenberg's explanation failed to convince Henry Dana Ward, who wrote in his *Diary* after attending one of the services:

The reverence paid to the Altar table in my opinion detracts from the worship of His name who sanctified the altar and especially the hearts of His faithful ones. To be saying the prayer into the chancel as if that were the place of the Lord's presence is a contempt of His presence in the midst of the congregation which goes far to inculcate the doctrine of transubstantiation, the delusion of a most holy place in the Church, the corruption of pictures and likenesses, (first to Adam) and then to inhabit that place and then a train of sympathies that have been instrumental of perverting the whole Church in ages past and perverting our learned Doctor in this age from the simplicity of the Gospel and of the Prayer Book to the baneful practice and corruptions of that great city which is the mistress of the kings of the earth.[63]

In this remark Ward was probably expressing contemporary Protestant opinion.

Another innovation which Muhlenberg made was to break up the long drawn-out Sunday service. It had become the custom to say the three services of Morning Prayer, the Litany, and the Ante-Communion—together with a sermon—as the regular Sunday morning service. There was no requirement on the part of the church that this be done but it had the authority of long-standing custom. The separation of the services made it possible to have more frequent celebrations of the Holy Communion and thus enabled working people to attend and be active communicants.[64] As might be expected these innovations also drew adverse comment in the diary of Ward but later on he admitted that this was one of Muhlenberg's novelties which he had come to approve.[65]

Muhlenberg was therefore regarded as a Tractarian by the general public during his early years at the Church of the Holy Communion and there is no way of determining when his reaction against the movement began. Dr. Harwood is undoubtedly correct in stating that during these years he was for the most part in the company of Tractarians. Among these was William Croswell, rector of the Church of the Advent, Boston, whose work in Boston somewhat paralleled that of Muhlenberg at the Church of the Holy Communion in New York.[66] He was also acquainted with Bishop Levi Silliman Ives of North Carolina who had succeeded him as rector of St. James, Lancaster, and who had consecrated the Church of the Holy Communion, and with John Murray Forbes, rector of St. Luke's, New York. The last two were officers of a society called the Ecclesiologists, whose purpose was to develop ritual in the Episcopal church.[67] Henry Dana Ward reports a conversation with him in 1854:

194

The Doctor [Muhlenberg] said he had at one time [been] in full sympathy with Newman and Co.—that he saw Newman's Doctrine led Romeward, but he was not afraid to follow truth though it led to Rome—that in this way he came to see Rome *in purvis naturalibus,* and he drew back and turned from her with horror as the masterpiece of Satan, and retreated to old Evangelical ground. He accompanied this with action of both hands and the whole body and followed it by referring to his Memorial to the House of Bishops, calling for a closer cultivation of our relations with all Prot. Evan denominations.[68]

Miss Ayres also says that Muhlenberg's disillusionment with the Tractarian movement came with the reading of Newman's book *The Development of Christian Doctrine,* the writing of which had led Newman to join the Roman Catholic church:

Mr. Newman's *Doctrine of Development* fully opened my eyes. I will remember, how, having read half through the book, I tossed it from me, exclaiming, "my mind is escaped as a bird from the snare of the fowler" and some of my then pupils, now in the ministry will recollect the emphasis with which I repeated to them these words: I was far out on the bridge . . . that bridges the gulf between us and Rome. I had passed through the mists of vulgar Protestant prejudices when I saw before me 'the mystery of Abomination'. I flew back, not to rest on the pier of High-Churchmen, from which the bridge of Puseyism springs, but on the solid rock of Evangelical truth, as republished by the Reformers.[69]

Muhlenberg began to evolve in the 1850's a system which he called Evangelical Catholicism. In this he was greatly influenced by one of his former students at St. Paul's College, Joseph Passmore, who at that time was an instructor at St. James College in Maryland. Muhlenberg and Passmore regarded protestantism and catholicism as different aspects of the Christian faith which supplemented but were not opposed to each other.[70] A tangible example of Evangelical Catholicism appeared in *The Evangelical Catholic:*

The other day we visited, in the Eastern part of the city, a humble little Church of the Old Lutheran School. There was the altar with the crucifix, with the tall candles, lighted during the Eucharist. There lay the service book, parts of which are intoned by the minister, fronting the altar, directing him to make the sign of the cross over the elements when repeating the Institution, there the communicants received the consecrated wafer, imprinted with the Agnus Dei—but there, too, stood the pulpit, from which sounds forth the reformation doctrine of Justification by Faith—there, every Sunday, the children are indoctrinated in Luther's catechism. The good pastor would have smiled had we expressed any fears of Popery from

195

what we saw. He would have told us that "Faith cometh by hearing" and that when a clear and scriptural faith is received, the symbolism of his altar and the ritual only tells of "the truth as it is in Jesus."[71]

Such views did not satisfy Muhlenberg's Low Church friend Henry Dana Ward. In his diary he summarized a sermon which he (Ward) preached in the Church of the Holy Communion:

> Never look on a picture and say "This is Jesus" — Never look on a Crucifix and say "This is Christ," neither kiss it nor bow before it. Jesus is glorified — no painter can set His likeness; Christ is glorified at the right hand of power on the throne of His Father and not on the Crucifix.
>
> The Dr. thanked me for my aid but regrets this notice of the "Crucifix;" lest it might be thought his people needed a caution. My reply was that all Christendom being infected with this error it is important to defend against the outward pressure even when no inward danger exists.
>
> The Dr. is naturally sensitive on this [matter?] from the existence of prejudice in the public mind. I am sorry to have hurt his sensibility; but every word was in harmony with the text and with Christian love.[72]

In his conception of the church also, Ward differed from Muhlenberg. Regarding a sermon he heard Muhlenberg preach, he wrote:

> The sermon was on the Kingdom of Christ on Earth. My spirit went with the preacher in all the current of his words until he came to say: "The hope of the world is the Church," from which I bolted, and the Doctor went on doubtfully to the end. It was a great sermon and only wanted the name *Christ* in place of "The Church" to have borne the Doctor and his hearers triumphantly together above the doubts of this sinful kingdom into the glorious liberty of the sons of God in the Kingdom of Heaven.[73]

When Muhlenberg presented his memorial to the House of Bishops in 1853 one of the pamphlets written on the subject agreed with the memorial's statement that the Episcopal church had failed to reach all sorts and conditions of men, but rejected the contention that it was the church's system that had failed; rather it was the rise of Puseyism that had caused people to suspect the Episcopal church and had thus retarded its growth. The writer of this pamphlet supported his argument by pointing out that the Tractarians had revived customs that had never before been used in the American church. In particular he singled out the practice of turning toward the communion table with the back to the congregation. He asserted, as did Ward, that this practice connived at the doctrine of transubstantiation. He further claimed that the leaders of the memorial movement were Tractarians and were trying to place the blame elsewhere in order to evade their own responsibility for the decline of the church's growth:

Let an American Churchman, of twenty years ago, or one who knows nothing of the changes since taken place in our church attend public worship
in the Church of the Holy Communion, in the City of New York, the amiable rector of which is understood to have taken the lead in the movement—will he find himself at home there? If he has ever witnessed the
service of the Church of Rome, will he be able to tell the difference? We
know there is a difference but would an unsophisticated man see it? Rely
upon it, his impression will be the impression of the whole American Protestant mind, in the presence of these exhibitions; and yet the mission of the
Protestant Episcopal Church of the United States is to the Protestant mind
of this country. Nothing can be more delicately sensitive than religious
sensitiveness, and the only safeguard of Protestantism is a jealousy of Rome.
We would not have it otherwise and we thank God for it.

We have been told, by an authority which puts the fact beyond doubt,
that a stranger in New York (a churchman) inquired the way on a Sunday
morning to St. Peter's Church, Twentieth St. and on his way made a mis-
take by going into the (Church of the) Holy Communion. After service he
asked what church it was; and declared that he thought it was a Papal
Church.[74]

The writer of the pamphlet later admitted that after reading Muhlenberg's *Exposition of the Memorial* he changed his mind about Muhlenberg
personally and realized that he was not a Tractarian but he believed
that Muhlenberg had unwittingly helped the Tractarians. He concluded
his second statement by saying in regard to Muhlenberg that "We are
glad, however, to observe that he will be on the side of Evangelical Catholicity which we ought to have known by the title and character of a
public journal he once had a hand in."[75]

The publication of *The Evangelical Catholic* in the years 1851–53—as
was noted in Chapter 7—helped to dispel the popular impression
that Muhlenberg was a Puseyite and it is in this paper that the first evidence appears of a trend altogether away from the Tractarian movement. *The Evangelical Catholic* in a long article, probably written by
Muhlenberg himself, described the growth of the Broad Church party
in England. Unlike the other parties this one had no organization and
no set doctrines or policies. It was more a state of mind than anything
else. Its one distinguishing characteristic, as opposed to the other parties, was that it upheld the comprehensive character of the Anglican
church, believing that this church could contain not only the catholicism
and protestantism represented by the older parties but liberalism or
modernism as well. Muhlenberg reprinted an article on church parties
from the *Edinburgh Review* and stated editorially that he was somewhat
disappointed in it because he had hoped that it would show how much
of their differences arose from mutual misunderstanding and confusion
of terms. This the article failed to do. Instead it merely caricatured the

old Evangelical party and the Tractarians. In Muhlenberg's opinion the writer had carried his fun too far. In both of these parties there were some of the most earnest men in the English church. In particular he believed that the writer should have mentioned Dr. Pusey whom Muhlenberg remembered so favorably from his interview in 1845. But the article's chief value according to Muhlenberg was its description of the Broad Church school for he declared that that movement could not be called a party:

> As a theological interest it is perhaps at present the major interest of the church. The Scholarship, the thought, the freedom, the eloquence in our church are moving in that line, are destined to reach a common, explicit consciousness essentially under that form. The exclusive, the self-satisfied, will stand by their old favorite formulas on the one side and on the other, while the fresher stream of life in the Church will sweep by in its force and leave them "High and Dry" or "Low and Slow." . . .
>
> This sketch of the Broad Church School . . . is quite to our mind, and we are glad to print it, as being very much what we should be content to accept as an exhibition of Evangelical Catholicism. "Broad Church" is not an inapposite term for a school or party marked by its comprehensiveness and we do not see why churchmanship may not be measured by latitude as well as altitude . . . though for our own part we should not choose to be considered Latitudinarian.
>
> One almost despairs of a Church thus marked by divisions and sub-divisions, in mutual conflict; but there is everything to hope for, as long as whether High or Low, Recordite or Tractarian, they are all content to say the same creeds, the same prayers, and read the Bible by the same calendar.[76]

On his second visit to England in 1853 Muhlenberg called on Frederick Dennison Maurice again and this time left a somewhat longer description of the Broad Church leader:

> Spent a pleasant hour with Maurice. He talks as he writes. They tell me his eyes resemble mine. Perhaps there is a likeness. I went on Sunday evening to his Bible Class for working men. He explained to them the third chapter of St. John's First Epistle having gone through the Gospel; he evidently felt at home in the writings of the beloved disciple and in an easy and familiar manner brought out the sense with great beauty. Afterwards the men asked him any questions they pleased and I was impressed at the intelligence and discrimination evinced. Maurice readily accepted them all with the meekness of wisdom. I accepted an invitation to breakfast with him next morning when I saw his family but had not much opportunity for conversation. He is a lovely man and just such as you would fancy from his books.[77]

The transition from sympathetic interest in the Tractarian movement—now generally referred to as the Anglo-Catholic party—to open opposition to it was a gradual one. Probably the most important alienating factor was the exclusiveness which Muhlenberg never accepted—an exclusiveness which unchurched all Protestant ministries. Ward states that:

> Dr. Muhlenberg preached a very fine sermon this morning in which he recognized the Lord's prophets in other sects and of every denomination known by their words and works—this was a degree of love not wholly expected, but much approved.[78]

Possibly the elaborate ritual introduced by the Anglo-Catholics was another element. Both Muhlenberg and the Anglo-Catholics derived their ideas about ritual from their contacts with the Roman Catholic church and they both wanted to introduce some beauty into the drab and dull services of their day but they developed quite different concepts of ritualism. The Anglo-Catholics regarded nineteenth-century Roman Catholic ritual as pure "Catholic" and this they uncritically superimposed on the services of the Book of Common Prayer. This ritual served to express their emphasis on the authority of the church, the priesthood, and the sacramental system.

Muhlenberg regarded ritual as a means to an end. It was one of the Catholic elements which he fitted into his concept of "Evangelical Catholicity." At his schools he used ritual to beautify the services. At the Church of the Holy Communion his ritual as well as liturgical experiments were designed to adapt the services of the church to the urban masses whom he was trying to reach. In this respect he anticipated many of the ideas of the modern liturgical movement. There is a widespread belief that his ritual was a result of his Lutheran background, but no evidence to support this belief has been found in the course of this research. On the contrary it appears that the Lutheran church of his boyhood was as simple in its ritual and as sermon-centered as the Episcopal.[79]

A third occasion for his turning against the Anglo-Catholics may have been the conversion to Roman Catholicism of several of his Anglo-Catholic colleagues. Among these were Bishop Levi Silliman Ives of North Carolina and Dr. John Murray Forbes of New York; also a former professor of St. Paul's College, Dr. Jebediah Huntington. The opposition of the old High Churchmen and Anglo-Catholics to his Memorial (see Chapter 8) may have been a further factor.

Muhlenberg never, however, took an extreme Protestant position in regard to the church. In a widely read sermon delivered at the Augustus Church, Trappe, Pennsylvania, the parish of his Lutheran ancestors, he criticized his Lutheran friends and relatives for having for the most part discarded the episcopate but pointed out that a few branches of the Lutheran church still retained it. The Lutherans at the time of the Reformation he said, were a liturgical church but they subsequently abandoned their liturgy. He then explained why he regarded the liturgy as such an extremely important part of the Episcopal church:

> True, we have adhered more constantly to our Liturgy — and would it not have been well (allow me to ask, as I do in the most brotherly spirit) if you also had adhered more constantly to yours — not to the exclusion of free prayer, but together with that, according to the practice of all the continental churches long after the Reformation, and to a great extent now, as also, I believe, in many of your congregations.

> It is not simply from partiality for that to which I am accustomed, that I think a Scriptural and unchanging service book greatly becomes a church, adoring her unchanging Lord. It secures the uniformity of her worship, and so manifests its unity in all her congregations. The Liturgy is her perpetual testimony of Jesus. (The English Liturgy is a grand witness for the objective faith of the whole church, while the Lutheran Hymns are a rich expression of the subjective faiths of individual believers. But each, of course, is more or less of the other.) It is a living creed, which, more than any dogmatic formulas, keeps alive the truth in the hearts and minds of the worshippers. Generation after generation takes it up unchanged. The Glorias and Litanies, uttered by our remotest ancestors, we repeat today, confident they will be the Glorias and Litanies, of the ages to come — the present church thus symbolizing and feeling her identity with the future and the past. "Never," says Mr. Cecil, "do I enter one of our old cathedrals without being deeply impressed with the thought, that for ages these vaults have resounded with the acclaim — 'Thou art the King of Glory, O Christ!'"

> Further, let me express my conviction (you will accord me the privilege of years) of the value of a Liturgy as a safeguard of the truth and a protection against lapsing into error. Without such inclosure, I cannot tell how far I might have been enticed by the subtleties of German rationalistic criticism, and of science falsely so-called, during a period of my ministry, peculiarly exposed to such danger. However it may be with others, I feel it a subject of devout gratitude to God that in the orderings of His providence my lot has been cast in a church, where I must needs confess "the Faith once delivered to the saints" — where it has not been left to my choice whether or not I should make the catholic ascription of glory to the Father, and to the Son, and to the Holy Ghost — where it has not been optional with me or my congregation, in offering our prayers, to plead the name of the One Mediator between God and man. Thankful am I that it did not rest with me to read or not as I pleased a set portion of God's Word to the people. Blessed constraint, if such it was, that whatever was the defect of my own discourses, the testimony of Jesus was proclaimed in the lessons, the psalms,

200

the creeds, and the prayers, so that the flock never went away unfed with the bread of life.

In this view of the subject, it is not mere Episcopalianism to maintain that in venerating our Liturgy we have done better than the reformed churches which have laid theirs aside. That cannot be, since, in all their important parts, the Liturgies are a common heritage from the early church. If you are offended by any among us, talking of *our* Te Deum, *our* Gloria in excelsis, you should excuse the ignorance occasioned by the disuse of those old treasures, and show by a practical appreciation of them that they are yours as much as ours.[80]

The war years 1861–1865 brought a lull in church affairs, and in 1865, when the war ended, Muhlenberg was a relatively old man. In his later years he was much engrossed in the affairs of St. Luke's Hospital and of a new project, St. Johnland, which he began the year the war ended (see Chapter 12). St. Johnland was to be a private enterprise under Episcopalian auspices but with the cooperation and participation of all Protestant denominations. Such a broad base was a far cry from the definitely denominational basis of his schools, the Church of the Holy Communion, and St. Luke's Hospital.

Muhlenberg intended the St. Johnland project to be, among other things, an example of his views on the church and its policy. The St. Johnland parish to which he gave the unique name of the Church of the Testimony of Jesus, was to be in communion with the Episcopal church, but certain rights and privileges were reserved since it was a private corporation not directly under the control of the church or supported by it. The first of these was "the Liberty of Conscience," by which the minister had the right to interpret the Scriptures according to his own private judgment and to omit anything from the services which, in his opinion, was contrary to the Scriptures. The second privilege was "the Liberty of Prayer," by which the minister had the right to compose additional prayers to supplement those of the prayerbook or to use extemporaneous prayers. Third, the minister had "the Liberty of Ministerial Fellowship," by which he had the right to invite ministers of Reformed and Evangelical churches to preach in the church from time to time.

These reservations placed Muhlenberg definitely on the Evangelical side in the controversies which followed the Civil War. The first reservation, "the Liberty of Conscience," undoubtedly related to the controversy over the doctrine of baptismal regeneration in which the Evangelicals wanted to drop certain words from the baptismal office which they believed were unscriptural. The second reservation, "the Liberty of Prayer," embodied the Evangelical desire to use extemporaneous prayer or to compose additional prayers, a liberty strongly opposed by High Churchmen. The third reservation reflected the desire of the Evangelicals to invite ministers of other Protestant churches to preach in their churches. Minor schisms were associated with two of these reservations. The attempt of a High Church bishop to prosecute a Low Church priest for dropping the words concerning regeneration from the baptismal office was a factor in bringing on the Reformed Episcopal schism of 1874. In 1908 the passage of a canon which allegedly relaxed restrictions on inviting ministers of other communions to preach in Episcopal churches led to the defection of a number of Anglo-Catholic clergy and laity to the Roman Catholic church.[81]

Two particularly sharp controversies occurred between Muhlenberg and Bishop Horatio Potter in 1865, the bitterness of which was probably increased by the fact that the two men had been friends. The first appears to have been caused by a misunderstanding. Muhlenberg loaned the Church of the Holy Communion to a group of German Lutherans for a service in the German Language, under the impression that he had obtained the consent of the bishop. The bishop apparently had not intended to give any such permission. Muhlenberg was further disconcerted when after criticizing him for his act the bishop permitted a priest of the Eastern Orthodox church to conduct services in an Episcopal church.[82] The incident was symptomatic of a resumption of party strife in the Episcopal church following the Civil War. Bishop Potter had been influenced by the Tractarian movement, particularly in its insistence on church order and discipline.[83] The old Evangelical party, on the other hand, was becoming increasingly fearful of this emphasis. In the same year a union service with several other denominations was conducted in New York by Dr. John Cotton Smith, an associate of Muhlenberg's, which was criticized in a pastoral letter by Bishop Horatio Potter. Replies to this pastoral were issued by several of the Evangelical clergy including besides Muhlenberg, Dr. John Cotton Smith and Dr. Stephen Tyng, Sr.[84]

Not only in practice but also in doctrine Muhlenberg moved away from his previous sympathy with Tractarianism. He refused to attend the consecration of his protégé, John Barrett Kerfoot, as bishop of Pittsburgh not only because of the distance and his advanced age but also because he felt repelled by some of the parts of the consecration service which he considered too narrow. Writing to Kerfoot in December, 1867, he said:

> You ask me to be present at your consecration. With all the love I bear you, I can hardly think of undertaking such a journey in midwinter, with my stay-at-home habits.

On one condition, however, I might. If, when you take that oath of conformity to the doctrine, discipline, etc. of the P.E. Church which in a narrow, sectistic spirit is made the first act in the consecration office... you
will make an audible reservation in words to this effect: "So long as I shall
believe that there is nothing in the same hindering my liberty and duty as
a bishop in the Universal Church of Christ," I should make an effort to
come and witness such an advance towards Catholic liberty in the Episcopate![85]

Three years later he wrote Kerfoot again:

You read about St. Johnland! and you'll read more. Please God, in the
same number of *Brotherly Words*. Before the year's out, you will have an
account of the dedication of St. Johnland — *one place in which our church will
not be a sect.* You pray against my church views — not very hard, I guess, for
you have so many badder things to pray against. . . .

I'll send you my talk at the Evangelical Conference in Philadelphia, in
which you will see what a good Catholic I am. Won't you put in for the
prize of $500 for the best tract on the unscripturalness of the doctrine of
the Apostolic Succession as held by a certain party in the Episcopal Church?[86]

Samuel Roosevelt Johnson, a High Churchman then living in New York,
wrote Kerfoot: "Our old friend, Dr. Muhlenberg, has the same conception of the Church as a Quaker."[87] Thus the evening of Muhlenberg's
life was clouded by the revival of party controversy. He read a paper
at an Evangelical conference in Philadelphia in 1869,[88] and his last
known public address was before the Evangelical Alliance in October,
1873.[89] The former paper defined his position with regard to the parties
within the Episcopal church, one not substantially different from that
he had held throughout his adult life, and refuted the statement of Dr.
Samuel Roosevelt Johnson, quoted above. First, discussing the meaning
of the word "Catholic" he says:

Our Church is Catholic in that she adheres to all of Faith, Doctrine, and
Order, which have been universal, always and from the beginning in the
"Holy Church throughout all the world." This is pure Catholicism, or primitive, seeing it embraces only that which has been held in the *Church from
the beginning.*

But Muhlenberg wrote on that "the primitive Catholic Church became corrupt and the reformation of the Sixteenth Century restored
primitive Catholicism." And this primitive Catholicism was what he
called "Evangelical Catholicism." It was necessary to make this distinction because in the popular mind the word Catholic was synonymous
with Roman Catholic.

Muhlenberg then raised the question of the value of Evangelical Catholicism when the Gospel itself was available. Its value, he replied, was that it was a corroboration of present understanding of the Gospel. "That which was the consent of all Christians in the earliest ages, touching the great facts and teachings of the Gospel can hardly have been wrong. Its universality and antiquity render its rightness in the highest degree probable."

A further value of Catholicism, Muhlenberg wrote, was in regard to institutions of the church. To these it could not give binding authority, but did accord invaluable testimony to their early existence:

> Thus, Infant Baptism, Episcopacy, the observance of the Christian Sabbath on the first day of the week and of the great memorial days of the Church, they have a hold upon us because of their 'Catholicity' over and above whatever ground we may find for them in the Scriptures. And as to the Scriptures themselves, how could we defend the accepted canon thereof independently of Catholicism?

In distinguishing between Catholicism and Evangelicism, he said, Catholicism was more objective, it considered the church as a visible and organized body, its minister an officer commissioned by external authority, its faith expressed in symbols, and its worship in forms and ceremonies. Evangelicism, on the other hand, was subjective for it dealt rather with the inward and spiritual. It viewed the church as the society of all true believers, the "blessed company of all faithful people." A minister of the Gospel was not ordained by man but had a call from the Lord. The various forms of worship were matters of comparative indifference as long as there was "worship in spirit and in truth." Further, Muhlenberg added:

> Agreeable to their distinction our Church is both Catholic and Evangelic— Catholic in adhering to the ancient documents of the faith; Evangelic in requiring the faith of the heart and immediately in Christ . . . as to her formulary, our Church is Catholic in her Creeds and liturgy, Evangelic in her articles and homilies, though both in each, Catholic in keeping to the Episcopate as the historic channel of the ministry, Evangelic in not denying the validity of ministers outside of that channel. Catholic as to the Sacraments in teaching that they are special means of grace, Evangelic in making faith in the recipient indispensable to their efficacy; Catholic in observing Holy Days and seasons, Evangelic in keeping those only of divine appointment and which relate to Christ and His apostles.

Both were essential to the church and mutually checked undersirable tendencies in the other. Without Evangelicism, Catholicism would degenerate into Romanism, and without Catholicism, Evangelicism would degenerate into the excess of private judgment, individualism, rationalism, and the infidel Christianity of his day. He suggested that Episcopalians keep the *via media,* not between Rome and Geneva but between genuine Catholic authority and the light and freedom of the Gospel. He went on to point out that in the advanced stage of criticism and science Episcopalians had advantages in the study of the scriptures unknown before his day. While they might thankfully approve such new light, they need not think this illumination throws all the bygone reading of the Bible into the dark.

So long as the church had Catholic safeguards—her creeds and liturgy, her festivals and feasts—he saw little danger from the Evangelical side that the church was in danger of drifting into latitudinarian heresy. Rather it was from the Catholic side that the church was in danger:

> It is then in our own Communion that we have Romanistic doctrine, worship, rite and ceremony, preaching and teaching, order and communities, catechisms and manuals of devotion, and what not, in extent of which the like, or a hundredth part, has never before been known. No one pretends that these un-Protestant phenomena are on the decrease.

To meet this danger, Muhlenberg proposed that if the church was to offer toleration to these trends it must also offer an equal toleration to the Evangelicals who took liberties with the church's doctrines, canons, and rubrics. Further he advocated the promotion of unity with other Protestant churches, fraternizing with other Protestant clergy, freedom of preaching in any place, liberty to use additional prayers in public worship, and the right to drop words or phrases from the services of the church that a clergyman believed contrary to the Scripture. Finally he proposed the organization of an Evangelical Catholic Union to promote these ideas.[90]

His speech before the Evangelical Alliance in 1873 was entitled "The Lord's Supper in its Relation to Christian Union." In it he advocated that Christians of various denominations receive communion in each other's churches. He commented on the fact that Protestant Christians were in the habit of receiving communion only in their own churches. He believed that Protestant Christians should make it a regular practice to receive communion in churches other than their own. When his speech was printed the following year he added a postscript in which he pointed out that a number of prominent Church of England clergymen together with Dr. George Cummins, the assistant bishop of Kentucky, had received communion in three different Presbyterian churches during the convention. Muhlenberg regarded this as a significant and encouraging fact "not the least of the good fruits of the Evangelical Alliance."[91]

The actions of these clergymen, however, loosed a storm of criticism from High Churchmen. At about the same time a Low Church clergyman in Chicago, Charles E. Chenney, was prosecuted by his bishop for omitting the word "regenerate" in the baptismal service—a practice that Muhlenberg provided for in the Directory of the church at St. Johnland which he was then building. As a result of these incidents and of the growing strength of the Anglo-Catholic party, a group of Evangelicals under the leadership of Bishop Cummins, seceded and founded the Reformed Episcopal church.[92] Muhlenberg although in sympathy with the grievances of these men was opposed to any secession.[93]

Muhlenberg's theology is central to his biography because it was the basis of his life and thought. Throughout his life he was consistently Evangelical but he freely used "Catholic" elements. He was therefore able to sympathize with the Tractarian movement without accepting all of its doctrines. Indeed, his development of the concept of Evangelical Catholicism was an attempt to merge these two systems. In later life he was repelled by the Anglo-Catholic party which developed out of the Tractarian movement and welcomed the emergence of the Broad Church movement. Despite his emphasis on Practical Christianity and his consistently Evangelical theology he is a significant figure in both the Catholic and Broad Church movements in the Episcopal church.

Muhlenberg's influence in the church was summed up thus by an Anglo-Catholic leader, George F. Seymour, who was professor of ecclesiastical history at the General Theological Seminary and later bishop of Springfield, Illinois:

> The Doctor's teaching, as far as I can recall the little of it which I was privileged to hear, implied and involved more than probably he himself knew at the time. He developed around him and within the range of his influence as a priest a depth and intensity of spiritual life which was far beyond the average in our Church of that day.[94]

CHAPTER 9

Toward Church Unity:
The Muhlenberg Memorial

The climax of Muhlenberg's life may well be regarded as the year 1853, for he then carried out the project with which his name is most frequently identified — the Muhlenberg Memorial. The fundamental purposes of the memorial in Muhlenberg's mind were the promotion of Christian unity and the reform of the church along lines that he had been advocating, but they led to developments that probably not even he anticipated.

In considering the divided and distracted state of American Protestantism Muhlenberg may have seen a basis for Christian unity in an incident in his own family history. His granduncle, Peter Muhlenberg — who has earlier appeared as the leader of the English language party in Philadelphia — entered the Lutheran ministry as a young man and was assigned a church in Virginia. Upon arriving there he found that the Lutheran parish required that its ministers be ordained in the Established English church so that the parish could be supported by taxation. With the consent of both Anglican and Lutheran authorities he went to London and was there ordained deacon and priest in the Anglican church by the bishop of London. On this occasion one of the other persons ordained was William White of Philadelphia.[1]

William Augustus Muhlenberg knew of this incident as well as of the rather close relationship between the Lutheran and Anglican clergymen in colonial America. He knew that a German Lutheran synod had made it a policy never to open an English-speaking Lutheran church in any community where an Anglican parish was located but merely advised its members to become members of the local Anglican church. He also knew that there had been a considerable interchange of Anglican and Lutheran clergymen in the colonial period.[2]

Muhlenberg grew to manhood in Philadelphia which had a wider variety of religious groups than any other American city and he came into personal contact with many of them: The Episcopal church in which he grew up; the Quaker faith of his first school and of his friends Dr. George B. Wood and Roberts Vaux; the Roman Catholic Church whose services he sometimes attended as a boy and a college student and which was the faith of his college friend, James Keating; the Lutheran church, the faith of his relatives and of Christian Crusé; and the staunch Presbyterianism of his first college friend, Joseph Engles.

Some years later in his valedictory sermon at Lancaster he remarked:

> Let the harmony continue which has existed between yourselves and your brethren of other denominations. Hitherto it has gone on delightfully. May it not be interrupted. Why should Christians quarrel about the little points in which they differ, instead of loving each other for the great ones wherein they agree? They all profess to be on the road to heaven, strange they should go fighting along the way. If we are children of the same Father, traveling toward the same home, and hoping to sit down, at last, to the same banquet, let us "love as brethren."[3]

As early as 1835 while still at Flushing he published a pamphlet entitled "Hints on Catholic Union" in which he suggested that the Episcopal church take the lead in promoting the union of all Protestant churches. This proposal is extremely important for it presents his ideas on Christian unity at an early date and is fundamental to an understanding of his later memorial to the House of Bishops and subsequent unity proposals. It is therefore necessary to discuss "Hints on Catholic Union" in some detail.

The first step toward unity, Muhlenberg said, would be the formation of a confederacy among the leading Protestant churches somewhat analogous to our federal government. If such a union should not be strong enough for all the important objects that would be desirable, it would be at least a nucleus of union. It would make the common ground of Protestants a visible and tangible thing and would be a catholic basis on which, from time to time, might be erected all the superstructure of a visible Catholic church.

The essential articles of agreement in the confederacy would relate to doctrine, the ministry, and public worship. As far as doctrine was concerned Muhlenberg saw no great difficulty. Nothing would be easier than to frame a set of articles asserting the fundamental doctrines of the Gospel to which nine-tenths of the Protestant world would assent. These articles would be based on the Apostles' Creed, but since this creed was too general it could be expanded to include the distinctively Protestant doctrine of the divinity and atonement of Jesus Christ, the fallen condition of man, the regeneration and sanctification of the soul by the Holy Spirit, the justification of the sinner by faith in Christ alone, and good works the necessary fruit of faith. Such primary doctrines would be adopted by Lutherans, Episcopalians, Presbyterians, Methodists, Baptists, the United Brethren, and others.

The chief obstacle to union would be in relation to the ministry. A mutual acknowledgment among the confederate churches of the full authority of their respective ministers and of the validity of their ministration would be essential to union. But the greatest difficulty arose from the various channels of an external commission to the ministry. Some churches place their channels in the presbytery, some in the congregation, and some in the episcopacy. The solution of this problem as Muhlenberg saw it was for all the churches to adopt that form of ordination "which all believe to be sufficient and not repugnant to the Word of God." He offered no arguments about the relative merits of the various forms of ordination. The single point to be determined should be: what form of ordination was acknowledged to be valid by all and might be received by all without any sacrifice of conscience. If no such ordination could be found then Muhlenberg admitted that union was impossible. But he firmly believed that a council of the churches keeping firmly to the above policy could find one.

Once a common ordination formula was found clergymen already ordained could be asked in the interest of unity to submit to a conditional reordination according to the agreed upon formula. New clergymen would all be ordained according to the formula and all would therefore be accepted as true ministers in all the churches. Christians of the different denominations could then listen to ministers of any denomination and on special occasions could receive Communion together.

Unity in public worship, Muhlenberg thought, might not be expedient immediately and certainly it was not essential. Each church could continue its own policy. But a common liturgy would be such a strong bond that one might well be developed which would incorporate biblical sources and common hymns while each church might use its own forms in addition.

Muhlenberg then turned to a consideration of union from the viewpoint of Episcopalians. The promotion of unity might be shown to be their peculiar duty, although two groups in the Episcopal church might not agree with this statement. The first would be those who believed that the Episcopal church was divinely ordered in every respect and who would oppose any union unless all other churches adopted every tenet, rite, and ceremony of the Episcopal church. A second group would not assert these exclusive claims but believed that the Episcopal church had only a restricted role to play in American Christianity. Other churches would better reach the masses of the people while the Episcopal church's mission was to the more staid, settled, educated, and reflecting part of the community operating as a barrier to enthusiasm and fanaticism. And if the Episcopal church was not as active as some of her younger sisters, neither was she as wild. This second group, Muhlenberg conceded, could not be interested in unity; they saw sufficient unity already. Where several churches were carrying on the work of the Gospel each in their own way, one did what another would not, or could not, and the generous rivalry among them produced far more fruit than would ever spring from union. Let us then, they said, be satisfied that we are right and not feel obliged to tell our neighbors that they are wrong.

The majority of Episcopalians did not fit into either of the above categories, Muhlenberg said. They were not opposed to union. This majority distinguished between the principles and the practices of the church. The principles they considered unalterable; the practices, a beautiful and edifying application of these principles, but not in their nature unalterable. The principles of the Episcopal church as Muhlenberg saw them were:

> First: the Doctrines of the Gospel as taught in the thirty-nine articles, including the leading principle, that the Scriptures alone are the rule of faith.
> Second: the obligation of adhering to Episcopacy as the channel of the ministry, and derived by succession from the Apostles.
> Third: the expediency, sanctioned by scriptural precedent, and the earliest usage, of precomposed prayer in some established liturgy.

Episcopalians are not being asked to give up their principles. Thus, in regard to episcopacy: having received it, as they believe, in a line of unbroken descent from the Saviour and His Apostles, they are not at liberty to recognize the conveyance of the ministry through any other medium. *They would cheerfully accede to one admitting it,* although considerable compromise was demanded in matters not involving a sacrifice of principle. Nor do these people believe that the Episcopal church is an aristocracy in American Christianity. They believe that the church should be extended on the basis of "Evangelical truth, and Apostolic order."

Muhlenberg therefore proposed that bishops be authorized to ordain men who did not accept the whole theological system of the Episcopal church. Bishops would be authorized to perform two types of ordination:

Candidates for the ministry in that Church will be ordained on the present terms of entire conformity to all its requirements, and this would be an act of the bishop in his double office, – as the minister of Christ and the chief officer of a particular body. Candidates for the ministry at large (to be amenable, however, to some ecclesiastical tribunal), or in other evangelical churches, might be ordained on the single condition of due qualification and soundness in the faith; and this would be an act of the bishop, simply in his office as a bishop of the Church Catholic and Apostolical. Not more than two or three omissions in the office of the ordinal for the ordering of priests and deacons, as they now stand, would be required by such an arrangement.

Muhlenberg then returned to the earlier problem of a form of ordination that would be acceptable to all denominations. This form should be episcopal ordination, he argued. Arguments based for or against episcopacy as a primitive and apostolic institution should be waived. Instead the following facts should be pointed out: 1) nine-tenths of all Christian ministers since the foundation of the church had episcopal ordination; 2) in the early ages heretics as well as Catholics adhered to episcopal ordination; 3) all who had it professed to have received it by transmission from the earliest ages, and the line of succession cannot be shown to end anywhere below the Apostles; 4) if the case for episcopacy could not be decided on the basis of the New Testament alone, early ecclesiastical history rather turned the scale in its favor; 5) eminent Christians favored it and those who opposed it did so because it appeared in the form of a corrupt prelacy or in alliance with political abuses. Thus Episcopalians should not be charged with bigotry if they urged their own form of ordination as a basis of unity but they were open to the charge if they required entire conformity to all the prescription of their particular sect when they offered episcopal ordination.

Muhlenberg then took up the problem of joint ordination which he had proposed as a basis of unity. This could be accomplished in two ways: either the candidate might be ordained first in one church and then in another or there might be ordaining councils composed of duly authorized ministers of the several churches.

Thus in each of our large cities, there might be such a council, consisting of two or three presbyters of the Presbyterian Church, the same from the Lutheran, Baptist or other churches, together with a bishop and two presbyters of the Episcopal Church. By this method all would meet on a perfect equality and there would be no compromise of principle. Each church would consider its own minister alone as sufficient, but would consent to the assistance of others to give validity to the act in the eyes of all.

211

Muhlenberg concluded his paper with a section entitled "The Catholic Spirit of the Episcopal Church." He pointed out that the Articles and liturgy of the Episcopal church are broad and comprehensive, deliberately designed to include as many points of view as possible and to give the fullest scope to a man's own reason and conscience under the guidance of the Holy Spirit. Muhlenberg further listed the great Protestant divines of the Church of England who were the common property of all Protestantism and concluded his article:

> The Catholic spirit of the Episcopal Church might be further shown in the enlightened liberty which generally characterizes her members. But on this head the writer forbears lest he be betrayed into an overestimate of the virtue of his brethren. He thinks he can say much for his Church as a center of union among Protestants, in several respects: but he is equally sure much might also be said by others for theirs.

Muhlenberg appended to the paper the "Introductory Essay" from Jeremy Taylor's *Liberty of Prophesying* and in a prefatory note said:

> An enlightened spirit of toleration must be at the foundation of all schemes of Christian union. But on that subject the attention of the reader has been reserved for the eloquent enforcement of it in the following extracts from the "Liberty of Prophesying." As this work of Jeremy Taylor has never been printed in America, the writer is sure that for this part of it, at least, his book is not unworthy of circulation.[4]

"Hints on Catholic Union," Muhlenberg says, was received rather harshly and he therefore dropped these ideas for the time being.[5] The year 1835 was not the most propitious time to bring forward a unity proposal because the High Church–Low Church controversy was still smouldering and the Tractarian movement was just beginning. Some years later when he came to New York he probably found the time and place more opportune to revive this proposal. As noted in Chapter 8 on the Tractarian movement, Muhlenberg defined his conception of the position of the Episcopal church on the controversial subject of the ministry in terms which the Tractarians might approve without passing judgment on the validity of Protestant ministries. His sermons at the Church of the Holy Communion, printed under the title of *Pastoral Tracts* (see Chapter 8), are therefore an important part of his continuing discussion of the subject of unity.

Upon assuming the editorship of *The Evangelical Catholic,* he began to explore the subject again. Scattered through the paper were such items as the following: "A friend, calling upon Archbishop Leighton one day, and not meeting him at home, learnt on inquiry, that he was gone to visit a sick Presbyterian minister, on a horse which he had borrowed from a Roman Catholic priest."[6]

In an editorial in *The Evangelical Catholic* to contributors of letters he wrote:

We cannot admit communications in which the religious bodies around us are not spoken of with Christian courtesy — "Ranting Methodists" "Bigoted Puritans" "Lying Papists" etc. is not the language suited to our taste to say the least of it. It savors of a want of charity, and even if it be true, where is the good of it? Do "Churchmen" expect to convert their "dissenting" brethren by calling them ugly names?

And in particular taking issue with the High Church party in the Episcopal church he wrote:

Most especially ought they who hold that our Church is the one and only Church in the land, to speak and act with the dignity which becomes such a belief — and which indeed would be natural if it really were their belief. People of ancient and illustrious families are generally remarkable for their civility to inferiors. They do not think it necessary to be always asserting their own superior standing in society, by deriding that of all others. It is folks who are just getting up in the world that are prone to be contemptuous towards their neighbors, and sensitive to every thing said against them. They feel that they are rivals who they affect to despise. If our church be *the* Church, then in proportion as her members are sure of it, they can afford to let the societies *think* they are churches; and if they wish to convince them of their error, they will attempt it by some more promising methods than the use of unchurchlike language. "But they are not very courteous towards us." "Very true — and what then?" Is "tit for tat" our church's rule? Abusive epithets are the petty anathemas of the spirit of Sect.[7]

To a discussion of religious controversy *The Evangelical Catholic* contributed this:

From the appearance of things it is not altogether improbable that the Church will find peace only through some awful pressure from without. In Germany, where the contest has been for the last seventy years between Christianity and infidelity, Christians have, in their zeal and labors to defend the Truth, forgotten the very serious differences among themselves. Hence, even Roman Catholic and Protestant polemics have assumed a degree of gentleness, of frankness, of courtesy, such as is not found either in England or America. Occasionally disputants among ourselves are enabled to treat each other handsomely and with a truly Christian spirit, but the rule is to doubt a man's orthodoxy unless he pours forth

213

vituperation and abuse upon an opponent, Be he Protestant or Roman Catholic, the viler his language, the louder are the plaudits of the party with which he is identified. He who calls the Romanist or the Puseyites, or the Evangelicals, or the Rationalists, the most abominable names is regarded as the bravest and firmest man among his fellow partisans. Think of the transition from the Bible to our ordinary theological polemics—nay of the transition from Leighton to the religious newspapers of the day.

It may be that the bigotry, the intolerance, the narrowmindedness, the zeal for words, which all are rending the Church at this moment, will go on and increase, until the force of some mighty form of infidelity will bid us be silent and lay aside our animosities and turn to the study of truth with a new spirit.

It may be that Christians will be whipped into charity—will be forced to love each other, and as a consequence, to listen kindly to what opposite schools have to say of Christian doctrine. Certainly we are moving within a circle of contradiction. We end where we begin. We are whirled round and round in assertions and denials—which tend to sever hearts and widen the breach already existing between Belief and Practice. Christian doctrine will grow less and less important to the minds of all unprofessional men. They will regard it just as legal and political abstractions are regarded now—entirely of no value for a man to live by. Bigots upon all sides are exclaiming against Latitudinarianism, and they are at present on the highway just to this goal. They are making ready the advent of Anti-Christ, in a new form. It is impossible for them to save the Church from spiritual lethargy—they account a man "good and true," just in as far as he swears in the words which they idolize. We need something very unlike what is at hand among us. And how are we to "have and hold" this something? This is the question.[8]

Muhlenberg again brought before the church public through the columns of *The Evangelical Catholic* the proposal he had made in his *Hints on Catholic Union*. He also began a campaign to broaden the forty-fifth canon, passed in 1832, which if strictly enforced would prohibit any experimentation in public worship, extemporaneous preaching, use of prayers or services not in the prayer book, simplified services, or any prayers for special occasions.[9] This canon was difficult enough for clergymen in established parishes and was a major impediment in carrying on church work in the western areas or among the masses in the cities. It also strengthened the distinctively class character of the Episcopal church for it automatically restricted the services to those who could read and those who could be reached by a liturgical service. It was probably a reflection of the fear of "enthusiasm" which was traditional to Anglicanism and a reaction to the revivalism that was so strong in the United States in the nineteenth century. This canon was also strongly supported by the High Church party which feared that any relaxation in its restrictions would be used by the Low Church party to promote evangelical practices.

The theological atmosphere of 1853 on the whole was more favorable to a proposal for Church unity and a relaxation of canon forty-five than 1835 when Muhlenberg first published "Hints on Catholic Union." The violence of the controversy aroused by the Tractarian movement was spending itself and the Episcopal church was becoming accustomed to the presence of the Anglo-Catholic party in its membership. Likewise, Muhlenberg, through his editorials in *The Evangelical Catholic* was no longer closely identified with any one party in the popular mind[10] and his leadership in establishing church institutions had won for him a measure of respect from members of all parties. Even his strongest opponents had to preface their arguments by an expression of their admiration for his good works.[11] Public opinion may also have been prepared for a concrete move in the direction of church unity by the appearance of a book by Muhlenberg's friend Bishop Thomas H. Vail of Kansas. This book entitled *The Comprehensive Church or, Christian Unity and Ecclesiastical Unity in the Protestant Episcopal Church* first published in 1841 held that the Episcopal church should take the lead in promoting unity because it alone was comprehensive enough to contain all theological positions held by American Protestants.[12] Bishop Vail's views were endorsed by Muhlenberg in his answer to Ellie Bowman when she asked his advice on the bishop's proposal of marriage (see Chapter 8).

Dr. Edwin Harwood, a close associate during the 1850's, wrote that the idea of a memorial to the House of Bishops had been germinating in Muhlenberg's mind for some time. The favorable atmosphere of the church in these years may have encouraged him. Furthermore, his own mind was now made up on various issues as to which he had formerly been somewhat uncertain.[13] By 1853 Jackson Kemper on a visit to New York in October of that year was able to write:

> Dr. Muhlenberg... took me into his study and read to me a petition he had drawn up and addressed to the Bishops in reference to Catholic Unity or rather opening the doors to the admission of various persons into our ministry without requiring conformity in all things and which he will probably get some of the clergy to sign and then read it to the House of Bishops.[14]

The petition to which Jackson Kemper referred was a memorial to the House of Bishops to be presented at the General Convention in 1853. This memorial first cited:

> The divided and distracted state of our American Protestant Christianity; the new and subtle forms of unbelief, adapting themselves with fatal suc-

cess to the spirit of the age; and the consolidated forces of Romanism, bearing with renewed skill and activity against the Protestant Faith; and, as more or less the consequence of these, the utter ignorance of the Gospel among so large a portion of the lower classes of our population making a heathen world in our midst;

The memorialists then raised the question as to whether the Episcopal church as then constituted was able to cope with these problems. They answered this question in the negative and thereupon proposed:

That a wider door must be opened for admission to the Gospel ministry than that through which her candidates for holy orders are now obliged to enter. Besides such candidates among her own members, it is believed that men can be found among the other bodies of Christians around us who would gladly receive ordination at your hands could they obtain it without entire surrender, which would now be required of them, of *all* the liberty in public worship to which they have been accustomed; men who could not bring themselves to conform in all particulars to our prescriptions and customs but yet are sound in the faith, and who having the gifts of preachers and pastors, would be able ministers of the New Testament.... The extension of orders to the class of men contemplated (with whatever safeguards, not infringing on evangelical freedom, which your wisdom might deem expedient), appears to your petitioners to be a subject supremely worthy of your deliberations.

In addition to helping the Church meet her responsibilities such a plan would be an important step toward Christian unity:

To become a central bond of union among Christians, who though differing in name, yet hold to the one Faith, the one Lord, and more primitive fellowship, is here believed to be the peculiar province and high privilege of your venerable body as a College of Catholic and Apostolic Bishops....

The memorialist concluded with a request that the proposal be submitted to a commission for further study. It was signed by twelve clergymen: W. A. Muhlenberg, C. F. Cruse, Phillip Berry, Edwin Harwood, G. T. Bedell, Henry Gregory, Alex H. Vinton, M. A. DeWolfe Howe, S. H. Turner, S. R. Johnson, C. W. Andrews, F. E. Lawrence "and others." In addition five more signed a postscript stating that they agreed with the main purpose of the memorial but could not agree with certain suggestions in it. They did join in the request that it be submitted to a commission. These signers with qualifications were John Henry Hobart, A. Cleveland Coxe, Ed Y. Higbee, Francis Vinton, Isaac C. Hubbard "and others."[15]

The division between those who signed without qualification and those who signed with some qualification is significant. The former were

216

for the most part close friends of Muhlenberg and Low or Broad Churchmen. C. F. Crusé was Muhlenberg's old college friend, member of the faculty of the Flushing Institute, and now librarian of the General Theological Seminary. Phillip Berry was rector of the Church of the Ascension, Esopus, Ulster County, New York. Edwin Harwood was rector of the Church of the Incarnation, New York City, a former associate editor of *The Evangelical Catholic,* and was later to become a leader of the Broad Church party and a pioneer in the introduction of biblical criticism. G. T. Bedell was rector of the Church of the Ascension, New York City, an alumnus of the Flushing Institute, and later became Bishop of Ohio. He was a militant Low Churchman. Henry Gregory was rector of St. James Church, Syracuse, New York. Alex H. Vinton was rector of St. Paul's Church, Boston, Massachusetts. M. A. DeWolfe Howe was rector of St. Luke's Church, Philadelphia, and later became bishop of Central Pennsylvania, now the diocese of Bethlehem. S. H. Turner had started out in the ministry in Philadelphia with Muhlenberg and was now professor of biblical learning and the interpretation of Scripture in the General Theological Seminary. S. R. Johnson was a former member of the faculty of the Flushing Institute and was now professor of Systematic Divinity at the General Theological Seminary. He was the only member of this group who could be called a High Churchman. C. W. Andrews was rector of Trinity Church, Shepherdstown, Virginia. F. E. Lawrence was Muhlenberg's assistant at the Church of the Holy Communion. He came from Flushing, was an alumnus of the Flushing Institute, and might be called a Broad Churchman.

The five who signed "with qualification" were all High Churchmen and were acquaintances rather than friends of Muhlenberg. John Henry Hobart, the son of Bishop Hobart, was on the staff of Trinity Church, whose rector was an opponent of the Memorial. Hobart was also on the board of trustees of St. Luke's Hospital. A. Cleveland Coxe was rector of St. John's Church, Hartford, Connecticut, and had family connections with the Church of the Holy Communion, and later became bishop of Western New York. Ed Y. Higbee, was assistant at Trinity Church, New York. Francis Vinton was rector of Grace Church, Brooklyn Heights, New York, and Isaac S. Hubbard of St. Michael's, Manchester, New Hampshire.[16] An interesting example of the way the Episcopal church divided on party lines in one family appeared among the signers. A. H. Vinton, a Low Churchman, signed without qualifications while his brother, Francis Vinton, who had High Church leanings, signed with qualifications.[17] The net effect of this division among the signers was to place the memorial above party in the public mind.

A comparison of the style of Muhlenberg's writings with that of the memorial clearly indicates that this document was drawn up either by

217

someone other than Muhlenberg or by a group. The artificial ecclesiastical style is definitely not Muhlenberg's despite the fact that the ideas in the memorial can be duplicated in his writings. It may have been drawn up in this style to please the High Churchmen who signed the memorial with qualifications.

The convention met in Trinity Church and St. John's Chapel, New York City, from October 5 to October 26, 1853. The memorial was presented to the House of Bishops on October 18, 1853 by Muhlenberg's friend, Jonathan Wainwright, provisional bishop of New York.[18] It should be remembered that Bishop Wainwright was a friend of long standing. He had been on the faculty of St. Paul's College and was acting head of the college when Muhlenberg took his trip to Europe. He had also been one of the clergymen who went with Muhlenberg to call on Bishop Onderdonk in regard to the bishop's alleged improprieties, and more recently had collaborated with Muhlenberg in drawing up *The Choir and Family Psalter.*

The memorial immediately provoked controversy in the House of Bishops. Jackson Kemper wrote in his Diary: "A paper from Dr. Muhlenberg, etc. warm dicussion—opposed by Meade, Doane, D. L. Eastburn; advocated by Johns, Burgess, Potter, Wainwright and Whittingham."[19] The non-partisan character of the memorial was again evident for party lines were split even in this preliminary debate. Of those opposed, Bishop George W. Doane of New Jersey was a militant High Churchman. The other two opponents were Bishop William Meade of Virginia, and Bishop D. L. Eastburn of Massachusetts who were equally militant Low Churchmen. Of those who spoke in favor, Bishop Whittingham of Maryland was a strong High Churchman; bishops Burgess of Maine, Alonze Potter of Pennsylvania, and Jonathan Wainwright of New York were moderates; and Bishop John Johns of Virginia was strongly Low Church. Bishop Doane had once approached Muhlenberg to have a branch of St. Paul's College established in his Diocese but Muhlenberg had turned him down fearing too much ecclesiastical control. Muhlenberg, however, had the invitation of Bishop Whittingham, another High Churchman, to found St. James' College in the diocese of Maryland. Another proponent and a moderate, Bishop Wainwright, who introduced the memorial, has been described above.[20]

Probably the most significant name among those in the opening debate is that of Alonzo Potter. As bishop of Pennsylvania he took the lead in establishing church institutions and had an influence in Philadelphia similar to that of Muhlenberg in New York. He founded a church hospital in Philadelphia which was in actual operation before St. Luke's and he also founded an Evangelical sisterhood. He took such an active part in the memorial movement that some sources regard him rather than Muhlenberg as its leader.[21]

Bishop George Burgess of Maine moved that the memorial be referred to a special commission of five and this was seconded by Bishop N. H. Cobbs of Alabama.[22] The motion did not come to a vote until October 24 when twenty bishops voted in favor and four opposed. Of the four opposed William Meade of Virginia and Martin Eastburn of Massachusetts have been described. George W. Freeman was missionary bishop of the Southwest and a High Churchman.[23] William H. DeLancey is the most interesting opponent. He began his ministry, like Muhlenberg, as an assistant to Bishop White in Philadelphia and was called by the trustees of the University of Pennsylvania to be provost when they deposed Dr. Beasley. He it was who restored order at that university. The twenty bishops who voted in favor of the resolution included High Churchmen, Low Churchmen, and middle-of-the-roaders. Since the bishops, both those in favor and those opposed, came from all parts of the country and from both parties, the memorial immediately became a national issue transcending party and sectional lines.

The committee on the memorial consisted of James H. Otey of Tennessee, a moderate High Churchman who was chairman; Alonzo Potter of Pennsylvania, a Broad Churchman; George Burgess of Maine, a moderate; John Williams, Bishop Coadjutor of Connecticut, a High Churchman; and Jonathan Wainwright of New York who has been described above.[24] On motion of George Freeman of the Southwest territory who had opposed the appointment of the commission a sixth bishop was added to the commission, this motion being seconded by William M. Green of Mississippi. On motion of Carlton Chase of New Hampshire the sixth bishop named to the commission was George W. Doane of New Jersey, a militant High Churchman.[25] Of the six bishops on the Commission only James Otey of Tennessee had been present but had not voted on the motion establishing the commission. He was an acquaintance of Muhlenberg and had visited St. Paul's College. Bishops Wainwright and Potter have already been described. Muhlenberg once mentioned Bishop Burgess as a supporter of the memorial. Bishop Williams of Connecticut was a High Churchman. Bishop Doane was a militant High Churchman and had opposed accepting the memorial. The commission was therefore fairly representative of the composition of the House of Bishops on party and geographical lines.[26]

The first meeting of the commission took place in St. Peter's Church, New York, on June 29, 1854 and subsequent meetings were scheduled for Hartford, Connecticut, in October, 1854, Savannah, Georgia, in February, 1855, and Philadelphia, in May, 1855. No information has been found as to how many of these meetings were actually held but there were several. Samuel Roosevelt Johnson, one of the signers of the memorial, was appointed secretary of the commission. He subsequently resigned and Daniel Kerdig of Philadelphia was elected in his place.

All members of the commission were present at its first meeting but Bishop Wainwright died shortly thereafter thus reducing the membership to five.[27] In order to obtain the opinion of the church at large on the issues raised by the memorial, the commission compiled a questionnaire which was sent out to a representative group of Episcopal clergy and laity and of clergy of other denominations.[28] In view of the facts that (a) the most active member of the commission was Bishop Alonzo Potter, Muhlenberg's friend, (b) most of the other members of the commission were friends or acquaintances, and (c) the questionnaire not only covered the issues raised by the memorial but all those Muhlenberg had been raising throughout his life, it seems a fair assumption that he himself had a hand in the drafting. The questionnaire is therefore given below in full:

1. Can the present method of preparing young men for the ministry in the P.E. Church be improved, in respect to learning, piety, intellectual power, or practical efficiency? If yes, please state how. Mention any remarkable facts respecting the training of ministers whom you have known to be especially useful and efficient.

2. Could any change be advantageously made in the prevalent character of our preaching? If yes, state what, and by what means. What modes of instruction, besides sermons from the pulpit, have you found especially beneficial and effective?

3. How can the influence of our ministry be made to reach the multitudes now living without the Gospel in our own land and neighborhood, (a) by social intercourse, (b) by extra-parochial services, (c) by philanthropic labours, etc. etc.

4. Ought we, or ought we not, to have itinerating Evangelists, as well as settled Pastors; also permanent Deacons, and a portion of the clergy more especially devoted to theological and Biblical studies?

5. Can any method for division of labour be suggested, by which persons of marked ability in a certain line shall have their useful gift especially exercised to the edification of the Church; and by which ministers thrown out of parish life may yet be advantageously occupied?

6. Is our present system of family, Sunday School, and catechetical instruction and training chargeable with any serious defects? If yes, please state them; suggest your opinion respecting the proper remedy.

7. Ought or ought not our parish Churches in large towns to be opened more frequently on the Lord's day; and to different congregations at different hours?

8. What can be done for the religious instruction of boys when they leave Sunday School?

9. Do the laymen and laywomen of our congregations cooperate sufficiently with the pastor in the work of winning souls? How can that co-operation be safely increased?

10. How can a spirit of true brotherly intercourse among our members be promoted?
11. Ought not young men to be seen in our churches in much larger numbers? Please suggest means.
12. How can the proper influence of our church over men engrossed in business be secured?
13. By what specific means can we increase adequately the pecuniary contributions of Churchmen to the work of evangelizing our own land, and the world at large? Do we instruct our people sufficiently on the dangers and responsibilities involved in the possession of property?

II

1. Could changes be advantageously made in our Liturgical services?
    (a) By lengthening, shortening, or dividing?
    (b) By adapting the lessons, anthems, etc., better to the different ecclesiastical seasons?
    (c) By a larger number of special.services and prayers for special occasions?
    (d) By a larger discretion in the use of hymns, and other sacred music?
    (e) By services specially fitted for missionary work at home or abroad?
    (f) By allowing the authorities of each Diocese larger liberty?
2. Ought the conditions now imposed on candidates who have been licensed or ordained in other Protestant communions, be relaxed?
    (a) as to term of time?
    (b) degree of conformity to the worship, discipline, etc., of the P.E. Church?
3. Should the conditions on which ministers are admitted to orders be prescribed exclusively by the General Convention?
4. Are any facts known to you indicating a preference, on the part of ministers of other Protestant bodies, for Episcopal ordination, if it were in their power?
5. Are any facts known to you indicating on the part of the members of such bodies, a disposition to make any sacrifices of sectarian feeling for the sake of restoring unity?
6. Are our Liturgical services, and the discretion accorded to our several Dioceses, as free as they were in the early Church?
7. Ought the Church to make better provision for training teachers, nurses, etc.?
8. Ought it to afford its female members who have leisure and inclination for benevolent labours, any more systematic means of pursuing them, than exist at present?[29]

Between the convention of 1853 and that of 1856 a vigorous pamphlet war ensued[30] in which Muhlenberg took an active part. He first published the memorial in pamphlet form in 1853 and then published an *Exposition of the Memorial of Sunday Presbyters of the Protestant Episcopal Church* "by one of the memorialists." This pamphlet appeared a year after the memorial was presented and four months after the first meeting of the commission. Since he was writing the pamphlet under his own signature he was able to give a definite presentation of his own views on the memorial.[31]

The pamphlet was intended, Muhlenberg wrote, to be a contribution to that discussion which it was a purpose of the memorial to stimulate. In order to come to any conclusion or to any progress in the consideration of the questionnaire, there must be free and open comparison of views genuinely entertained by differing yet honest minds. The memorial and this exposition of it were based on his matured judgment since he had proposed the same ideas in his essay on catholic union in 1835. He might have added that much of the material that he used in this and succeeding pamphlets is to be found in *The Evangelical Catholic,* which ceased publication about the time he presented the memorial.

Muhlenberg contended that it was an acknowledged fact that the Protestant Episcopal church was not effectual in dispensing the Gospel to all sorts and conditions of men. He discussed the distinctively class position of the Episcopal church in terms almost repetitive of the articles in *The Evangelical Catholic* and "Hints on Catholic Union." "But what can we do about this situation?" he asked. Two courses were open to the bishops in order to their having room for the exercise of their Episcopal commission in its Catholic context. The first was to bring about changes in the system and administration of the church which are lets and hindrances to her efficient action. The second was for the bishops over and above their duty to their communion, and leaving its system untouched, to act upon some broad and more comprehensive system.

To carry out the first course of changing the system he suggested the restoration of the old minor orders of the ministry or their equivalent, such as subdeacons, readers, catechists, etc. — inferior ecclesiastics, who by having also some temporal calling, could serve the church without taxing it. The advantage would thus be obtained of the lay agency so largely employed among our Protestant brethren. (It should be remembered that Joseph Engles, Muhlenberg's friend, had become a colporteur among the Presbyterians.) Second, in the matter of public worship much might be done by setting forth shorter services and a larger variety of them — by allowing a discretionary use of parts of the prayer Book and also, within certain limits, "free" prayer.

Muhlenberg admitted that it was easy to suggest measures by which the church's adaptability and popular efficiency might be increased but less so to secure a sufficient agreement to secure their adoption. Both party feeling and the conservative character of the church would resist change. Thus it was unlikely that the church by legislation would ratify what the memorial confessed to be its ultimate scope and design—the reunion of Protestant Christianity. But the memorial looked to a higher end—an end that required the adoption of the second of the two courses proposed.

Muhlenberg then advanced the plan which he had previously suggested in *Hints on Catholic Union* and in *The Evangelical Catholic* and which is implied in the memorial: The ordination of men outside the Episcopal church without obliging them to relinquish all their existing ecclesiastical relations on the following three conditions:

1. That they declare their belief in the Holy Scriptures and the Word of God in the Apostles' and Nicene Creed, in the divine institution of the two sacraments, and in the "doctrine of grace" substantially as they are set forth in the thirty-nine Articles.
2. That they would use certain parts of the liturgy including the essential parts of the administration of the Holy Sacraments.
3. That they will make report of their ministry once, at least, in every three years to the bishop or some approved ecclesiastical tribunal.

In sum, Muhlenberg contended that the memorial submitted the "practicality of an ecclesiastical system broader and more comprehensive than that of the Protestant Episcopal church, including that church as it now is . . . yet providing for as much freedom in opinion, discipline, and worship as is consistent with the essential faith and order of the Gospel." No one believed that the Episcopal church in its present form would ever supply that grand desideratum. The great law, Diversity in Unity, forbade it. If there was ever to be an American Catholic church, that law of diversity in unity would prevail. The most to be hoped for, or desired, was the acceptance of that old and true canon of catholicity: *In rebus necessariis, unitas; in non necessariis, libertas; in omnibus, charitas.* (In essentials, unity; in non-essentials, liberty; in all things, charity.)

Muhlenberg then tried to anticipate some of the objections to this proposal and finally in an addendum commented further on the proposed reform. Here he attacked the rigidity of the present services and advocated more flexibility in morning and evening prayer but did not advocate any change in the Holy Communion service because it was already flexible enough. Despite his deep reverence for the prayer book as it stood, he advocated an appendix containing additional liturgical material.

He concluded the addendum by returning to the ordination proposal. He argued that this would mean the emancipation of the Protestant Episcopate. In the early church, he wrote, the Episcopate had been free but then it had become enthralled by the papacy; the Reformation liberated the English Episcopate from this thralldom only to subject it to the state; the American Episcopate liberated from both papacy and state was yet in bondage to sect.[32]

Muhlenberg addressed a second public letter to Bishop Otey two years later in 1856 in which he endeavored to meet the charge that the memorial had been too vague, a charge which was made not only by his opponents in the 1850's but subsequently by historians. He claimed that if the memorial had been more definite it probably would have been laid on the table. But its very vagueness led to its first objective: the appointment of the commission. Then on behalf of some of the signers an exposition of the memorial was put forth; this was followed by other publications on the issues raised; and articles on these issues appeared in church journals of all parties. Thus, the memorial with all its vagueness had succeeded in eliciting a large amount of well defined views and opinions.

The time had now arrived, he said, for those memorialists for whom he spoke to be more specific. The memorial had a double bearing: one on the Episcopal church as such; the other on its ultimate target, that church, considered in its essential elements as the norm of a broader and more catholic system.

Muhlenberg took up the two reforms that he advocated within the Episcopal church as such. They related to Canon XLV which read:

> Every minister shall, before all sermons and lectures, and on all other occasions of public worship, use the Book of Common Prayer, as the same is or may be established by the authority of the General Convention of this Church; and in performing said service no other prayers shall be used than those provided by the said Book.

Muhlenberg's first proposal was that the canon be amended by striking out the clause, "and in performing said service, no other prayers shall be used than those prescribed by the said book." He asserted that this clause restricted the minister to those prayers that were already in the book but that there were innumerable occasions when special prayers were needed that were not covered by any prayers in the prayer book. He pointed out that this clause rendered the Episcopal church more restricted than any other church in Christendom. He suggested that with the repeal of this clause deacons applying for priest's orders might very properly be required by the bishops to give examples of their ability to frame occasional prayers such as might be needed in their parochial ministrations and could not be furnished by the bishop.

224

He then proposed as a second amendment that the canon should apply only to duly organized congregations. The requirement that the prayer book services be used on all occasions severely restricted the efforts of the clergy in the West in their missionary work for the prayer book had been drawn up for established parishes where it could be assumed that all the congregation were accustomed to its use.

These two changes, he said, along with the provision already existing for the admission to the ministry of men not possessing the ordinary academic or theological learning, might be used as a basis for an order of evangelists. This seemed all that needed to be done *in the way of legislation* for the greater effectiveness of the church upon the population at large and where there were no organized congregations. In his opinion, no legislation was needed to implement a lay agency because there were no canons restricting such a thing. The next proposal along the lines of making the Episcopal church more effective to the masses of the people likewise required no further legislation. It could be brought about by the House of Bishops authorizing a more flexible use of the office of morning and evening prayer by which these could be shortened or lengthened to adapt them to various circumstances. He then went into an extended discussion of the opportunity for a wide enrichment of the church services.

He concluded as to these reforms that the memorialists had not asked for any change in the doctrine of the church, nor in the prayer book, nor in the discipline of the church; they upheld the church's ideal of order but believed that order and freedom went together, order without freedom merely meant a rigid uniformity which was a sure means of destroying the spirit of the one and drying up the sources of the other.

Muhlenberg then proceeded to the second object of the memorial: that of constituting the Episcopal church the norm of a broader and more catholic system. And here he made an important change in strategy from his previous pamphlets: instead of asking for the ordination of men outside the Episcopal church he asked for the appointment of a permanent commission on church unity. This commission should consist of a certain number of bishops and have for its object the consideration of measures for the promotion of unity among Christians; and further, should be the authorized organ of the Protestant Episcopal church for holding communication with all bodies and individuals adhering to the Catholic faith with whom it might be advisable to hold communications.

In commenting on this proposal Muhlenberg said that he was well aware that unity among Christians was not likely to be the product of ecclesiastical negotiations. The commission, however, would be the continuing protest of the Episcopal church against the divided body of

Christ in our land. It would be a testimony and a witness for unity which could not be without its effect. He concluded by calling upon the church not to center her whole concern upon herself but to take thought for the common good of the great congregation—the single brotherhood in Christ.[33] Muhlenberg did not abandon the ordination proposal, however, for in a subsequent pamphlet he stated that the commission might be the preparatory body for this reform.[34]

An appendix to this pamphlet gave long quotes from two other memorial supporters. The first was a pamphlet by E. A. Washburn entitled *The Catholic Work of the Protestant Episcopal Church in America — By a Presbyter* in which Dr. Washburn defended the memorial on much the same grounds as Muhlenberg did. The second long quote was from Muhlenberg's old friend, Bishop Bowman, a High Churchman, who from a highly conservative point of view supported the memorial.[35] Muhlenberg followed the foregoing pamphlets with a sequel in the same year entitled *What the Memorialists Do Not Want* in which he repeated much of the same argument defending the memorial from charges of radicalism and concluding with the same specific requests as in the preceding pamphlet. This pamphlet also contained an addendum listing various writers who supported the memorial.[36]

The final pamphlet was Muhlenberg's reply to Bishop Potter's questionnaire. After recapitulating the arguments in the three previous pamphlets he concluded with further remarks on the appointment of a permanent Episcopal commission on church unity. In the controversy as it developed over the three years between the presentation of the memorial in 1853 and the report of the commission in 1856 this final pamphlet appeared to be the least controversial that he had put forward. He proposed that the commission should be no more than the authorized organ of communication with surrounding Christian bodies or individuals who were sound in the faith. Any further action on the part of the commission would require further instructions from the House of Bishops or the whole convention. As far as the specific proposal for granting holy orders on evangelical terms he argued for the commission as the necessary *preparatory* measure with the understanding that the commission would, until further instruction, confine itself to preliminary or rather tentative action.[37]

The memorial commission's report to the convention of 1856 was signed by all five of the remaining members including Bishop G. W. Doane, the militant High Churchman who had originally opposed the setting up of the commission. The commission came to the unanimous conclusion that some of the improvements which were most loudly called for and which commended themselves to the commission's judgment might be attained without legislation. There was nothing in the rubrics or canons which required that when the holy communion was administered it should be preceded by the offices of morning prayer. The practice rested merely on usage and there were occasions when the right of omitting morning prayer should be exercised. To secure this, nothing more would be needed, it was thought, than a declarative resolution of the House. The same discretion seemed allowable in respect to the time of using the litany and the ante-communion office. Canon XLVII of 1832 already provided for special services to be set forth by bishops in their own dioceses, and the commission concluded that by exercising the power thus given, provision could be made for these local necessities which resulted from peculiarities in the character of the population or in the circumstances under which the church was to be extended.

In the preamble to its resolution it acknowledged that the church's present order of worship had been framed with special reference to established parishes and to a population incorporated with the church while the actual work of the Church was or should be among many not yet connected with the Church or its established parishes. It also acknowledged there might be in different dioceses peculiar emergencies arising out of the character and condition of certain portions of the population.

The commission, therefore, recommended that practically all the requests of the memorialists as outlined in Muhlenberg's pamphlets be granted. Morning prayer, the holy communion, the litany, and evening prayer should be recognized as distinct services and might be used separately if desired. Ministers should be allowed to use parts of the Book of Common Prayer and the Holy Scriptures on special occasions and at extraordinary services. Bishops should be authorized to provide special services for any class or portion of the population within their dioceses that needed such services. The fifth recommendation was probably the most important of all in the eyes of Muhlenberg:

That to indicate the desire of this church to promote union among Christians and as an organ of Communication with different Christian bodies or individuals who may desire information or conference on the subject it is expedient that five bishops be appointed by ballot at each General Convention as Commissioners for the foregoing to be entitled The Commission on Church Unity.

The commission further recommended that Canon XLV be so amended as to give the bishops power to authorize the use of services other than those in the Book of Common Prayer. The effect of this amendment, the report explained, would be to enable particular dioceses under the direction of its ecclesiastical authority during such seasons as Passion

227

Week, Christmas, and the like to substitute lessons, anthems, or canticles more appropriate to the occasion and also to bring the provisions of this canon into harmony with those of Canon XLVII of 1832. The commission also proposed the authorization of nine new prayers one of which was for Christian unity.[38]

A reading of the minutes of the House of Bishops of this convention indicates that it was a foregone conclusion that the House would take favorable action on these recommendations since on every test vote the side favorable to the recommendations won by a large majority. The High Churchmen who were the most critical therefore tried to amend them by giving the bishops more authority over the greater freedom they offered and they were occasionally joined by an extreme Low Churchman. Among them were some of Muhlenberg's old friends such as Bishop Whittingham of Maryland, Kemper of Wisconsin, and DeLancey of Western New York. Significant also among this group was a new bishop, Horatio Potter of New York, who had succeeded Bishop Wainwright. He was a brother of Alonzo Potter of Pennsylvania but was much more conservative in churchmanship. While Alonzo Potter was a very active supporter of the memorial, his brother Horatio was extremely critical of it,[39] and a few years later he became involved in a number of controversies with Muhlenberg. (See Chapter 8 on the Tractarian Movement.)

Minor modifications were accepted but the only major amendment was offered by Bishop Alonzo Potter himself. This amendment cautioned that in setting up the commission on unity it was to be distinctly understood that it was clothed with no authority to mature plans of union with other Christian bodies or to propound expositions of doctrine or discipline. The recommendations as amended were carried without opposition.[40] The House then elected the following bishops to serve on the Commission on Church Unity: Thomas Church Brownwell of Connecticut, John Henry Hopkins of Vermont, Stephen Elliot of Georgia, George Burgess of Maine, and Charles P. MacIlvaine of Ohio. Bishops Brownwell and Hopkins of Vermont were High Churchmen, Elliot and MacIlvaine were Low Churchmen and Bishop Burgess was a moderate.[41]

The pastoral letter issued by the bishops at the close of the convention commented on the fact that it was the most widely attended convention that had yet been held and had been marked throughout with an admirable degree of fraternal kindliness, unity of feeling, and Christian courtesy. In particular the bishops rejoiced to see its perfect freedom from the plague of party spirit.[42]

Following the convention Alonzo Potter published a selection from the vast correspondence that the commission received on the memorial.

It should be remembered that the questionnaire went out before Muhlenberg dropped the proposal for the ordination of clergymen outside the Episcopal church and the committee therefore received replies to this question. For the most part there was only indifference or hostility to that proposal. The only persons who endorsed it were two of the memorialists, M. A. DeWolfe Howe, a Low Churchman, and Francis Vinton who had High Church leanings.[43]

Of those opposing the proposal Dr. William Henry Odenheimer, an alumnus of St. Paul's College, reported that he had discussed the matter with the Rev. Albert Barnes and other Protestant clergymen and that he believed that the facts were against the "amiable theory" of this part of the memorial. From conversation with intelligent laymen of other Protestant bodies "he believed that they had no idea of unity as connected with or dependent on the Episcopate." Other negative replies supported Dr. Odenheimer's remarks.[44] Most interesting were the replies of the clergymen from other churches, none of whom even mentioned the ordination proposal. Their replies were courteous in tone, however, and displayed genuine sympathy for the aims of the memorialists.[45]

On matters other than unity the answers to the commission's questionnaire indicated a widespread unrest in the church and support for many of the proposals which Muhlenberg had advocated in *The Evangelical Catholic* or which he had put into effect in New York. The commission itself made an exhaustive report on the answers to the questionnaire and Bishop Potter in his book gave samples of them. As far as unity was concerned the report emphasized the comprehensive character of the Episcopal church holding that it was broad enough to contain many different points of view without compromising its fundamental unity and that by practicing comprehensiveness, it could become the basis of unity, a point of view that had been developed by Muhlenberg, Dr. Washburn, and Bishop Vail.[46]

The commission then addressed itself to the major problems which it saw as facing the Episcopal church in the United States. The services of the church had been drawn up and its system or organization developed to meet conditions in England where there was an established church and where nearly every person was already a member of the church and was trained from childhood in her services. The reverse, however, was true in the United States:

> In no country in the world will there be found united under the same form of government, so great a variety of people, and so much diversity in intellectual, moral, social, and religious character as in this land. Immigration annually brings in its vast contribution to the elements of division in the religious sentiment and practice of our countrymen. In the popula-

tion of the same state, and not infrequently in the same town will be found all these varieties.... Out of this anomalous condition of things arises the necessity of that diversity in our modes of operation which had not been heretofore sufficiently appreciated, and the need of that versatility of talents in the ministry which in our case is more or less indispensable and which is always found to be eminently useful.[47]

Muhlenberg himself said much the same thing in his contribution to the Memorial Papers:

> Our Church has both a Catholic and denominational character. Which shall we now seek to develop? This, in reference to all the wants of the Memorialists is the question before you in making your report. If it be her denominational character that she is most concerned for your report may be very brief: Dismiss the Memorial. Take your stand on the prudential maxim: Let well enough alone. Our well doing Church will continue to do well in her own sphere and peculiar mission; with her stern integrity, her conservative policy, her refined taste and dignified bearing, she will always be most acceptable in the upper walks of life where, indeed, as well as in the lower, there are souls to be gathered into the kingdom; while also she will always have a goodly number of retainers in her beneficiaries among the poor. As she is, she can thus prosper—confessedly the most respectable denomination in the land. But if, without compromising any real advantages in that character she is mainly bent on developing the Catholic elements in her constitution, then give her ample room for so glorious a design.
>
> Bid her look over this vast continent, filled in with people of all nations and languages and tongues, and see the folly of hoping to perpetuate among them an *Anglican Communion* that will ever be recognized as naught more than an honorable sect. Bid her give over her vain attempt to cast all men's minds into one mould.
>
> Bid her cherish among her own members mutual tolerance of opinion in doctrine and taste in worship; remembering that uniform sameness in lesser matters may be the ambition of a society, a party, a school, in the church, but is far below any genuine aspirations of the church herself.[48]

There thus appeared to be general agreement that the memorial was correct in stating that the Episcopal church in its present form did not reach the masses of the American people. There were a few conservatives who claimed that there was nothing drastically wrong with the church but even they admitted that some reforms were desirable.[49] Another fairly conservative group claimed that there was nothing essentially wrong but that many customs had grown up which could be corrected without any change in the church's canons or constitutions. And a third group called for drastic reforms involving changes not only in the constitutions and canons but also in the liturgy.[50]

Chief among the complaints was as to the length of the service but it was recognized that this abuse could be corrected by dividing morning prayer, the holy communion and the litany into three separate services as Muhlenberg had already done at the Church of the Holy Communion. The evils of the pew system and the fact that the church could not attract the masses unless the rich and the poor worshiped together in the same church building was brought out. Several of the answers advocated sisterhoods for women similar to the Sisterhood of the Holy Communion. There was general opposition to the lowering of the educational requirements for the clergy but several suggested the formation of lower orders of the clergy in the form of permanent deacons or traveling evangelists. High standards for the seminaries were suggested, better training in preaching, and an internship for the younger clergy. A greater participation in the church by the laity was also suggested.

Others demanded more drastic changes including revision of the prayerbook itself and greater flexibility in its use. Southern correspondents were especially concerned for special services adapted to the religious life of Negro slaves. Others wanted to give missionaries greater freedom in using the prayer book and in extemporizing services to cope with varying conditions. The bishops, it was argued, should also be given the right to use discretion in improvising services.[51]

The replies from clergymen of other denominations raised similar questions. A "Venerable Divine of the Presbyterian Church (Old School)" stated that the Episcopal church had the best government of all the Protestant churches, a form which protected it from "enthusiasm." It could become a powerful influence as an agency of conciliation among the Protestant churches if it continued in an Evangelical direction. Therefore he welcomed the memorial.

A Congregational clergyman advised the Episcopal church to adopt the practice of traveling evangelists and colporteurs; otherwise it would lose the masses. He also suggested the relaxation of requirements for a liturgical service. A Baptist divine believed that religion and Christianity were on the decline in the United States because Americans had gone mad over a learned clergy, thus creating a clerical caste. "Rouse the masses," he said, "and set as many as possible to preaching." The Episcopal church had been considered as the head of the view which he deplored but it did have some facilities such as deacons and responsive readings. If it would turn and strike for the masses it could be "the leader of a revival" and "I will join hands with you if you take the lead." A German Reformed clergyman told of a movement in his own church to formulate a liturgy. He was evidently a personal friend of Muhlenberg and had a considerable knowledge of movements

231

within the Church of England. A Methodist clergyman stated that Episcopalians were too rigid with their set forms while the Methodists went too far in the opposite directions. He suggested that Episcopalians allow more informal services while the Methodists should compile a liturgy. It is noteworthy that none of these even mentioned the proposal for the ordination of Protestant clergy but dealt with other questions in which Episcopalians were interested.[52]

Probably more typical of the general reaction of the Protestant world than the sympathetic replies published by Bishop Potter was a pamphlet issued in Philadelphia by a Presbyterian minister writing under the name of "A Plain Presbyter." He declared that "the proposal for ordination of non-Episcopalian clergy is a proposition for the most wholesale proselytism in ecclesiastical history." He pointed out that of the six leading Protestant denominations, Episcopal, Methodist, Baptist, Congregational, Presbyterian, and Lutheran, the Episcopal Church was by far the smallest. This proposition, A Plain Presbyter admitted, may have been made in all Christian conscientiousness and candor. "But it will be exceedingly difficult for the Christian Public to allow to those who make it, a great share either of unpretending modesty or of a just appreciation of the conscientious conviction of those who differ with them. It is as if Rhode Island or Delaware should cooly and modestly plan to swallow up New England and New York." He further declared that the Episcopalian conception of a bishop was in agreement with that of the Roman Catholics and in opposition to that held by the great majority of Protestants. He denounced the use of the word "churchman" by American Episcopalians; the term could logically be used only where there is an established church.

After an exhaustive review of the controversy between Presbyterianism and Episcopacy in England the Plain Presbyter went on to charge that most members of Bishop Potter's diocese were against our present republican form of government and favored a system resembling an English aristocracy. He further alleged that the Episcopal church was the most worldly minded of all churches, and concluded by defining what he believed should be an American church as one that was grounded in Evangelical doctrine and associated with a republican form of government and republican traditions.[53]

The Convention of 1859 produced a backfire against the memorial. A resolution was introduced in the House of Deputies by Milo Mahan, a former student of Muhlenberg's and a former member of the faculty of St. Paul's College which read as follows:

Whereas, the Preamble and Resolutions adopted by the House of Bishops on the 18th day of the last session of the General Convention

232

in relation to the use of the Book of Common Prayer and published in the Journal of the said convention have disturbed the minds of many in our Church creating doubts both as to the effect of said Preamble and Resolutions and as to the constitutionality of the mode in which they were adopted and published; therefore, Resolved that the House of Bishops is hereby respectfully requested to reconsider the said Preamble and Resolutions and to throw the subject matter into such shape as will admit of the joint action of both Houses of this convention.[54]

This resolution carried. Milo Mahan was typical of the younger instructors of St. Paul's College who had been deeply influenced by the Tractarian movement and who in later life became Anglo-Catholics and thereby opponents of their old schoolmaster. The House of Bishops refused to reconsider the subject, however, and there the matter dropped.[55]

The report of the Commission on Church Unity was presented by Bishop MacIlvaine of Ohio:

> The Commission on Church Unity reports that they have had one meeting during the recess of the General Convention and have not seen cause for more. In consequence of the restricted nature of the powers committed to them no occasion for action consistent therewith has been presented. At the same time, however, your committee have seen with much gratification and encouragement impressive evidence that among several of the various forms and confessions which divide the Protestant Christian Community not only of this country, but of Europe, also especially of Great Britain, there is an increasing sense of the magnitude of the evils involved in or resulting from the present divisions, a growing desire and searching of heart not only for more of the unity of the spirit, but also for the unity of the spirit in that "bond of peace" which nothing but a close harmony and communion in visible Church institutions can create. Your committee perceives this increase in a more active inquiry into the nature and extent of the evils of which our present separation are the cause, in books which have recently been issued on the subject, which, whatever the soundness of their views evince an encouraging earnestness to discover the true remedy and its most effective application in the nearer drawing together of brethren of differing ecclesiastical institutions, but essentially the same Christian faith, on grounds common to all, for affectionate intercourse, sympathy, and prayer....[56]

Despite the lack of immediate results Muhlenberg continued to explore possible steps toward unity. He had an opportunity to continue the discussion in 1860 on a rather dramatic occasion. The historic Lutheran Augustus Church, at Trappe, Pennsylvania, which his great-grandfather, Henry Melchior Muhlenberg, had founded, was restored through a gift of William Augustus and his sister, Mrs. John Rogers, and other members of the family. The Lutheran church thereupon invited Muhlenberg to deliver the sermon when the church was reopened. (This sermon has already been discussed in Chapter 8 on the Tractarian movement.) On this occasion Muhlenberg suggested a rapprochement between the Episcopal church and the Lutheran on the basis of the revival of the order of Evangelist. He said that the early Christians were all evangelist—both apostles and laymen—and that the evangelical office did not depend on the Apostolic Succession. He claimed that the evangelical office had eventually merged into the priesthood and had become almost dormant during the Middle Ages but was revived by the Reformation. Muhlenberg proposed that both Lutherans and Episcopalians join in developing the "preacherhood" which would include both layman and clergy. It could be a step toward unity by encouraging Evangelists of both denominations to preach in each other's churches. In an addendum to the published version of this sermon he defended this proposal from an Episcopalian point of view—Muhlenberg must have coined the term "preacherhood." It is not found in any of his other writings. He obviously used it in contrast to "priesthood." Commenting on his proposal of a "preacherhood" as contrasted with his ordination proposals in the memorial he said:

> The measures proposed in the Memorial for a free extension of Episcopal orders looks to a Catholic organization of the Evangelical Churches and is advocated in my Exposition of that document on the ground of consistency in our Church. What is here pleaded for is independent of that, and might, on our part be preparatory to it.[57]

At the close of the Civil War, Muhlenberg took the lead in compiling "The Christian Circular," a public statement calling for a better observance of Good Friday which was signed by prominent clergymen of New York representing many Protestant denominations. Included among the signers were not only the leading Protestant clergymen of New York but some High Church Episcopalians as well, including Dr. Morgan Dix, an Anglo-Catholic leader and rector of Trinity Church. On this occasion Muhlenberg preached in the Madison Avenue Presbyterian church for which he was censured by Bishop Horatio Potter.[58]

Efforts toward Protestant unity after the Civil War received a setback with the increasing influence of the Anglo-Catholic party and its emphasis on Church order and a strict interpretation of the Doctrine of the Apostolic Succession. With these trends Bishop Horatio Potter of New York, Brother of Alonzo Potter and successor of Jonathan Wainwright, was in sympathy. As noted in Chapter 8 on the Tractarian movement this brought him into conflict with the Evangelical party and on one occasion with Muhlenberg personally. The Evangelical party

234

favored intercommunion among Protestants, interdenominational cooperation, and the exchange of pulpits with the clergy of other denominations which the bishop, backed by the High Churchmen, considered a violation of Church order. Muhlenberg also tried to make his last project, St. Johnland, an interdenominational project as free as possible from what he considered sectarian policies. In his last public paper, which he read at the convention of the Evangelical Alliance in Philadelphia in 1873, he advocated that as a step toward unity Protestants should receive communion in each other's churches. (For further discussion of these topics see Chapter 8 on the Tractarian movement and Chapter 10 on St. Johnland.)

Viewers with alarm in Muhlenberg's lifetime as well as historians since that time have regarded him variously as a transplanted Lutheran, a man who was warmhearted but a little vague, an Evangelical who had little understanding of the Catholic elements in the Episcopal church, and as a well-meaning idealist who did not know exactly where he himself stood or what he was doing. The evidence examined as a basis for this biography does not support these opinions. On the contrary, as he himself claimed, his views were remarkably consistent from the publication of *Hints on Catholic Union* in 1835 to this paper before the Evangelical Alliance in 1873. An examination of his writings on Christian unity shows that he regarded the doctrines of the Episcopal church as the basis of a broader unity. So did Bishops Vail and Alonzo Potter and other Anglicans since their time. In his schemes for unity he always regarded the episcopate as essential. In the published version of his speech before the Evangelical Alliance he added a postscript in which he criticized the Alliance for not including the Apostles' and Nicene Creeds and a statement concerning the divine origin of the Lord's Supper, baptism, and the ministry as part of its basic principles.[59] In his sermon before the Lutheran church at Trappe he criticized the Lutherans for not retaining the episcopate and their liturgy (see Chapter 8).[60]

Despite its disappointing immediate results the memorial movement had a lasting influence in the life of the Episcopal church and on the development of the Ecumenical movement. The dramatic manner of its presentation to the House of Bishops and the fact that it was signed by men prominent in all parties and from all sections of the country attracted national attention. Bishop Potter's action in sending out a questionnaire precipitated widespread discussion and broadcasted Muhlenberg's ideas on a national scale. Vigorous discussion at two general conventions, in the church press, and in numerous pamphlets also helped to popularize his ideas.[61] It is the consensus of church historians that this episode started movements for church unity and church reform that survived and that eventually reached fruition. Many of the reforms suggested during the course of the controversy over the memorial have since then been enacted.[62] A canon providing for the ordination of clergy from outside the Episcopal church was actually passed in 1922 but it failed to have the widespread effect that Muhlenberg anticipated. The pew system has been abolished except in a few isolated parishes, services have been shortened, a certain amount of ritual is used in all Episcopal churches, the standards of theological education have been raised, orders of deaconesses and sisterhoods have been established, the social service aspect of the church's life has been fully developed and an order of permanent deacons has been instituted. The discussion of the memorial also began the improvement of the character of church controversy from the vitriolic exchanges of the 1840's and 1850's to the magnanimous tone of the late 1850's. The debate centered the church's attention on problems of broader scope than the partisan wrangling of the earlier period. The most recent history of the Episcopal church (1965) assesses the long range influence of the memorial in the following terms:

> Although the immediate results were small, the memorial aroused a new critical approach and gave a new direction to the life of the Episcopal Church. As a result, liturgy, canons, and Christian Unity have been considered by every succeeding General Convention. Muhlenberg's stimulation led eventually to the Prayer Books of 1892 and 1928 and to the present canonical structure undergirding Episcopal Church polity. . . . Muhlenberg was not alone in supporting such advanced ideas, although few of his contemporaries supported so many of them so effectively.[63]

The memorial may be counted far more of a success than Muhlenberg and his contemporaries realized.

Despite the few tangible results that appeared during his lifetime he never lost hope that the church would eventually rouse itself to the problems and opportunities that confronted it. In *Brotherly Words,* a magazine that he published at St. Johnland in the 1870's, he wrote:

> "The liberal deviseth liberal things, and by liberal things he shall stand." Now is the day for the Church, through those who sway her councils to devise liberal things, that she may stand in her undivided strength, and have no let or hindrance of her own making in doing her full share of the work of the Lord in evangelizing the land.
>
> Vain hope, it may be said, If so now, not always. Church power will learn to unloose as to bind; and that ere long, if wise to discern the signs of the times.[64]

CHAPTER 10

Slavery and War

Muhlenberg began his life as the grandson of a prominent politician whose political affiliations though somewhat vacillating were generally Federalist.[1] He himself grew up in the aristocratic and Federalist atmosphere of Christ Church and the University of Pennsylvania even though his family was not quite from the upper-upper class of Philadelphia society. There is, however, little evidence that he had any particular interest in politics beyond the fact that in early life he regarded himself as a Federalist.[2] His first political decisions were forced upon him when he faced military service in the War of 1812 at the conclusion of his studies at the University of Pennsylvania. When the British army under General Ross took Washington, Philadelphia began to prepare to meet attack and Muhlenberg put in a day's work on the fortifications. This emergency was quickly over, however, with the news of the repulse of the British at Baltimore. Miss Ayres in her biography writes:

> War was abhorrent to him and his mind was fully impressed that the existing one was unnecessary. He had a strong bias towards the Quaker doctrine of nonresistance, and in order to confirm himself in this theory if tenable, or to correct his presuppositions if he were wrong he wrote an essay on the subject. . . . In the present case, all his pains did not settle the vexed question. Nonresistance and public protection could not be made compatible.

Later he wrote in his diary: "The British have been repulsed at Baltimore. General Ross killed. Querie — Is it Christian-like to rejoice in the death of an enemy? New Testament says 'Love your enemies.'"[3]

Although he did not take part in politics, he was a genuinely patriotic American. He even went so far as to permit the performance of a tableau at St. Paul's College on Washington's birthday which greatly astonished his students. This tableau was very much like a play and they knew of Muhlenberg's abhorrence of the theater.[4] He had a great admiration for the English nation as well as its church. Perhaps he imbibed these sentiments from his old schoolmaster, Dr. James Abercrombie, who was a forceful Federalist and anglophile.[5]

In his public ministry, however, Muhlenberg conformed to the prevailing opinion of the Episcopal clergy of his day that the clergy should not engage in politics. This view barred activity in various reform movements such as the temperance and antislavery movements. Some of the Episcopal clergy even carried this policy to the extreme of refusing to vote in elections.[6] This attitude may have arisen from experience. Before the revolution the Episcopal church had been an established church in some of the colonies and had suffered severely as a result. Probably the more important cause, however, was the reaction of Episcopalians to the very emotional denominations which played such an important role in American religious and political life. Writing in *The Evangelical Catholic* Muhlenberg admitted that clergymen had a right to vote and take part in politics if they wished. But he pointed out that doing so led to dissention within the parish and frequently to its disruption. He quoted with approval the late Bishop Griswold, who stated that as a clergyman he himself had no necessary concern with political matters. Muhlenberg stated that some objector might raise the case of Bishop White, who as Muhlenberg knew from his Philadelphia background very definitely did take part in politics. To such an objection Muhlenberg replied that "Bishop White was no common man, that he began his career under peculiar circumstances; and that his high position and unbounded influence enabled him to do with safety what it would be indiscreet and wrong in others to attempt."[7] (It should be borne in mind that voting was public and that a congregation could very easily find out how its rector voted.)

He was not, however, as indifferent to the reform movements as his writings might suggest. As was true of many clergymen he saw in the colonization of free Negroes in Africa the only solution to the slavery problem. Early in his ministry, while still Bishop White's assistant in Philadelphia, he preached a sermon in memory of two agents of the American Colonization Society who had died in Africa. It should be remembered that in the year that this sermon was preached — 1820 — the United States was convulsed by the controversy over the admission of Missouri as a slave state. Since it so well illustrates the thought of many church leaders of this period it is quoted at length.

238

This is practical philanthropy; [the Colonization Society] to carry to that quarter of the globe, which Europe and America have hitherto united in degrading, all the comforts and arts and decencies of civilized life.

Our departed friends were eminently engaged in the cause of philanthropy in as much as the abolition of the slave trade was an important object of their mission; it being evident that this traffic will be most effectually destroyed by the increase of colonies on the coast. Brethren, you have heard much of the slave trade. It has been the theme of every advocate of humanity. It has roused the eloquence of senates—our newspapers daily depict its evils. But I do not know that you have heard one word too much. I do not know that the subject has ever been exaggerated—for it is doubtful whether imagination could exaggerate this mighty outrage on humanity. I am not, however, going to try my powers of description, I have not accumulated a host of epithets and execrations, to darken the colours of this blackest of national crimes, because the simple story of many an African in this land of liberty is enough. Go to him, and he will tell you, that when he was a boy at home . . . that . . . after one of the village festivals had ended, in the dead of night they were awakened by the flames of their dwellings; a band of white men had set fire to the village—the people were driven to the coast, and in a crowded slave ship were transported to this soil of freedom. This is a very common tale. Thousands might tell one more heart rending. For it is a fact, that for two hundred years, the nations of Christendom agreed in sanctioning this crime; And that in some of these years, more than one hundred thousand Africans were enslaved. It is a fact, that at this very time, no less than three hundred vessels are engaged in the trade; and it is another fact, to be remembered in hell forever, that at the will of the trader, whole vessels, full of these miserable victims, after having been thus torn from their homes, have been poisoned or plunged into the ocean. God of vengeance! if I dare, I would ask, why did Thy thunders sleep? Why did the red-winged lightning stay its shaft?

In what laver of expiation the nations implicated in this crime shall wash their hands of its pollution, I know not. The sufferings of Europe seem to be a portion of that retributive cup of vengeance, the dregs of which it is to be feared they have yet to drink. In the mission of our friends our country has taken one step towards making her amends for the sin. If we can transmit to Africa the blessings of our arts, our civilization, and our religion, perhaps we may extinguish a part of the great moral debt. . . .

We may say, without taking any part in the political questions of the day that slavery is an immense national evil. The danger need not, for it cannot be concealed. The physical power of some sections of the union, lies in its black population. Nothing may be now apprehended; for the same reason that we do not fear the natural strength of the brute creation although far exceeding that of the human race. But should this physical power be thrown under the command of an able leader, as it might be in the event of invasion or of civil discord, would not the worst anticipations be realized?

This is not an imaginary danger. It lowers on the horizon of our political prospects; and may not the occasional insurrections in the South be viewed as the precursive lightnings which play about a thunder cloud; portending the storm it carries within. Slavery, my brethren, is not a few withered leaves on the fair tree of freedom, merely spoiling its verdure; it must be jealously watched as a canker worm eating at the root.

But how is the danger to be averted? Our southern brethren lament the evil equally with ourselves. Emancipation under present circumstances, is a wild scheme of philanthropy. To retransport the slaves at once is impossible and, if possible would be almost as cruel as the crime which gave rise to the evil. The proposed colony, as an asylum for free Africans and emancipated slaves, is the most plausible scheme that has yet been proposed. Whether or not it succeeds—for it is an experiment—the men who have been willing to devote themselves to an experiment so interesting to their country, deserved well of their fellow citizens—richly merit the reputation of patriot.

Let no one detract from the reputation of these men, by saying that they entered on a visionary scheme. We cannot now discuss the merits of the colonization system. Wise and able men have pronounced it worthy of a fair experiment.[8]

Muhlenberg did not see the church as entirely divorced from the world. Writing again in *The Evangelical Catholic* in an article entitled "Christianity and the Social Question of the Age" he asked the question "What relation does Christianity sustain to the social questions and leading movements of the age?" Muhlenberg said that he knew the answer that he would get "from many a comfortable parsonage and from innumerable stately Christian residences":

Christianity in its organic form has nothing to do with such matters. It is the peculiar and exclusive prerogative of the clergy to prepare man for another world; they have but one message to deliver and but one work to perform. The safety of the Church depends upon her keeping aloof from the excitements of the day.

On the whole Muhlenberg admitted that he agreed with this opinion for most Episcopalians at this time were pleased that their Church was not torn into factions by political questions. He allowed that reform movements might have their moral phases and they might be the indirect result of Christianity but:

they become so identified with political action, they are pushed to such outrageous excesses, and in some cases are based upon such an unsound foundation, that no place can be found for their consideration in the councils of the Church. There is but one Protestant Communion in the land that has kept entirely clear of the distractions and divisions which these topics occasion; and many a weary Christian now turns a wistful eye to that Church as a refuge from the storm which is thundering and raging in every quarter.[9]

Admitting all this Muhlenberg claimed that there remained some great moral movements which the church should support and noted that although Christian men have been leaders in these movements they were not organically connected with the Church. These movements had therefore been infiltrated by infidelity which apparently wanted to show that it could out-reform Christianity itself. As an example Muhlenberg cited the Temperance and Lyceum movements. The first he pointed out had become a substitute for the church in the minds of many people and the weekly meetings of the temperance societies had taken the place of Sunday worship. The Lyceum movement was moulding public opinion more effectively than the pulpit and its lecturers were a band of secular clergy who give a great deal of theological teaching of a questionable sort under the guise of science. He concluded that "It is useless to deny that our most enlightened forms of Christianity have shamefully failed in respect of that duty which the blessed Savior made most prominent in his earthly Mission."[10]

While still at St. Paul's College he received a letter from Jackson Kemper asking his assistance in obtaining men to work in Missouri. In replying Muhlenberg gave his view of slavery:

> I read your letter to one of the men most devoted. After he heard it with great attention—and although he has chosen foreign missions—he said after some thought "I would really take it into consideration if Missouri were not a slave state." And this with many a young man would be a serious objection—For my own part, I confess it would be unsurmountable—I am no abolitionist—but I am thoroughly persuaded of the iniquity of the system of slavery as established in our country—As a Christian minister I might find but little difficulty in a slave state—confining myself solely to the truth of the Gospel—Indeed I think I could do my duty (at least if my cunning were equal to my zeal) without coming into conflict with the political institutions of the land. But not so as a preceptor of the young. Then every subject is within the range of instruction and I should think myself signally deficient in truth if I carefully concealed from my pupils what I thought of making cattle of my fellow creatures. But "Au bono" [sic] say you to all? . . . Cogswell—is disengaged at present—and in some respects would be a first rate man—He is somewhat broken down in the service and I believe has objections to dealing with the sons of slaveholders—having found them as I have done—Impatient and undisciplined.[11]

Through the pages of *The Evangelical Catholic* Muhlenberg continued to give his support to the colonization society[12] but on other occasions took pains to emphasize that he was not an abolitionist. On his first trip to Europe in 1843 he took the lead among the passengers in counteracting the influence of a Quaker abolitionist Arnold Buffam, who was on his way to an antislavery convention in London.[13] Nonetheless, he used St. Luke's as a station on the Underground Railroad with the aid of one of the sisters from the South.[14]

Muhlenberg's associates were divided on this question. Samuel Seabury was an open apologist for slavery and during the Civil War he and Milo Mahan sympathized with the South.[15] Bishop Wittingham was not an abolitionist but he upheld the Union in the critical state of Maryland.[16] Muhlenberg's former student and friend, John Jay, however, was about the nearest that the Episcopal church came to producing a lay abolitionist. His resolutions calling for the suppression of the slave trade were repeatedly voted down by the diocesan convention of New York on the ground that they dealt with "political matters."[17]

Muhlenberg perhaps unwittingly produced the only clerical Abolitionist in the Episcopal church who has appeared in the course of this research. He was John McNamara, who entered the ministry under Muhlenberg's influence and who volunteered for missionary work in the West.[18] He eventually went to Geneva Lake, Wisconsin, where he founded the Church of the Holy Communion.[19] There he persuaded the congregation to pass a rule expelling any person who believed in the abstract right of one human being to hold another in bondage.[20] Later he was censured by Bishop Kemper for excommunicating a communicant for voting the Democratic ticket.[21] He also started a paper called *The Anti-Slavery Churchman*. Bishop Kemper received a letter of protest from Bishop Mercer Green of Mississippi that so well expresses the outlook of Episcopal clergy toward antislavery agitation and the "sects" in the Pre-Civil War period that it is here reproduced in full:

> How shall I describe the pain and fear and mortification with which I received through the P. Office a day or two since a printed paper purporting to be the "4th No" of the "I Vol." of the *Anti-Slavery Churchman*, edited by a clergyman of our own dear and undivided church and published from "Geneva Lake, Wisconsin."
>
> Oh, what is that mistaken brother about that he would thus cast a firebrand into the very penetralia of our temple — I do not charge him with any wanton motive in what he is doing, but knowing the only issue to which it cannot fail to come, I would entreat and beseech him by the love which we equally bear to our dear Mother, to stay the blow which he is aiming, as I trust unconsciously, at her peace. What can he hope to accomplish in that way? Will he allay the sectional prejudice and animosity which unhappily for all is daily growing up between the hitherto united sections of our country? Will he make his slave-holding brethren any better Christians than they

now are? No! No! Every line that he writes will rivet the chains and draw tighter the cords of those whose cause he advocates; will stir up more and more ill blood between the North and the South; will rend assunder our hitherto United Zion; and put us upon a level with the jarring and inter-meddling sects around us.

I rejoice at the prompt and decided, though kind rebuke given to this undertaking by that most sound and judicious Print, the *"Gospel Messenger."* God grant that its friendly warning may not be given in vain.

I know my dear brother that you must look with equal regret upon this fatal movement. Is there no way in which you could by your influence (I do not say authority) stop it where it is? If it goes on, what is to become of the present peace and unity of the Church?

Will not our dear Nashotah be the first to suffer? Is she not suffering from it now? Oh I dread to take up any of the sectarian prints that swarm the land but my eye should meet the shout of triumph which they will raise when they find that we too have fallen into this snare of the Evil one and cannot claim the respect of the moderate and just and conservative of the land.

Let me hear from you my dear brother on this subject. I know that it is a painful one and a delicate one to you—and that you see dangers and difficulties on both sides. But I have all confidence in your judgment and prudence and I feel that God will guide you to what is right.[22]

McNamara later became Muhlenberg's assistant at St. Johnland in New York.[23] One of the later rectors of the Church of the Holy Communion at Geneva Bay was Richard Kerfoot, brother of John Barrett Kerfoot.[24]

A review of Episcopal church history in the pre-Civil War period indicates that for the most part its clergy practiced a withdrawal from affairs of the world, particularly politics, and remained engrossed in their religious work. Only rarely have examples of interest in politics turned up. But by 1860 excitement was so intense that it affected even Muhlenberg. He writes in his diary concerning the election in which he voted for Lincoln:

Tuesday, November 6, 1860—So I did my duty as I felt and believed it was. I am no party politician, but I am much interested in the success of the Republicans as opposed to slavery. I have not voted for years, before, and but seldom in my life.

Wednesday, November 7. Lincoln elected! huzza! I am glad I shared in the victory. And why? I have no interest in the Republican success save that I believe it a triumph of humanity—of principles—over Mammon.[25]

Later on he wrote:

This war, this war! How do I feel about it? Alternately with horror and then with a conviction that it is so righteous, I am glad to have my boys in it. It ought not to cost me nothing. . . . The whole city is wild with a military delirium. I have always been almost a Quaker but I have fallen into the universal sentiment—that there must be fighting, at least in defense of the government, the capital must be held. . . . But oh, the passions which the war spirit engenders—I falter in the thought. But if ever there was a just war, this is one. For our country and against the slave power—that power which declares that it means to be perpetual! If the war relieves the country of that, I shall rejoice, should all my boys fall in battle.[26]

During most of the war Muhlenberg remained at his post as superintendent of St. Luke's Hospital. The only events of immediate concern were the admission to the hospital of wounded and sick soldiers and the threat to the hospital during the three day riot of 1863 (see Chapter 6). Muhlenberg's niece and only close collateral descendent married a South Carolinian, William Chisholm, but he made his home in the North for many years. William Chisholm had a brother, however, who had been educated at St. Paul's College, who served in the Confederate Army, and died on active duty.[27] This connection did not influence Muhlenberg for he became a great admirer of Lincoln and supported the war effort. He published in 1863 "The President's Hymn," a metrical setting of Lincoln's first Thanksgiving proclamation.[28]

During the course of the war the major preoccupation of the Northern Episcopalians was to prevent a schism with the Southern dioceses.[29] Upon the outbreak of the war the Southern dioceses had formed their own church and Northern church leaders were determined that nothing should be done that would block a reconciliation once the war was over. This task was made easier because some of the Northern church leaders were pro-South in their sympathies and some Southern bishops were Unionist.[30] A militant minority of Northerners, however, was definitely pro-Union and throughout the war supported the Lincoln administration. Among these were Muhlenberg's friends, Bishops Potter[31] of Pennsylvania, Whittingham of Maryland,[32] and Horace Binney of Philadelphia.[33] Despite his support of the Union cause, Muhlenberg favored a benevolent approach to the Southern dioceses and passed around an anonymous letter supporting a rapprochement.[34] This was accomplished at the general convention of 1865 and among the leaders in bringing it about were Bishop Whittingham and John Barrett Kerfoot. The leader of the opposition group who wanted an endorsement of the Union position even at the expense of estranging the Southern dioceses was Horace Binney, Muhlenberg's octogenarian friend from Philadelphia. The defeat of Binney's resolution made reunion possible and avoided a North-South schism in the church.[35]

Kerfoot, in his speech against Binney's resolution, stated that he himself agreed with the words of the resolution but that he was voting against it.

Why? Because this *Church Convention* was not the place for declarations on these or any distinctly national topics; not on any topics whatever, civil or social, except in direct and necessary connection with ecclesiastical and religious work. Only mischief, confusion, grief, and distraction could ensue if such resolutions and such discussions were brought into our Church Conventions. Their duty as a Church legislature was limited to topics of religious doctrine and worship and the spread of the Gospel.

This was too much for Muhlenberg; in a letter to Kerfoot about another matter he added the following postscript:

I send you our Thanksgiving songs. Let your college boys sing them. It will be a further demonstration of the loyalty which you had to vouch so emphatically to cover the shame of that mean—yes, I will say it—that mean vote of yours in the General Convention. "Connecticut voted solid," exulted a Copperhead. I was not proud of you then. "Not the proper work of the Church" O Transcendental, sublimated, superspiritual Church! —too far up in the third heavens to care about what is doing on earth.[36]

Four years after the end of the war Muhlenberg and St. Luke's Hospital were involved in a controversy of which the following letter from Muhlenberg to his pro-Southern and proslavery friend, Samuel Seabury, is self-explanatory:

Dear Doctor:

Supposing that the real object of your letter is to call me to account in the matter of Mr. James—I proceed dutifully to give it—Wm. J. . . . held his place here under me and I relieved him for having officiated at the reinterment of the Assassin Booth—using the whole Burial Office—the psalms, lessons, . . . and the two concluding prayers. The "Governing Board" had nothing to do with the removal, except to pass a resolution thanking me for it. I liked Mr. James, in most respects very much, and gave him a kind letter in parting—nor as he was soon to leave would I have dealt so promptly with his offence—outrage as it was upon the feelings of all Loyal and Christian men—but for the appearance in the public prints that the "Chaplain of St. Luke's Hospital" was the minister "on the occasion of glorifying this villain of villains"—James did not look at it in that light but I felt that the honor of the Hospital was to be vindicated and I left him to tell his own story in the papers—No harm has been done him—He will fare all the better at the South—for this act of persecution as they will call it Hoping the above is satisfactory and that you will not bring me under ecclesiastical censure, I am sincerely yours.[37]

CHAPTER 11

St. Johnland:

The Church's Answer to Socialism

With the close of the Civil War, Muhlenberg, at the age of sixty-nine, became deeply engrossed in the last of his projects—the Society of St. Johnland. This was the least successful but also the most characteristic of all his projects. He referred to it as the Benjamin of his life. In it he tried to create a concrete example of all that he had stood for during his lifetime not only in practical Christianity but also in theology and church policy.

The objects of St. Johnland as listed in the constitution and by-laws were as follows:

First: To provide cheap and comfortable homes together with the means of social and moral improvement, for deserving families from among the working classes, particularly of the city of New York and such as can carry on work at St. Johnland; but this provision shall never be used for pecuniary emolument, either to the society or to any of the agents in its employ.

Second: To maintain a home for aged men in destitute circumstances, especially communicants who are esteemed entitled to it by the churches to which they belong, to care for friendless children and youths and especially cripples by giving them home, schooling, Christian training, and some trade or occupation by which they can earn their future livelihood; and generally to do such other Christian offices as shall from time to time be required and are practicable by the society consistently with its benevolent designs.

246

Third: To assist indigent boys and young men who desire literary education with a view to the Gospel Ministry by affording them the opportunity for such education and at the same time means of self-support by some useful employment. An Evangelical School or College chiefly for training for the ministry would come within the scope of the society.

Lastly and as embracing its whole, to give form and practical application to the principle of Brotherhood in Christ in an organized Congregation or parish, constituted by settled residents of St. Johnland.[1]

To begin this project Muhlenberg purchased a tract of land on Long Island Sound in the county of Suffolk with his own private funds. He then, in 1864, issued a Retro-prospectus in which, using the looking backward device, he described how St. Johnland would look in 187 . This pamphlet, dedicated to his old friend "Robert B. Minturn, the Poor Man's Friend and Mine," gave in detail Muhlenberg's ideas on how the project would look when completed.[2]

He first described an idyllic community whose purpose was to enable certain classes of the industrious poor to exchange their slum dwellings in the city for comfortable rural homes and at the same time to have some way of earning a living. There were two leading officials of the community: a pastor and a superintendent. The pastor was the rector of the St. Johnland Parish Church and all the inhabitants for the time being were his parishioners. The superintendent had charge of the business management of the project and an important part of his business was to secure employment for the industrial workers who settled there. Most of the people living in the community worked for clothing and finishing businesses in the city. The material was shipped out to them by railroad and the finished product shipped back. He did not go into any greater detail concerning this work. He did stipulate that St. Johnland was to do business only with firms that paid fair wages to their employees. The cottages were financed by individuals who were interested in the enterprise. Donors were encouraged to build these cottages for some family in which they were particularly interested. In this way interested people furnished a family with separate home-like dwellings at much lower rents than they were paying for dismal rooms in the city. Tenants retained their homes on the condition of continued satisfactory behavior.

The settlement in its main features was a church industrial community. Muhlenberg declared that the working people almost without exception were contented. They could live at St. Johnland only in habits of industry which forestalled discontent; most of them had experience which taught them to value their present circumstances. Some of the sewing machines were owned by the corporation and loaned

247

to the workers; others, however, were owned outright by the workers who had received them as gifts from friends. Providing homes and employment for industrial workers was the main feature of the project according to the retro-prospectus. The pamphlet spoke of the evils of the slum. The only way that Muhlenberg saw of financing St. Johnland was for benevolent rich people to donate cottages.[3]

St. Johnland had additional features. The care of orphans was an important one. They lived in houses under the care of a poverty-stricken woman and were organized as a family unit. Muhlenberg referred to this plan as "the family mode" of caring for orphans. The boys were occupied as workers in self-supporting industries when they grew old enough, and the girls were taught needlework and sewing, or ladies took some of them into their homes teaching them to be good housemaids. There was an evening school with lectures in the arts and sciences. All orphans were taught to sing and some of the boys were formed into a band.[4]

Another activity of the colony provided an infirmary for chronic invalids and incurables. These people had been discharged from hospitals or were not eligible for admission to them. They were disabled in various ways yet too comfortable in health to need treatment or nursing. They could not pursue the occupations on which they once depended for support and yet might live on for years with destitution all the while staring them in the face. There were always some of these in St. Luke's Hospital, which departed from its rules by retaining them as long as there was room enough to do so in the wards. When the hospital was filled with regular patients, some of its friends started the infirmary at St. Johnland, which had now something of an endowment. There was also a home for aged people.[5]

In fulfillment of Muhlenberg's lifelong interest in forming a semi-monastic order for men he included in his retro-prospectus a society of "The Christian Brothers of St. Johnland"—young men preparing for the ministry or teaching—drawn from several different denominations. They were not considered monks in any way. They wore grey uniforms and were unmarried for the time being but were not bound by vows of celibacy or to continue in the society forever. They were expected to complete the term for which they entered, at the end of which matrimony would be a matter of choice. If, as missionaries, they judged a single life best for them for a while at least, the discipline to which they had been used would be a good preparation. The family idea pervaded the place throughout—the monastic or ascetic spirit was foreign to its genius. No state of life was allowed which was out of tune with God's appointments. Roman Catholicism might have its convents; it was for Evangelical Catholicism to create St. Johnland.[6]

This passage is the only specific description that we have of the type of organization that Muhlenberg had in mind in his frequent references to a semimonastic order. There are vague descriptions in his correspondence with Bishop Kemper and in his fragmentary comments about the never-started Cadet's Hall. James Lloyd Breck in attempting to found a monastic order at Nashotah seems to have drawn some of his inspiration from Muhlenberg and some sources — but not Muhlenberg — speak of "the brotherhood" when referring to the faculty of St. Paul's College. He always thought of his brotherhoods in terms of sending men to work out West or in the slums of the cities. He was never able, however, to form such an order for men as he did in the case of the Sisterhood of the Holy Communion for women.

Although he was as strongly opposed to the Catholic conception of monastic orders for men as for women he involuntarily influenced the formation of such orders although less directly than in the case of the Sisterhood of St. Mary. One of Muhlenberg's students at St. Paul's College was George H. Houghton, who later became his assistant at the Church of the Holy Communion. He has already appeared in this book as the founder of the Little Church around the Corner — The Church of the Transfiguration. He it was who advised the Reverend James O. S. Huntington, the founder of the Order of the Holy Cross, in the early years of Father Huntington's life.[7] No source shows any direct Muhlenberg influence, however, on the formation of this order. The Christian Brothers of St. Johnland followed the same general outline for men that the Sisterhood of the Holy Communion followed for women.

St. Johnland was not to become larger than a moderate-sized parish — rather it was hoped that it would serve as a model for similar communities throughout the nation. It epitomized Muhlenberg's lifelong interest in the problems of the city and what he believed at this time the Protestant churches could do toward solving them. This is the real significance of the Retro-prospectus. In actual fact the community never worked out as Muhlenberg hoped and was the least successful of his projects. By 1865 when the Retro-prospectus was written Muhlenberg was already sixty-nine years old and he was active only for the next seven years. Thus the Retro-prospectus gives us a picture of the focus of Muhlenberg's interests at the end of his life.

Muhlenberg contributed the remainder of his personal fortune to the project as well as his salary from St. Luke's and he received generous contributions from his sister.[8] The list of the original organizers, contributors, and directors reads like that of St. Luke's Hospital. It is obvious that at the start the backers were Muhlenberg's old friends and associates. As the project developed, however, a number of new and interesting names were added. Two were clergymen, who were to take a leading part in church affairs in the 1870's and 1880's, Edward A. Washburn and John Cotton Smith. Another newcomer to the enterprise was the banker J. P. Morgan and lastly there was Henry Codman Potter, rector of Grace Church and later bishop of New York. Other contributors were Dr. G. B. Wood and Horace Binney from Philadelphia. The names of prominent New York families such as Astor, Vanderbilt, Van Cortland, and Roosevelt were also listed. Muhlenberg himself issued a revised version of his perennially popular hymn, "I Would Not Live Alway," which he "evangelized," the profits going to St. Johnland.[9]

Papers of incorporation were taken out in 1868[10] and in 1869 Muhlenberg made his first report which recorded that expenditures for land and other purposes amounted to $60,340.00. He transferred title to the St. Johnland property to the board of trustees in 1870 subject to a reservation of a homestead for the Sisterhood of St. Luke's upon the property.[11] In his 1871 report he suggested that the completion of the railroad now being built on Long Island would make it possible to sell "villa" lots to persons who were in harmony with St. Johnland and were interested in being a part of the community. In regard to the actual progress of the community Muhlenberg reported:

> The delay in the advance of the railroad and other circumstances have given an impetus to the establishment of the charitable institutions of St. Johnland in advance of its tenant cottages—but these are only waiting the right time. A true St. Johnland as conceived by the founder cannot exist without them and in the conception of such a community there enters not only the good St. Johnland itself will do but the hope that it may be an example and stimulus to similar settlements in different parts of the country.[12]

In the meantime much had been done in the line of charitable institutions and he recognized that these would probably become the main feature of the project. He listed them as follows:

St. John's Inn—The Old Men's Home
Extension of St. John's Inn for orphan girls and sisters
The Children's House for crippled and orphan children
The Boy's House for older Orphan Boys
The Typesetting room
The Church of the Testimony of Jesus[13]

Farming was the first activity to start at St. Johnland and then the stereotype foundry was set up to employ crippled children. Next came the home for crippled and destitute children. Twenty-five such children who were formerly patients at St. Luke's were the first to be admitted. Then followed the Old Men's Home in 1869. Muhlenberg also refers to Kinderland, the home for very young children.[14]

He commented again, however, on the failure of St. Johnland to develop in the direction originally outlined in the prospectus:

> Some may be disappointed in finding in the foregoing pages so little mention of what was set forth in the Prospectus as a chief design, viz. the accommodation of poor industrious families with cheap and comfortable homes (in exchange for their tenement apartments in the city) in which they could continue their accustomed employment for support. This, of course, could apply only to those pursuing certain kinds of handicraft and to but few of these compared with the large numbers for whom philanthropy should make such provisions. The purpose was, by the establishment of one industrial Christian Colony, to show what might be done for the relief of a large portion of our Protestant working population by the multiplication of such colonies within a moderate distance of the city. This, of which a small beginning has been made, we trust will yet be accomplished to the extent anticipated when the nearer proximity of the railroad and other facilities will make it sufficiently practicable. In the meanwhile the place is growing in the list of charitable and useful institutions more than was at first contemplated—although such were more or less included in the original plan.[15]

In building St. Johnland he continued to have the services of Anne Ayres. She served as one of the original members of the board of trustees and the Sisterhood of St. Johnland was organized under her direction.[16] A seal for St. Johnland was also adopted. At the meeting of the trustees in 1871 Muhlenberg announced that he had conveyed 110 acres in addition to the seventy acres already conveyed together with the buildings thereon, on condition that the corporation would give or lease to him and Anne Ayres for the term of their natural lives the Mansion House and so much of the adjoining ground as may be agreed upon by the parties concerned.[17]

St. Johnland continued to expand in the direction of its secondary purpose—that of providing homes for the orphans and aged. The need of additional housing for the children was soon felt. The schools, according to the report of 1872, had competent men and women teachers with scholars of various grades. The principal branches of mechanical industry established were typesetting and stereotyping. These activities returned a profit to the community and only young workmen trained on the spot were employed.[18] The report for the following year described the training in trades of the children of St. Johnland and their placement in the outside world when they grew up. There was a wide

251

range of national groups represented among them: Norwegian, Swedes, Russian, Polish, Germans, Swiss, Italian, English, Scotch, Irish, Cubans, Mexicans, and "Central Americans."[19]

Likewise a plan was put forward to build a house named Rest-Awhile for the use of working women from the city who could take a vacation there.[20] A gift for this purpose was announced in 1873:

> An advance of another kind has been the maturing of a work for many years imperfectly done by means of the "Fresh Air Fund." We refer to the opening of the House given by Mr. William H. Aspinwall as a summer holiday retreat for poor children and worked-out women. Successive parties of these in the months of July and August enjoyed this refreshment under the care of a volunteer Christian lady admirably qualified to be the housemother to such an adopted family. Several of our charitable institutions have availed themselves of the House. This provision for which St. Johnland is peculiarly adapted might be largely expanded and, as time goes on, give a value to the place for that purpose alone.[21]

The report of the following year lists among the organizations making use of Rest-Awhile, the Missions of Grace Church, the Incarnation, St. Mark's, Anthon Memorial, the Sisters of the Church of the Holy Communion, the Sisters of St. Barnabas House with their children, the Children of the Sheltering Arms, and convalescents from St. Luke's Hospital.[22]

Announcement was also made in the third annual report that Muhlenberg's lifelong friend, Dr. Crusé, had left his library to St. Johnland. The books were mostly in ancient languages and the report suggested that they would prove valuable when part of the original St. Johnland program, a training school for candidates for the ministry, was carried out.[23]

The trustees of St. Johnland met in 1874 for the first time without Muhlenberg. The deficit for the preceding year of ten thousand dollars was made up by his sister. It was resolved that henceforth he should be relieved of all responsibility for the financial support of the enterprise. "This is the least we owe to his advanced years, his abundant labors in the Church, and the unremitting care and amount of personal means which he had expended on this particular work," the resolution read. To implement this resolution it was decided to make an appeal for funds to relieve Muhlenberg from further anxiety concerning the future of St. Johnland, and John McNamarra, Muhlenberg's abolitionist protégé, was appointed assistant pastor and superintendent of St. Johnland.[24] The year 1874 appears to have marked the end of Muhlenberg's active ministry for he never again attended a meeting of the trustees.[25]

The annual report of 1875 gives a comprehensive picture of the project ten years after it was started and two years before Muhlenberg's death. The physical plant comprised 565 acres of land, 225 of which were arable and 125 of which were under thorough cultivation; the other 240 were wooded though some might be cleared for tillage. The remaining 100 were salt meadow on which stood old farm buildings. The total value of the property consisted of land, $40,000; buildings, $94,933; stock, furniture, etc., $20,000; total in round numbers $150,000. The number of persons at St. Johnland was 209. These were broken down into the following groups:

Beneficiaries of the various houses	159
Cottage Children	12
Employees	27
Individuals in Employees' families	11
	209

St. Johnland required an average of $1,900.00 per month for current expenses but this sum would not be materially affected by either an increase or diminution of beneficiaries to the extent of 15 to 20 per cent as the most considerable expenses were for the general maintenance of the place and would go on whether this number was maintained or not. Assured income amounting to about $11,000 per year was derived as follows:

By payments for beneficiaries and Donations	$ 4,500.00
Interest on Wolfe Memorial Fund	4,500.00
Net returns of stereotyping	1,000.00
Dr. Muhlenberg's Annual Gift	1,000.00
	$11,000.00

Commenting on the children who in the years to come were to be the most important part of St. Johnland's work, the report described two classes of children at St. Johnland. The first were either fatherless or motherless children whose parents must work to earn a living and therefore could not take care of them but who nonetheless contributed partially to their support. The second class were deformed, crippled, or feebly constituted young convalescents from St. Luke's Hospital. The report continued:

The children are not huddled together in one vast building like so many pieces of a great machine, knowing nothing beyond its own groove or niche They are divided according to circumstances into households numbering from thirty to forty each. Their houses are not alike but each in different ways pleasant and picturesque. The children are not dressed alike nor in any manner ground into an artificial uniformity by unnecessary routine or cold repression. They have room for spontaneity. They have their own little possessions and predilections. The little girls especially take pride in the care and ornamentation of their home and in the cultivation of their gardens. While the hardier divisions in the true boy fashion find only too much scope on the out of door range. Nothing is more commonly remarked by strangers visiting the settlement than the natural, open manners of our young people — Quite recently a member of the State Charities Aid Society after a somewhat close inspection of the work spoke with warm admiration of this feature of it, adding "Your Children all look as though they had Mothers."

In regard to the original purpose of the community it was reported that there was now a St. Johnland station about a mile and a half from the village. This now made possible the carrying out of the original plan of providing cottages for industrial workers. If the necessary money could be raised cottages could be built for the right sort of tenants, who, it was presumed, would gladly exchange their miserable tenement quarters for neat country homes with much smaller rent and with incalculable advantages in every way. The report said that this would be an example of what might be done extensively toward lessening a dark element in our city if each of the leading Protestant denominations had a settlement "more or less like that which we trust, ours is destined to become."[26]

Despite the completion of the railroad, the trend toward making St. Johnland primarily a collection of charitable institutions continued although occasional mention is still made of the dream of its becoming an industrial colony. Following the death of Muhlenberg in 1877, St. Johnland continued to operate an orphanage, rest house, home for cripples and incurables, and old peoples' home.[27] As other institutions absorbed some of these functions, St. Johnland remained with an orphanage, home for children from broken homes, and old peoples' home.[28] In 1955 the orphanage and children's work was discontinued and it embarked on a new career as an old peoples' home only.[29]

Muhlenberg took particular interest in the establishment of the parish church of St. Johnland to be called the Church of the Testimony of Jesus. For just as its other institutions were to set an example of practical Christianity, so this was to be a model parish for the church. Although the parish was to be related to the Episcopal church it was the chapel of a private corporation and therefore Muhlenberg believed that he could reserve certain liberties for the parish that he could not have if it were organized as a regularly constituted parish. As noted in the chapter on the Tractarian movement, Muhlenberg through these "liberties" was putting into practice the controversial policies that were being demanded by the Evangelical party in the Episcopal church. He suggested that these privileges should be made generally available in all parishes in the church. Only in this way, he wrote, could her parties and schools of thought live in peace and could she come closer to her separated brethren. And he expressed his confident hope that this would eventually happen.[30]

In line with his enduring interest in liturgical reform Muhlenberg published a *Directory in the Use of the Book of Common Prayer for the Church of the Testimony of Jesus* (1871). This directory of only fifty-six pages proposed a flexible use of the prayer book with some additional material. He revised the offices of morning and evening prayer, the litany, the catechism, and the burial office, as well as the holy communion service and baptism. In a supplement he added additional canticles and hymns. In the concluding part of the book he added a litany in the form of "Collects of the Passion." This book is important for it shows Muhlenberg's ideas on a possible revision of the Book of Common Prayer and it is evident that he hoped that the directory would come into general use as a supplement to it.[31] The directory is the last example of his lifelong effort to improve the service of the church, which he began when he chopped away the clerk's desk at St. James as a young man, and which he continued in his Lancaster ministry when he brought about the adoption of a new hymnbook, in his services in the chapels of the Flushing Institute and St. Paul's College, in his pastoral tracts at the Church of the Holy Communion, and in the worship at St. Luke's Hospital.

Muhlenberg also started a magazine for St. Johnland titled *Brotherly Words* which reflected his interest in church journalism. No copy of this magazine has been found but several articles from it were published[32] and it is frequently referred to in his correspondence. Like its predecessors it was not only a house organ but also a means by which Muhlenberg sought to bring his views before the church. The journalistic bug seems to have bitten Muhlenberg quite early in life, for Dr. Abbe says that when Muhlenberg and Dr. George B. Wood were students at the University of Pennsylvania they tried to found a magazine for which they collected subscriptions but were never able to publish the first number.[33] As a young clergyman in Philadelphia he had experience with publishing church papers (see Chapter 1). Later on he published *The Journal of the Institute at Flushing*. The material in this journal reflects many of the interests which were to develop later. After the founding of St. Paul's College he continued this journal as the *Journal of St. Paul's College*. His next publication was *The Evangelical Catholic*, which has been discussed in Chapter 8. He also projected at one time a publication for St. Luke's Hospital but this apparently never materialized. *Brotherly Words* was thus the last of Muhlenberg's journalistic efforts.

Muhlenberg withdrew from active participation in church affairs in the last twelve years of his life (1865–1877) and with the exception of his speeches at the Evangelical Catholic Conference and the Convention of the Evangelical Alliance was preoccupied with the affairs of St. Luke's Hospital and St. Johnland. He was regarded with great veneration in New York largely because of the charitable institutions he had founded. And this aspect of his life overshadowed all others in the minds of his contemporaries.[34] Bishop Horatio Potter in 1863, for example, in listing the numerous institutions that had been established in the diocese of New York pointed out that the movement had been started by Muhlenberg.[35] A survey of charitable undertakings in the greater New York area was dedicated to Muhlenberg as the leader in the movement to establish charities.[36] His St. Johnland project was regarded by the general public as an experiment in Christian socialism and the Christian answer to secular socialism.[37] Other aspects of his life such as his work in the fields of education, church unity, church music, and hymnology, were largely overlooked. He visited Europe again in 1872 and 1873, this time including France and Germany on his itinerary.[38]

He enjoyed the acquaintance of many men prominent in the social and cultural life of New York, among whom were William Cullen Bryant, the poet and editor; the philanthropist Peter Cooper;[39] and Henry Raymond of the *New York Times*.[40] Dr. Phillip Schaff, formerly president of the Mercersberg Seminary and now on the faculty of Union Seminary was a continuing friend.[41] And among a list of those who visited St. Johnland in 1876 was the name of Mr. Theodore Roosevelt.[42] Muhlenberg died on April 8, 1877, and was buried at St. Johnland.[43] On his gravestone is the following inscription:

Here sleeps the Earthly Part of
William Augustus Muhlenberg, Doctor in Divinity
He was born September 16th, 1796. Ended
his work April 8th, 1877

"I know whom I have believed"

In testimony of those Evangelical Catholic
Principles to which as the Founder of St. Johnland he
consecrated it.

CHAPTER 12

The Man and His Influence

Contemporaries testify that Muhlenberg was a striking man in appearance and possessed a remarkable personality. In his twenty-first year he spent several days with the family of his Quaker friend Dr. George Wood. In his journal Dr. Wood commented, "During his stay he pleased all the family and I believe was pleased with us."[1] When Muhlenberg was fifty-eight years old in 1854, Henry Dana Ward, the diarist, records his wife's reaction to a conversation with Muhlenberg: "Having parted, Mrs. Ward was in rapture with his beautiful face, heavenly smile, delightful squeeze of hand; and made no wonder that the ladies sometime go mad for his beauty."[2] Speaking of him in the declining years of his life, William Wilberforce Newton said that "Muhlenberg was tall and well-proportioned. His head was of massive structure, well set, and crowned with an abundance of curling locks. Both in face and in bearing he was marvelously impressive. When animated or interested in any of his benevolent designs, there was a peculiar radiancy in his countenance and manner."[3]

Bishop Kemper thus describes him in 1860:

> Clarkson has been very attentive and very useful but his manners are not equal to Dr. Muhlenberg's who belongs to the old school and by his courtesy towards me reminds me very much of the way he and I used to act towards Bp. White.[4]

At Flushing and St. Paul's he was regarded as a severe disciplinarian; even the Kemper boys held him in awe.[5] Behind his back he was referred to as "Old Billy."[6] A more prosaic description comes from the

257

diary of Lewis Manigault of Charleston, South Carolina, a former student who passed through New York on his return from Europe in 1854:

> I thought it might be interesting to pass one of my Sundays in going to hear my old School Master Dr. Muhlenberg preach at his Church of the Holy Communion—I have always thought that the 18 Months I spent at College Point were amongst the pleasantest of my life.—Yale College was not to be compared to it.—I often think of the skating, and sleighing, and then in summer the many pleasant afternoons we'd spend in our boats.—So off I went to see what Billy would have to say for himself.—
>
> Before I went to Europe I did not understand Billy's idea of building a church at all.—Says I, Who in the devil ever heard of building a Church with the steeple 'way off on one side.'—I knew it was one of Billy's Crazy notions.—in fact I took a dislike to the Church just from the manner in which it was built.—But now in what a different light I viewed this little structure.—I'd been to Italy, and seen the Ancient style of building Churches, I had now had an opportunity of studying the various orders of Grecian Architecture and here, with pleasing recollections of a European Tour, I stood once more beside this Chapel—not indeed to sneer at what I saw but rather to admire as it were an old Italian Church and Campanile.—This is Man—He often retains his prejudiced ideas 'till error stares him in the face.
>
> I found Billy's service pretty much the same as what we used to have at St. Paul's College.—Just as much Resembling the Catholic as ever.—Turning his back to the congregation during the whole Litany, and looking up to the Cross above and the open Bible upon the Altar.—Billy also commenced Service with the Litany, having read the first and second lessons early in the morning.—I recognized one or two old faces at the Church but as there is Communion every Sunday at this Church, and as most of these acquaintances of mine partook of the Lord's Supper I did not remain to see them.—Billy had always been accustomed to preach to boys, and Consequently used very plain language, in fact the boys used to say that he could not preach to grown persons.—I remembered this, and thought there was some truth in my former opinions for I Can't say that there was much eloquence on this occasion in our address.[7]

There are three known portraits of Muhlenberg. The earliest is by the Pennsylvania Dutch painter, Jacob Eicholtz, who came to Flushing in 1836 for the express purpose of painting Muhlenberg's portrait when Muhlenberg was forty years old. It had been in the possession of descendants of his mother's family, the Sheaffs, and was presented by them to St. Luke's Hospital.[8] The second, a crayon drawing is by a popular artist, H. F. Darby, and was drawn in 1854.[9] It is also at St. Luke's Hospital. The third was painted in 1865 by the fashionable painter Daniel Huntington, who was a personal friend of Muhlenberg and one of his staunch supporters. There are two copies of this third portrait:

one is in the possession of St. Luke's Hospital and the other is in the possession of Mrs. Henry Chisholm, a direct descendant of Muhlenberg's sister Mary.[10] There is a photograph of Muhlenberg by the Civil War photographer, Mathew Brady, also at St. Luke's. A comparison of the Brady photograph with the Huntington portrait indicates that Huntington painted his portrait from this photograph rather than from life. There are several other pictures made from photographs but none of the originals have been located.[11]

One of the most striking characteristics of Muhlenberg was his ability to win the support of businessmen. This ability first came to the fore when he organized the Flushing Institute. The activities of the Church of the Holy Communion were backed by such men as Robert Minturn and John H. Swift. With the building of St. Luke's Hospital came the names of Astor, Vanderbilt, John P. Wolfe, and with the building of St. Johnland are added the names of J. P. Morgan and the Roosevelts. Nor should Muhlenberg's ability as a money raiser by public appeals be underestimated. He it was who carried out the drive for the building of St. Luke's and St. Johnland, and his vigorous sermons helped to raise money for the Midnight Mission and for Bishop Kemper's work in the West.[12] *The Fifth Annual Report of St. Johnland* remarked that contributions had fallen heavily because the powerful voice of Dr. Muhlenberg has not been heard due to his advanced age.[13]

The aid that Muhlenberg received from his inheritance and from his wealthy sister should not be overlooked. He himself was able to buy some of the shares in the Flushing Institute and with his own money he started St. Paul's College. His sister built the Church of the Holy Communion from her private fortune and contributed generously to the work of St. Luke's and St. Johnland. Muhlenberg used the balance of his private fortune to start St. Johnland. He did not accept a salary from any of his projects until late in life, when he received $3,000 a year from St. Luke's which he turned over to St. Johnland.[14]

No evidence has been found that Muhlenberg was ever again interested in marriage after the break-up of his romance with Sarah Coleman, although he once had to write his friends in Lancaster denying his interest in the daughter of a prominent clergyman.[15] Miss Ayres thus describes his final decision in this matter:

> On his way to keep an appointment with a lady, he passed a Roman Catholic Church, and stopping in for a moment, these words of the preacher fell upon his ear: 'We have but one heart. If we had two hearts, we might give one to God, and the other to the world; having but one, God must have it all.'
> 'If celibacy has been the destiny of my life, it was not its program. I never advocated the unmarried status preferably for a clergyman, though in my

own case, in the orderings of Providence, it has enabled me to do various tasks in the Church, which otherwise I might not have undertaken, or even have thought of.'

Photograph of Muhlenberg by Mathew Brady. (Courtesy St. Luke's Hospital)

260

He believed indeed, and inspired others to believe, that in all ages, and in all parts of Christendom, there have been individuals who, from supreme love to God, chose to forego the ordinary ties of earth, remembering our Lord's words: 'He that is able to receive it, let him receive,' but he condemned entirely the imposition of rules to this end, upon organizations or classes, either of men or women, and always spoke with the strongest reprehension, of the enforced celibacy of the Roman clergy.[16]

Dr. Edwin Harwood, Muhlenberg's close friend and supporter whose perceptive biography has been frequently quoted, describes Muhlenberg as not a scholar himself but as an admirer of scholarship.[17] This statement must be qualified in some respects. Thoroughly grounded in Greek and Latin, Muhlenberg had a sound classical education. He was particularly facile in handling Latin quotations, which he often used. He displayed a wide knowledge of the Bible, the early Church Fathers, the English Reformers, and later theologians of the Church of England. He was familiar with contemporary literature in England and the United States. His sermons were carefully constructed and a number were published in pamphlet form or in *Evangelical Catholic Papers*. For this very reason he forfeited the reputation of being a "great preacher" since he did not indulge in "pulpit eloquence." This explains perhaps the somewhat apologetic remarks made about his preaching by Dr. Harwood and the statement of Henry Dana Ward that his sermons were disappointing.[18] Yet Muhlenberg's published sermons and other articles are quite readable and have a contemporary flavor.

He was sufficiently a scholar to support the efforts of F. D. Maurice in England and of Dr. Harwood in this country to adjust the thought of the church to the impact of biblical criticism from Germany and to the scientific discoveries of Sir Charles Lyell and later of Charles Darwin. This was illustrated in *The Evangelical Catholic* in 1852–1853 and in his sermon in 1869 entitled *Christ and the Bible; Not the Bible and Christ*. Dr. Harwood reports that this sermon was in accord with the best biblical scholarship of the time. In his address before the Evangelical Alliance in 1870 Muhlenberg pointed out that criticism and science gave us advantages in the study of the Scriptures unknown before his day.

Muhlenberg did not claim to be a systematic theologian but his theological position throughout his lifetime was remarkably consistent. Personally he was deeply evangelical, but he could bring in, appreciate, and use, Catholic elements. The label that he gave his own theological system, Evangelical Catholicism, best summarizes his own position for he did not see Protestantism and Catholicism as antithetical but as different aspects of the same truth.

Although Muhlenberg did not claim to be a social philosopher, he had

261

a fairly well defined social philosophy which he summed up in the phrase "practical Christianity." The good works in which he engaged were the practical consequences of his Evangelical Catholicism. He never divorced his social reform from his theology: each was an integral part of the other.

In many ways he was a man of his times. His benevolent projects usually had an eleemosynary cast. They were something that the wealthier classes could do for the poorer classes. Although he saw only too clearly the social evils of his age, he sometimes candidly admitted that he saw no solution for them beyond attempts at amelioration by wealthy Christians. It might be asked why he did not advocate that the government accept responsibility for these problems which he admitted were too large for private charity. Muhlenberg himself probably answers this question in a sentence in his appeal for St. Johnland when he states that it would be impossible for the politicians to handle honestly the large sums required.[19] It should be remembered that these were the days of the Tweed Ring in New York local politics and of the Grant administration in national politics. A reformer contemplating the existing corruption might have believed that giving the government new administrative money would merely open new sources of corruption.

Muhlenberg was in strong sympathy with the Temperance Movement despite the traditional occupation of his mother's family.[20] He was an opponent of the "Continental Sabbath" but insisted that a strict observance of the Sabbath did not mean a Puritan Sabbath. He blamed the deterioration of Sabbath observance on the foreigners who swarmed in our cities.[21] He never abated one jot his opposition to the theater.[22] His hymns—one of the major factors in promoting his personal popularity—are definitely period pieces. Only one is still retained in the Episcopal church hymnbook. A commentator has remarked that the less said about Muhlenberg's hymns the better and this is confirmed by a reading of them. Nonetheless as late as 1900 he was still regarded as a great hymnographer and the hymn which caused him much embarrassment, "I Would Not Live Alway," was widely popular.[23]

The Lutheran Church Review published in 1890 an article by Dr. H. E. Jacobs, professor of Church history at the Lutheran Theological Seminary in Philadelphia, entitled "A Commonplace Lutheran." Dr. Jacobs argued that Muhlenberg was Lutheran in background and that most of the ideas that he promoted in the Episcopal Church came from Lutheran sources.[24] This theory has been generally accepted by historians of the Episcopal church.[25] Little evidence to support it can be found, however. Muhlenberg was less than nine years old when he began to attend the Episcopal church. Furthermore, the

Lutheran services which he did attend when he was very young were in German, a language that he did not understand and never learned. As late as 1855, when he was fifty-nine years old, he had to apologize for hiring a German translator.[26] He first went to a school run by an English-speaking Quaker and later changed to Dr. Abercrombie's school, from which he graduated at the age of eleven. The formative influences in his early life were unquestionably the clergy of the United Parish: Dr. Abercrombie, Bishop White, Jackson Kemper, and Dr. James Milnor, and each of these men in his own way was an important influence on young Muhlenberg. There is very little in Muhlenberg's work which can be called Lutheran in origin although there were some parallel efforts within the Lutheran church as there were in other churches. In 1820, for example, Muhlenberg led the movement for an enlarged hymnal in the Episcopal church. He knew that one had recently been adopted in the Lutheran church under the leadership of Philip Mayer but he used an Evangelical church of England hymnal as a basis for his hymnbook. He was interested in developing a ritual which could be consistent with his Evangelical principles, but the Lutheran church in Philadelphia in his early years had no more ritual than the Episcopal church.[27] It is more probable that he got his ritualistic ideas from the Roman Catholic services in Philadelphia which he attended during his youth and early manhood.[28] So also in the case of the establishment of sisterhoods, he was influenced by Dr. Passavant but he had already "set aside" his first sister before Dr. Passavant went to Kaiserwerth and brought back the German deaconesses. As Jackson Kemper's letters indicate, there had also been some prior discussion of such a project in the Episcopal church. There is no question that Muhlenberg had a deep affection for the church of his fathers[29] but in the formative years of his life the strongest influence was that of the Philadelphia churches—especially the Episcopal, Quaker, and Roman Catholic.

It cannot be claimed, strictly speaking, that Muhlenberg originated his ideas—rather there are usually to be found precedents for them, especially in his Philadelphia background and in the New York environment in which he spent the latter part of his life. And there were movements parallel to those he initiated both in the Episcopal church and in other denominations during his lifetime. His primary significance is that he was able to discern those movements which were to mature following the Civil War when the United States became more industrialized and urbanized and to support them far more effectively than any of his contemporaries.

Muhlenberg's influence was not confined to one denomination. It is true that he lived and worked within the context of the Episcopal church and it is in that church that his influence is chiefly felt. Indeed, recent Episcopal church historians rank him as the most influential figure produced by their church in the nineteenth century. But the movements to which he gave impetus became interdenominational and ecumenical in scope.

Thus his work in developing hymnody from the publication of *Church Poetry* in 1823 to the publication of *Hymns for Church and Home* in 1861 promoted hymnody both in the Episcopal church and in American Christianity generally. The public school system of which he was an early proponent is now an accepted fact in our national life. Private schools on the Muhlenberg plan are now operated by both church and secular groups. The Institutional Church of which the Church of the Holy Communion was an early example became the most conspicuous aspect of the social Gospel in all denominations. Deaconesses on the order of the Sisters of the Holy Communion were widely employed by several denominations in education, nursing, and social work, and helped to develop those fields into salaried professions with specialized training. As the first pastor and superintendent of St. Luke's he was a pioneer in hospital administration. His articles in *The Evangelical Catholic* called attention to the problem of housing and the related problem of slums and his St. Johnland project was an attempt to find a practical solution to this problem.

Many of Muhlenberg's activities qualify him as a pioneer of the social Gospel but his influence is broader. His efforts to develop a ritual along Evangelical Catholic lines gave impetus to ritualism in the Episcopal church and in Protestantism generally. His efforts to obtain a more flexible use of the Book of Common Prayer and to provide additional material not in the prayer book mark him as a protagonist of the Liturgical movement. These efforts began with his chapel services in his schools and continued throughout his pastorate at the Church of the Holy Communion and his plans for the parish at St. Johnland. His memorial to the House of Bishops set in motion a debate on church unity which has merged into the Ecumenical movement. Many of the issues that are being debated today in this movement were explored by Muhlenberg from his first paper *Hints on Catholic Union* in 1835 to his last paper before the Evangelical Alliance in 1873. He and his colleague Dr. Edwin Harwood anticipated the impact that Biblical criticism would make on the churches.

The fact that his activities were centered in New York, then the center of the church as well as of the secular affairs of the nation, made him an influence throughout the entire country. And this influence was strengthened by the manner in which the memorial was presented, the questionnaire sent out, and the ensuing controversy conducted. But his most notable achievement was that he profoundly influenced a group of younger men who were to play an important part in the life of the Episcopal church in the years after the Civil War. He left behind no party in the church nor any group indoctrinated with partisan principles. The men whom he influenced were instead imbued with his concern for social justice and his belief in the comprehensive character of the church. The last is undoubtedly the most striking element of Muhlenberg's character: That he believed that Christians of widely different theological opinions could all be united in one church, and this in an age in which not only members of one denomination but of one party within a denomination supposed themselves to be absolutely right and that those who held different opinions were either fools or scoundrels.

Probably the best known of the Muhlenberg men was Henry Codman Potter, the son of Muhlenberg's colleague of the Memorial movement, Bishop Alonzo Potter of Pennsylvania. He came to New York in 1868 as rector of Grace Church and modeled that parish after the Church of the Holy Communion taking Muhlenberg as his own model. He succeeded his uncle Horatio Potter as bishop of New York in 1887 and in this position was a forceful advocate of the social Gospel and exercised a conciliatory influence during the bitter controversies over the Anglo-Catholic movement, and the acceptance of Biblical Criticism and the Darwinian theory of evolution.[30] Other Muhlenberg men who exerted a similar influence were Edward A. Washburn,[31] Edwin Harwood,[32] John Cotton Smith,[33] Heber Newton,[34] William Wilberforce Newton,[35] and Bishop Thomas Hubbard Vail.[36]

The clergyman, however, who best typifies the continuing Muhlenberg tradition was not, as far as can be discovered, associated with Muhlenberg during his lifetime. William Reed Huntington (1838–1909) was approximately forty years old at the time of Muhlenberg's death and had lived the greater part of his life in Boston. He came to New York in 1883 as rector of Grace Church to succeed Henry Codman Potter when the latter was elected bishop of New York. Huntington, as rector of Grace Church, filled much the same position that Muhlenberg did before the war. He was interested in most of the causes in which Muhlenberg had been interested. Although he did not know Muhlenberg personally he was largely influenced by Dr. Edward A. Washburn who had been one of Muhlenberg's associates and who after the war became one of Dr. Huntington's close friends. A contemporary historian who has done extensive research on these three men says that the influence of Muhlenberg on Dr. Huntington although indirect was profound.[37]

In summarizing Muhlenberg's significance it is difficult to fit him into any one frame of reference. It is possible to regard him as one of a group of men who tried to broaden and adjust the thought and policies of their respective churches to the problems of the nineteenth century. It might be argued that Muhlenberg was to the Episcopal church what Samuel Schmucker and William A. Passavant were to the Lutheran; Albert Barnes and Stephen Colwell to the Presbyterians; Horace Bushnell to the Congregationalists; and possibly Cardinal James Gibbons to the Roman Catholics. However the principal objective of Muhlenberg was that the Christian church, in general, and the Episcopal church in particular, might meet the problems that were rising in nineteenth-century United States. To focus his interests further it should be pointed out that his principal attention was to the problems of people living in cities since he lived his early and formative years in Philadelphia, then the leading urban center of the country, and the greater part of his days in and around New York which succeeded Philadelphia as the leading urban center. Although he maintained a concern for the work of the church in the West, it was as a prominent urban clergyman recognizing the westward trend of the population. His absorbing interest was in the life of the church in the city. For this reason if any designation were to be chosen for Muhlenberg, that of Church Leader in the Cities best sums up his life and work.

NOTES

CHAPTER 1: PHILADELPHIA 1796–1820

1. *Report of the Centennial, 1806–1906* (Philadelphia: St. John's Evangelical Lutheran Church, 1906), p. 10.

2. James Mease, *The Picture of Philadelphia, giving an account of its Origin, Increase and Improvements, in Arts, Sciences, Manufactures, Commerce, and Revenue, with a Compendious view of its societies, literary, benevolent, patriotic, and religious, its police, the public buildings, the prison and penitentiary systems, its institutions, monied and civil* (Philadelphia: Kite and Co., 1811), pp. 202–208.

3. William B. Sprague, *Annals of the American Pulpit* (New York: R. Carter and Bros., 1857–1861), IX, 47.

4. Documents concerning the language controversy at St. Michael and Zion Parish are in the library of the Lutheran Theological Seminary, Mt. Airy, Pennsylvania. They will be referred to as Documents in the Language Controversy.

5. M. L. Stoever, *Memorial of the Rev. Philip Mayer, D.D.* (Philadelphia: James Kite and Co., 1859), pp. 13–14.

6. *Trial of Frederick Eberle and Others, at a Nisi Prius Court, held at Philadelphia, July, 1816, before the Honorable Jasper Yeates, Justice, for illegally conspiring together by all means lawful and unlawful "with their bodies and lives" to prevent the introduction of the English Language into the Service of St. Michael's and Zion Church Belonging to the German Lutheran Congregation in the City of Philadelphia. Taken in shorthand by James Carson, Attorney at law.* (Philadelphia: Published for the reporter, 1871), p. 12.

7. Paul A. Wallace, *The Muhlenbergs of Pennsylvania* (Philadelphia: The University of Pennsylvania Press, 1950), *passim*.

8. H. M. M. Richards, "Descendents of Henry Melchio Muhlenberg," in *Proceedings and Addresses of the Pennsylvania-German Society*, X (January, 1900), 5–12, 30–33. Will of John Rogers, April 29, 1841, Hall of Records, New York County, Liber 83, p. 270. Will of Mrs. William Sheaff, December 4, 1817, Recorder's Office, Philadelphia County Courthouse, No. 117. *Philadelphia Directories*, 1785–1821, various authors and publishers (1799–1804 directories missing from the file in the Pennsylvania Historical Society Library).

9. Henry Melchior Muhlenberg had four daughters who are not mentioned in this book.

10. These men had other children not mentioned in this book.

11. Letters of Administration of the Estate of Henry William Muhlenberg, Recorder's Office, Philadelphia County Courthouse, Case A-13, DL. – 128.

12. Will of William Sheaff, February 22, 1803, Recorder's Office, Philadelphia County Courthouse, No. 65.

13. William Garnett Chisholm, *Chisholm Genealogy* (New York: Knickerbocker Press, 1914), p. 41.

14. *Dunlaps American Daily Advertiser,* August 5, 1795.

15. Anne Ayres, *Life and Work of William Augustus Muhlenberg* (5th ed. New York: T. Whittaker, 1894).

16. *The Philadelphia Directory for* 1797, p. 133; *The Philadelphia Directory for* 1805, p. 126.

17. George W. Sheaff to John F. Steinman, September 29, 1807, in Sheaff Papers, Pennsylvania Historical Society; Poulson's *American Daily Advertiser,* Philadelphia, October 1, 1805.

18. Letters of Administration for the Estate of Henry William Muhlenberg, Recorder's Office, Philadelphia County Courthouse, Case A-13, DL 128; Ayres, *Life of Muhlenberg,* pp. 10–13.

19. Will of Mrs. William Sheaff, December 4, 1817, Recorder's Office, Philadelphia County Courthouse, No. 117.

20. Ayres, *Life of Muhlenberg,* p. 14; *The Philadelphia Directory for* 1812, p. 76.

21. *Minutes of the United Parish,* October 8, 1806.

22. Will of George David Seckel, November 30, 1798, Recorder's Office, Philadelphia County Courthouse, No. 3100; *The Philadelphia Directory for* 1785, p. 71.

23. *The Philadelphia Directory for* 1795, p. 163.

24. *Ibid.,* p. 163; Mease, *Picture of Philadelphia,* pp. 235, 239, 247.

25. Documents in the Language Controversy.

26. Will of George David Seckel, November 30, 1798, Recorder's Office, Philadelphia County Courthouse, No. 3100.

27. *Supra,* this chapter.

28. Will of William Sheaff, February 22, 1803, Office of the Recorder, Philadelphia County, No. 65.

29. A review of the Philadelphia Directories from 1785 to 1805 indicates that although the Sheaffs and Seckels had various occupations the usual one was wine merchant.

30. George Sheaff, Subscription list for a present for Commander Isaac Hull, Archives of the Pennsylvania Historical Society.

31. Minutes of the United Parish, January 30, 1807; *Catalogue of St. Paul's College,* 1839, p. 13; *First Report of the Society of the Advancement of Christianity in Pennsylvania* (Philadelphia: Published by the Society, 1813).

32. Documents in the Language Controversy.

33. Minutes of the United Parish, December 29, 1806; January 30, 1807; March 23, 1807; May 25, 1807.

34. *Ibid.,* September 21, 1912.

36. Ayres, *Life of Muhlenberg,* pp. 15-16.

36. Anonymous description of Philadelphia, Kemper Papers, Wisconsin State Historical Society Library, vol. VII, no. 6. (Probable author: Elizabeth Kemper, daughter of Jackson Kemper.)

37. Ayres, *Life of Muhlenberg,* pp. 10-11.

38. *Ibid.,* p. 14.

39. James Abercrombie, *A Charge delivered after a public examination on July 27, 1804, to the senior class of the Philadelphia Academy, upon their having completed*

the course of study prescribed by that institution (Philadelphia: Privately printed, 1804), p. 7. Hereafter these annual addresses will be referred to as Abercrombie, *Charge to the class of...*

40. Oliver Oldschool, ed., *The Port Folio* V (November, 1810), 393-396.

41. Abercrombie, *Charge to the class of 1805* p. 4.

42. Abercrombie, *Charge to the class of 1804* p. 8.

43. *Ibid.*, p. 4.

44. Ayres, *Life of Muhlenberg*, p. 19.

45. Abercrombie, *Charge to the class of* 1808, *passim.*

46. Abercrombie, *Lectures on the Catechism, on Confirmation, and on the Liturgy of the Protestant Episcopal Church; Delivered to the students of that denomination in the Philadelphia Academy* (Philadelphia: Privately printed, 1807), p. 15. Abercrombie, *Charge to the class of* 1804, p. 9.

47. Sprague, *Annals of the American Pulpit*, V, 392-395.

48. *Ibid.*, p. 395.

49. "Prospectus," The Quarterly Theological Magazine, I (February, 1813). (The Prospectus was republished in the second issue.)

50. Abercrombie, *Prospectus of an Edition of Johnson's Works* (Philadelphia: n.p., n.d.).

51. Abercrombie, *A Sermon on the Liturgy of the Protestant Episcopal Church* (Philadelphia: Smith and Maxwell, 1808), *passim.*

52. Abercrombie, *The Mourner Comforted* [A Sermon] (Philadelphia: Bradford and Inskeep, 1812), *passim.*

53. Abercrombie, *Charge to the class of* 1806, p. 120.

54. Abercrombie, *A Sermon Occasioned by the Death of Alexander Hamilton, who was killed by Aaron Burr, in a duel, July* 11, 1804. *Preached in Christ Church and St. Peter's, Philadelphia, on July* 22, 1804 (Philadelphia: H. Maxwell, 1804), *passim.*

55. Abercrombie, *Charge to the class of* 1808, p. 2.

56. Abercrombie, *A Sermon Preached in Christ Church and St. Peter's, Philadelphia, on May* 9, 1798. *Being the day appointed by the President as a Day of Fasting, Humiliation and Prayer, throughout the United States of America* (Philadelphia: Printed by John Ormond, 1798).

57. *The Gazette of the United States,* August 30, 1800.

58. Abercrombie, *Charge to the class of* 1810, p. 16.

59. Ayres, *Life of Muhlenberg*, p. 19.

60. Minutes of the board of Trustees of the University of Pennsylvania, January 5, 1807.

61. *Ibid.*, April 7, 1812.

62. Pennsylvania, University of, *University Papers,* vol. VIII (1811–1813).

63. Ayres, *Life of Muhlenberg*, pp. 20-23.

64. Pennsylvania, University of, *Biographical catalogue of the matriculates of the college, together with lists of the members of the college faculty and trustees, officers, and recipients of honorary degrees,* 1749–1893 (Philadelphia: Published by the Alumni Association, 1894), p. 48.

65. Minutes of the board of Trustees of the University of Pennsylvania, November 23, 1813.

66. *Biographical catalogue of the matriculates of the college of the University of Pennsylvania,* p. 48.

67. Engel's letters are in the files of the Presbyterian Historical Society. They reflect this interest in particular.

68. *Biographical catalogue of the matriculates of the college of the University of Pennsylvania,* p. 49.

69. *Ibid.,* p. 52; Ayres, *Life of Muhlenberg,* p. 20.

70. *University Papers,* vol. VI (1808–1810), January 5, 1808; Minutes of the board of Trustees of the University of Pennsylvania, October 10, 1810, June 21, 1811; *Philadelphia Directory,* 1808, p. 11; *The Port Folio,* III (1814), 520.

71. Minutes of the board of Trustees of the University of Pennsylvania, June 21, 1811.

72. *Philadelphia Directory,* 1808, p. 42.

73. Edward Potts Cheyney, *A History of the University of Pennsylvania* 1740– (Philadelphia: University of Pennsylvania Press, 1940), pp. 176-177.

74. *Ibid.,* pp. 177-180.

75. Minutes of the board of Trustees of the University of Pennsylvania, October 10, 1810.

76. *University Papers,* VI, 1808–1810; VIII, 1814–1816: February 1, 1814; March 3, 1812; April 6, 1813; VII, 1811–1813: June 30, 1813; Minutes of the board of Trustees of the University of Pennsylvania, February 1, 1814; June 30, 1813; April 6, 1813; January 2, 1810.

77. Cheyney, *History of the University of Pennsylvania,* pp. 182-195.

78. Ayres, *Life of Muhlenberg,* p. 26.

79. *University Papers,* VIII, 1814–1816: April 4, 1814; VII, 1811–1813: March 2, 1813; VI, 1808–1810, n.d.; Minutes of the board of Trustees of the University of Pennsylvania, October 10, 1810; February 21, 1814; January 30, 1813; April 6, 1813; *Archives General of the University of Pennsylvania. Grammar School,* 1814–1821.

80. Muhlenberg to Samuel Seabury, August 22 (no year given), Oliver Papers. The family papers of Mr. Andrew Oliver, a direct descendant of Samuel Seabury. In General Theological Seminary Library, 175 9th Avenue, New York, N.Y. When William Augustus Muhlenberg, the subject, is cited, he will be referred to simply as "Muhlenberg," except when he is cited along with another person named Muhlenberg. The same rule will be followed in regard to his close associates, Jackson Kemper and Samuel Seabury, whose letters are frequently cited in this biography.

81. One of the persons arrested at the time of the riot in St. Michael and Zion Church was a Frederic Crusé. *See Trial of Frederic Eberle,* fn. 6. He may have been the father of Muhlenberg's friend.

82. *Catalogue of the Philomathean Society Instituted in the University of Pennsylvania,* MDCCCXIII (Philadelphia: Ringwall and Co., Printers, 1859), 2, 5; Frederick Beasley to the Trustees, January 3, 1815, *University Papers,* vol. VIII, 1814–1816; Muhlenberg to Samuel Seabury, July 14, 1843, Oliver Papers; Report of the Pastor Superintendent of St. Luke's Hospital, 1865, p. 16.

83. *Biographical catalogue of the matriculates of the college of the University of Pennsylvania,* p. 46.

84. George B. Wood, *An Address Delivered Before the Philomathean Society of the University of Pennsylvania* (Philadelphia: Published by the Society, 1826), p. 12.

85. George Bacon Wood, *Journal of Dr. George B. Wood, No. 1st [sic] 1817 to 1829* (Philadelphia: Privately published, 1839), April 21, 1823; August 14, 1823; September 1824; August 4, 1827.

86. *Biographical catalogue of the matriculates of the college of the University of Pennsylvania,* p. 55.

87. Ayres, *Life of Muhlenberg,* pp. 27-28.

88. Philo [the name of a student society]. *Addresses delivered before the Philomathean Society of the University of Pennsylvania, on the occasion of the semi-centenial* [*sic*] *celebration, October* 6, 1863. (Philadelphia: Published by the Society, 1864), p. 16.

89. *University Papers*, 1789–1827; June, 1815; August 1, 1821.

90. *Addresses Delivered before the Philomathean Society*, p. 23; Ayres, *Life of Muhlenberg*, pp. 28-29.

91. Ayres, *Life of Muhlenberg*, pp. 33-37.

92. Minutes of the board of Trustees of the University of Pennsylvania, January 7, 1815; Dr. Frederick Beasley to the Trustees of the University of Pennsylvania, January 3, 1815; *University Papers*, VIII, 1814–1816; *United States Gazette*, January 13, 1815; Dr. Frederick Beasley to the Trustees of the University of Pennsylvania, April 1, 1817, in Archives General of the University of Pennsylvania. Students and activities, 1789–1827.

93. Greenough White, *An Apostle of the Western Church* (New York: Thomas Whittaker, 1911), pp. 1-6. Minutes of the United Parish, September 21, 1812.

94. Minutes of the United Parish, May 13, 1811; August 3, 1814; January 11, 1815. Ayres, *Life of Muhlenberg*, pp. 24-26.

95. Minutes of the United Parish, June 28, 1816.

96. *Ibid.,* August 5, 1816.

97. The Kemper Papers in the State Historical Society of Wisconsin Library contain many letters from Muhlenberg to Kemper. Kemper died in 1870.

98. Ayres, *Life of Muhlenberg*, p. 38. Muhlenberg to Bishop White, 1828, Kemper Papers Book IV, nos. 124, 133.

99. William White, "Copy of a letter to Bishop Hobart, September 1, 1819, relating, at his request, the incidents of the early part of my life, together with twenty-one notes connected with my Letter to Bp. Hobart added December 21, 1830," Walter H. Stowe, ed., reprinted in the *Historical Magazine of the Protestant Episcopal Church*, XXII, IV (December, 1953), 383-417. This letter will be referred to as White, *Autobiography;* Bird Wilson, *Memoir of the Life of the Rt. Rev. William White* (Philadelphia: Hayes and Fell, 1839), p. 12. This book will be referred to as Wilson, *Memoir of Bishop White;* William White, "The Case of the Episcopal Churches in the United States Considered," Richard G. Salomon, Editor, reprinted in *Historical Magazine of the Protestant Episcopal Church*, XXII, No. 4 (December, 1953), 435-494; Walter H. Stowe, "William White, Ecclesiastical Statesman," in *Historical Magazine of the Protestant Episcopal Church*, XXII (December, 1953), 372-383.

100. Mease, *Picture of Philadelphia*, pp. 161, 235, 239, 243, 244, 246, 247; *Pennsylvania Journal of Prison Discipline and Philanthropy*, II, 1; William White, "An Address delivered at the Laying of the Cornerstone of the Building for the Deaf and Dumb on the 15th of June, 1824," in *National Gazette*, June 17, 1824; Henry U. Onderdonk, *Appendix to a discourse Delivered in Christ Church, Philadelphia at the funeral of the Rt. Rev. William White* (Philadelphia: Jaspar Harding, printer, 1836), *passim;* Minutes of the United Parish, May 2, 1812, March 5, 1819.

101. Ayres, *Life of Muhlenberg*, pp. 41, 48.

102. Wood, *Journal*, August 8, 1817; August 31, 1817; September 21, 1817; May 19, 1818.

103. Ayres, *Life of Muhlenberg*, p. 41. Robert Abbe, "A New View of the Boyhood of the Rev. Dr. Muhlenberg," reprinted from the *Medical Journal and Record* for November 17, 1926, p. 6.

104. Wood, *Journal,* September 18, 1817.

105. Minutes of the United Parish, September 30, 1818; October 29, 1819; October 4, 1820.

106. Unsigned Document in the Kemper Diary, Kemper Papers, November 18, 1832, July 12, 1833.

107. Ayres, *Life of Muhlenberg,* p. 54; Abercrombie, *Charge to the Class of* 1808, p. 16.

108. Ayres, *Life of Muhlenberg,* pp. 40-47; Minutes of the United Parish, April 6, 1812.

109. Ayres, *Life of Muhlenberg,* p. 55.

110. Minutes of the United Parish, May 27, 1809; April 30, 1810; April 13, 1816.

111. Minutes of the United Parish, March 26, 1813; *First Report of the Society for the Advancement of Christianity in Pennsylvania* (Philadelphia: Privately printed, 1813), pp. 7-8.

112. *Fifth Annual Report of the Trustees of the Society for the Advancement of Christianity in Pennsylvania* (Philadelphia: Privately printed, 1817), pp. 8-9.

113. *Seventh Annual Report of the Society for the Advancement of Christianity in Pennsylvania* (Philadelphia: Privately published, 1819), pp. 10-11.

114. Minutes of the Vestry of the United Parish, September 3, 1817; *First Annual Report of the Episcopal Missionary Society of Philadelphia* (Philadelphia: Privately printed, 1817), pp. 6-7.

115. *Circular of the Episcopal Education Society* (Philadelphia: Privately printed, 1825), pp. 3, 5; *Circular of the Episcopal Education Society* (Philadelphia: Privately printed, 1826), pp. 3-4.

116. *Fifth Annual Report of the Society of the Protestant Episcopal Church for the Advancement of Christianity in Pennsylvania* (Philadelphia: Privately printed, 1817), pp. 10-11.

117. Ayres, *Life of Muhlenberg,* p. 39; Anonymous, Appeal For Funds For The General Theological Seminary Giving an Account of Its History, February 10, 1824, Kemper Papers, vol. VII, no. 10; A True Copy of the Will of J. Sherred, April 23, 1821, Kemper Papers, vol. V, no. 114.

118. Clifford P. Morehouse, "The Origens of the Episcopal Church Press from Colonial Days" *Historical Magazine of the Protestant Episcopal Church* XI (September, 1942), 199-318.

119. *Second Annual Report of the Protestant Episcopal Sunday and Adult School of Philadelphia* (Philadelphia: Privately printed, 1819), pp. 6-7; *Constitution of the Protestant Episcopal Sunday School Society of Philadelphia* (Philadelphia: Privately printed, 1818), *passim.*

120. *Supra,* this chapter.

121. Henry Caswall, *America and the American Church* (London: Gilbert and Rivington, Printers, 1839), pp. 331-337.

122. Kemper Papers, 1817, vol. II, nos. 6, 16, 42, 52.

123. Muhlenberg to Kemper, Kemper Papers, February 17, 1820, vol. V, no. 120.

124. *Ibid.,* September 2, 1820, vol. V, no. 134.

125. *Ibid.,* September 12, 1820, vol. V, no. 136.

126. Ayres, *Life of Muhlenberg,* p. 47.

127. Muhlenberg to Kemper, Kemper Papers, February 17, 1820, vol. V, no. 120.

128. *Ibid.,* June 12, 1820, vol. V, no. 123.

129. Hobart to Kemper, Kemper Papers, December 28, 1820, vol. V, no. 155.

130. Muhlenberg to Kemper, Kemper Papers, September 2, 1820, vol. V, no. 134.

131. *Ibid.,* September 12, 1820, vol. V, no. 136.

132. *Ibid.,* August, 1820, vol. V, no. 131.

133. *Ibid.,* July 5, 1820, vol. V, no. 129.

134. *Ibid.,* August, 1820, vol. V, no. 131.

135. Muhlenberg to Kemper, Kemper Papers, September 12, 1820.

136. Wilson, *Memoir of Bishop White,* p. 237.

137. *The Philadelphia Directory for* 1806, p. 18; *The Philadelphia Directory for* 1811, *passim.*

138. *The Philadelphia Directory for* 1806, p. 18.

CHAPTER 2: LANCASTER, 1820–1827

1. Ayres, *Life of Muhlenberg,* pp. 55-58.

2. *Journal of the Diocese of Pennsylvania,* 1820, p. 10; Muhlenberg to Kemper, December 18, 1820, Kemper Papers, vol. V, no. 152; *Lancaster Journal,* June 6, 1801.

3. Sprague, *Annals of the American Pulpit,* IX, 61.

4. *Biographical catalogue of the matriculates of the college of the University of Pennsylvania,* p. 86.

5. Henry Melchior Muhlenberg, *Journals,* II, 240.

6. H. M. J. Klein, *Lancaster's Golden Century,* 1821–1921 (Lancaster: Hager and Brother, 1922), pp. 21-45.

7. Sprague, *Annals of the American Pulpit,* IX, 61.

8. James Stuart, "Three Years in North America," 11,303, quoted in *Lancaster Historical Society Proceedings,* XXXII (1928), 154.

9. Minutes of the Vestry of St. James Church, Lancaster, Pennsylvania, October 3, 1744. These will be referred to as Minutes of St. James, Lancaster.

10. *Journal of the Diocese of Pennsylvania,* 1820, p. 10.

11. Minutes of the Vestry of St. John's Church, Pequea, Pa., December 27, 1821.

12. Muhlenberg to Kemper, December 18, 1820, Kemper Papers, vol. V, no. 152.

13. Minutes of the Vestry of St. James, Lancaster, September 29, 1826.

14. Philip Shriver Klein, "James Buchanan and Ann Coleman," in *Pennsylvania History,* XXI, (January, 1954), 1-20.

15. Catherine Yeates to Kemper, July 19, 1826, Kemper Papers, vol. VIII, no. 32; Franklin Ellis and Samuel Evans, *History of Lancaster County* (Philadelphia: Everts and Peck, 1883), pp. 226, 627.

16. Henry Wilder Foote, *Three Centuries of American Hymnody* (Cambridge: Harvard University Press, 1940), chs. V, VI; Louis F. Benson, *The English Hymn, Its Development and Use in Worship* (New York: George H. Doran Company, 1915), 390-402.

17. William White, *Memoirs of the Protestant Episcopal Church, in the United States of America, from its organization up to the present day,* 2d ed. (New York: Swords, Stanford & Company, 1836), pp. 43-45, 34, 103, 108, 385-395, 21-23, 256-257.

18. White, "Thoughts on the Singing of Psalms and Anthems in Churches," (Signed "Silas") in the *Christian Journal,* May and June, 1808.

19. White, *Autobiography,* p. 384.

20. I have been unable to find any reference to this story in source materials, but it is entirely plausible, for it fits in well with what we know about Dr. Abercrombie and Bishop White.

21. Muhlenberg to Kemper, October 15, 1821, Kemper Papers, vol. VI, no. 49.

22. Muhlenberg, "A Plea for Christian Hymns," in *Evangelical Catholic Papers,* ed. by Anne Ayres (New York: T. Whittaker, 1875, 1877), II, ll. This two-volume collection of articles by Muhlenberg will be referred to as E.C.P. to distinguish them from *The Evangelical Catholic,* a newspaper that Muhlenberg published from 1851 to 1853.

23. White, *Memoirs,* p. 265.

24. Muhlenberg, "A Plea for Christian Hymns," *E.C.P.,* II, ll.

25. This book will be referred to as Muhlenberg, *Church Poetry.*

26. *Lancaster Journal,* February 13, 1824.

27. Thomas Cotterill, *A Selection of Psalms and Hymns For the Use of St. Paul's and St. James Churches,* 9th ed. (Sheffield: Printed by J. Montgomery, 1820).

28. Muhlenberg, *Church Poetry,* p. iii.

29. *Ibid.,* pp. iii-iv, vi.

30. *Ibid.,* VI; John Julian, *A Dictionary of Hymnology* (London: John Murray, 1925), pp. 503-504.

31. *Philadelphia Recorder,* May 10, 1823.

32. Ayres *Life of Muhlenberg,* pp. 63-64.

33. White, *Memoirs,* p. 261.

34. *Ibid.,* p. 267.

35. Muhlenberg to Kemper, December 28, 1826, Kemper Papers, vol. VIII, no. 144.

36. Circular, signed by Bishop John Henry Hobart, April 10, 1827, The Hobart Papers, New York Historical Society Collection.

37. White, *Memoirs,* p. 256.

38. Benson, *The English Hymn,* pp. 399-401.

39. Julian, *Dictionary of Hymnology,* pp. 774-775.

40. *Infra,* this chapter.

41. *Philadelphia Recorder,* June, 1826.

42. *Evangelical Catholic,* II, vi.

43. Kemper to Muhlenberg, Kemper Papers; Letter Book, May 25, 1853.

44. Muhlenberg, *"I Would Not Live Alway" and other pieces in verse, by the same author* (New York: Robert Craighead, Printer, 1860); Muhlenberg, *"I Would Not Live Alway," evangelized by its author with the story of the hymn and a brief account of St. Johnland* (New York: T. Whittaker and Co., 1871).

45. Julian, *Dictionary of Hymnology,* pp. 774-775.

46. *Supra,* ch. I.

47. Ayres, *Life of Muhlenberg,* pp. 59-60.

48. Minutes of St. James Church, Lancaster, March 24, 1821; C. H. Brewer, *A History of Religious Education in the Episcopal Church to 1835* (New Haven: Yale University Press, 1924), p. 166.

49. Ayres, *Life of Muhlenberg,* pp. 59-60; First Annual Report of the Female Sunday School Society of St. James Church, Lancaster, May 27, 1882; Constitu-

tion and Minutes of the Sunday School Society of St. James Church, February 24, 1822.

50. Mark Twain, *The Adventures of Tom Sawyer* (New York: Grossett and Dunlap, 1946), pp. 11-45.

51. Joseph Lancaster to Roberts Vaux, November 26, 1818, Roberts Vaux Papers, Historical Society of Pennsylvania Library.

52. Constitution and Minutes of the Sunday School Society of St. James Church, (Lancaster, Pa., n.p., 1820).

53. Mease, *Picture of Philadelphia*, p. 27; Ayres, *Life of Muhlenberg*, p. 62.

54. Thomas J. Wharton, *Address Delivered at the Opening of the New Hall of Athenaeum*, October 18, 1812. (Philadelphia, 1812), *passim.*

55. *Ibid.*, pp. 61-62; *Second Annual Report of the Controllers of the First School District of the State of Pennsylvania, with their accounts. And a list of its Controllers and Directors* (Philadelphia: Printed by order of the Board of Controllers, 1820), p. 20.

56. J. J. McCadden, *Education in Pennsylvania 1801–1805, and its Debt to Roberts Vaux* (Philadelphia: University of Pennsylvania Press, 1937), pp. 178-233.

57. Commonwealth of Pennsylvania, *Laws of the Commonwealth of Pennsylvania . . .* (Philadelphia: published under the authority of the legislature, 1808), pp. 193-194. This collection will be cited as *Laws of Pennsylvania*.

58. *Laws of Pennsylvania*, 1818, pp. 124-130.

59. Joseph Lancaster, *The Lancastrian system of Education with improvements* (Baltimore: The Lancastrian Institute, 1821), p. 28.

60. Joseph Lancaster, *Epitome of some of the chief events and transactions in the life of Joseph Lancaster containing an account of the rise and progress of the Lancastrian system of Education and the Author's Prospects of future usefullness to mankind* (New York: Baldwin and Peck, 1833), *passim.*

61. Hall Harrison, Life of the Rt. Rev. John Barrett Kerfoot (New York: James Pott and Co., 1886), p. 4; Ellis-Evans, *History of Lancaster County*, p. 409.

62. McCadden, *Education in Pennsylvania*, pp. 183-192.

63. Lancaster to Vaux, November 20, 1818, Vaux Papers.

64. Emlen to Vaux, October 15, 1818, Vaux Papers.

65. Lancaster to Vaux, November 20, 1818, Vaux Papers.

66. *Supra*, fn. 58.

67. Ellis-Evans, *History of Lancaster County*, p. 407.

68. *Laws of Pennsylvania*, 1822, p. 49; Abbe, *A New View of Muhlenberg*, p. 8.

69. *Laws of Pennsylvania*, 1822, p. 52.

70. Ellis-Evans, *History of Lancaster County*, p. 408.

71. *Infra*, fn. 78.

72. *Infra*, ch. III.

73. *Biographical catalogue of the matriculates of the college of the University of Pennsylvania*, p. 76; Ellis-Evans, *History of Lancaster County*, p. 402.

74. *Lancaster Intelligencer*, April 22, 1823.

75. Ellis-Evans, *History of Lancaster County*, pp. 407-409.

76. Constitution and Minutes of the Sunday School Society of St. James Church, February 24, 1822; *Lancaster Journal*, January, 1817.

77. Ellis-Evans, *History of Lancaster County*, pp. 408-409.

78. *Laws of Pennsylvania*, 1824, p. 81.

79. Ellis-Evans, *History of Lancaster County*, pp. 408-410.

80. *Ibid.*, p. 410.

81. *Tenth Annual Report of the Controllers of the First School District of Pennsylvania.* . . . (Philadelphia: Printed by order of the Controller, 1828), p. 7.

82. Muhlenberg to Vaux, January 14, 1822, Vaux Papers.

83. *Ibid.*

84. *Ibid.,* June 25, 1822.

85. *Ibid.,* September 30, 1822.

86. *Ibid.,* February 11, 1823.

87. *Ibid.,* February 18, 1823.

88. *Ibid.,* March 27, 1826.

89. *Tenth Annual Report of the Controllers of the First School District of Pennsylvania.* . . . (Philadelphia: Printed by order of the Controller, 1828), p. 31; Ellis-Evans, *History of Lancaster County,* p. 409.

90. Muhlenberg to Vaux, September 19, 1821, Vaux Papers.

91. Harrison, *Life of Bishop Kerfoot,* I, 4.

92. Muhlenberg, *A valedictory sermon preached in St. James Church, Lancaster, On Sunday Evening, July 23,* 1826 (Jamaica, L.I.: Sleight and Tucker, Printers, 1826), p. 13.

93. Muhlenberg to Kemper, December 29, 1824, Kemper Papers, vol. VII, no. 63.

94. *Ibid.*

95. *Ibid.*

96. Ayres, *Life of Muhlenberg,* pp. 68-69.

97. *Infra,* fn. 113.

98. *Ibid.*

99. Phillip Shriver Klein, "James Buchanan and Ann Coleman," in *Pennsylvania History,* XXI (January, 1954), pp. 1-20.

100. *Lancaster Journal,* December 13, 1819.

101. Minutes of St. James Church, Lancaster, October 30, 1820.

102. *Ibid.,* October 17, 1820.

103. First Annual Report of the Female Sunday School Society of St. James Church, Lancaster, Pennsylvania, May 22, 1822.

104. Minutes of St. James Church, April 23, 1821.

105. *Ibid.,* April 8, 1822.

106. *Ibid.,* April 20, 1822.

107. *Ibid.,* April 6, 1823.

108. Muhlenberg to Kemper, January 13, 1825, Kemper Papers, vol. VII, no. 124.

109. Will of Robert Coleman, April 6, 1822, Lancaster County Court House, Book 0.1, pp. 347-352.

110. *American Daily Advertiser,* Philadelphia, October 4, 1825, November 7, 1825.

111. *Lancaster Journal,* November 4, 1825.

112. Minutes of St. James Church, June 19, 1825, June 20, 1826.

113. *Ibid.,* June 28, 1826; Letters of Administration of the Estate of Sarah Hand Coleman, November 30, 1825, Lancaster County Court House, Book C − 1 − 143.

114. Minutes of St. James Church, June 28, 1826.

115. *Ibid.,* June 30, 1826.

116. *Ibid.,* August 1, 1826.

117. Muhlenberg, *Valedictory Sermon,* p. 36.

118. Minutes of the Vestry of St. James Church, Lancaster, August 18, 1826.

119. *Ibid.*, September 21, 1826.

120. Muhlenberg to Margaret and Catherine Yeates, February 14, 1827, Archives of St. James Church, Lancaster.

121. Klein, *James Buchanan and Ann Coleman*, p. 72.

122. The Rev. John B. Clemson to the Rev. Frederic M. Bird, July 19, 1889, in Union Theological Seminary Library.

123. Mrs. Martha J. Nevin to the Rev. Frederic M. Bird, October 17, 1881, in Union Theological Seminary Library.

124. Klein, James Buchanan and Ann Coleman, pp. 15-20.

125. Ayres, *Life of Muhlenberg*, pp. 194-195.

126. White, *Apostle of the Western Church*, p. 76, Kemper to Muhlenberg, September 17, 1835, Kemper Papers, Letter Book.

127. Wilson, *Memoir of Bishop White*, p. 327.

CHAPTER 3: FLUSHING INSTITUTE

1. Ayres, *Life of Muhlenberg*, pp. 81-82. Minutes of the Vestry of St. George's Church, Flushing, L.I., N.Y., July 1, 1826. These will be referred to as Minutes of St. George's Church, Flushing.

2. Benjamin F. Thompson, *The History of Long Island From Its Discovery and Settlement to the Present Time* (New York: Gould, Banks, and Co., 1843), p. 67; Thomas Kelah Wharton, Unpublished Diary, in the Manuscript Division of the New York Public Library, August 24, 1831. This document will be referred to as Wharton, Diary.

3. Wood, *Journal*, August 4, 1827.

4. J. Carpenter Smith, *History of St. George's Parish, Flushing, Long Island* (Flushing: Sword and Shield, 1897), p. 116.

5. Minutes of St. George's Church, Flushing, July 30, 1828.

6. *Ibid.*, July 1, 1826.

7. Muhlenberg to Kemper, December 28, 1826, Kemper Papers, vol. VIII, no. 144.

8. *Ibid.*, December 14, 1826, no. 137.

9. Minutes of St. George's Church, Flushing, April 8, 1828, May 5, 1828.

10. Smith, *History of St. George's Church*, Flushing, p. 95.

11. Muhlenberg to Margaret and Catherine Yeates, February 14, 1827. Letter in the Archives of St. James Church, Lancaster, Pa.

12. *Laws of the State of New York passed at the Fiftieth Session of the Legislature begun and held at the City of Albany, the Second Day of January, 1827* (Albany: E. Croswell, 1827), pp. 360-363. These volumes will be referred to as *Laws of New York*.

13. *Catalogue of the Officers and Students of the Flushing Institute, Flushing, L.I., N.Y.* (Flushing: French and Wheet, 1862), p. 4.

14. Works Progress Administration, *Historical Collections of the Borough of Queens, New York City*. Project #465-97-3-20. In the Long Island Collection The Queensboro Public Library, Jamaica, Long Island, N.Y., 1938. 7:45, 153. This collection will be cited as *W.P.A. Collections. Catalog of St. Paul's College* (New York: printed by Charles E. Smith, 1847).

15. *W.P.A. Collections*, 6:42, 43; Minutes of St. George's Church, Flushing, February 15, 1825.

16. *W.P.A. Collections,* 9:47. Minutes of St. George's Church, Flushing, April 8, 1818.

17. *W.P.A. Collections,* 6:208; 7:22, 26. Minutes of St. George's Church, Flushing, April 15, 1827. Statement of the Rev. William McLean, Rector of St. George's in 1956.

18. Minutes of St. George's Church, Flushing, April 15, 1827.

19. *W.P.A. Collections,* 8:165. Minutes of St. George's Church, Flushing, July 1, 1826.

20. *W.P.A. Collections,* 6:204.

21. Minutes of St. George's Church, Flushing, April 15, 1827. W.P.A. records do not indicate his profession.

22. *Catalogue of the Officers and Students of the Flushing Institute,* Flushing, L.I., N.Y. (Flushing: French and Wheet, 1862), p. 4.

23. Muhlenberg to Kemper, July 25, 1827, Kemper Papers, vol. IX, no. 59.

24. G. Henry Mandeville, *Flushing, Past and Present, an Historical Sketch* (Flushing, N.Y.: J. Egbert Printer, 1860), p. 125.

25. William Augustus Muhlenberg, *The Application of Christianity to Education, being the Principles and Plan of Education to be adopted in the Institute* at Flushing, L.I. (Jamaica, N.Y.: Sleight and George, 1828).

26. For a detailed discussion of Muhlenberg's philosophy of Education and the similarity and difference to that of John Dewey *see* John F. Woolverton, "William Augustus Muhlenberg and the Founding of St. Paul's College" in *Historical Magazine of the Protestant Episcopal Church,* XXIX (September, 1960), 192-218.

27. Muhlenberg, *Application of Christianity to Education,* p. 10.

28. *Ibid.,* pp. 12-13.

29. Muhlenberg to the Honorable P. Van Rensselaer, March 19, 1835, Historical Society of Pennsylvania Library.

30. Muhlenberg, *Application of Christianity to Education,* p. 17.

31. *Ibid.,* pp. 6-7.

32. *Ibid.,* Muhlenberg, *Valedictory Sermon,* p 10.

33. Muhlenberg, *Application of Christianity to Education,* p. 7.

34. *Ibid.,* pp. 6-7.

35. Thomas Kelah Wharton, Diary, December 1, 1832, December 29, 1832; Samuel Kemper to Jackson Kemper, October 15, 1842, June, 1842, February 23, 1843. Collection of letters in the possession of Mrs. Charles Jackson, Nashotah, Wisconsin. These letters will be referred to as the Jackson Letters.

36. Nelson Munford Blake, *A History of American Life and Thought* (New York: McGraw-Hill Book Co., Inc., 1963), p. 233. Used with permission of McGraw-Hill Book Company.

37. Muhlenberg, *Application of Christianity to Education,* pp. 9-10.

38. *Ibid.,* p. 8.

39. *Ibid.,* pp. 9-10, 17.

40. *Ibid.,* pp. 13-16.

41. Muhlenberg to Kemper, February 11, 1828, Kemper Papers, vol. IX, no. 123.

42. Muhlenberg to Vaux, February 12, 1828, Vaux Papers.

43. Muhlenberg to Bishop William White, February 14, 1828, Kemper Papers, vol. IX, no. 124.

44. Muhlenberg to Bishop William White, n.d., 1828, Kemper Papers, vol. IV, no. 133.

45. Muhlenberg to Kemper, April 2, 1828, Kemper Papers, vol. IX, no. 145.

46. *Ibid.*, August 3, 1827, vol. IX, no. 72.

47. Muhlenberg, *Application of Christianity to Education*, p. 18.

48. Muhlenberg to Kemper, April 2, 1828, Kemper Papers, vol. IX, no. 145.

49. Bishop John Croes to Bishop John Henry Hobart, February 14, 1828. In the New York Historical Society Collection, vol. XXXIV, no. 21.

50. *Journal of the Diocese of New York*, 1829, p. 14.

51. Sprague, *Annals of the American Pulpit*, V, 381; *Journal of the Institute at Flushing*, November 1832, p. 15.

52. Muhlenberg to Seabury, n.d., no place (probably ca. 1829). Oliver Papers in General Theological Seminary Library, 175 9th Ave., New York, N.Y. Edward Waylen, *Ecclesiastical Reminiscences of the United States* (New York: Wiley and Putnam, 1846), p. 279.

53. Minutes of St. George's Church, Flushing, January 2, 1829.

54. Muhlenberg, *Christian Education: Being an address delivered after a public examination of the students of the institute at Flushing, L.I.* (July 28, 1831) pp. 1-3.

55. *Ibid.*, pp. 3-4.

56. *Ibid.*, p. 5.

57. Lewis Kemper to Mrs. Relf, April 12, 1843, Jackson Papers.

58. *Ibid.*, p. 11.

59. Muhlenberg, *Tabella Sacra for the Vacation* (St. Paul's College, 1839).

60. Muhlenberg, *Christian Education*, p. 13.

61. *Ibid.*, p. 16.

62. *Journal of the Institute at Flushing* August, 1833, pp. 14–22; November, 1832, p. 13.

63. Muhlenberg to Bishop (Croes), February 11, 1828, Hobart Papers; Muhlenberg to Kemper, February 11, 1828, Kemper Papers, vol. IX, no. 123.

64. William King, *What DeFellenberg has done for Education* (London: Saunders and Oakley, 1839), pp. xi-xlii.

65. "Joseph G. Cogswell to Elizabeth Tichnor," September 1, 1818; "Joseph G. Cogswell to Mrs. Prescott," August 28, 1819; "Joseph G. Cogswell to Elizabeth Tichnor," May 28, 1818; "George Tichnor to S. A. Elliot," February 1, 1823; quoted in Anna Elliott Tichnor, *Life of Joseph Green Cogswell as sketched in his letters* (Cambridge: The Riverside Press, 1874), pp. 87–88, 81, 105–106, 135.

66. Joseph G. Cogswell and George Bancroft, *Some account of the school for the Liberal Education of Boys, established at Round Hill, Northampton, Mass.* (Northampton: 1826), *passim.*

67. Joseph G. Cogswell, *Outline of the system of education at the Round Hill School, with a list of the present instructors and of the pupils from its commencement until this time June* 1831 (Boston: N. Hale's Press, 1831), *passim.*

68. Marshall Delancey Haywood, *Lives of the Bishops of North Carolina* (Raleigh, N.C.: Alfred Williams & Co., 1910), p. 104.

69. Muhlenberg to Kemper, January 4, 1838, Kemper Papers, vol. XIX, no. 141.

70. Joseph G. Cogswell, *Outline of the system of education at the Round Hill School, with a list of the present instructors and of the pupils from its commencement until this time June* 1831 (Boston: N. Hale's Press, 1831), p. 41.

71. Orie W. Long, *Literary Pioneers; early American Explorers of European Culture* (Cambridge: Harvard University Press, 1935), pp. 102–107.

72. *Catalogue of the Professors, Instructors, and Students of St. Paul's College and Grammar School, for the session of* 1838–39 (New York: William Osborne, 1839),

passim. This catalogue will be referred to as *Catalogue of St. Paul's College* 1838–1839.

73. Wharton, Diary, December 1832.

74. Wharton, Diary, *passim;* there is a summary of the author's life by an anonymous writer on the first page of this manuscript.

75. Wharton, Diary, May 3, 1830-October 15, 1834.

76. Muhlenberg, *Christian Education*, p. 16.

77. Ayres, *Life of Muhlenberg*, p. 130.

78. Muhlenberg, *The Ceremony and Address at the Laying of the Corner-stone of St. Paul's College* (1836), *passim*. This pamphlet will be referred to as Muhlenberg, *Address at St. Paul's College*.

79. Ayres, *Life of Muhlenberg*, p. 131.

80. Muhlenberg, *Address at St. Paul's College*, p. 14.

81. Muhlenberg, *Address at St. Paul's College*, p. 12.

82. *Ibid.*, p. 6.

83. *Ibid.*, p. 5.

84. *Evangelical Catholic*, I, 1; *Journal of the Diocese of New York*, 1837, pp. 29–30; 1838, pp. 46, 54, 66.

85. *New York State Laws*, 1840, p. 197.

86. *Catalogue of St. Paul's College* 1838–1839, *passim*.

87. *Ibid.*, p. 12; Joseph G. Cogswell, *Outline of the system of education at the Round Hill School, with a list of the present instructors and of the pupils from its commencement until this time June*, 1831 (Boston: N. Hale's Press, 1831), pp. 12–14.

88. *Catalogue of St. Paul's College*, pp. 3–4.

89. *Ibid.*, p. 3.

90. *Ibid.*, p. 5.

91. Muhlenberg to Kemper, April 2, 1828, Kemper Papers, vol. IX, no. 145; July 12, 1841, vol. X, no. 125; *Catalogue of St. Paul's College*, 1842, pp. 12–17; Muhlenberg to Stephen Van Rensselaer, May 5, 1836, American Hymn Writers Collection, Historical Society of Pennsylvania.

92. Muhlenberg, *Address at St. Paul's College*, 1836, *passim; Evangelical Catholic*, I, 1.

93. Muhlenberg, *Address at St. Paul's College*, p. 93.

94. Muhlenberg to the Hon. G. C. Verplanck, December 4, 1838, in the New York Historical Society Archives. Charles A. Brind, counsel of the Board of Regents of the State of New York to the author, May 17, 1956.

95. Muhlenberg to the Hon. G. C. Verplanck, November 15, 1839, New York Historical Society Library.

96. Letter from Muhlenberg, addressee not given, June 4, 1840, Manuscript Division, New York Public Library; *New York State Laws*, 63d Sess., 1840, p. 197; Harrison, *Life of Bishop Kerfoot*, p. 50.

97. Sam Kemper to Jackson Kemper, March 8, 1841, Kemper Papers, vol. XXIV, no. 45; November 20, 1841, vol. XXV, no. 99; June, 1842, vol. XXVI, no. 72; February 3, 1843, vol. XXVII, no. 31; "Henry A. Coit to his Father," November 21, 1842, quoted in W. E. Piers, *History of St. Paul's School* (Concord, N.Y.) (New York: Harper Brothers, 1940, p. 26; "Bishop Whittingham to Muhlenberg, November 5, 1843," quoted in Harrison, *Life of Bishop Kerfoot*, pp. 97–99.

98. Kemper to Muhlenberg, March 10, 1841, Kemper Papers, vol. XXIV, no. 53.

99. *St. Paul's College Catalogue* (New York: William C. Martin, Printer, 1846), p. 3.

100. The Rev. Benjamin Mottram, Rector, St. Paul's Church, College Point, N.Y., in conversation with the author (1956).

101. *Evangelical Catholic,* September 13, 1852, I, 1; Statement to the author by Mrs. Henry Chisholm, descendant of Muhlenberg's niece (1956).

102. George Harvey Gentzmer, "George Washington Doane," in *Dictionary of American Biography,* Dumas Malone, et al; ed. (New York: Charles Scribner's Sons, 1930), V, 333–334; Ayres, *Life of Muhlenberg,* p. 216.

103. Edward Dwight Eaton, "John Henry Hopkins," in *Dictionary of American Biography,* pp. 212–213.

104. *Evangelical Catholic,* I, xxii.

105. Albert Sidney Thomas, "Christopher Edward Gadsden" (1785–1852), in *Historical Magazine of the Protestant Episcopal Church,* XX, 308–314.

106. Marshall Delancey Haywood, *Lives of the Bishops of North Carolina* (Raleigh: Alfred Williams and Co., 1910), p. 104; *Catalogue of the Episcopal School for Boys* (Raleigh, N.C., 1836), p. 34.

107. Muhlenberg to Kemper, January 4, 1838, Kemper Papers, vol. XIX, no. 141.

108. Mrs. Samuel Relf to Kemper, February 28, 1839, Kemper Papers, vol. XX, no. 152; R. R. Menail to Kemper, January 13, 1837, Kemper Papers, vol. XVI, no. 142.

109. Minutes of the Trustees of Kemper College, April 10, 1837, Kemper Papers, vol. XVII, no. 53.

110. Kemper College Circular, May 15, 1839, Kemper Papers, vol. XXI, no. 41; 1839–1840, vol. XXII, nos. 139, 155, 156, 159.

111. Correspondence between Kemper and Faculty Members, Kemper Papers, 1840–1843, vol. XXIII, nos. 9, 32; vol. XXVI, nos. 140, 141; *Episcopal Recorder,* August 30, 1845; Muhlenberg to Kemper, May 17, 1841, July 9, 1841, Kemper Papers, vol. XXIV, nos. 102, 146.

112. Jackson Kemper Diary, December 25, 1844, Kemper Papers, no vol. or manuscript no.

113. William Mercier Green, *Memoir of James Hervey Otey* (New York: James Pott and Co., 1885), p. 127.

114. *Catalogue of St. Paul's College,* 1838, p. 3.

115. Ayres, *Life of Muhlenberg,* p. 113; Tichnor, *Life of Joseph G. Cogswell,* p. 231.

116. *Catalogue of St. Paul's College,* 1838, p. 3.

117. Lewis Kemper to Jackson Kemper, October 7, 1843, Kemper Papers, vol. XXL, no. 34; Francis Lester Hawks, *Circular of St. Thomas Hall* (New York: privately published, 1840), *passim.*

118. Thomas March Clark, *Reminiscences* (New York: Thomas Whittaker, 1895), pp. 34–37.

119. Harrison, *Life of Bishop Kerfoot,* II, 126.

120. *Appleton's Cyclopedia of American Biography,* James Grant Wilson and John Fiske, eds. (6 vols.) (New York: D. Appleton and Co., 1888), III, 324. *Catalogue of St. Paul's College,* 1839–1840, pp. 4–5.

121. *Appleton's Cyclopedia,* III, 444–445.

122. Harrison, *Life of Bishop Kerfoot,* I, 12; Waylen, *Ecclesiastical Reminiscences,* I, 237.

123. Muhlenberg to Kemper, December 28, 1826, Kemper Papers, vol. VIII, no. 144; *Ibid.,* April 12, 1843.

124. Harrison, *Life of Bishop Kerfoot,* I, 4; *Catalogue of St. Paul's College,* 1838, p. 3.

125. Muhlenberg to Kemper, August 1, 1843, Kemper Papers, vol. XX, no. 6.

126. Muhlenberg to Bishop Whittingham, March 9, 1841, quoted in Harrison, *Life of Bishop Kerfoot*, I, 33.

127. *Ibid.*, p. 35.

128. Harrison, *Life of Bishop Kerfoot*, I, 12.

129. Muhlenberg to Kemper, May 12, 1841, Kemper Papers, vol. XXIV, no. 102; *Evangelical Catholic*, I, xxii.

130. "Bishop Whittingham to Kerfoot," December 30, 1841, quoted in Harrison, *Life of Bishop Kerfoot*, I, 37.

131. "Kerfoot to Bishop Whittingham," January 3, 1842, quoted in Harrison, *Life of Bishop Kerfoot*, I, 38.

132. *Ibid.*, pp. 40–41.

133. *Ibid.*, p. 152.

134. Harrison, *Life of Bishop Kerfoot*, I, 48–49, II, 44.

135. Frederick Joseph Kinsman, *Salve Mater* (New York: Longmans Green and Co., 1920), p. 15.

136. William Adams, "Historical Paper," *Report of the Jubilee Ceremonies of Nashotah House* (Nashotah: Published by the Alumni, 1892, *passim*.

137. Charles Breck, *The Life of the Reverend James Lloyd Breck* (New York: E. and J. B. Young and Co., 1883), pp. 2–3. This book will be referred to as Charles Breck, *Life of J. L. Breck*.

138. J. L. Breck to Kemper, March 16, 1843, Kemper Papers, vol. XXVII, no. 58; J. L. Breck to Mr. G. French, March 3, 1843, Nashotah House Archives.

139. The Rev. F. F. Peake to Kemper, May 31, 1841, Kemper Papers, vol. XXIV, no. 123.

140. T. I. Holcombe, *An Apostle of the Wilderness* (New York: Thomas Whittaker, 1903), *passim*. This book will be referred to as Holcombe, *Apostle of the Wilderness*.

141. J. L. Breck to the Rev. William G. French, March 6, 1848, Nashotah House Archives.

142. Holcombe, *Apostle of the Wilderness*, p. 10.

143. Kemper to Muhlenberg, April 14, 1852, Kemper Papers, Letterbook; February 10, 1853, December 18, 1852, December 27, 1849; Lewis Kemper to Jackson Kemper, November 20, 1847, Kemper Papers, vol. XXXII, no. 27; *Evangelical Catholic*, I, iv; I, vii; I, xvii; II, i. Lewis Kemper to Jackson Kemper, November 20, 1847, Kemper Papers, vol. XXXII, no. 27; Kemper Diary, June 3, 1852, Kemper Papers.

144. J. L. Breck to Kemper, September 22, 1847, Kemper Papers, vol. XXXII, no. 12.

145. J. L. Breck to Kemper, September 23, 1847, Kemper Papers, vol. XXXII, no. 13.

146. Lewis Kemper to Jackson Kemper, November 20, 1847, Kemper Papers, vol. XXXII, no. 27.

147. J. L. Breck to Kemper, September 23, 1841, Kemper Papers, vol. XXXII, no. 13.

148. Bishop L. S. Ives to Jackson Kemper, January 4, 1848, Kemper Papers, vol. XXXIII, no. 87.

149. Sprague, *Annals of the American Pulpit*, V, 687–697; W. R. Whittingham

to J. Kemper, September 13, 1862, Kemper Papers, vol. XLII, no. 79; *Racine College Bulletin*, December 1859, Kemper Papers, vol. XL, no. 143.

150. Holcombe, *Apostle of the Wilderness*, pp. 19-25; Breck to the Rev. J. G. Barton, June 6, 1846, Breck Papers, Nashotah House Archives.

151. Kemper to Muhlenberg, December 27, 1849, January 22, 1850,Kemper Papers, Letter Book.

152. Holcombe, *Apostle of the Wilderness*, p. 104.

153. J. L. Breck to Kemper, January 25, 1850, quoted in Charles Breck, *Life of J. L. Breck*, p. 112; Kemper to Muhlenberg, April 18, 1850, Kemper Papers, Letter Book.

154. William Adams, "Historical Paper," in *Report of the Jubilee Ceremonies of Nashotah House* (Nashotah: Published by the Alumni, 1892), pp. 11–17.

155. James Lloyd Breck to Charles Breck, January 2, 1855, quoted in Breck, *Life of J. L. Breck*, p. 287.

156. Charles Breck, *Life of J. L. Breck*, pp. 443–446.

157. Henry H. Shires, "History of the Church Divinity School of the Pacific," in *Historical Magazine of the Protestant Episcopal Church*, XI, (June, 1942), 179-188.

158. James Lloyd Breck to Miss Edwards, December 11, 1856, quoted in Breck, *Life of J. L. Breck*, p. 317.

159. Breck to the Lay-Brothers and other members of St. Paul's College, November 6, 1866, Breck Papers, Nashotah House Archives.

160. Breck to the Rev. J. G. Barton, June 6, 1866, Breck Papers, Nashotah House Archives.

161. Breck to the Church of the Holy Communion, February 16, 1856, quoted in Breck, *Life of J. L. Breck*, p. 299.

162. James Lloyd Breck to Charles Breck, May 23, 1871, quoted in Breck, *Life of J. L. Breck*, p. 482.

163. *Ibid.*, James Lloyd Breck to Miss Edwards, May, 1849, p. 241.

164. *Ibid.*, January 2, 1853, p. 234.

165. *Appleton's Cyclopedia*, I, 215.

166. *Ibid.*, IV, 556-557.

167. *Catalogue of St. Paul's College*, 1838, p. 7; 1847, p. 3.

168. "Houghton Obituary," *New York Times*, November 18, 1897.

169. Joseph Jefferson, *Autobiography* (London: Reinhart and Evans, Ltd., 1949), pp. 260-261.

170. Christopher Wilkinson Knauff, *Doctor Tucker, Priest-Musician* (New York: A. F. D. Randolph Co., 1897), p. 17.

171. *Catalogue of St. Paul's College*, 1838, p. 3.

172. Knauff, *Doctor Tucker, Priest-Musician*, p. 18.

173. Ayres, *Life of Muhlenberg*, p. 185.

174. Muhlenberg to Seabury, August 1, 1836, Oliver Papers; *Evangelical Catholic*, II, xxxiii, xli.

175. *Appleton's Cyclopedia*, III, 443-444.

176. Muhlenberg to Seabury, n.p., n.d., Oliver Papers.

177. *Catalogue of St. Paul's College*, 1838–1846, *passim.*

178. Ayres, *Life of Muhlenberg*, p. 105.

179. Diary of Lewis Manigault, Unpublished manuscript in the possession of the Rev. Robert Emmett Gribben, University of Alabama, Tuscaloosa. This manuscript will be referred to as the Manigault Diary. Elizabeth Kemper to Jackson Kemper, June 6, 1844, Kemper Papers, vol. XXIV, no. 31.

CHAPTER 4:
THE CHURCH OF THE HOLY COMMUNION

1. *Census of the United States*, 1820, p. 15.
2. *Census of the state of New York for* 1875, p. 41.
3. *Map of the City of New York*, 1845. In Map Room of the New York Public Library.
4. Daniel Curry, New York, *A Historical Sketch of the rise and progress of the Metropolitan City of America* (New York: Carleton and Phillip, 1853), p. 206.
5. *Ibid.*, p. 209.
6. Citizens Association of New York, *Report of the Council of Hygiene and Public Health* (New York: 1865), p. 300; *Census of the State of New York*, 1845, Schedules 29-1 and 23-1.
7. Muhlenberg, *The Rebuke of the Lord, A sermon preached in the Chapel of the Institute at Flushing, L.I. on the Sunday after the great fire in New York on the 16th and 17th of December 1835* (Jamaica: I. F. Jones and Co., 1835), pp. 1-16.
8. Muhlenberg, *The Voice of the Church and the Times Chiefly addressed to churchmen in the middle and upper Walks of Life* (New York: R. Sears, 1840).
9. Charles Haynes Haswell, *Reminiscences of an Octogenarian of the City of New York* (New York: Harper and Bros., 1896), pp. 212, 421. *Journal of the Diocese of New York*, 1846, pp. 101, 258-59; Ezekiel Porter Belden, *New York, Past, Present, and Future. Comprising a history of the City of New York, a description of its present condition and an estimate of its future increase* (New York: Pratt, Lewis, and Co., 1850), pp. 96-97.
10. Curry, *New York—Historical Sketch*, p. 240; C. S. Francis, *Francis's New Guide to the Cities of New York and Brooklyn and the vicinity* (New York; C. S. Francis and Co., 1853), p. 105; Belden, *New York, Past, Present, and Future*, pp. 96-97; *Evangelical Catholic*, II, iii; An English Layman, *Recent Recollections of the Anglo-American Church in the United States. By an English Layman five years resident in the Republic* (London: Rivingtons, 1861), pp. 66-67. This book will be referred to as English Layman, *The Anglo-American Church*.
11. *Map of New York*, 1845, Map Room of the New York Public Library. C. S. Francis, *Francis's New Guide to the Cities of New York and Brooklyn and the vicinity* (New York: C. S. Francis and Co., 1853), p. 115.
12. Will of John Rogers, April 29, 1841, Liber 83, 270, Hall of Records, County of New York; Muhlenberg, "Address at the Laying of the Cornerstone of the Church of the Holy Communion," in *Evangelical Catholic Papers*, II, 75. These papers will be referred to as *E.C.P.*
13. Everard M. Upjohn, *Richard Upjohn, Architect and Churchman* (New York: Columbia University Press, 1939), pp. 87-88, fig. 37, p. 87. Used with permission of Columbia University Press.
14. Wayne Andrews, *Architecture, Ambition and Americans* (Glencoe, Ill.: The Free Press, 1964), pp. 127-128. Used with permission of Harper and Row, copyright owners.
15. Haswell, *Reminiscences*, pp. 199-200; Clark, *Reminiscences*, pp. 41-42; English Layman, *The Anglo-American Church*, I, 147; Henry Caswall, *America and the American Church* (London: Gilbert and Rivington, 1839), pp. 280-82. This will be referred to as Caswall, *The American Church*.
16. Muhlenberg to Seabury, no date, Oliver Papers. Probably written when Seabury was planning the Church of the Annunciation in New York.

17. Caswall, *America and the American Church*, p. 66; *C. S. Francis's New Guide to the Cities of New York and Brooklyn and the Vicinity*, p. 115. Sketch in the Archives of the Church of the Holy Communion; Henry Dana Ward, Diary (unpublished manuscript in the Manuscript Room of the New York Public Library); English Layman, *The Anglo-American Church*, I, 136.

18. Muhlenberg, *The Weekly Eucharist, No. IV, or Pastoral Tracts; Printed chiefly for the members of the Church of the Holy Communion* (New York: Pudney and Russell, 1848), pp. 7, 12; Ward, Diary, June 25, 1854; Haswell, *Reminiscences*, p. 213.

19. English Layman, *The Anglo-American Church*, I, 162; Ayres, *Life of Muhlenberg*, pp. 223-224. Ward, Diary, June 25, 1854.

20. Lewis Kemper to Mrs. Samuel Relf, May, 1845, Kemper Papers, vol. XXVII, no. 60.

21. Muhlenberg, *The Psalter, or Psalms of David; together with the Canticles of the Morning and Evening Prayer, and Occasional Offices of the Church. Figured for Chanting. To which are prefixed an explanatory preface and a selection of chants* (New York: D. Appleton and Company, 1849; Muhlenberg and Jonathan Wainwright, *The Choir and Family Psalter* (New York: Stanford and Swords, 1851; Muhlenberg, *The People's Psalter* (New York: Stanford and Swords, 1854).

22. W. A. Muhlenberg, G. T. Bedell, G. J. Geer (eds.), *A Tune-Book proposed for the use of Congregations of the Protestant Episcopal Church, Compiled by a Committee Appointed for that Purpose* (New York: Published by the Committee, 1859).

23. W. A. Muhlenberg *et al. Hymns for Church and Home Compiled by members of the Protestant Episcopal Church as a contribution to any addition that may be made to the hymns now attached to the Prayer Book* (Philadelphia: J. B. Lippincott and Company, 1861).

24. Muhlenberg, "Congregational Singing, A Lecture Delivered in Several Episcopal Churches about 1860," in *E.C.P.*, II, 263; *Evangelical Catholic*, II, xlvi.

25. Jackson Kemper Diary, August, 1847, Kemper Papers; Muhlenberg to Bishop Bowman, November 6, 1847, Church Historical Society Archives; Ward, Diary, August 8, 1854; Lewis Kemper to Mrs. Samuel Relf, n.d. Kemper Papers, vol. XXII, no. 139; English Layman, *The Anglo-American Church*, I, p. 136; Robert Abbe, *A New View of the Rev. Dr. Muhlenberg*.

26. *Evangelical Catholic*, I, 1.

27. Clark, *Reminiscences*, pp. 34-37.

28. C. S. Francis, *Francis's Guide to the Cities of New York and Brooklyn*, p. 104.

29. Edwin Harwood, *In Memory of William Augustus Muhlenberg, 1796–1877, D.D. LL.D.[sic]* (New York: T. Whittaker, 1877), p. 20.

30. *E.C.P.*, II, pp. 261-444. Wharton, Diary, August 26, 1852; Ward, Diary, February 26, 1854, November 18, 1855, *passim*.

31. Muhlenberg, *Pastoral Tracts Printed for the Use of the Members of the Church of the Holy Communion* (New York: G. W. Wood, Printer, 1847), no. 1-4.

32. *In Memoriam John S. Swift*, Pamphlet in the Archives of St. Luke's Hospital.

33. Caswall, *America and the American Church*, II, 304-307.

34. Jackson Kemper to Samuel Roosevelt Johnson, April 16, 1836, Kemper Papers, vol. XVI, no. 11; *Ibid.*, Sketch of Proposed Church, L. 40; *Ibid.*, Jackson Kemper to James Milnor, October 19, 1816, Kemper Papers, vol. V, no. 2.

35. Waylen, *Ecclesiastical Reminiscences of the United States*, pp. 282-283.

36. Caswall, *America and the American Church*, pp. 281-282.

37. Gospel Advocate, August, 1822, II, no. 7, 232.

38. *Christian Journal and Literary Register*, August, 1824.

39. *Ibid.*, September, 1826.

40. *Journal of the Diocese of New York*, 1847, p. 92.

41. *Ibid.*, 1833, p. 264.

42. Map of New York, 1845.

43. *Journal of the Diocese of New York*, 1833, p. 264.

44. *Ibid.*, 1835, pp. 27-28; 1836, p. 48; 1847, p. 92.

45. *Ibid.*, 1847, p. 90.

46. Gardiner C. Tucker, "Impressions of the Episcopal Church in 1867" *The Historical Magazine of the Episcopal Church*, XX (March, 1951), 67-70.

47. Muhlenberg, *Pastoral Tracts*, no. 1; *Journal of the Diocese of New York*, 1844, p. 89.

48. *Laws of the State of New York*, 1813, p. 212.

49. W. A. Muhlenberg to Dr. Samuel Jarvis, June 18, 1847, Church Historical Society Archives.

50. Muhlenberg, "An Exposition of the Memorial of Sundry Presbyters to the House of Bishops," *E.C.P.*, I, 88; "An address at the Laying of the Cornerstone of the Church of the Holy Communion, New York," *E.C.P.*, II, 75; *Journals of the Diocese of New York*, 1846–1849. These journals list Muhlenberg in attendance, but do not list a lay delegate from the Church of the Holy Communion; Ayres, *Life of Muhlenberg*, p. 118.

51. Minutes of the United Parish, October 29, 1819, April 15, 1816. Minutes of St. James Church, Lancaster, May 15, 1820.

52. Catherine Yeates to Jackson Kemper, July 19, 1826, Kemper Papers, vol. VIII, no. 32.

53. Minutes of St. George's Church, Flushing, New York, May 5, 1828.

54. *Journals of the Diocese of New York*, 1846–1858.

55. Muhlenberg, *Pastoral Tracts*, no. I, iii.

56. Ward, Diary, August 18, 1853.

57. English Layman, *The Anglo-American Church*, I, 135.

58. Ward, Diary, April 27, 1850, April 14, 1851, May 31, 1851, November 14, 1852, November 6, 1855, December 4, 11, 1853.

59. *Ibid.*, October 1, 1853, November 6, 1853, November 19, 1854.

60. Map of New York, 1845.

61. *Ibid.*, 1847.

62. Drawing in the Church of the Holy Communion Archives, New York; Robert Dale Owen, *Hints on Public Architecture.... Prepared on behalf of the building committee of the Smithsonian Institute* (New York: George D. Putnam, 1849), p. 71.

63. *Census of the State of New York*, 1845 (Albany: Printed by the Secretary of State, 1846), pp. 116-118.

64. *Census of the State of New York*, 1855 (Albany: Printed by the Secretary of State, 1856), pp. 116-118.

65. Clarence E. Walworth, *The Oxford Movement in America, or Glimpses of Life in an Anglican Seminary* (New York: The Catholic Book Exchange, 1895), p. 108.

66. *Census of the State of New York*, 1845, Schedule 29, pp. 1-2; *New York, Department of the Sanitary Commission* (New York: Board of Health, 1879), p. 71.

67. Ayres, *Life of Muhlenberg*, pp. 194-96; Caswall, *America and the American Church*, I, 11; Waylen, *Ecclesiastical Reminiscences*, I, pp. 281-282; English Layman, *The Anglo-American Church*, I, pp. 142-147.

68. Ayres, *Life of Muhlenberg*, pp. 208–11.

69. Henry J. Carman and Hugh N. Camp, *The Charities of New York, Brooklyn and Staten Island* (New York: Hurd and Houghton, 1868), pp. 200–208.

70. *Ibid.*, p. 95.

71. *Evangelical Catholic*, I, vi.

72. *Journal of the Diocese of New York*, 1865, p. 121.

73. Muhlenberg, *The Woman and her Accusers, A Plea for the Midnight Mission, Delivered in several of the churches of New York and Brooklyn* (New York: P. F. Smith, 1871), p. 40.

74. Carman-Camp, *Charities of New York*, p. 208.

75. Muhlenberg, *The Woman and her Accusers, passim*.

76. *Journal of the Diocese of New York*, 1864, pp. 90–91.

77. *Ibid.*, p. 93.

78. John Punnett Peters (ed.), *Annals of St. Michael's, Being the History of St. Michael's Protestant Episcopal Church, New York for One hundred years, 1807–1907* (New York: G. P. Putnam Sons, 1907), p. 113. This book will be referred to as Peters, *Annals of St. Michael's*.

79. *St. Luke's Hospital; Annual Report*, 1864 (New York: Published by the Managers, 1864), p. 15; Peters, *Annals of St. Michael's*, pp. 447-454.

80. Peters, *Annals of St. Michael's*, p. 307.

81. *Journal of the Diocese of New York*, 1843, pp. 39, 49; 1866, p. 108. Carman-Camp, *Charities of New York*, p. 447; Ayres, *Life of Muhlenberg*, pp. 196, 197, 201–2, 392–96; Jackson Kemper, Pastoral Letter, November 28, 1865, Kemper Papers, vol. XXV, no. 23; Robert B. Minturn to Jackson Kemper, December 2, 1841, Kemper Papers, vol. XXV, no. 111; December 6, 1841, vol. XXV, no. 119; March 24, 1857, vol. XXXVIII, no. 66; August 3, 1866, Letter Book. *Dictionary of American Biography*, XIII, 32.

82. Ayres, *Life of Muhlenberg*, p. 421. *Report of the Board of Trustees of St. Johnland*, 1875, p. 14. *Dictionary of American Biography*, XX, 449–451.

83. Ayres, *Life of Muhlenberg; Report of the Board of Trustees of St. Luke's Hospital*, 1859, pp. 4–5; "In Memoriam" Adam Norrie, Archives of St. Luke's Hospital.

84. Ayres, *Life of Muhlenberg*, pp. 258, 294; *Report of the Board of Trustees of St. Luke's Hospital*, 1859, p. 45; *Report of the Board of Trustees of St. Johnland*, 1875, p. 13.

85. *Report of the Board of Trustees of St. Luke's Hospital*, 1859, p. 45. *Dictionary of American Biography*, I, 401.

86. Minutes of the Board of Trustees of St. Johnland, December 27, 1857; *Report of the Board of Trustees of St. Luke's Hospital*, 1869, p. 4; *Dictionary of American Biography*, XIII, 175–180.

87. *Supra*, Chap. I; Minutes of the Board of Trustees of the Church of the Holy Communion, March 13, 1873, January 2, 1868.

88. Will of John Rogers, April 29, 1871, Liber 83, p. 27, Hall of Records, County of New York.

89. *Supra*, Chap. III; Lewis Kemper to Jackson Kemper, November 16, 1845, Jackson Papers.

90. Ayres, *Life of Muhlenberg*, p. 314.

91. Minutes of the Trustees of the Church of the Holy Communion, January 2, 1868.

92. *Ibid.*, November 3, 1879.

93. Communicant List, 1869, Church of the Holy Communion Archives.

94. Church of the Holy Communion, Papers of Incorporation, June 25, 1867, File 118, 1867, County Clerk, New York County.

95. *Ibid.*, December 18, 1886.

96. *Ibid.*, June 25, 1867.

97. Church of the Holy Communion, Minutes of the Trustees, January 2, 1868.

98. *Ibid.*, November 17, 1887.

99. *Ibid.*, May 4, 1874.

100. *Ibid.*, May 12, 1879, November 3, 1879; Communicant List, Church of the Holy Communion, January, 1869.

101. *Chronicles of the Church of the Holy Communion*, 1883–1901. (In some years referred to as a *Yearbook*) *passim.*

102. Harwood, *In Memory of Muhlenberg*, p. 21.

CHAPTER 5:
DEACONESSES AND SISTERHOODS

1. Jackson Kemper to Elizabeth Kemper, November 23, 1841, Kemper Papers, vol. XXV, no. 100.

2. Elizabeth Kemper to Jackson Kemper, February 5, 1842, Kemper Papers, vol. XXVI, no. 144.

3. Muhlenberg to Kemper, July 9, 1841, Kemper Papers, vol. XXIV, no. 146; Muhlenberg to Dr. Samuel Jarvis, January 16, 1843, Church Historical Society Library.

4. John Tracy Ellis, *American Catholicism* (Chicago: University of Chicago Press, 1956), pp. 53-57; Annabelle M. Melville, *Elizabeth Bayley Seton* (New York: Charles Scribner's Sons, 1951), pp. 82-102, 153-184, 208-227.

5. Anne Ayres, *Evangelical Sisterhoods, In two letters to a friend,* edited by W. A. Muhlenberg (New York: T. Whittaker, 1867). This pamphlet will be referred to as Ayres, *Evangelical Sisterhoods.*

6. Anon., *Life of Anne Ayres,* in the Archives of St. Luke's Hospital.

7. Ayres, *Evangelical Sisterhoods,* pp. 16-17.

8. *Ibid.*, pp. 11-18.

9. *Ibid.*, pp. 22-32.

10. Alonzo Potter (ed.), *Memorial Papers, The Memorial with circular and questions of the Episcopal Commission; Report of the Commission; contributions of the Commission; and communications from Episcopal and non-Episcopal Divines* (Philadelphia: E. H. Butler Co., 1857), p. 61.

11. Muhlenberg, *Protestant Sisterhoods, originally introductory to two letters on Evangelical Sisterhoods* (New York: 1852), p. 12.

12. Ayres, *Life of Muhlenberg,* p. 284.

13. Ward, Diary, January 15, 1854.

14. *Evangelical Catholic,* I, vii, xvii; II, xvii, xx; Ayres *Evangelical Sisterhoods,* p. 40.

15. Harwood, *In Memory of Muhlenberg,* p. 27.

16. G. H. Gentzer, "W. A. Passavant," in the *Dictionary of American Biography,* XIV, 289.

17. Ayres, *Evangelical Sisterhoods,* p. 48.

18. W. A. Passavant to Muhlenberg in *The Evangelical Catholic,* I, viii.

19. *Annual Report of the Trustees of St. Luke's Hospital*, 1859, pp. 20-21; *Evangelical Catholic*, II, ii.

20. "Resident Physician's Report," in *Annual Report of the Trustees of St. Luke's Hospital*, 1860, p. 9.

21. M. Adelaide Nutting and Lavinia Doch, *A History of Nursing* (G. P. Putnam's Sons, New York and London, 1907) II, 326-347, 355-357. Miss Emma Edwin to the author, May 15, 1956.

22. Health Department of New York City, *Report of the Proceedings of the Sanitary Committee of the Board of Health in Relation to the Cholera, as it Prevailed in New York in 1849, passim.*

23. "Beginnings of Some Famous Schools," *Trained Nurse and Hospital Review*, August, 1938.

24. Manuscript in the Archives of St. Luke's Hospital.

25. George F. Seymour, "Mother Harriet of the Sisterhood of St. Mary," *The Church Eclectic, June*, 1896. Reprinted in *Mount St. Gabriel Series No. 1, Historical Papers* (St. Mary's Convent, Peekskill, N.Y.: 1931), pp. 8-9; Peters, *Annals of St. Michael's Church*, pp. 313-315.

26. Sister Mary Hillary, C.S.M., *Ten Decades of Praise. The Story of the Community of Saint Mary During its First Century: 1865-1965* (DeKoven Foundation, Racine, Wis., 1965).

27. Peters, *Annals of St. Michael's Church*, pp. 338-361; *Journals of the Diocese of New York*, 1865, pp. 111-112; 1871, pp. 93-110.

28. *Ninth Annual Report of St. Luke's Hospital*, 1867, p. 10; *Fifteenth Annual Report of St. Luke's Hospital*, 1873, p. 331; *Journal of the Diocese of New York*, 1871, pp. 93-100.

29. *Twentieth Annual Report of St. Luke's Hospital*, 1878, pp. 11-12.

30. "Beginnings of Some Famous Schools," *Trained Nurse and Hospital Review*, August, 1938, *Passim.*

31. Aaron I. Abell, *The Urban Impact on American Protestantism*, 1865-1900. (Cambridge: Harvard University Press, 1943). This book will be referred to as Abell, *Urban Impact on American Protestantism*. Charles Howard Hopkins, *The Rise of the Social Gospel in American Protestantism*, 1865-1915 (New Haven: Yale University Press, 1940), pp. 6, 154, 155.

32. *Journal of the Diocese of New York*, 1865, pp. 93-100.

CHAPTER 6: ST. LUKE'S HOSPITAL

1. W. W. Newton, *Dr. Muhlenberg* (New York: Houghton, Mifflin Co., 1890), p. 78.

2. *Ibid.*, p. 79; New York City, *Report of the Sanitary Committee* (New York: Board of Health; Published by the city, 1849), p. 6.

3. *Census of the State of New York of 1845* (Albany: The Secretary of State, 1846), p. 12.

4. *Journal of the Diocese of New York*, 1848, p. 31; Moses Marcus, *Address to the Members of the "United Church of England and Ireland" and of the Protestant Episcopal Church in the United States of America on the subject of Emigration* (New York: 1846), p. 6; *Evangelical Catholic*, I, vi.

5. Carman-Camp, *Charities of New York*, pp. 43-49.

6. *Ibid.*, pp. 48-49.

7. Ayres, *Life of Muhlenberg*, p. 214; Jackson Kemper to Elizabeth Kemper Adams, October 19, 1860, Kemper Papers, vol. XLI, no. 63; Muhlenberg, "Sketch of the History of St. Luke's Hospital," *E.C.P.*, II, 137.

8. Ayres, *Evangelical Sisterhoods*, fn. 7; Ayres, *Life of Muhlenberg*, p. 214.

9. Infirmary Register, Sisters of the Holy Communion, 1857, Archives of St. Luke's Hospital.

10. Muhlenberg, *A Plea For a Church Hospital in the city of New York in two Lectures*. (New York: Stanford and Swords, 1850), pp. 53-55.

11. *Ibid.*, p. 55.

12. *Ibid.*, fn. 7.

13. Incorporation Papers of St. Luke's Hospital in New York City, Municipal Reference Library, File 31, 1850.

14. *Evangelical Catholic*, I, vi.

15. *Ibid.*, I, xvii.

16. St. Luke's Hospital Subscription Book, May 30, 1852, in Archives of St. Luke's Hospital.

17. *Evangelical Catholic*, I, vi; St. Luke's Hospital, *Service at the Laying of the Cornerstone of St. Luke's Hospital, May 6, 1854* (New York: Phair and Co., 1854), *passim*.

18. Ayres, *Life of Muhlenberg*, p. 216.

19. *First Annual Report of St. Luke's Hospital* (New York, 1859), pp. 37-40.

20. Ayres, *Life of Muhlenberg*, pp. 282-283, 285.

21. Samuel Cooke, *The Morals of Bethesda: A sermon preached in the Chapel of St. Luke's Hospital on the occasion of opening the hospital for Patients, Ascension Day, May 13, 1858* (New York: Published by the manager of the Hospital, 1858), p. 5.

22. *First Report of the Board of Trustees of St. Luke's Hospital* (New York: Published by the Board of Trustees, 1859).

23. Eigenbrodt, David, Life of, Manuscript in the Archives of St. Luke's Hospital; Thirty-second Annual Report, St. Luke's Hospital (New York, 1892), p. 7.

24. Papers of Incorporation of St. Luke's Hospital, Municipal Reference Library, File 31, 1850, New York, N.Y.

25. *First Annual Report of St. Luke's Hospital*, p. 45.

26. *Ibid.*, pp. 32-33.

27. *Ibid.*, pp. 41-44.

28. Mease, *Picture of Philadelphia*, p. 48.

29. *First Annual Report of St. Luke's Hospital*, pp. 32-33.

30. *Ibid.*, pp. 28-29.

31. *Junior Association of St. Luke's Hospital in the Parish of St. Thomas, Constitution and By-laws* (New York, 1863), *passim; St. Luke's Hospital First Report of the manager* (New York, 1859), p. 37.

32. Muhlenberg, *Plea for a Church Hospital*, p. 54; *Evangelical Catholic*, I, xi.

33. *Annual Reports, St. Luke's Hospital*, 1859-1877, *passim*.

34. *First Report of the Managers of St. Luke's Hospital* (New York, 1859), p. 28.

35. *Ibid.*, pp. 18-19.

36. *Second Annual Report, St. Luke's Hospital* (New York, 1860), pp. 12-13.

37. *Third Annual Report of St. Luke's Hospital* (New York, 1861), pp. 23-25.

38. *Ibid.*, 1862, pp. 10-11; 1863, p. 5; 1864, p. 6; 1865, p. 14; 1866, p. 15; 1868, p. 21; 1873, p. 16; 1874, p. 18; 1875, p. 18; 1877, p. 19.

39. *Annual Report of St. Luke's Hospital, 1860* (New York, 1860), p. 6.

40. *Second Annual Report, St. Luke's Hospital,* p. 18; Ibid., 1859, p. 13; 1860, p. 5.

41. *Ibid.,* 1868, p. 7; 1869, p. 7; 1871, p. 7; 1872, p. 8; 1873, p. 12; 1874, p. 10; 1875, pp. 9-10; 1876, pp. 11-14; 1877, p. 10.

42. *Ibid.,* 1868, p. 10.

43. *Ibid.,* p. 16.

44. *Ibid.,* 1872, p. 10.

45. *Ibid.,* 1875, p. 17.

46. *Ibid.,* p. 12.

47. *Ibid.,* p. 9, 12.

48. *Harper's Weekly* XXXI (January, 1887).

49. *Nineteenth Annual Report of St. Luke's Hospital,* 1876, p. 6.

50. *Annual Report of St. Luke's Hospital* (New York, 1866); p. 6.

51. *Ibid.,* 1866, p. 15.

52. *Ibid.,* 1862 (Appendix), pp. 13, 19-20.

53. *Ibid.,* 1877, pp. 44-45.

54. *Ibid.,* 1871, p. 41.

55. Waylen, *Ecclesiastical Reminiscences,* p. 230.

56. Muhlenberg, manuscript in the Archives of St. Luke's Hospital on the choice of his successor.

57. *Annual Report, St. Luke's Hospital* (New York, 1862), p. 5.

58. James Bennett Fry, *New York and the Conscription Act of 1863; a Chapter in the History of the Civil War* (New York: G. Putnam and Sons, 1885), *passim.*

59. Ayres, *Life of Muhlenberg,* p. 220.

60. *Evangelical Catholic* II, xxv.

61. E. Clowes Chorley, *Men and Movements in the American Episcopal Church* (New York: Charles Scribner's Sons, 1946), pp. 24, 238, 232, 153.

62. Henry Mottet, *In Commemoration of Rev. William Augustus Muhlenberg* (New York: The Church of the Holy Communion, 1927).

CHAPTER 7:
THE EVANGELICAL CATHOLIC

1. "Muhlenberg to Kerfoot," September 25, 1849, quoted in Harrison, *Life of Bishop Kerfoot,* p. 133; Ayres, *Life of Muhlenberg,* pp. 479, 490.

2. Mary L. Booth, *History of the City of New York from its earliest settlement to the present time* (New York: W. R. C. Clark and Meeker, 1859), p. 734.

3. *Evangelical Catholic,* I, i; Ayres, *Life of Muhlenberg,* pp. 235-237.

4. *Evangelical Catholic,* I, i.

5. *A Pastoral Letter to the Clergy and Members of the Protestant Episcopal Church in the United States of America, from the Bishops of the same, Assembled in General Convention, in the City of Philadelphia, August 1835* (New York, 1835), pp. 14-15.

6. *Evangelical Catholic,* I, i.

7. *Ibid.,* I, i.

8. Harwood, *In Memory of Muhlenberg,* p. 19; Karl Christian Wilhelm Felix Bahr, *The Book of the Kings,* translated, enlarged, and edited by Edwin Harwood and W. G. Sumner (New York: Scribner, Armstrong, and Co., 1872). This volume is one of a series entitled *A Commentary on Holy Scripture* by J. P. Lange and translated from the German and edited by Phillip Schaff.

9. *Evangelical Catholic*, I, xii; I, vi; I, iii.

10. *Ibid.*, II, xxii.

11. *Ibid.*, II, vii.

12. *Ibid.*, II, xix.

13. *Journal of the Diocese of New York*, 1841, p. 95.

14. *Evangelical Catholic*, I, vii.

15. *Ibid.*, I, vii.

16. *Ibid.*, I, v.

17. *Ibid.*, I, vi; II, vi; II, xv.

18. *Journal of the Diocese of New York*, 1846, pp. 26-27, 54; 1850, pp. 32-33; 1853, p. 45.

19. *Evangelical Catholic*, II, xxiv.

20. *Ibid.*, I, iv; I, v; II, xxxix; II, i.

21. *Ibid.*, I, v.

22. *Ibid.*, I, iv, v.

23. *Ibid.*, I, iii.

24. *Ibid.*, I, xii.

25. *Ibid.*, I, xvi.

26. *Ibid.*, I, xvii.

27. *Ibid.*, I, viii.

28. Henry F. May, *Protestant Churches and Industrial America* (New York: Harper and Brothers, 1949), pp. 18-20.

29. *Evangelical Catholic*, I, iii.

30. *Ibid.*

31. *Ibid.*, I, iv; I, v; II, iii.

32. *Ibid.*, I, vii.

33. *Ibid.*, II, iii.

34. *Ibid.*, I, xxiii.

35. *Ibid.*, II, xlii.

36. *Ibid.*, I, xii.

37. *Ibid.*, II, v.

38. *Ibid.*, II, xl.

39. *Ibid.*, I, iv.

40. *Ibid.*, II, xliv.

41. *Ibid.*, I, v.

42. *Ibid.*, I, viii.

43. *Ibid.*, I, x.

44. *Ibid.*, I, xii.

45. *Ibid.*, II, vi.

46. *Ibid.*, IV, xx; David S. Schaff, *The Life of Phillip Schaff* (New York: Charles Scribner's Sons, 1879), 322, 329; Muhlenberg, "*I Would Not Live Alway" evangelized by its author with the story of the hymn And a brief account of St. Johnland* (New York: T. Whittaker and Co., 1871).

47. James Thayer Addison, *The Episcopal Church in the United States, 1789-1931* (New York: Charles Scribner's Sons, 1951), pp. 249, 284.

48. *Evangelical Catholic*, II, ii.

49. *Ibid.*, II, xxv.

50. *Ibid.*, I, xxii.

51. *Ibid.*, II, xlix.

52. Muhlenberg to Seabury, June 1, 1843, Oliver Papers.

53. *Evangelical Catholic*, I, iv.

54. *Ibid.*, I, xvi.

55. *Ibid.*, I, xxi.

56. *Ibid.*, II, xxv.

57. *Ibid.*, I, v.

58. Muhlenberg to Kemper, February 17, 1820, Kemper Papers, vol. V, no. 18.

59. Samuel H. Turner, *Autobiography of the Rev. Samuel H. Turner, D.D.* (New York: A. D. F. Randolph, 1864), *passim.*

60. *Evangelical Catholic*, II, xlcix, xlvii.

61. *Ibid.*, II, xi.

62. *Ibid.*, I, xxii.

63. *Ibid.*, I, iv.

64. *Ibid.*, II, i.

65. *Ibid.*, II, xlv.

66. *Ibid.*, II, xivii.

67. James Lloyd Breck to Charles Breck, February 23, 1852, quoted in Charles Breck, *Life of J. L. Breck*, p. 190.

68. Kemper to Muhlenberg, June 26, 1853, Kemper Papers, vol. XXXIV, no. 38.

69. Harry Croswell, *Memoir of William Croswell* (New York: D. Appleton and Co., 1854), p. 472.

70. Muhlenberg to Kerfoot, January 6, 1873, quoted in Harrison, *Life of Bishop Kerfoot*, I, 153.

71. Harwood, *In Memory of Muhlenberg*, p. 19.

CHAPTER 8: THE LITURGICAL MOVEMENT

1. Muhlenberg to Seabury, July 17, 1843, Oliver Papers.

2. Muhlenberg, "Hints on Catholic Union," in *E.C.P.*, I, 10-16.

3. Muhlenberg to Kemper, December 31, 1827, Kemper Papers, vol. IX, no. 102.

4. *Ibid.*, February 17, 1820, vol. V, no. 117.

5. *Ibid.*, March 17, 1828, vol. VII, no. 22.

6. *Appleton's Cyclopedia*, I, 339.

7. Thomas H. Vail, *The Comprehensive Church or Christian Unity and Ecclesiastical Union in the Protestant Episcopal Church* (New York: P. Appleton and Co., 1879), *passim;* Muhlenberg to Mrs. Vail, February 29, 1872, Church Historical Society Collections.

8. Muhlenberg to Ellie Bowman, January 8, 1857, Church Historical Society Collections.

9. Muhlenberg, *A Valedictory Sermon*, pp. 9-10.

10. *Evangelical Catholic*, I, i.

11. *Account of the True Nature and Object of the late Protestant Episcopal Clerical Association of the City of New York together with a defense of the Association from Objections which have been urged against it, and an explanation of the Reasons which have led to its Dissolution, By Members of the Association* (New York, 1829), *passim;* Dr. Samuel Turner to Jackson Kemper, March 12, 1829, Kemper Papers, vol. X, no. 96.

12. James Abercrombie, *Sermon on the Liturgy* (Philadelphia, 1808), *passim.*

13. Muhlenberg to Seabury, August 22 (no year), Oliver Papers.

14. Samuel Hollingsworth to Jackson Kemper, January 30, 1868, Kemper Papers, vol. X, no. 96.

15. Waylen, *Ecclesiastical Reminiscences*, p. 279.

16. Harrison, *Life of Bishop Kerfoot*, I, p. 29.

17. Muhlenberg to Seabury, June 1, 1843, Oliver Papers.

18. Muhlenberg to Kerfoot, November 26, 1852, quoted in Harrison, *Life of Bishop Kerfoot*, I, 139-141.

19. *Ibid.*, September 24, 1826, p. 16.

20. *Evangelical Catholic*, I, i.

21. Harwood, *In Memory of Muhlenberg*, p. 24; "The Proposed Reform of the Episcopal Church." Reprinted from *The Episcopal Quarterly Review*, April, 1855 (New York: Anson D. F. Randolph, 1855).

22. Ayres, *Life of Muhlenberg*, pp. 161-163; Harrison, *Life of Bishop Kerfoot*, I, 29.

23. *Journal of St. Paul's College*, vol. I, no. i; Sam Kemper to Jackson Kemper, March 18, 1842, Kemper Papers, vol. XXVI, no. 23; Easter (n.d.) Jackson Papers; Wharton, Diary, April 1, 1833.

24. Muhlenberg to Seabury (n.d.), Oliver Papers; Samuel Kemper to Jackson Kemper, September 14, 1844, Kemper Papers, vol. XXIX, no. 39.

25. Ayres, *Life of Muhlenberg*, pp. 17-18, 29.

26. Wharton, Diary, April 1, 1833; *Catalogue of the Flushing Institute*, 1835, p. 6; Knauff, *Life of Dr. Tucker*, p. 16.

27. Elizabeth Kemper to Jackson Kemper, April 8, 1841, Kemper Papers, vol. XXIV, no. 72.

28. Chorley, *Men and Movements*, pp. 194, 167, 228; George E. DeMille, *The Catholic Movement in the American Episcopal Church* (Philadelphia: Church Historical Society, 1949), pp. 82, 95-97.

29. John Tracey Ellis, *American Catholicism* (Chicago: University of Chicago Press, 1956), pp. 95-96, 65-68.

30. Calvin Colton, *The Genius and Mission of the Protestant Episcopal Church in the United States* (New York: Stanford and Swords, 1853), chapter xiii; Benjamin Parham Aydelott, *The Condition and Prospects of the Protestant Episcopal Church* (Cincinnati: W. H. Moore and Co., 1848), pp. 3-7, 44-54, 105-119, 121.

31. Muhlenberg to Seabury, July 17, 1843, Oliver Papers.

32. John Henry Newman, *Apologia Pro Vita Sua* (New York: Longmans, Green, and Co., 1901), pp. 133-134, 156-158, *passim*.

33. Muhlenberg to Seabury, July 17, 1843, Oliver Papers.

34. Ayres, *Life of Muhlenberg*, pp. 166-167.

35. Newman, *Apologia*, pp. 181-215.

36. *Journal of the Diocese of New York*, 1841, pp. 80-86.

37. *Ibid.*, 1843, pp. 72-81; 1844, p. 76.

38. Muhlenberg to Seabury, April 30, 1844, Oliver Papers.

39. Kemper Diary (n.d.), Kemper Papers, vol. XLVIII, no. 76.

40. *Ibid.*, December 24, 1844, vol. XLVIII, no. 78.

41. *Ibid.*, December 19, 1844, November 9, 1844, February 8, 1845.

42. *The Proceedings of the Court Convened Under the Third Canon of 1844 in the City of New York, on Tuesday, December 10, 1844. For the trial of the Rt. Rev. Benjamin T. Onderdonk, D.D., Bishop of New York; on a Presentment made by the Bishops of Virginia, Tennessee, and Georgia. By Authority of the Court* (New York: D. Appleton and Co., 1845), p. 85.

43. Chorley, *Men and Movements*, p. 209; Richard S. Salomon, "The Episcopate on the Carey Case," *Historical Magazine of the Episcopal Church*, XVIII (September, 1949), 240-281.

44. Bishop Kemper's Notes, December 31, 1844, Kemper Papers, vol. XXIX, no. 18.

45. Salomon, "The Episcopate on the Carey Case," *op. cit. supra* fn. 43.

46. Muhlenberg to Seabury, Friday (n.d.), Oliver Papers.

47. *Ibid.*, January 3, 1845.

48. *Ibid.*, January 6, 1845, Oliver Papers.

49. *Journal of the Diocese of New York*, 1845, pp. 30-52, 77-139.

50. Harwood, *In Memory of Muhlenberg*, p. 24.

51. *Ibid.*, p. 24.

52. Clarence E. Walworth, *The Oxford Movement in America, or Glimpses of Life in an Anglican Seminary* (New York: The Catholic Book Exchange, 1895), p. 108.

53. *Church Eclectic*, XXIII (1895), 387, as quoted in Chorley, *Men and Movements*, p. 383.

54. Muhlenberg, *Pastoral Tracts*, no. 1, p. 1.

55. DeMille, *Catholic Movement*, p. 101.

56. Muhlenberg, *Pastoral Tracts*, no. 1, p. 9.

57. *Ibid.*, p. 1.

58. *Ibid.*, p. 9.

59. *Ibid.*, p. 10.

60. *Ibid.*, p. 12.

61. *Ibid.*, pp. 15-16.

62. *Ibid.*, p. 16.

63. Ward, Diary, September 11, 1853.

64. Muhlenberg, *Pastoral Tracts*, no. 4, Preface.

65. Ward, Diary, November 19, 1854.

66. *Evangelical Catholic*, I, vi; I, vii; William Croswell, *A Memoir of the late Rev. William Croswell* (New York: D. Appleton and Co., 1853), p. 404.

67. Muhlenberg to Kerfoot, November 12, 1845, October 30, 1849, in Harrison, *Life of Bishop Kerfoot*, I, 126, 135; *Evangelical Catholic*, II, xxiv.

68. Ward, Diary, January 15, 1854.

69. Ayres, *Life of Muhlenberg*, p. 173.

70. Muhlenberg to Kerfoot, 1852, quoted in Harrison, *Life of Bishop Kerfoot*, I, 139.

71. *Evangelical Catholic*, I, xvii.

72. Ward, Diary, May 17, 1854.

73. *Ibid.*, January 6, 1856.

74. *The Proposed Reform of the Protestant Episcopal Church* (New York: Anson D. F. Randolph, 1855), pp. 17-19.

75. *Ibid.*, pp. 21-22.

76. *Evangelical Catholic*, II, xii.

77. Ayres, *Life of Muhlenberg*, pp. 283-284.

78. Ward, Diary, November 27, 1853.

79. Dr. Theodore Tappert, professor of American church history at the Lutheran Theological Seminary, Mt. Airy, Pennsylvania, in conversation with the author.

80. Muhlenberg, "The Testimony of Jesus, the Spirit of Prophecy." A sermon preached at the reopening of the Church of Augustus (Evangelical Lutheran), Trappe, Montgomery County, Pennsylvania, September 5, 1860, *E.C.P.*, II,

236-239. This sermon will be referred to as Muhlenberg, "The Testimony of Jesus."

81. Muhlenberg, *Directory in the Use of the Book of Common Prayer for the Church of the Testimony of Jesus* (New York: T. Whittaker, 1871), p. 5; Chorley, *Men and Movements*, pp. 355, 410-422; *infra*, Chap. IX.

82. Ward, Diary, April 8, 1853; Muhlenberg, *Letters to a Friend Touching the Late Pastoral of the Rt. Rev. Bishop Potter* (New York, 1865), *passim*.

83. Horatio Potter, "Annual Address to the Diocese of New York" in *Journal of the Diocese of New York*, 1857.

84. Horatio Potter, *Pastoral Letter to the Clergy of the Diocese of New York, with the replies of the Rev. S. H. Tyng, E. H. Canfield, John Cotton Smith and W. A. Muhlenberg* (New York, 1865).

85. Muhlenberg to Kerfoot, December, 1865, quoted in Harrison, *Life of Bishop Kerfoot*, II, 417-418.

86. *Ibid.*, January 17, 1870, II, 152.

87. Samuel Roosevelt Johnson to John Barrett Kerfoot, quoted in Harrison, *Life of Bishop Kerfoot*, I, 483.

88. Muhlenberg "Suggestions for the formation of an Evangelical and Catholic Union," a paper read at the Evangelical Conference in Philadelphia, November 9, 1869 in *E.C.P.*, vol. I, no. IX, pp. 433-459. This paper will be referred to as Muhlenberg, "Suggestions for the formation of an Evangelical and Catholic Union," *E.C.P.*, I.

89. *Ibid.*, p. 454; Muhlenberg, "The Lord's Supper in Relation to Christian Union," a paper read at the Conference of the Evangelical Alliance, New York, October 11, 1873, *E.C.P.*, I, 461-482. This paper will be referred to as Muhlenberg, "The Lord's Supper in Relation to Christian Union," *E.C.P.*, I.

90. Muhlenberg, "Suggestions for the formation of an Evangelical and Catholic Union," *E.C.P.* I, 433-459.

91. Muhlenberg, "The Lord's Supper in Relation to Christian Union," *E.C.P.*, I, 480.

92. Chorley, *Men and Movements*, pp. 410-422.

93. Ayres, *Life of Muhlenberg*, pp. 459-461.

94. George F. Seymour, "Mother Harriet of the Sisterhood of St. Mary," *The Church Eclectic*, June, 1896. Reprinted in *Mount St. Gabriel Series, No. 1 Historical Papers*, St. Marys Convent, Peekskill, N.Y., February 2, 1931.

CHAPTER 9:
THE MUHLENBERG MEMORIAL

1. Ayres, *Life of Muhlenberg*, p. 4.
2. Muhlenberg, "The Testimony of Jesus," *E.C.P.*, II, 209.
3. Muhlenberg, *Valedictory Sermon*, p. 13.
4. Muhlenberg, "Hints on Catholic Union" 1835, *E.C.P.*, I, 9-76.
5. *Ibid.*, p. 9.
6. *Evangelical Catholic*, I, iv.
7. *Ibid.*, I, xiii.
8. *Ibid.*, I, vi.
9. *Evangelical Catholic*, I, xii; I, xliv; II, xvi.

10. Harwood, *In Memory of Muhlenberg*, p. 19.

11. William Berrian, *To the Commission of Bishops on the Memorial of the Rev. Dr. Muhlenberg, etc. to the House of Bishops at the late General Convention* (New York: For Private Distribution, 1854).

12. Thomas H. Vail, *The Comprehensive Church, or Christian Unity and Ecclesiastical Union in the Protestant Episcopal Church* (New York: D. Appleton and Co., 1879).

13. Harwood, *In Memory of Muhlenberg*, pp. 22-26.

14. Kemper Diary, October 11, 1853, Kemper Papers, vol. XXXV, no. 135.

15. Muhlenberg, *Memorial of Sunday Presbyters of the Protestant Episcopal Church, Presented to the House of Bishops, October 18, 1853* (New York: Published by the Author, 1853), *passim*.

16. "Appendix M.1, List of the Clergy of the Protestant Episcopal Church in the United States, October, 1853," in *Journal of the General Convention, 1854,* Philadelphia: published by the Convention, 1854), pp. 404-444.

17. The party background of the signers has been examined by E. R. Hardy in "Evangelical Catholicism, William Augustus Muhlenberg and the Memorial Movement," *Historical Magazine of the Episcopal Church*, XIII (June, 1944), 155-192. There are biographies of Alex H. Vinton, Francis Vinton, M. A. DeWolfe Howe, S. H. Turner, and A. C. Coxe in both *Appleton's Cyclopedia* and the *Dictionary of American Biography*. There are biographies also of C. F. Crusé, G. T. Bedell, and John Henry Hobart in *Appleton's Cyclopedia*.

18. *Journal of the General Convention*, 1853, pp. 181-182.

19. Kemper Diary, October, 1853 in Kemper Papers.

20. *See* biographies in *Appleton's Cyclopedia* and *Dictionary of American Biography*.

21. Thomas March Clark, *Reminiscences* (New York: Thomas Whittaker, 1895), p. 88.

22. *Journal of the General Convention*, 1853, p. 183.

23. *See* biography in *Appleton's Cyclopedia* and *Dictionary of American Biography*. There are biographies of Bishop DeLancey in both *Appleton's Cyclopedia* and the *Dictionary of American Biography*. There is a short biography of Bishop Freeman in *Appleton's Cyclopedia*.

24. *Journal of the General Convention*, 1853, p. 231.

25. *Ibid.*, p. 232.

26. *Journal of the General Convention*, 1853, p. 231. *See* biographies in *Appleton's Cyclopedia* and *Dictionary of American Biography*.

27. *Journal of the General Convention*, 1856, p. 340.

28. Alonzo Potter, *Memorial Papers*, pp. 37-40.

29. *Ibid.*

30. These pamphlets may be found in the Bibliography under the following names: W. H. Barnwell, William Berrian, Catholicus, C. M. Parkman, A Plain Presbyter, Southern Presbyter, and Edward Abiel Washburn.

31. These pamphlets will be found listed in that section of the Bibliography entitled "Published Works of William Augustus Muhlenberg."

32. Muhlenberg, *An Exposition of the Memorial*, 1854, E.C.P., I, 77-198.

33. Muhlenberg, *What the Memorialists Want* (1854), E.C.P., I, 199-286.

34. Muhlenberg, *What the Memorialists Do Not Want* (1856), E.C.P., I, 287-307.

35. Muhlenberg, *What the Memorialists Want* (1854), E.C.P., I, 199-286.

36. Muhlenberg, *What the Memorialists Do Not Want* (1856), E.C.P., I, 287-307.

37. *Ibid.*

38. *Journal of the General Convention*, 1856, pp. 339-353.

39. *Journal of the General Convention*, 1856, pp. 181, 183.

40. *Ibid.*, pp. 191-192, 203-204.

41. *Ibid.*, pp. 206-207. *See* biographies in *Appleton's Cyclopedia* and *Dictionary of American Biography.*

42. *Journal of the General Convention*, 1856, pp. 18-19.

43. Alonzo Potter, *Memorial Papers*, pp. 254, 329-331.

44. *Ibid.*, pp. 207-219, 323-328, 169-187, 251-254.

45. *Ibid.*, pp. 417-444.

46. *Ibid.*, pp. 101-102.

47. *Ibid.*, pp. 51-52.

48. "Dr. Muhlenberg's Contribution," Alonzo Potter, *Memorial Papers*, pp. 287-289.

49. Alonzo Potter, *Memorial Papers*, pp. 83-100, 188-204, 323-328; Berrian, *To the Commission of the House of Bishops*, pp. 3-5; Parkman, *A Counter-Memorial*, pp. 3-9; Southern Presbyter, *The Memorial Viewed From a Different Standpoint*, pp. 3-4, 22.

50. Alonzo Potter, *Memorial Papers*, pp. 50-60, 83-112, 140-150, 169-187, 207-219, 220-225, 226-229, 231-237, 238-245, 246-249, 251-254, 261-273, 290-296; Anon., *Proposed Reform of the Episcopal Church*, pp. 4-7, 12-13; Barnwell, *Letter to Alston*, pp. 1-4, 6-7; Catholicus, *A Few Thoughts*, pp. v-vi, 2, 10-17, 20-24, 30-33, 46, 54-55, 62-63.

51. Alonzo Potter, *Memorial Papers*, pp. 83-416.

52. *Ibid.*, pp. 422-435.

53. A Plain Presbyter, *A response to Bishop Potter in relation to the designs of the recent Episcopal Memorial Papers* (Philadelphia: Joseph M. Wilson, 1858).

54. *Journal of the General Convention*, 1859, pp. 101-105.

55. *Ibid.*, pp. 215-216.

56. *Ibid.*, p. 382.

57. Muhlenberg, "The Testimony of Jesus," *E.C.P.*, II, 261.

58. Muhlenberg, "The Three Crosses," *E.C.P.*, I, 311; Muhlenberg, "Letters to a Friend Touching the Late Pastoral of the Rt. Rev. Bishop Potter of New York" (1865), *E.C.P.*, I, 380.

59. Muhlenberg, "The Lord's Supper in Relation to Christian Union," *E.C.P.*, I, 480–481.

60. Muhlenberg, "The Testimony of Jesus," *E.C.P.*, II, 236–237.

61. Alonzo Potter, *Memorial Papers*, p. 48; Anon, *Proposed Reform of the Episcopal Church*, p. 6; Barnwell, *Letter to Alston*, p. 1; Harwood, *In Memory of Muhlenberg*, p. 24.

62. James Thayer Addison, *The Episcopal Church in the United States, 1789–1931* (New York: Charles Scribner's Sons, 1951), pp. 164-188. E. Clowes Chorley, *Men and Movements in the American Episcopal Church* (New York: Charles Scribner's Sons, 1946), pp. 58, 285. George E. DeMille, *The Catholic Movement in the American Episcopal Church* (Philadelphia: Church Hostorical Society, 1949), pp. 103-104. William W. Manress, *A History of the American Episcopal Church* (New York: Morehouse Publishing Co., 1935), pp. 266-290. Raymond W. Albright, *A History of the Protestant Episcopal Church* (New York, The Macmillan Co., 1964), pp. 352-353.

63. Albright, *History of the Episcopal Church*, pp. 352-353. Used with permission of the Macmillan Company.

64. Muhlenberg, *Directory in the Use of the Book of Common Prayer for the Church of the Testimony of Jesus* (New York: T. Whittaker, 1871), p. 5.

CHAPTER 10: SLAVERY AND WAR

1. Wallace, *The Muhlenbergs of Pennsylvania*, pp. 274-320.
2. Ayres, *Life of Muhlenberg*, p. 21.
3. Muhlenberg Diary, September 13, 1814, September 24, 1814, quoted in Ayres, *Life of Muhlenberg*, pp. 34-35.
4. Lewis Kemper to Jackson Kemper, March 28, 1842, Kemper Papers, vol. XXVI, no. 24.
5. Muhlenberg to Seabury, August 1, 1843, June 19, 1843, Oliver Papers.
6. English Layman, *Recollections of the Anglo-American Church*, p. 320; *Evangelical Catholic*, II, i; White, *Apostle of the Western Church*, p. 18.
7. *Evangelical Catholic*, II, xxxviii.
8. Muhlenberg, *A Sermon in Memory of the Rev. Samuel Bacon and John P. Bankson, Agents of the United States Under the Direction of the American Colonization Society Who Died on the Coast of Africa, May, 1820* (Philadelphia: Published by friends of the deceased, 1820).
9. *Evangelical Catholic*, I, xviii.
10. *Ibid.*, I, x.
11. Muhlenberg to Kemper, January 4, 1838, Kemper Papers, vol. XXI, no. 17.
12. *Evangelical Catholic*, II, xxv.
13. Ayres, *Life of Muhlenberg*, pp. 163-165.
14. Ibid., pp. 333-334.
15. Samuel Seabury, *American Slavery Distinguished from the Slavery of the English Theorist, and Justified by the Laws of Nature* (New York: Mason Brothers, 1861), passim; Milo Mahan, *Collected Works*, ed. John Henry Hopkins, Jr., 3 vols. (New York: Pott, Young, and Co., 1875), I, *passim*.
16. Harrison, *Life of Bishop Kerfoot*, I, 198.
17. *Journal of the Diocese of New York*, 1860, pp. 75-76, 87-88.
18. *Evangelical Catholic*, II, xlviii.
19. Edwin A. Batchelder, *1850–1950, Centennial Observance of the Church of the Holy Communion, Lake Geneva, Wisconsin* (Published by the Parish, 1950), pp. 7-11.
20. Church of the Holy Communion, Geneva Lake, Wisconsin, Resolution of the Congregation, Kemper Papers, December 14, 1857, vol. XXXIX, no. 34.
21. Kemper to Muhlenberg, November 21, 1857, Kemper Papers, Letter Book.
22. W. M. Green to Jackson Kemper, December 20, 1856, Kemper Papers, vol. XXXVIII, no. 28.
23. *Report of the Board of Trustees of St. Johnland*, 1871.
24. Edwin A. Batchelder, *1850–1950, Centennial Observance of the Church of the Holy Communion, Lake Geneva, Wisconsin*, p. 12.
25. Muhlenberg Diary, November 6, 1860, November 7, 1860 quoted in Ayres, *Life of Muhlenberg*, pp. 336-337.
26. *Ibid.*, n.d., pp. 340-341.
27. William Garnett Chisholm, *Chisholm Genealogy, being a Record of the name from A.D. 1254* (New York: The Knickerbocker Press, 1941).
28. Muhlenberg, *The President's Hymn* [contains Lincoln's Proclamation of October 3, 1863, and a facsimile of the words and music of Muhlenberg's "The President's Hymn"].

29. J. H. Otey to Jackson Kemper, May 1, 1861, Kemper Papers, vol. XLI, no. 101; J. Kemper to W. R. Whittingham, September 23, 1862, Kemper Papers, Letter Book.

30. Henry C. Lay to T. C. Brownwell, September 20, 1861, Kemper Papers, vol. XLI, no. 139; John Henry Hopkins, Sr., *A Scriptural, Ecclesiastical and Historical View of Slavery from the Days of the Patriarch Abraham to the Nineteenth Century, addressed to the Right Rev. Alonzo Potter, D.D.* (New York: W. I. Pooley and Company, 1864), *passim.*

31. Alonzo Potter, *The Voice of the Clergy* (Philadelphia, 1863), a manuscript in the Pierpont Morgan Library, New York. (An answer to the book by J. H. Hopkins, Sr., *supra* fn. 30.)

32. Harrison, *Life of Bishop Kerfoot,* p. 198.

33. *Ibid.,* pp. 392-393.

34. Ayres, *Life of Muhlenberg,* pp. 374-379.

35. Harrison, *Life of Bishop Kerfoot,* I, 316, 399, 406.

36. *Ibid.,* p. 406.

37. Muhlenberg to Seabury, August 19, 1869, Oliver Papers.

CHAPTER 11: ST. JOHNLAND

1. Minutes of the Board of Trustees of St. Johnland, May 30, 1870.

2. Muhlenberg, *St. Johnland, A retro-prospectus in two letters supposed to be written in the year* 187 (New York: R. Craighead, printer, 1864).

3. *Ibid.,* pp. 13-16.

4. *Ibid.,* pp. 16-19.

5. *Ibid.,* pp. 25-26.

6. *Ibid.,* pp. 32-33.

7. Vida Dutton Scudder, *Father Huntington* (New York: E. P. Dutton and Company, 1940), pp. 76, 93, 144.

8. Minutes of the board of Trustees of St. Johnland, May 2, 1874; "Minutes of the Executive Committee of the Board of Trustees of St. Johnland," in *Third Annual Report,* 1873, pp. 15-17.

9. Minutes of the board of Trustees of St. Johnland, July 9, 1868; *First Annual Report of St. Johnland* (New York: Published by the Society, 1871), p. 36; Muhlenberg, *"I Would Not Live Alway" evangelized by its author with the story of the hymn and a brief account of St. Johnland* (New York: T. Whittaker and Co., 1871).

10. Papers of Incorporation, Society of St. Johnland, File 400, 1868, Clerks Office, County of New York.

11. Minutes of the Board of Trustees of St. Johnland, May 30, 1870.

12. *Ibid.,* January 9, 1871.

13. Muhlenberg, *"I Would Not Live Alway" evangelized,* p. 22.

14. Muhlenberg, "History of St. Johnland Prior to 1871," in *First Annual Report of the Society of St. Johnland* (New York: Published by the Society, 1871), pp. 15-19.

15. *First Annual Report of St. Johnland,* p. 24.

16. Minutes of the board of Trustees of St. Johnland, May 26, 1871; *Fifth Annual Report of St. Johnland* (New York: Published by the Society, 1875), p. 29.

17. Minutes of the board of Trustees of St. Johnland, May 26, 1871.

18. *Second Annual Report of St. Johnland,* 1872, p. 6.

19. *Fourth Annual Report of St. Johnland,* 1874, pp. 6-7.

20. *Second Annual Report of St. Johnland,* 1872, p. 8.

21. *Third Annual Report of St. Johnland,* 1873, p. 5.

22. *Fourth Annual Report of St. Johnland,* 1874, pp. 6-7.

23. *Ibid.,* p. 7.

24. Minutes of the board of Trustees of St. Johnland, April 8, 1874, May 2, 1874.

25. *Fourth Annual Report of St. Johnland* (New York: Published by the Society 1874), pp. 5-7.

26. *Fifth Annual Report of St. Johnland,* 1875, pp. 7-15.

27. *Tenth Annual Report of St. Johnland,* 1880, p. 7.

28. *Annual Report of the Board of Trustees of St. Johnland* (New York: Published by the Society, 1948), pp. 30-36.

29. *Annual Report of the Board of Trustees of St. Johnland* (New York: Published by the Society, 1955), pp. 12-13.

30. Muhlenberg, *Directory in the Use of the Book of Common Prayer for the Church of the Testimony of Jesus, St. Johnland, Long Island* (New York: T. Whittaker, 1871), pp. 1-6.

31. *Ibid.,* pp. 7-46.

32. *E.C.P.,* II, 365.

33. Abbe, *A New View of Dr. Muhlenberg,* p. 6.

34. Kemper to Muhlenberg, October 19, 1860, Kemper Papers, vol. XLI, no. 63; October 1, 1868, vol. XLVI, no. 37.

35. *Journal of the Diocese of New York,* 1865, pp. 111-112.

36. Camp-Carman, *Charities of New York, Brooklyn, and Staten Island,* p. ii.

37. "Dr. Muhlenberg," in *The Atlantic Monthly,* XLVI (July, 1880), 564-566. Minutes of the Board of Trustees of St. Luke's Hospital, April 11, 1877.

38. Ayres, *Life of Muhlenberg,* p. 444.

39. *Ibid.,* p. 479.

40. Harrison, *Life of Bishop Kerfoot,* II, 426.

41. Schaff, *Life of Dr. Phillip Schaff,* pp. 205, 322, 329.

42. Minutes of the Board of Trustees of St. Johnland, May 25, 1876.

43. Obituary, *New York Times,* April 9, 1877.

CHAPTER 12:
THE MAN AND HIS INFLUENCE

1. Wood, *Journal,* April 8, 1817.

2. Ward, Diary, August 8, 1854.

3. Newton, *Dr. Muhlenberg,* pp. 14-15.

4. Jackson Kemper to Elizabeth Kemper Adams, May 8, 1860, Kemper Papers, vol. XLI, no. 24.

5. Lewis Kemper to Jackson Kemper, March 2, 1846, Jackson Papers; Samuel Kemper to Mrs. Relf, January 11, 1843, April 12, 1843, Jackson Papers.

6. Harrison, *Life of Bishop Kerfoot,* I, 126-127.

7. Manigault Diary, pp. 13-14.

8. Mrs. Henry R. Higgins to the author, April 25, 1956.

9. George C. Groce and David H. Wallace *Dictionary of Artists in America, 1564–1860* (New York: The New York Historical Society, 1957), p. 165.

10. Church of the Holy Communion: Minutes of the Vestry, May 12, 1894. Ayres, *Life of Muhlenberg,* pp. 313, 392-393.

11. Abbe, *A New View of Dr. Muhlenberg*, pp. 11-12.
12. *Supra*, chs. VI, XI.
13. *Fifth Annual Report of St. Johnland*, p. 12.
14. Abbe, *New View of Dr. Muhlenberg*, pp. 4-6.
15. Muhlenberg to Margaret and Catherine Yeates, February 14, 1827, Archives of St. James Church, Lancaster.
16. Ayres, *Life of Muhlenberg*, pp. 392-393.
17. Harwood, *In Memory of Dr. Muhlenberg*, p. 20.
18. Ward, Diary, August 8, 1854.
19. Muhlenberg, *St. Johnland, A retro-prospectus in two letters supposed to be written in the Year 187–*, p. 23.
20. *Evangelical Catholic*, I, xii; II, xxv.
21. *Ibid.*, II, iii, iv.
22. Wharton, Diary, January 21, 1833; *Evangelical Catholic*, II, vi.
23. Julian, *A Dictionary of Hymnology*, pp. 774-775.
24. H. E. Jacobs, "A Common Place Lutheran," in *The Lutheran Church Review* XXI (April, 1890), 117-129.
25. Frank J. Klingberg, "Colonial Anglo-Lutheran Relations," in *Historical Magazine of the Protestant Episcopal Church* XVI (June, 1947), 217-220; DeMille, *The Catholic Movement*, p. 78.
26. W. A. Muhlenberg to H. M. Muhlenberg, August 13, 1853, Church Historical Society Archives.
27. Dr. Theodore Tappert, professor of American church history at the Lutheran Theological Seminary, Philadelphia, Pa., in conversation with the author, September, 1956.
28. Ayres, *Life of Muhlenberg*, p. 29.
29. Muhlenberg, "The Testimony of Jesus," *E.C.P.*, II, 209; W. A. Muhlenberg to H. M. Muhlenberg, August 13, 1853, Church Historical Society Archives.
30. George Hodges, *Henry Codman Potter, Seventh Bishop of New York* (New York: The Macmillan Co., 1915), pp. 201-220; *Dictionary of American Biography*, XV, 127.
31. Hopkins, *Social Gospel in American Protestantism*, pp. 34-37; E. A. Washburn, *Sermon in Memorial [sic] of William Augustus Muhlenberg* (New York: T. Whittaker, 1877), p. 22; *Dictionary of American Biography*, XIX, 498.
32. *Supra*, ch. VII.
33. Chorley, *Men and Movements*, pp. 311, 312, 397-398, 408; *Dictionary of American Biography*, XVIII, 300.
34. Heber Newton, "Obituary of Dr. Muhlenberg," *New York Times*, April 9, 1877; Hopkins, *Social Gospel in American Protestantism*, pp. 32-34, 35, 93, 72-73, 91, 94, 107; Abell, *Urban Impact on American Protestantism*, pp. 48, 50, 59, 60, 70, 81, 247; May, *Protestant Churches and Industrial America*, pp. 176-177, 183-184, 221-225; *Dictionary of American Biography*, XII, 474.
35. Newton, *Dr. Muhlenberg*, p. 281; *Dictionary of American Biography*, XII, 478.
36. Vail, *The Comprehensive Church, passim;* R. Rouse and L. C. Neill, *A History of the Ecumenical Movement 1517–1948* (London: S. P. C. K., 1954).
37. Raymond W. Albright in conversation with the author, December, 1964. Albright, *History of the Episcopal Church*, pp. 352-353; Charles J. Minifie, "William Reed Huntington and Church Unity," in *Historical Magazine of the Protestant Episcopal Church*, XXXV, ii; Raymond W. Albright, "When We Talk about Unity . . . ," The Episcopalian, August, 1963, p. 14; *Dictionary of American Biography*, IX, 420.

BIBLIOGRΛPHICΛL ESSΛY

The best single source on the life of Muhlenberg is the biography written by Anne Ayres shortly after his death. It went through five editions and has been used as the principal and sometimes the only source by most persons who have written about him. Acting on the directions of Muhlenberg given before his death, Miss Ayres destroyed all his papers after publishing the first edition. His was apparently no idle whim for he once wrote in *The Evangelical Catholic* a long editorial denouncing writers who used the private papers of friends to write biographies. Miss Ayres apparently did a thorough job; not a single item has been found that can be identified as part of his private papers.

Despite certain obvious shortcomings, her book is extremely valuable for she had unrivaled opportunities for collecting information. She herself was Muhlenberg's close associate during the last thirty-two years of his life—from the time of his coming to New York in 1845 to his death. For the twenty previous years she had the collaboration of Libertus Van Bokellin, who had been with Muhlenberg from his Lancaster ministry as a student and instructor throughout his entire career as an educator. For Muhlenberg's early life in Philadelphia she drew on the reminiscences of Mrs. John Rogers, Muhlenberg's sister, who survived him by two years. Thus the only period of Muhlenberg's life for which she did not have firsthand sources was the relatively short period of his stay in Lancaster. For the period in which she had not known Muhlenberg she took down his reminiscences during their trip to Europe in 1872–1873. In addition to these sources she used the voluminous diary and journals which he kept from boyhood.

The information given in this biography when checked against other sources has been found remarkably accurate except for two items. Miss Ayres gives as the reason for the refusal of the Board of Regents of the University of the State of New York to grant degree-granting powers to St. Paul's College that it was their policy to refuse such powers to denominational colleges. This statement is also made in Hall Harrison's biography of Bishop Kerfoot but he probably got his information from

Miss Ayres's biography. Mr. Charles Brind, when counsel for the Board of Regents, reported in 1956 that he searched the records of the board thoroughly and found no evidence of any such policy; on the contrary, he pointed out that a number of denominational colleges were chartered by the board during this period. A letter written by Muhlenberg himself in 1843 indicated that it was the lack of an adequate endowment that caused the rejection of his request for degree-granting powers.

The second item may reflect a certain anti-Roman Catholic attitude on the part of Miss Ayres. She wrote that of the "inner circle" of Muhlenberg's college friends only one, James Keating, a Roman Catholic, did not remain a lifelong friend. Nothing more was heard of him after the class graduated, she said, implying that there was some break because of religious differences. The biography of Keating in the matriculates of the University of Pennsylvania reveals that he died two years after the class graduated, thus accounting for his failure to appear in Muhlenberg's later life.

Despite its accuracy, there are serious drawbacks to the Ayres biography. Miss Ayres selected only that material in which she was personally interested and suppressed all that she considered of a private nature. Thus she only hinted at his romance in Lancaster and at his part in the trial of Bishop Onderdonk. Nor did she discuss his deep interest in the problems of the westward-moving population. The entire book is extremely mawkish and whole sections are given over to sentimentalizing on inconsequential matters while important ones are dismissed in a few sentences. Furthermore, she missed the overall significance of Muhlenberg's work, regarding him merely as a great and good man. Thus this biography, while valuable as source material, is deficient in most other respects.

A second collection of letters has apparently also been destroyed. Hall Harrison in his biography of Bishop Kerfoot stated that he had the entire correspondence between Kerfoot and Muhlenberg, but a search of the archives of Trinity College, Hartford, and the diocese of Pittsburgh failed to locate them. The headmaster of St. James School, Maryland, where they were last known to be, suggests that they were probably destroyed with other records of the school when the original building burned some years ago. Harrison used about one-third of these letters in his biography and these he quotes verbatim. His book is to this extent a valuable source but like Miss Ayres he probably used only the letters that interested him.

A third loss is the correspondence between Muhlenberg and Dr. George Wood. Dr. Robert Abbe in his article, *A New View of the Boyhood of Dr. Muhlenberg*, refers to a packet of letters containing this correspondence at St. Luke's Hospital, but a search by the librarian of the hospital failed to locate it. Her predecessor was consulted and replied that she knew of these letters but that they were kept in the director's office. The present director has made a thorough search of the office but has been unable to find them. This loss is particularly regrettable because Dr. Wood was a Quaker and the letters might throw light on Muhlenberg outside the general range of church affairs. Miss Ayres also mentions correspondence between Muhlenberg and Joseph Engles. There are some letters of Joseph Engles in the files of the Presbyterian Historical Society but none from Muhlenberg, and there are none in the Pennsylvania Historical Society Library.

Miss Ayres's biography is thus the only source on Muhlenberg's early life but it is amply supplemented by much background material in Philadelphia. The pamphlets issued in the language controversy of St. Michael and Zion Church are in the Lutheran Theological Seminary Library at Philadelphia. The papers of the Sheaff and Seckel families—Muhlenberg's relatives through his mother—are in the Pennsylvania Historical Society Library. A contemporary guide book, Mease's *Picture of Philadelphia,* gives a comprehensive picture of Philadelphia in the years in which Muhlenberg grew to manhood. The Philadelphia Directories of the period supplement Mease's more general account and much family information is to be found in the wills in the Philadelphia County Courthouse.

There is considerable material on Bishop White and Dr. Abercrombie in the archives of Philadelphia. The archives of the University of Pennsylvania and the Minutes of the Board of Trustees are useful for Muhlenberg's college years. A still more valuable source is the description of the university given by Muhlenberg's classmate, Dr. George B. Wood, in his *History of the University of Pennsylvania.* Dr. Wood's own journal and papers are in the George B. Wood Room of the College of Physicians in Philadelphia. There is no material on William Augustus Muhlenberg in the library of the Pennsylvania Philosophical Society although there is some relating to previous generations of Muhlenbergs.

The Minutes of the Vestry of Christ Church, St. Peters, and St. James, contain some reference to Muhlenberg as well as to the purchase of the land from his mother on which St. James was built. Philadelphia archives in general have many pamphlets dealing with the various societies which flourished in Philadelphia during Muhlenberg's early ministry. There is a considerable amount of material on music both church and secular in early nineteenth century Philadelphia but exhaustive research has failed to turn up any reference to Muhlenberg himself or to his musical education. Mr. Donald W. Krummel of the Library of Congress, who is doing his doctoral dissertation on music in early nineteenth century Philadelphia, has found, however, that a person living in Philadelphia at that time would have had opportunities for acquiring such an education.

As a result of Muhlenberg's association with Jackson Kemper we have what is undoubtedly the best source next to Miss Ayres on his entire life. These are the some forty bound copies of Kemper's papers and miscellaneous items in the State Historical Society of Wisconsin library in Madison, Wisconsin. Kemper began keeping his papers as a small boy and continued this practice to the end of his life. Since he went West quite early while Muhlenberg remained in the East there is a considerable correspondence between them. This collection is also valuable for a general background of church history in the years up to Kemper's death in 1870. Another source for Kemper's life is the biography by Greenough White, *Apostle of the Wilderness,* which is based on the reminiscences of Elizabeth Kemper, the bishop's daughter.

The sources on Muhlenberg's Lancaster ministry are sparse. The Minutes of the Vestry of St. James Church are in the archives of that church together with other documents. The letters of Roberts Vaux and Muhlenberg are in the Vaux Letters in the Pennsylvania Historical Society Library. Another serious loss was that of the reports to the Court of the Board of Trustees of the Lancaster School District. All other official papers of these years are intact in the Lancaster County Courthouse; these alone are missing. They are quoted verbatim in Ellis and Evans, *History of Lancaster County,* but I am unable to confirm my opinion that they were written by Muhlenberg himself. There is an adequate amount of material relating to his efforts to found a public school system and to promote a new hymnal but the story of his romance with Sarah Coleman has to be pieced together from various sources. The only complete account appears in the letters to Frederick Bird from John B. Coleman and Mrs. Martha J. Nevin which were written more than fifty years after the event.

There is a large amount of material available on Muhlenberg's career as an educator: pamphlets, catalogues, minutes, reminiscences, and so forth, but two are of peculiar interest. The first is the diary of Thomas K. Wharton, who was an instructor at the Flushing Institute in 1832–1833. This diary is in the Manuscript Room of the New York Public Library together with some of Wharton's sketches. Some of the sketches have been published in a textbook by Ralph Volney Harlow, *The United States From Wilderness to World Power* (3d ed.; New York: Henry Holt and Co., 1957). The second of these sources is the letters of Kemper's two sons, who were students at St. Paul's College. They are in the private collection of Mrs. Charles Jackson, a great-granddaughter of Bishop Kemper at Nashotah, Wisconsin. Mrs. Jackson still lives in the original farmhouse where Kemper spent the last years of his life. These letters give a schoolboy's view of Muhlenberg—"justice without mercy." Valuable source material on the relationship of Muhlenberg and Breck is found in the Archives of Nashotah House, and on his relationship with Kerfoot in Harrison's biography.

The material on the beginning of the Church of the Holy Communion and about the New York of the 1840's and 1850's is voluminous. The one thing lacking is a set of minutes for the Church of the Holy Communion during these years. Although it was founded in 1845 it was not incorporated until 1867, and throughout these formative years it had neither vestry nor board of trustees. Possibly the most interesting record of this period is to be found in the Manuscript Room of the New York Public Library. This is the diary of Henry Dana Ward, who lived in the neighborhood of the Church of the Holy Communion and attended its services. His reactions to Muhlenberg's "novelties" are typical of the average church member of that period. A biography of this clergyman appears in the *Dictionary of American Biography*. Another source is the speech delivered before an association of clergymen at the time of Muhlenberg's death by Dr. Edwin Harwood, Muhlenberg's scholarly associate. This speech has been ignored by other writers, perhaps because its title gives the impression that it is merely an obituary notice. It is a remarkably perceptive biography, however, and comes nearer to assessing the significance of Muhlenberg than any other contemporary writer.

The chapters on deaconesses and sisterhoods, St. Luke's Hospital, and St. Johnland are derived largely from the minutes of St. Luke's and St. Johnland, *The Evangelical Catholic*, and numerous pamphlets. St. Luke's Hospital has a very carefully organized historical section in its Medical Library. The best source on the highly controversial topic of the formation of the Sisterhood of St. Mary is Peters' *Annals of St. Michael's Church*. The author was the son of Muhlenberg's friend and most of his information is based on his own knowledge of these events or the reminiscences of his father. A second source is a history of the Sisterhood of St. Mary published in 1965 entitled *Ten Decades of Praise* by Sister Mary Hilary. The author evidently had access to source material not available to this writer.

Material for the chapter on *The Evangelical Catholic* comes largely from the paper itself. The best sources on the Tractarian movement as it touched Muhlenberg are his letters to his friend, Samuel Seabury. These are in the collection of Mr. Andrew Oliver, Seabury's great-grandson, and are now in the General Theological Seminary Library. In addition to these there are the numerous pamphlets published during this controversy. Muhlenberg himself in the style of the Tractarians published a series of Pastoral Tracts in which he presented his position on this movement. Chapter 10 dealing with the Muhlenberg memorial has the most voluminous source material of all—a doctoral dissertation could be written on this chapter alone. The most valuable source on the memorial is the *Memorial Papers* edited and published by Bishop Alonzo Potter. These papers written by clergymen and laymen from all over the United States supply extensive material about American Christianity in the 1850's. Sources on Muhlenberg and national issues are mainly those already cited.

Miss Ayres published a selection of Muhlenberg's sermons and pamphlets in 1875 and shortly after his death she published a second volume. Most of these had already been published in pamphlet form but some have not been found elsewhere. These papers are entitled *Evangelical Catholic Papers*, Vols. I (1875) and II (1877), and should not be confused with the two volumes of *The Evangelical Catholic*, a weekly paper which Muhlenberg published from 1851 to 1853. The former are referred to in the notes as *E.C.P.* to avoid confusion.

Muhlenberg is frequently mentioned in *The Diary of George Templeton Strong*, edited by Allan Nevins and M. H. Thomas, but it is evident that Strong did not know Muhlenberg personally but only as a public figure. This diary as well as that of Philip Hone (1851) is valuable as background material for Muhlenberg's New York career. Dr. William Wilberforce Newton wrote a biography of Muhlenberg in 1890 based on his reminiscences of Muhlenberg whom he remembered when he (Newton) was a young clergyman. This biography is largely homiletical but has some value as source material.

A considerable number of secondary sources deal with Muhlenberg but usually with those aspects of his career in which the authors were interested. As noted in the Preface, two standard works, Abell, *The Urban Impact on American Protestantism,* and Hopkins, *The Rise of the Social Gospel in American Protestantism,* recognize Muhlenberg as a leader in urban church activities before the Civil War. A recent urban history of the United States, Glaab and Brown, *A History of Urban America,* also discusses Muhlenberg's activities in New York in the 1840's and 1850's. In summarizing their book they state that our cities are facing the same problems today and give as illustration Muhlenberg's struggle with "slumlords" in the 1850's.

Two generations of the Muhlenberg family have been portrayed by Wallace: *The Muhlenbergs of Pennsylvania,* but since Henry William and his son, William Augustus, were of the third and fourth generations respectively they are mentioned in this book only incidentally. There are no definitive biographies of Bishop White, James Abercrombie, nor Jackson Kemper.

Muhlenberg's place in the field of hymnody is discussed in three works: Foote, *Three Centuries of American Hymnody;* Julian, *A Dictionary of Hymnology;* and Benson, *The English Hymn, Its Development and Use in Worship.* Ellinwood, *The History of American Church Music,* cites Muhlenberg as a significant figure in the development of church music but does not go into detail. His role in the movement to establish a public school system in Pennsylvania is described in McCadden, *Education in Pennsylvania, 1801–1805, and Its Debt to Roberts Vaux.* His romance with Sarah Coleman is mentioned in a few paragraphs in an article by Dr. Philip Shiver Klein, "James Buchanan and Ann Coleman," *Pennsylvania History,* January, 1954.

Muhlenberg's schools have received some notice: Brewer, *A History of Religious Education in the Episcopal Church to 1835* gives an extensive account of the Flushing Institute but ends too early to mention St. Paul's College. His philosophy of education has been examined by Dr. John F. Woolverton in an article "William Augustus Muhlenberg and the Founding of St. Paul's College" in the *Historical Magazine of the Episcopal Church,* XXIX (September, 1960). Dr. Woolverton in this article compares the educational philosophy of Muhlenberg with that of John Dewey, noting that there were significant similarities as well as differences between the two.

The Church of the Holy Communion is cited in the standard works listed in the bibliography as well as in the denominational histories as an early example of the Institutional Church. Many histories of hospitals, nursing, and social work variously cite Muhlenberg, St. Luke's Hospital, and the Sisterhood of the Holy Communion as pioneers in their respective fields. Since there is a large number of such books giving essentially the same information, only the following have been listed in the bibliography: Bremner, *From the Depths; the Discovery of Poverty in the United States* (1956); Ernst, *Immigrant Life in New York City, 1825–1863,* (1949); Nutting and Doch, *The Development of Nursing in America* (1907); Roberts, *American Nursing History and Interpretation* (1954); and Doyle, "Nursing by Religious Orders in the United States," in *American Journal of Nursing,* V (February, 1929). Muhlenberg's social philosophy has been examined by the Rev. Richard G. Becker in an article in the *Historical Magazine of the Episcopal Church* entitled "The Social Thought of William Augustus Muhlenberg," XXVII (December, 1958).

Nichols, *Romanticism in American Theology, Nevin and Schaff at Mercers-*

berg (1961) alleges that Muhlenberg drew his concept of Evangelical Catholicism from Nevin and Schaff but offers no documentation for the statement. This is quite possible, however, because according to David S. Schaff, *The Life of Phillip Schaff* (1879) Muhlenberg and Phillip Schaff were close friends. Shepherd on *The Reform of Liturgical Worship* (1961) examines Muhlenberg's contribution to the liturgical movement and prayer book revision. In the opinion of this author Muhlenberg and Huntington prevented the Episcopal church from becoming a sect.

Muhlenberg is presented as an ecumenical leader in John T. McNeill, *Unitive Protestantism: A Study in Our Religious Resources* (1930); in Hardy, "Evangelical Catholicism, William Augustus Muhlenberg and the Memorial Movement," in the *Historical Magazine of the Episcopal Church;* and in Rouse and Neill, *A History of the Ecumenical Movement, 1517–1948* (1954). George Tavard states that Muhlenberg was an advocate of "Concentric Churches" in his book *Two Centuries of Ecumenism: The Search for Unity* (1962).

Muhlenberg receives detailed treatment in Episcopal church histories, Addison, *The Episcopal Church in the United States, 1789–1931* (1951), and Albright, *History of the Protestant Episcopal Church* (1964). Earlier Episcopal church histories also give Muhlenberg some space: Manross, *A History of the American Episcopal Church* (1935); DeMille, *The Catholic Movement in American Episcopal Church* (1949); and Chorley, *Men and Movements in the American Episcopal Church* (1949). There are numerous articles in the *Historical Magazine of the Episcopal Church* that deal with Muhlenberg's life or are valuable for background material. Particularly valuable are articles from this magazine by Morehouse, "Origin of the Episcopal Church Press from Colonial Days," (September, 1942); Satcher "music in the Episcopal Church in Pennsylvania in the Eighteenth Century," XVII (December, 1949); Douglas, "Early Hymnody of the American Episcopal Church," X (June, 1941); Klingberg, "Colonial Anglo-Lutheran Relations," XVI (June, 1947); and Tucker, "Impressions of the Episcopal Church in 1867," XX (1951). Also valuable are three pamphlets issued by the National Council—now the Executive Council—of the Episcopal Church. Two of these are by Harry Boone Porter: *William Augustus Muhlenberg: Pioneer of Christian Action* (1959) and *Sister Anne, Pioneer in Women's Work* (1960). The third is by Robert Bosher, *James Lloyd Breck on the Frontier* (1955).

Muhlenberg never married and therefore has no direct descendants. His sister Mary, however—who married John Rogers—had one daughter. She married William Chisholm and there are a number of Chisholms today who are her descendants. Mrs. Henry Chisholm of Thornbury, Westchester, New York, has all the Muhlenberg family portraits except the one by Eicholtz. The other members of the Chisholm family referred me to her as the family historian.

There are also descendants of the Sheaffs, the family of Muhlenberg's mother. Only one, however, answered my letters of inquiry. She was Mrs. Henry R. Higgins of Rehoboth Beach, Delaware, who gave the portrait by Eicholtz to St. Luke's Hospital, but she has no documents on Muhlenberg.

Three biographical encyclopedias have been of great value. The Rev. William Sprague's eleven-volume set of biographies of clergymen of all denominations published in the years 1857–1861 includes the clergymen who were influential in the first half of Muhlenberg's life. Dr. Sprague may have been personally acquainted with Muhlenberg for there is a note in one of Kemper's letters which requests him to "Send Sprague a sketch of Bishop White." If Muhlenberg wrote this sketch Sprague did not use it.

The second, a six-volume work generally referred to as *Appleton's Cyclopedia* was edited by the philosopher-historian, John Fiske, and a professional biographer, James Grant Wilson. The latter lived in New York from 1860 to the end of his life, was an active layman of the Episcopal church, and edited among other works a four-volume history of the Diocese of New York. He thus knew New York during the closing years of Muhlenberg's life and may have known him personally. The third is the twenty-three-volume *Dictionary of American Biography* published under the auspices of the American Council of Learned Societies from 1928 to 1937 with Dumas Malone and others as editors.

Most of the persons mentioned in this book were important in their own right and have biographies in at least one or two of the above and in some cases, all three. Muhlenberg as a prominent Philadelphian and New Yorker evidently knew everybody who was anybody in those two cities.

BIBLIOGRAPHY

PUBLISHED MATERIAL

Abell, Aaron Ignatius. *The Urban Impact on American Protestantism, 1865–1900.* Cambridge: Harvard University Press, 1943.

Abercrombie, James. *Charges to the Senior Classes of the Philadelphia Academy:*
Philadelphia: Privately Printed   July 27, 1804
Philadelphia: Privately Printed   July 31, 1805
Philadelphia: John Watts   July 31, 1806
Philadelphia: H. Maxwell   July 31, 1807
Philadelphia: John Watts   July 30, 1808
Philadelphia: Smith and Maxwell   July 27, 1809
Philadelphia: John Watts   July 26, 1810

———. *Lectures on the Catechism, on Confirmation, and on the Liturgy of the Protestant Episcopal Church, delivered to the students of that denomination, in the Philadelphia Academy.* Philadelphia: Published by the Author, 1807.

———. *The Mourner Comforted.* (A Sermon). Philadelphia: Bradford and Inskeep, 1812.

———. *Prospectus of an Edition of Johnson's Works,* Philadelphia, n.p., n.d.

———. *A sermon occasioned by the death of Alexander Hamilton, who was killed by Aaron Burr, in a duel, July 11, 1804, preached in Christ Church and St. Peter, Philadelphia, on July 22, 1804.* Philadelphia: H. Maxwell, 1804.

———. *A sermon preached in Christ Church and St. Peter, Philadelphia, on May 9, 1798, being the day appointed by the President, as a day of fasting, humiliation and prayer, throughout the United States of America.* Philadelphia: Printed by John Ormond, 1798.

———. *A sermon on the Liturgy of the Protestant Episcopal Church, preached before the convention held in Christ Church, Philadelphia, June 15, 1808.* Philadelphia: Smith and Maxwell, 1808.

———. *Thanksgiving sermons in Christ Church and St. Peters, May 9, 1798.* Philadelphia: Published by the Author, 1798.

———. *Two compends for the use of the Philadelphia Academy: Elocution and Natural History.* Philadelphia: Published by the Author, 1803.

Account of the True Nature and Object of the late Protestant Episcopal Clerical Association of the City of New York together with a defense of the Association from Objections which have been urged against it, and an explanation of the reasons which led to its dissolution. New York: Published by members of the Association, 1829.

Adams, William. "Historical Paper," *Report of the Jubilee Ceremonies of Nashotah House.* Nashotah: Published by the Alumni, 1892.

Addison, James Thayer. *The Episcopal Church in the United States, 1789–1931.* New York: Charles Scribner's Sons, 1951.

Albion, Robert G. *The Rise of New York Port.* New York: Charles Scribner's Sons, 1939.

Albright, Raymond W. *A History of the Protestant Episcopal Church.* New York: The Macmillan Co., 1964.

Andrews, Wayne. *Architecture, Ambition and Americans.* Glencoe, Illinois: The Free Press of Glencoe, 1964.

Annual Reports of the Controllers of the First School District of the State of Pennsylvania. Philadelphia: Printed by order of the Board of Controllers, various dates.

"*Appendix* M.–1, List of the Clergy of the Protestant Episcopal Church in the United States, October, 1853" in *Journal of the General Convention,* 1854.

Aydelott, Benjamin Parham. *The Condition and Prospects of the Protestant Episcopal Church.* Cincinnati: W. H. Moore and Co., 1848.

Ayres, Anne. *Two letters on Protestant Sisterhoods.* 3d ed. New York: R. Craighead, printer, 1856.

———. *Evangelical Sisterhoods, In two letters to a friend.* Edited by W. A. Muhlenberg. New York: T. Whittaker, 1867.

———. *Life and Work of William Augustus Muhlenberg.* 5th ed. New York: T. Whittaker, 1894.

———. *Practical Thoughts on Sisterhoods. In reply to a letter of inquiry. With extracts from the Principles of Association and rules of the Sisterhood of the Holy Communion; now at St. Luke's Hospital.* New York: T. Whittaker, 1864.

Ayres, Anne. *Two letters on Protestant Sisterhoods.* Edited by W. A. Muhlenberg. New York: Hobart Press, 1852.

Bahr, Karl Christian Wilhelm Felix. *The Books of the Kings,* translated, enlarged, and edited by Edwin Harwood and W. G. Sumner. New York: Scribner, Armstrong and Co., 1872. This volume is one of a series entitled *A Commentary on the Holy Scripture* by J. P. Lange, translated from the German and edited by Phillip Schaff.

Baltzell, E. Digby. *Philadelphia Gentlemen: The Making of A National Upper Class.* New York: Free Press, 1966.

Barnwell, W. H. *Letter to the Honorable R. F. W. Alston, a Lay Delegate to the General Convention of the Protestant Episcopal Church.* Beaufort, S.C.: Published by the Author, September 8, 1856.

313

Batchelder, Edwin A. 1850–1950, *Centennial Observance of the Church of the Holy Communion, Lake Geneva, Wisconsin.* Lake Geneva, Wis.: Published by the Parish, 1950.

Belden, Ezekiel Porter. *New York: Past, Present and Future. Comprising a history of the City of New York; a description of its present condition and an estimate of its future increase.* New York: Pratt, Lewis and Co., 1850.

Benson, Louis F. *The English Hymn: Its Development and Use in Worship.* New York: George H. Doran Company, 1915.

Berrian, William. *To the Commission of Bishops on the Memorial of the Rev. Dr. Muhlenberg, etc., To the House of Bishops, at the late General Convention.* New York: For Private Distribution, 1854.

Blake, Nelson Mumford. *A History of American Life and Thought.* New York: McGraw-Hill Book Co., Inc. 1963.

Booth, Mary Louise. *History of the City of New York from its earliest settlement to the present time.* New York: W. R. C. Clark and Meeker, 1859.

Bosher, Robert S. *James Lloyd Breck on the Frontier.* New York: National Council of the Episcopal Church, 1955.

Brand, William Francis. *Life of William R. Whittingham.* New York: E. and J. B. Young and Co., 1886.

Breck, Charles. *The Life of the Rev. James Lloyd Breck.* New York: E. and J. B. Young and Co., 1883.

Bremner, Robert. *From the Depths: The Discovery of Poverty in the United States.* New York: New York University Press, 1956.

Brewer, Clifton Hartwell. *A History of Religious Education in the Episcopal Church to 1835.* New Haven: Yale University Press, 1924.

Bridenbaugh, Carl. *Cities in Revolt.* New York: Alfred A. Knopf, Inc., 1959.

———. *Cities in the Wilderness.* New York: The Ronald Press Co., 1938.

Bridenbaugh, Carl and Jessica. *Rebels and Gentlemen, Philadelphia in the Age of Franklin.* New York: Reynar and Hitchcock, 1942.

Bristed, John. *Thoughts on the Anglican and Anglo-American Churches.* New York: J. P. Haven, 1822.

Burchard, John, and Albert Bush-Brown. *The Architecture of America: A Social and Cultural History.* Boston: Little, Brown & Co., 1961.

Callow, Alexander B., Jr. *The Tweed Ring.* New York: Oxford University Press, 1966.

Carmann, Henry J., and Hugh N. Camp. *The Charities of New York, Brooklyn and Staten Island.* New York: Hurd and Houghton, 1868.

Caswall, Henry. *America and the American Church.* London: Gilbert and Rivington, Printers, 1839.

Catalogue of the Episcopal School for Boys. Raleigh, N.C., 1836.

Catholicus. *A Few Thoughts on the Duties, Difficulties and Relations of the Protestant Episcopal Church in the United States, in a letter to the Commission of Bishops, to whom was referred the memorial of Dr. Muhlenberg and others.* New York: Stanford and Swords, 1855.

Cheyney, Edward Potts. *History of the University of Pennsylvania, 1740–1940.* Philadelphia: University of Pennsylvania Press, 1940.

Chisholm, William Garnett. *Chisholm Genealogy being a Record of the Name from A.D. 1254.* New York: The Knickerbocker Press, 1914.

Chorley, E. Clowes. *Men and Movements in the American Episcopal Church.* New York: Charles Scribner's Sons, 1946.

Citizens Association of New York, *Report of the Council of Hygiene and Public Health.* New York: 1865.

Clark, Thomas March. *Reminiscences.* New York: Thomas Whittaker, 1895.

Cogswell, Joseph Green. *Outline of the system of education at the Round Hill School, with a list of the present instructors and of the pupils from its commencement until this time, June 1831.* Boston: N. Hale's Press, 1831.

———. *Prospectus of a school to be established at Round Hill, Northampton, Mass., by Joseph S. Cogswell and George Bancroft.* Cambridge: Harvard University Press, 1823.

Cogswell, Joseph Green, and George Bancroft. *Some account of the school for the liberal education of boys, established at Round Hill, Northampton, Mass. (Northampton, 1826).*

Colton, Calvin. *The Genius and Mission of the Protestant Episcopal Church in the United States.* New York: Stanford and Swords, 1853.

Cooke, The Rev. Samuel, D.D. *The Morals of Bethesda! A sermon preached in the Chapel of St. Luke's Hospital on the occasion of opening the Hospital for Patients, on Ascension Day, May 13, 1858.* New York: Published by the Managers of the Hospital, 1858.

Cotterill, Thomas. *A Selection of Psalms and Hymns for the use of St. Paul's and St. James' Churches.* 9th ed. Sheffield: J. Montgomery, 1820.

Cross, Robert D., ed. *The Church and the City, 1865–1910.* Indianapolis: Bobbs-Merrill Company, Inc., 1967.

Croswell, Harry. *Memoir of William Croswell.* New York: D. Appleton and Co., 1854.

Curry, Daniel. *New York, a Historical sketch of the rise and progress of the Metropolitan City of America.* New York: Carlton and Phillip, 1853.

DeMille, George E. *The Catholic Movement in the American Episcopal Church.* Philadelphia: Church Historical Society, 1949.

Doane, William Cromwell. *A memoir of the Life of George Washington Doane.* New York: D. Appleton and Co., 1860.

Douglas, George Williams. *Essays in Appreciation.* New York: Longmans, Green, and Co., 1917.

Dunlap, George. *The City in the American Novel, 1789–1900.* New York: Russell and Russell Publishers, 1965.

Eaton, Edward Dwight. "John Henry Hopkins," in *Dictionary of American Biography.* Dumas Malone, et al. eds. New York: Charles Scribner's Sons, 1930.

Ellinwood, Leonard. *The History of American Church Music.* New York: Morehouse-Gorham Co., 1958.

Ellis, Franklin, and Samuel Evans. *History of Lancaster County.* Philadelphia: Everts and Peck, 1883.

Ellis, John Tracy. *American Catholicism.* Chicago: University of Chicago Press, 1956.

English Layman. *Recent Recollections of the Anglo-American Church in the United States.* London: Rivingtons, 1861.

Episcopal Education Society. *Annual Reports, 1–12.* Philadelphia: Various Publishers, 1821–1833.

Episcopal Female Tract Society of Philadelphia. *Religious Tracts.* Philadelphia: William Stavely, 1823.

Episcopal Missionary Society of Philadelphia. *Annual Reports, 1817–1825.* Philadelphia: Various Publishers, 1817–1825.

Episcopal School of North Carolina. *The Prospectus.* Raleigh: Privately Printed, 1830.

Ernst, Robert. *Immigrant Life in New York City, 1825–1863.* New York: Kings Crown Press, 1949.

Fiske, John, and James Grant Wilson (editors). *Appleton's Cyclopedia of American Biography.* New York: D. Appleton and Co., 1889. Vols I–VI.

Flushing Institute, Flushing, N.Y. *Catalogue of the officers and students of the Flushing Institute, Flushing, L.I., N.Y.* Flushing: French and Wheet, 1862.

Foote, Henry Wilder. *Three Centuries of American Hymnody.* Cambridge: Harvard University Press, 1940.

Foster, George S. *New York by Gaslight.* New York: Dewitt and Davenport, 1850.

———. *New York in Slices by an experienced slicer. Being the original slices published in the New York Tribune,* New York, 1849.

Francis, C. S. *Francis's New Guide to the Cities of New York and Brooklyn and the vicinity.* New York: C. S. Francis and Co., 1853.

Fry, James Bennett. *New York and the Conscription Act of 1863; a Chapter in the History of the Civil War.* New York: G. Putnam and Sons, 1885.

Geberding, C. H. *Life and Letters of W. A. Passavant: D.D.* Greenville, Pa.: The Young Lutheran Co., 1906.

Gelfant, Blanche H. *The American City Novel.* Norman: University of Oklahoma Press, 1954.

Gentzmer, G. H. "George Washington Doane" in *Dictionary of American Biography.* Dumas Malone, et al. eds. New York: Charles Scribner's Sons, 1930.

———. "W. A. Passavant," in the *Dictionary of American Biography.* Dumas Malone, et al. eds. New York: Charles Scribner's Sons, 1930.

Glaab, Charles N. *The American City: A Documentary History.* Homewood, Ill.: Dorsey, 1963.

———. and A. Theodore Brown. *A History of Urban America.* New York: The Macmillan Co., 1967.

Green, Constance McL. *American Cities in the Growth of the Nation.* New York: John de Graff, Inc., 1967.

———. *The Rise of Urban America.* New York: Harper & Row Publishers, 1965.

Green, William Mercier. *Memoir of James Hervey Otey.* New York: James Pott and Co., 1885.

Greenlief, Jonathan. *A History of the Churches of all denominations in he city of New York, from the first settlement to the year, 1846.* New York: E. French, 1846.

Groce, George C., and David H. Wallace, *Dictionary of Artists in America, 1564–1860,* New York: The New York Historical Society, 1957.

Handlin, Oscar, and John Burchard, eds. *The Historian and the City.* Cambridge: Massachusetts Institute of Technology Press, 1966.

Handy, Robert T., ed. *The Social Gospel in America, 1870–1920: Gladden, Ely Rauschenbusch.* New York: Oxford University Press, Inc., 1966.

Harlow, Ralph Volney. *The United States From Wilderness to World Power.* 3d ed. New York: Henry Holt and Co., 1957.

Harrison, Hall. *Life of the Rt. Rev. John Barrett Kerfoot.* New York: James Pott and Co., 1886.

Harwood, Edwin. *In Memory of William Augustus Muhlenberg, 1796–1877, D.D. LL.D.*[sic] *A discourse by Edwin Harwood, D.D., and a poem by George D. Wildes, D.D., read before an association of Clergymen, of which he was the senior member, May 15th, 1877.* New York: T. Whittaker, 1877.

Haswell, Charles Haynes. *Reminiscences of an Octogenarian of the City of New York (1816–1860).* New York: Harper and Bros., 1896.

Hawks, Francis Lister. *Circular of St. Thomas's Hall.* New York: Privately Published, 1840.

Haywood, Marshall Delancey. *Lives of the Bishops of North Carolina.* Raleigh: Alfred Williams and Co., 1910.

Hillary, Sister Mary, C.S.M. *Ten Decades of Praise. The Story of the Community of St. Mary During its First Century.* 1865–1965. Racine, Wisconsin: DeKoven Foundation, 1965.

Hodges, George. *Henry Codman Potter, Seventh Bishop of New York.* New York: The Macmillan Co., 1915.

Holcombe, T. I. *An Apostle of the Wilderness.* New York: Thomas Whittaker, 1903.

Holy Communion, Church of, New York. *Working Men's Clubs in Great Britain and Ireland.* New York: Published by the Church, 1875.

————. *Chronicles and Year-books* 1883–1901. New York: Published by the Church, 1883–1901.

Hone, Phillip. *The Diary of Phillip Hone with an Introduction by Bayard Tuckerman.* New York: Dodd, Meade and Co., 1889.

Hopkins, Charles Howard. *The Rise of the Social Gospel in American Protestantism, 1865–1915.* New Haven: Yale University Press, 1940.

Hopkins, John Henry, Sr. *A Scriptural, Ecclesiastical, and Historical View of Slavery from the Days of the Patriarch Abraham, to the Nineteenth Century, Addressed to the Right Rev. Alonzo Potter, D.D.* New York: W. I. Pooley and Company, 1864.

Hansen, Philip M., and Leo F. Schnore, eds. *The Study of Urbanization.* New York: John Wiley & Sons, Inc., 1965.

Howe, M. A. DeWolfe. *Memoirs of the Life and Service of Alonzo Potter.* Philadelphia: J. B. Lippincott and Co., 1871.

Hymns of the Protestant Episcopal Church in the United States of America set forth in the General Convention of said church in the year of our Lord, 1789, 1808, and 1829. This book is sometimes referred to as *The Hymnal of 1827* or *The Hymnal of 1828* in source material.

Ingraham, Rev. J. P. "Early Reminiscences of Nashotah,' *Nashotah Jubilee Report.* Nashotah: Published by the Alumni, 1880.

Jefferson, Joseph. *Autobiography.* London: Reinhart and Evans, Ltd., 1949.

Journal of the Diocese of New York, various dates and publishers.

Journal of the Diocese of Pennsylvania, various dates and publishers.

Journal of the General Conventions of the Protestant Episcopal Church, various dates and publishers.

Journal of the Institute at Flushing, November, 1832–December, 1835. The only known file of this publication is at the Virginia Theological Seminary, Alexandria, Virginia.

Journal of St. Paul's College, February 1844. The only known copy of this publication is at the General Theological Seminary, New York, N.Y.

Julian, John. *A Dictionary of Hymnology, Setting Forth the Origin and History of Christian Hymns of all Ages and Nations.* London: John Murray, 1925.

King, William. *What De Fellenberg has done for Education.* London: Saunders and Oakley, 1839.

Kinsman, Frederick Joseph. *Salve Mater.* New York: Longmans, Green and Co., 1920.

Kip, William Ingraham. *The Early Days of My Episcopate.* New York: T. Whittaker, 1892.

Klein, H. M. J. *Lancaster's Golden Century, 1821–1921.* Lancaster: Hager and Brother, 1922.

Klein, H. M. J., and W. F. Diller. *The History of St. James' Church, 1744–1944.* Lancaster, Pa.: Published by the Vestry, 1944.

Knauff, Christopher Wilkin. *Doctor, Teacher, Poet, Musician, A. Sketch which concerns the doings and thinkings [sic] of the Rev. John Ireland Tucker, S.T.D., including a brief converse about the rise and progress of church music in America.* New York: A. D. F. Randolph and Co., 1897.

Kupta, August. *Reverend William Augustus Muklenberg [sic] Clergyman, educator, philanthropist, founder and Administrator.* Flushing, New York: Flushing Historical Society, 1907.

Lancaster, Joseph. *Epitome of some of the chief events and transactions in the life of Joseph Lancaster, containing an account of the rise and progress of the Lancastrian system of Education, and the author's future prospects of usefulness to mankind.* New York: Baldwin and Peck, 1833.

———. *The Lancastrian system of Education, with improvements by the founder.* Baltimore: The Lancastrian Institute, 1821.

Lawrence, Francis Effingham. *A Man after God's Own Heart. Loving Words to the dear Memory of William Augustus Muhlenberg, D.D., April 22, 1877.* New York: Printed for Private Circulation, 1877.

Levine, Daniel. *Varieties of Reform Thought.* Madison: State Historical Society of Wisconsin, 1964.

Livingood, James W. *The Philadelphia-Baltimore Trade Rivalry.* Harrisburg: Pennsylvania Historical and Museum Commission, 1947.

Long, Orie William. *Literary Pioneers; early American Explorers of European Culture.* Cambridge: Harvard University Press, 1935.

McCadden, J. J. *Education in Pennsylvania, 1801–1805, and Its Debt to Roberts Vaux.* Philadelphia: University of Pennsylvania Press, 1937.

McKelvey, Blake. *The Emergence of Metropolitan America, 1915–1966.* New Brunswick: Rutgers University Press, 1968.

———. *The Urbanization of America, 1860–1915.* New Brunswick: Rutgers University Press, 1963.

McNeil, John T. *Unitive Protestantism: A Study in Our Religious Resources.* New York: The Abingdon Press, 1930.

Mahan, Milo. *Collected Works.* Ed. by John Henry Hopkins, Jr. 3 vols. New York: Pott, Young and Co., 1875.

Malone, Dumas, ed., et al. *Dictionary of American Biography.* New York: Charles Scribner's Sons, 1928–1937, Vols. I–XX.

Mandelbaum, Seymour J. *Boss Tweed's New York.* New York: John Wiley & Sons, Inc., 1965.

Mandeville, G. Henry. *Flushing, Past and Present, An Historical Sketch.* Flushing: J. Egbert, Printer, 1860.

Manross, William Wilson. *A History of the American Episcopal Church.* New York: Morehouse Publishing Company, 1935.

Marcus, Moses. *Address to the Members of the "United Church of England and Ireland" and of the Protestant Episcopal Church in the United States of America on the subject of Emigration.* New York: 1846.

May, Henry F. *Protestant Churches and Industrial America.* New York: Harper and Brothers, 1949.

Mease, James. *The Picture of Philadelphia. Giving an account of its Origin, Increase and Improvements, in Arts, Sciences, Manufacturers, Commerce and Revenue; with a Compendium view of its societies, literary, benevolent, patriotic and religious; its police; the public buildings; the prison and penitentiary system; the institutions, monied and civil.* Philadelphia: Rite and Co., 1811.

Melville, Annabelle M. *Elizabeth Bayley Seton, 1774–1821.* New York: Charles Scribner's Sons, 1951.

The Memorial viewed from a different standpoint from that occupied by "One of their Number." New York, 1856.

Morehouse, F. C. *Some American Churchmen.* Milwaukee: Morehouse Publishing Company, 1892.

Mottet, Henry. *In Commemoration of Rev. William Augustus Muhlenberg.* New York: The Church of the Holy Communion, 1927.

Mowry, George E. *The Urban Nation, 1920–1960.* New York: Hill & Wang, Inc., 1965.

Muhlenberg, Henry A. *The Life of Major-General Peter Muhlenberg of the Revolutionary Army.* Philadelphia: Cary and Hart, 1849.

Muhlenberg, Henry Melchior. *The Journals of Henry Melchior Muhlenberg.* Translated by Theodore S. Tappert and John W. Doberstein. Philadelphia: The Evangelical Lutheran Ministerium of Pennsylvania and adjacent states and the Muhlenberg Press, 1945.

Mumford, Lewis. *The Brown Decades.* New York: Dover Publications, Inc., 1955.

———. *The Culture of Cities.* New York: Harcourt Brace & World, Inc., 1938.

Newman, John Henry. *Apologia Pro Vita Sua.* New York: Longmans, Green, and Co., 1901.

Newton, William Wilberforce, D.D. *Yesterday with the Fathers.* New York: Cochrane Publishing Company, 1910.

———. *Dr. Muhlenberg.* New York: Houghton, Mifflin Co., 1890.

Nichols, James Hastings. *Romanticism in American Theology, Nevin and Schaff at Mercersberg.* Chicago: The University of Chicago Press, 1961.

Nutting, M. Adelaide, and Lavinia L. Doch. *The Development of Nursing in America, A History of Nursing.* New York: G. P. Putnam, Inc., 1907. Vol. II.

Onderdonk, Henry U. *Appendix to a discourse delivered in Christ Church, Philadelphia, at the funeral of the Rt. Rev. William White.* Philadelphia: Jaspar Harding, printer, 1836.

Owen, Robert Dale. *Hints on Public Architecture, containing among other illustrations, views and plans of the Smithsonian Institution, .ogether with an appendix relative to building materials.* Prepared on behalf of the building committee of the Smithsonian Institute. New York: George D. Putnam, 1849.

Parkman, Rev. C. M. *A counter-memorial to the House of Bishops of the Protestant Episcopal Church.* Philadelphia: Henry B. Ashmead, 1856.

Pennsylvania, University of. *Biographical catalogue of the matriculates of the college, together with lists of the members of the college faculty, and the trustees, officers, and recipients of honorary degrees, 1749–1893.* Philadelphia: Published by the Alumni Association, 1894.

———. *General Alumni Ca. alogue of* 1922. Compiled by W. J. Maxwell under the direction of the Alumni Association of the University, H. M. Lippincott, Secretary.

Perry, William Stevens. *The History of the American Episcopal Church, 1587–1883.* Boston: James R. Osgood, 1885.

Peters, John Punnett. *Annals of St. Michael's Being the History of St. Michael's Protestant Episcopal Church, New York, for one hundred years, 1807–1907.* New York: G. P. Putnam and Sons, 1907.

Philadelphia Directory. Philadelphia: Various compilers and publishers, 1785–1821.

Philo [the name of a student Society]. *Addresses delivered before the Philomathean Society of the University of Pennsylvania, on the occasion of the semi-centennial [sic] celebration, October 6, 1863.* Philadelphia: Published by the Society, 1864.

———. *Catalogue of the Philomathean Society, instituted in the University of Pennsylvania, MDCCCXIII.* Philadelphia: Ringwalt and Co., 1859.

Piers, W. E. *History of St. Paul's School.* New York: Harper Brothers, 1940.

Plain Presbyter. *A response to Bishop Potter in relation to the designs of the recent Episcopal Memorial Papers.* Philadelphia: Joseph M. Wilson, 1858.

Porter, Harry Boone. *Sister Anne, Pioneer in Women's Work.* New York: The National Council of the Episcopal Church, 1960.

———. *William Augustus Muhlenberg, Pioneer of Christian Action.* New York: The National Council of the Episcopal Church, 1959.

Potter, Alonzo, ed. *Memorial Papers, The Memorial with circular and questions of the Episcopal Commission; Report of the Commission; contributions of the Commissioners; and communications from Episcopal and Non-Episcopal Divines.* Philadelphia: E. H. Butler Co., 1857.

Potter, Henry C. *Sisterhoods and Deaconesses, at Home and Abroad.* New York: Dutton, 1873.

Potter, Horatio. *Pastoral Letter to the Clergy of the Diocese of New York, with the replies of the Rev. S. H. Tyng, E. H. Canfield, John Cotton Smith, and W. A. Muhlenberg.* New York, 1865.

BIBLIOGRAPHY

The Proceedings of the Court Convened under the third canon of 1844 in the City of New York, on Tuesday, December 10, 1844. For the trial of the Rt. Rev. Benjamin T. Onderdonk, D.D., Bishop of New York; on a presentment made by the Bishops of New York; on a presentment made by the Bishops of Virginia, Tennessee, and Georgia. By authority of the court. New York: D. Appleton and Co., 1845.

Protestant Episcopal Church. *Journal of the General Convention.* Various publishers, titles, and dates.

Protestant Episcopal Sunday and Adult School Society of Philadelphia with constitution and by-laws, Reports. Philadelphia: Published by the Society, 1821.

Protestant Episcopal Sunday School Society of Philadelphia, Annual Reports. Philadelphia: Published by the Society, 1818–1821.

Protestant Episcopal Sunday School, Society of, Philadelphia, Constitution of. Philadelphia: Published by the Society, 1818.

Reichman, Felix. *The Muhlenberg Family,* A bibliography compiled from the (subject union) catalogue (of) American Germanica of the Carl Schultz Memorial Foundation. Philadelphia: Carl Schultz Memorial Foundation Incorporation, 1943.

Roberts, Mary. *American Nursing, History and Interpretation.* New York: The Macmillan Company, 1954.

Rosenberg, Charles. *The Cholera Years.* Chicago: University of Chicago Press, 1962.

Rouse, R., and L. C. Neill. *A History of the Ecumenical Movement, 1517–1948.* London: S.C.P.K., 1954.

St. James Church, Lancaster Sunday School Society of. Lancaster: Published by the Society, 1820.

St. James Church, Lancaster. *First Annual Report of the Female Sunday School Society.* Lancaster: Published by the Society, 1822.

St. Johnland, Society of. *Annual Reports.* Nos. 1–13 (1871–1883). Kings Park, New York: Published by the Society, 1871–1883.

Saint Luke's Hospital. *A Venture in Faith.* New York: St. Luke's Hospital, 1952.

St. Luke's Hospital. *Annual Reports of St. Luke's Hospital.* Various publishers and titles, 1860–1892.

St. Luke's Hospital Bulletin. Vol. II. New York: April, 1950.

St. Luke's Hospital. *History of the Saint Luke's Hospital Training School for Nurses.* New York: St. Luke's Hospital, 1938.

St. Luke's Hospital. *Service at the Laying of the Cornerstone of St. Luke's Hospital, May 6, 1854.* New York: Phair and Co., 1854.

———. *Junior Associations of St. Luke's Hospital in the Parish of St. Thomas, New York. Constitution and by-laws.* New York: 1863.

St. Paul's College, College Point, N.Y. *Catalogue of the Professors, Instructors, and Students of St. Paul's College and Grammar School, for the session of 1838–39.* New York: William Osborne, 1839.

St. Paul's College, College Point, N.Y. *Catalogues of the Professors, Instructors, and Students of St. Paul's College and Grammar School, for the session,* 1839–40. New York: 1840.

———. *An Account of the Grammar School, or Junior Department.* New York: Printed by F. C. Gutierrez, 1842.

———. *Catalogue,* 1846. New York: William C. Martin, Printer, 1846.

———. *Catalogue,* 1847. Printed by Charles E. Smith, 1847.

Saunders, Frederick. *New York in a Nutshell, or a visitor's Handbook to the City.* New York: T. W. Strong, 1853.

Schaff, David S. *The Life of Phillip Schaff.* New York: Charles Scribner's Sons, 1879.

Schlesinger, Arthur M., and Dixon Ryan Fox, eds. *The History of American Life.* 13 vols. New York: Macmillan Company, 1927–1948.

Schroeder, John Frederick. *Religion and the State or Christianity the safeguard of civil liberty. An oration delivered before the members of St. Paul's College and St. Ann s Hall, at St. Paul's College, College Point, N.Y., on the fifth of July, A.D.,* 1841. New York: Published by St. Paul's College, 1841.

Scudder, Vida Dutton. *Father Huntington.* New York: E. P. Dutton and Company, 1940.

Seabury, Samuel. *American Slavery Distinguished from the Slavery of the English Theorist, and Justified by the Law of Nature.* New York: Mason Brothers, 1861.

Shepherd, Massey H. *The Reform of Liturgical Worship.* New York: Oxford University Press, 1961.

Smith, J. Carpenter. *History of St. George's Parish, Flushing, Long Island.* Flushing: Sword and Shield, 1897.

Smith, Wilson. *Cities of Our Past and Present.* New York: John Wiley & Sons, Inc., 1964.

Society of [*sic*] the Advancement of Christianity in Pennsylvania. *Annual Reports,* 1813–1822, 1–10. Philadelphia: Published by the Society, 1813–1822.

Southern Presbyter. *The Memorial viewed from a different standpoint from that occupied by One of their Number.* Philadelphia: H. Hooker and Co., 1856.

Sprague, William B. *Annals of the American Pulpit.* New York: R. Carter and Bros., 1857–1861. Vols. I–XI.

Stanton, Phoebe B. *The Gothic Revival and American Church Architecture: An Episode in Taste,* 1840–1856. Baltimore: Johns Hopkins Press, 1968.

Still, Bayrd. *Mirror for Gotham.* New York: New York University Press, 1956.

Stoever, M. L. *Memorial of the Rev. Philip F. Mayer, D.D.* Philadelphia: James Hite and Co., 1859.

Stone, John. *Memoirs of the Life of James Milnor.* New York: A. D. F. Randolph, 1848.

Stone, William Leete. *The Centennial History of New York City. From the Discovery to the Present Day.* New York: R. D. Cooke, 1876.

Strauss, Anselm L., ed. *The American City: A Sourcebook of Urban Imagery.* Chicago: Aldine Publishing Co., 1968.

———. *Images of the American City.* Glencoe, Ill.: Free Press, 1961.

Strong, George Templeton. *The Diary of George Templeton Strong.* Allan Nevin and Milton Halsey Thomas, eds. New York: The Macmillan Co., 1952.

Tavard, George H. *Two Centuries of Ecumenism: The Search for Unity.* New York: New American Library, 1962.

Tewkesbery, Donald S. *The Founding of American Colleges and Universities before the Civil War.* New York: Teacher's College, 1932. (In Teacher's College, Columbia University. Contribution to Education, no. 543.)

Thompson, Benjamin F. *The History of Long Island from Its Discovery and Settlement to the Present Time.* New York: Gould, Banks, and Co., 1843.

Ticknor, Anna Elliot. *Life of Joseph Green Cogswell as sketched in his letters.* Cambridge: The Riverside Press, 1874.

Tiffany, Charles Comfort. *A History of the Protestant Episcopal Church in the United States of America.* New York: The Christian Literature Company, 1895.

Turner, Samuel H. *Autobiography of the Rev. Samuel H. Turner, D.D.* New York: A. D. F. Randolph, 1864.

Twain, Mark. *The Adventures of Tom Sawyer.* New York: Grossett and Dunlap, 1946.

Upjohn, Everad M. *Richard Upjohn, Architect and Churchman.* New York: Columbia University Press, 1939.

Vail, Thomas Hubbard. *The Comprehensive Church or Christian Unity and Ecclesiastical Union in the Protestant Episcopal Church.* New York: D. Appleton and Co., 1879.

Wade, Richard C. *Slavery in the Cities: The South, 1820–1860.* New York: Oxford University Press, 1967.

Wade, Richard C. *The Urban Frontier 1790–1830.* Cambridge: Harvard University Press, 1959.

Wallace, Paul A. *The Muhlenbergs of Pennsylvania.* Philadelphia: University of Pennsylvania Press, 1950.

Walworth, Clarence E. *The Oxford Movement in America, or Glimpses of Life in an Anglican Seminary.* New York: The Catholic Book Exchange, *1895.*

Washburn, Edward Abiel. *The Catholic Work of the Protestant Episcopal Church in America. A contribution to the cause of the Memorial, by a Presbyter.* New York: R. Craighead, 1855.

———. *Sermon in Memorial [sic] of William Augustus Muhlenberg, D.D.* New York: T. Whittaker, 1877.

Waylen, Edward. *Ecclesiastical Reminiscences of the United States.* New York: Wiley and Putnam, 1846.

Weber, Adna Ferrin. *The Growth of Cities in the Nineteenth Century.* Ithaca: Cornell University Press, 1963.

Weld, Ralph. *Brooklyn Village*. New York: Columbia University Press, 1938.

Wentz, Abell Ross. *The Lutheran Church in American History*. Philadelphia: The United Lutheran Publication House, *1940*.

Wharton, Thomas J. *Address Delivered at the Opening of the New Hall of the Athenaeum, October 18, 1812*. Philadelphia: 1812.

White, Greenough. *An Apostle of the Western Church*. New York: Thomas Whittaker, 1911.

White, Morton and Lucia. *The Intellectual Versus the City: From Thomas Jefferson to Frank Lloyd Wright*. New York: New American Library, Inc., 1964.

White, William. *The Case of the Episcopal Churches in the United States considered*. Philadelphia: Printed by David C. Claypoole, MDCCCXXXII.

————. *Memoirs of the Protestnat Episcopal Church in the United States of America, from its organization up to the present day*. 2d ed. New York: Swords, Stanford and Co., 1836.

————. *Sermon on the Assembly of the Sunday Schools of Philadelphia at the festival of the Holy Innocents (December 28, 1817) St. James' Church*. Philadelphia: 1818.

Wilson, Bird. *Memoir of the Life of the Rt. Rev. William White*. Philadelphia: Hayes and Fell, 1839.

Wilson, James Grant. *The Centennial History of the Protestant Episcopal Church in the Diocese of New York, 1785–1885*. New York: D. Appleton and Company, 1886.

Wood, George Bacon. *Journal of Dr. George B. Wood, No. 1st [sic] 1817–1829*. Philadelphia: Privately published, 1839.

————. *The History of the University of Pennsylvania, from its origin to the Year 1827. Read before the council of the Historical Society of Pennsylvania, October 29, 1827, and printed by order of the Council*. Philadelphia: McCarty and Davis, 1834.

————. *An Address delivered before the Philomathean Society of the University of Pennsylvania*. Published by order of the Society, 1826.

Works Progress Administration. *Historical Collections of the Borough of Queens, New York City*. Project #465-97-3-20. In the Long Island Collection, The Queensborough Public Library, Jamaica, Long Island, N.Y., 1938.

THE PUBLISHED WORKS OF WILLIAM AUGUSTUS MUHLENBERG

Muhlenberg, William Augustus. *An Account of St. Johnland*. New York: T. Whittaker, 1870.

————. *Address at the laying of the cornerstone of the Church of the Holy Communion*. New York: Published by the Parish, 1854. Also in *E.C.P.*, II.

————. *Address by the Rev. W. A. Muhlenberg, D.D., at the laying of the cornerstone of Kemp Hall*. Fountain Rock, Md., 1851.

——. *The Application of Christianity to Education being the Principles and Plan of Education to be adopted in the Institute at Flushing, L.I.* Jamaica, N.Y.: Sleigh and George, 1828.

——. *The Ceremony and Address at the Laying of the Cornerstone of St. Paul's College.* Flushing, N.Y., 1836.

——. *Christian Education: Being an address delivered after a public examination of the students of the institute at Flushing, L.I.* (July 28, 1831). New York: 1831.

——. *Christian Education.* Flushing, N.Y., 1840.

——. *Church Poetry, being portions of the Psalms in verse and hymns suited to the festivals and fasts and various occasions of the church. Selected and altered from various authors.* Philadelphia: Published by S. Potter and Co., 1823.

——. *The Claims of the Holy Week. A plain address to churchmen.* New York: Protestant Episcopal Tract Society, 1840.

——. *"Collectanea Sacra Latina," The use of Sacred Latin in Schools.* Flushing, N.Y., 1840.

——. *Directory in the Use of the Book of Common Prayer for the Church of the Testimony of Jesus. St. Johnland, L.I.* New York: T. Whittaker, 1871. Also in *E.C.P.*, I.

——. *Evangelical Catholic Papers.* Ed. by Anne Ayres. New York: T. Whittaker, 1875, 1877. (A collection of Muhlenberg's papers listed below.) These two volumes have been referred to in the notes as *E.C.P.* to prevent confusion with *The Evangelical Catholic,* a newspaper that he published.

Volume I

No. I. "Hints on Catholic Union." 1835.

No. II. "An Exposition of the Memorial of Sundry Presbyters of the Protestant Episcopal Church, presented to the House of Bishops during the General Convention of said church, 1853." 1854.

No. III. "What The Memorialists Want. A Letter to the Right Rev. Bishop Otey, Chairman of the Commission, on the Memorial presented by Sundry Presbyters to the House of Bishops during the General Convention of 1853." 1856.

No. IV. "What The Memorialists Do Not Want." 1856.

No. V. "A Further Communication of the Memorial to the Right Rev. Bishop Otey, Chairman of the Commission of Bishops." 1857.

No. VI. "A Word For Good Friday." 1864.

No. VII. "Letters To A Friend, Touching the Late Pastoral of the Right Rev. Bishop Potter of New York." 1865.

No. VIII. "Christ And The Bible: Not The Bible And Christ." 1868.

No. IX. "Suggestions For The Formation of an Evangelic and Catholic Union. A Paper read at the Evangelical Conference in Philadelphia, November 9, 1869." 1870.

No. X. "The Lord's Supper in Relation to Christian Union. A Paper read at the Conference of the Evangelical Alliance, New York, October 11, 1873."

No. XI. "St. Johnland: A retro-prospectus in two Letters, supposed to be written in the year 187–. 'Your old men shall dream dreams.' – Acts ii. 18." 1864.

No. XII. "Directory In The Use of The Book of Common Prayer for the Church of the Testimony of Jesus, St. Johnland, L.I." 1871.

Volume II

No. I. "A Plea for Christian Hymns. Addressed to a member of the special General Convention which met in Philadelphia, October 30th, 1821."

No. II. "The rebuke of the Lord. A Sermon preached in the Chapel of the Institute at Flushing, L.I., on the Sunday after the great fire in New York, on the 16th and 17th December, 1835."

No. III. "An Address Delivered at the Laying of The Corner-Stone of St. Paul's College, College Point, L.I., October 15, 1836."

No. IV. "Address at the Laying of the Corner-Stone of the Church of the Holy Communion, New York, July 24, 1844."

No. V. "A Plea for a Church Hospital in the City of New York. In two lectures, delivered in the Church of the Holy Communion, St. Paul's Church, New York, and St. John's Church, Brooklyn. 1850."

No. VI. "Sketch of The History of St. Luke's Hospital and Pastoral Report of 1871."

No. VII. "Protestant Sisterhoods, originally introductory to "Two Letters on Evangelical Sisterhoods." 1852.

No. VIII. "A Sermon Preached at the Reopening of the Church of Augustus (Evangelical Lutheran), Trappe, Montgomery Co., Pa., September 5, 1860."

No. IX. "Congregational Singing, A lecture delivered in several Episcopal Churches about 1860."

No. X. "One Way of Keeping Lent and the Claims of Holy Week."

No. XI. "The Three Crosses. A Sermon preached in Madison Ave. Presbyterian Church. On Good Friday 1864."

No. XII. "The Woman And Her Accusers. A Sermon preached for The Midnight Mission." 1863.

No. XIII. "The Church. A Brotherhood." An Unfinished Article From "Brotherly Words." 1868.

No. XIV. Six Sermons. I. Christmas And The World. II. The Lord's Prayer A Discipline and Model of Prayer. III. Idle Words. IV. Brief Comments On The Fifty-First Psalm. V. David's Prayer For Self- Knowledge. VI. Self-Distrust. (Sequel to A Sermon on Self-Knowledge.)

———. *An exposition of the memorial of Sundry Presbyters of the Protestant Episcopal Church by one of the memorialists.* New York: Stanford and Swords, 1854. Also in *E.C.P.* I.

———. *"I Would Not Live Alway,"* and other verses, by the same author. n.d.; n.p.

———. *"I Would Not Live Alway,"* and other pieces in verse, by the same author. New York: R. Craighead, printer, 1860.

———. *"I Would Not Live Alway,"* evangelized by its author with the story of the hymn and a brief account of St. Johnland. New York: T. Whittaker and Co., 1871.

———. "Letter to Bishop Otey," in Alonzo Potter *Memorial Papers.*

———. *The Liturgy in no Danger.* 1843. (Although this pamphlet is listed in some libraries under Muhlenberg's name I doubt that Muhlenberg wrote it.)

———. *The Lord's Supper in relation to Christian Union.* A paper read at the conference of the Evangelical Alliance, New York, October 11, 1873. New York: T. Whittaker [1873]. Also in *E.C.P.,* I.

———. *Memorial of Sundry Presbyters of the Protestant Episcopal Church Presented to the House of Bishops, Oct. 18, 1853.* New York: Published by the author, 1853.

———. *The order of a special service for the season of Lent.* New York: Published by the parish [Church of the Holy Communion] 1854.

———. *Our school-fathers Carol.* New York, 1856.

———. *Pastoral Tracts Printed for the use of the members of the Church of the Holy Communion. No. I. The Catholic faith, hole [sic] and undefiled; sentence of Consecration; Reasons for the altar; posture of the minister in prayer.* New York: George W. Wood, 1847.

———. *Pastoral Tracts No. III. Morning Prayer restored or the reasons for the division of the service on Sunday Morning, as practiced at the Church of the Holy Communion. Printed for the use of the members of this Church.* New York: George W. Wood, 1847.

———. *Pastoral Tracts No. II. Anthems and Devotions for Passion Week and Easter. For the use of the members of the Church of the Holy Communion.* New York: George W. Wood, 1847.

———. *Pastoral Tracts No. IV. The Weekly Eucharist, or Pastoral Tract Printed chiefly for the members of the Church of the Holy Communion.* New York: Pudney and Russell, 1848.

———. *The people's Psalter being the Psalms of David, arranged for chanting, with an appendix containing hymns from Holy Scripture, and a selection of chants.* New York: Stanford and Swords, 1854.

———. *A Plea for a Church Hospital in the city of New York, in two lectures. Delivered in the Church of the Holy Communion, St. Paul's Church, New York and St. John's Church, Brooklyn.* New York: Stanford and Swords, 1850. Also in *E.C.P.,* II.

———. *Prayer and Praise for Passion Week, Good Friday, and Easter.* New York: W. H. Kelly and Brother, 1864.

————. *The President's Hymn.* (Contains Lincoln's Proclamation of October 3, 1863, and a facsimile of the words and music of Muhlenberg's "The President's Hymn.")

————. *A Primer of Church Music.* New York: S. W. Benedict, 1845.

————. *Protestant Sisterhoods. Originally introductory to two letters on Evangelical Sisterhoods.* New York, 1852. Also in *E.C.P.,* II.

————. *The Psalter, or Psalms of David: together with the Canticles of the Morning and Evening Prayer, and Occasional Offices of the Church. Figured for Chanting. To which are prefixed an explanatory preface and a selection of chants. A new edition, revised and corrected.* New York: D. Appleton and Company, 1849.

————. *The rebuke of the Lord. A sermon preached in the Chapel of the Institute at Flushing, L.I., on the Sunday after the great fire in New York, on the 16th, and 17th, of December, 1835.* Jamaica: I. F. Jones and Co., 1835. Also in *E.C.P.,* II.

————. *St. Johnland, (A Church Industrial Community) A retrospectus in two letters supposed to be written some years hence.* New York: T. Whittaker, 1864.

————. *St. Johnland, A Retrospectus in Two Letters Supposed to be written in the year 187-.* New York: R. Craighead, Printer, 1864. Also in *E.C.P.,* I.

————. *St. Johnland: Ideal and Actual.* New York: T. Whittaker, 1867.

————. *St. Paul's College, Prospectus.* New York, 1835.

————. *A sermon in memory of the Rev. Samuel Bacon and John P. Bankson, Agents of the United States, Under the Direction of the American Colonization Society, Who Died on the Coast of Africa, May, 1820.* Philadelphia: Published by friends of the deceased, 1820.

————. *"Shout the Glad Tidings," A Christmas Hymn.* Bristol, England: P. J. Smith, printer, N.D.

————. *The Studies and Discipline of the Institute at Flushing, L.I., August, 1830.*

————. *Suggestions for the formation of an Evangelical and Catholic Union.* New York: T. Whittaker, 1870. Also in *E.C.P.,* I.

————. *Tabella Sacra For the Vacation.* St. Paul's College, 1839.

————. *The Testimony of Jesus, the Spirit of Prophecy. A sermon preached at the reopening of the Church of Augustus (Evangelical Lutheran), Trappe, Montgomery Co., Pennsylvania, September 5, 1860.* New York: R. Craighead, 1861. Also in *E.C.P.,* II.

————. *"The True Mary"* being Mrs. Browning's poem *"The Virgin Mary to the Child Jesus."* With comments and notes edited by William Augustus Muhlenberg, 1869.

————. *A valedictory sermon preached in St. James Church, Lancaster on Sunday evening, July 23, 1826.* Jamaica, L.I.: Sleight and Tucker, printer, 1826.

————. *The Voice of the Church and the Times, Chiefly addressed to Churchmen, in the Middle and Upper Walks of Life.* New York: R. Sears, 1840.

————. *What The Memorialists Want. A Letter to the Rt. Rev. Bishop Otey by One of Their Number.* New York: R. Craighead, 1856. Also in *E.C.P.,* I.

———. *The Woman and her Accusers, A Plea for the Midnight Mission. Delivered in several of the churches of New York and Brooklyn.* New York: P. F. Smith, 1871. Also in *E.C.P.*, II.

Muhlenberg, William Augustus, *et al. Hymns for Church and Home compiled by members of the Protestant Episcopal Church as a contribution to any addition that may be made to the hymns now attached to the Prayer Book.* Philadelphia: J. B. Lippincott and Co., 1861.

Muhlenberg, William Augustus, and Jonathan Wainwright. *The Choir and Family Psalter, being the Psalms of David; together with the canticles of the Morning and Evening Prayers, and Occasional Offices of the Church, Arranged for Chanting, to which is Prefixed a Selection of Chants.* New York: Stanford and Swords, 1851.

Muhlenberg, William Augustus, G. T. Bedell, and G. J. Geer. *A Tune Book Proposed for the Use of Congregations of the Protestant Episcopal Church, Compiled by a Committee, Appointed for the Purpose by the House of Bishops.* New York: Published by the Committee, 1859.

ARTICLES FROM PERIODICALS

Abbe, Robert. "A New View of the Boyhood of the Rev. Dr. Muhlenberg,' reprinted from *Medical Journal and Record,* November 17, 1926. Notes of an address to St. Luke's Alumni, May, 1922. Published by St. Luke's Alumni Association, 1927.

Abercrombie, James, "Prospectus," *The Quarterly Theological Magazine, I* (February, 1813).

Albright, Raymond W. "When We Talk About Unity . . . " *The Episcopalian,* CXXVIII (August, 1963), 12–16.

Becker, Richard G. "The Social Thought of William Augustus Muhlenberg," *Historical Magazine of the Protestant Episcopal Church,* XXVII (December, 1958), 307–323.

"Beginnings of some Famous Schools," *Trained Nurse and Hospital Review,* I (August, 1938), 20–27.

Bosher, Robert S. "The Episcopal Church and American Christianity, A Bibliography," *Historical Magazine of the Protestant Episcopal Church,* XIX (December, 1950), 368–384.

Croll, P. C. "William A. Muhlenberg, Clergyman," *Pennsylvania German,* VI (December, 1905), 243–252.

"Dr. Muhlenberg," *Atlantic Monthly,* XLVI (July, 1880), 564–566. (A review of Anne Ayres, *The Life and Work of William Augustus Muhlenberg.*)

"Dr. Muhlenberg," *The Dial,* II (June, 1891), 87–88 (An anonymous review of W. W. Newton's biography of Muhlenberg).

Douglas, Winfred. "Early Hymnody of the American Episcopal Church," *Historical Magazine of the Protestant Episcopal Church,* X (June, 1941), 202–218.

Doyle, Ann. "Nursing by Religious Orders in the United States," *American Journal of Nursing*, XXIX (July and August, 1929), 775–786, 959–969.

Halsted, N. O. "Dr. Muhlenberg and St. Johnland," *Pennsylvania German*, IV–V (April, 1905), 261–265.

Hardy, Edward Roche. "Evangelical Catholicism. William Augustus Muhlenberg and the Memorial Movement," *Historical Magazine of the Protestant Episcopal Church*, XIII (June, 1944), 155–192.

Jacobs, H. E. "A Commonplace Lutheran," *Lutheran Church Review*, XXI (April, 1890), 117–129.

Klein, H. M. J. "St. James Church, Lancaster, Pa.," *Historical Magazine of the Protestant Episcopal Church*, XIII (March, 1944), 26–35.

Klein, Phillip Shriver, "James Buchanan and Ann Coleman" in *Pennsylvania History*, XXI (January, 1954), 1–20.

Klingberg, Frank J. "Colonial Anglo-Lutheran Relations," *Historical Magazine of the Protestant Episcopal Church*, XVI (June, 1947), 217–220.

McCadden, Joseph J. "Joseph Lancaster and the Philadelphia Schools," *Pennsylvania History*, III (December, 1936), 225–239.

Minifie, Charles J. "William Reed Huntington and Church Unity," *Historical Magazine of the Protestant Episcopal Church*, XXV, (June, 1966), 155–166.

Morehouse, Clifford P. "Almanacs and Year Books of the Episcopal Church," *Historical Magazine of the Protestant Episcopal Church*, X (December, 1941), 330–353.

————. "Origins of the Episcopal Church Press from Colonial Days," *Historical Magazine of the Protestant Episcopal Church*, XI (September, 1942), 199–318.

Oldschool, Oliver (ed), *The Portfolio*, V (November, 1810), 393–396.

"The Proposed Reform of the Episcopal Church." Reprinted from *The Episcopal Quarterly Review*, (April, 1855). New York: Anson D. F. Randolph, 1855.

Salomon, Richard S. "The Episcopate on the Carey Case" In *Historical Magazine of the Episcopal Church*, XVIII (September, 1949), 240–281.

Satcher, Herbert B. "Music in the Episcopal Church in Pennsylvania in the Eighteenth Century," *Historical Magazine of the Protestant Episcopal Church*, XVIII (December, 1949), 372–413.

Seymour, George F. "Mother Harriet of the Sisterhood of St. Mary," *The Church Eclectic*, June, 1896. Reprinted in *Mount St. Gabriel Series, No. 1, Historical Papers*, Peekskill, New York: St. Mary's Convent, 1931.

Shires, Henry H. "History of the Church Divinity School of the Pacific," *Historical Magazine of the Protestant Episcopal Church*, XI (June, 1942), 179–188.

Theodore, Sister Mary. "The Foundation of the Sisterhood of St. Mary," *Historical Magazine of the Protestant Episcopal Church*, XIV (March, 1945), 38–52.

Thomas, Albert Sidney. "Christopher Edward Gadsden (1785–1852)" *Historical Magazine of the Protestant Episcopal Church*, XX (September, 1951), 294–324.

Tucker, Gardiner C. "Impressions of the Episcopal Church in 1867," *Historical Magazine of the Protestant Episcopal Church*, XX (March, 1951), 67–70.

West, Edward M. "History and Development of Music in the American Church," *Historical Magazine of the Protestant Episcopal Church*, XIV (March, 1945), 15–37.

White, William. "Copy of a letter to Bishop Hobart, September 1, 1819, relating, at his request, the incidents of the early part of my life, together with twenty-one notes connected with my Letter to Bp. Hobart added December 21, 1830," Walter H. Stowe, ed., reprinted in the *Historical Magazine of the Protestant Episcopal Church*, XXII (September, 1953), 383–417.

———. "Thoughts on the singing of Psalms and Anthems in Churches," *The Christian Journal*, May and June, 1808.

Williams, Thomas J. "The Beginnings of Anglican Sisterhoods," *Historical Magazine of the Protestant Episcopal Church*, XVI (December, 1947), 350–372.

Woolverton, John Frederick. "William Augustus Muhlenberg and the Founding of St. Paul's College," *Historical Magazine of the Protestant Episcopal Church*, XXIX (September, 1960), 192–218.

MANUSCRIPTS

Breck Papers. In Nashotah House Archives, Nashotah, Wis.

Christ Church, Philadelphia. Minutes of the Vestry of the United Parish of Christ Church, St. Peter and St. James, 1807–1821. In the archives of the church.

Eigenbrodt, David, Life of. Manuscript in the archives of St. Luke's Hospital, New York, N.Y.

Engles, Joseph P. Correspondence, 1849–1868. In the Presbyterian Historical Society Library, 231 South 44th Street, Philadelphia, Pa.

Hobart Papers. In the New York Historical Society Library, New York, N.Y.

Holy Communion, Church of, Geneva Lake, Wisconsin. Minutes of the Vestry. In the archives of the church.

Holy Communion, Church of, New York. Minutes of the Vestry, 1867–1882. In the archives of the church.

Jackson Papers. In the home of Mrs. Kemper Jackson [sic], Nashotah, Wis.

Kemper, Bishop Jackson. Papers. In the State Historical Society of Wisconsin Library, Madison, Wis.

Manigault Diary. Diary of Lewis Manigault. Manuscript in the possession of the Reverend Emmett Gribben, Tuscaloosa, Ala.

Muhlenberg's advice to the board of Trustees on the choice of his successor. Manuscript in the archives of St. Luke's Hospital, New York, N.Y.

Muhlenberg's Library [Catalogue]. Manuscript dated 1852 in General Theological Seminary Library, 175 Ninth Avenue, New York, N.Y.

Oliver Papers. In General Theological Seminary Library, 175 Ninth Avenue, New York, N.Y.

Passmore, Joseph Clarkson. Manuscript Letters, 1834–1840. In General Theological Seminary Library, 175 Ninth Avenue, New York, N.Y.

Pennsylvania, University of, Archives General,
Grammar School 1814–1821
Students and activities, 1789–1827

Pennsylvania, University of. Minutes of the Board of Trustees. Vol. V., November 8, 1791, to June 20, 1811; Vol. VI., June 21, 1811, to May 27, 1822. In the office of the secretary of the Board of Trustees, 34th and Walnut Streets, Philadelphia, Pa.

Pennsylvania, University of, University Papers, Vol. III, 1811–1913.

St. George's Church, Flushing, New York. Minutes of the Vestry, 1826–1845. In the archives of the church.

St. James Church, Lancaster, Pennsylvania. Minutes of the Vestry, 1820–1830. In the archives of the church.

St. Johnland, Society of. Minutes of the Trustees. King's Park, Long Island, New York. Vol. I, July 9, 1868 to May 21, 1895. In the archives of St. Johnland. King's Park, Long Island, N.Y.

St. Johnland, Society of. Reports. In the archives of St. Johnland. King's Park, Long Island, N.Y.

St. Luke's Hospital. Subscription book of St. Luke's Hospital, May 30, 1852. In the archives of St. Luke's Hospital.

St. Michael and Zion Church: documents concerning the language controversy. Manuscripts in the library of the Lutheran Theological Seminary, Mt. Airy, Pa.

Seckel Family Papers. In Historical Society of Pennsylvania Library.

Sheaff Family Papers. In Historical Society of Pennsylvania Library.

Sisters of the Holy Communion Infirmary Register, 1857, No. 2. In St. Luke's Hospital Medical Library.

Vaux, Roberts. Letters. In the Historical Society of Pennsylvania Library.

Verplank Letters. In New York Historical Society Library, New York, N.Y.

Ward, Henry Dana. Diary. Manuscript Division, New York Public Library, Astor, Lenox, and Tilden Foundations.

Wharton, Thomas Kelah. Diary. May 3, 1830–October 15, 1834. Manuscript Division, New York Public Library, Astor, Lenox, and Tilden Foundations.

Wood, Dr. George Bacon. Papers and books. In the George Bacon Wood Room of the Library of the College of Physicians, Philadelphia.

PUBLIC DOCUMENTS

New York, City of. *Report of the proceedings of the Sanitary Commission of the Board of Health in relation to the Cholera as it prevailed in New York in* 1849.

New York, State of. *Census of the State of New York for* 1845.

———. *Census of the State of New York for* 1855.

———. *Census of the State of New York for* 1875.

New York State Laws. *Thirty-sixth Session,* 1813.

———. *Fiftieth Session,* 1827.

———. *Sixty-third Session,* 1840.

———. *Seventy-seventh Session,* 1854.

Pennsylvania, Commonwealth of, *Laws of the Commonwealth of Pennsylvania . . .* Published under the Authority of the General Assembly, 1808, 1817, 1818, 1821.

———. *Annual Reports of the Controllers of the First School District of Pennsylvania.* Philadelphia: Published by order of the Controller, 1819–1844.

United States. *Second Census of the United States,* 1800.

———. *Fourth Census of the United States,* 1820.

———. *Seventh Census of the United States,* 1850. Printed summaries: *Manuscript schedule of the Fourth, Sixth and Tenth Wards of New York City.*

———. *Eighth Census of the United States,* 1860. Printed summaries.

INDEX